owned by: Kimberly Cleary Stethem

THIS BOOK IS THE PROPERTY OF		
ST. JOSEPH'S SCHOOL, PRESCOTT.		
Date Rec'd 6/90 Book No. _____		
Price 26.98 Condition		
Issued to	Year	Issue	Return

DO NOT WRITE ON ANY PAGE OF THIS BOOK.
CONDITION: NEW/GOOD/FAIR/POOR/BAD

DISCOVERING CANADA

Settling a land

EDITOR AND SENIOR AUTHOR
Ronald C. Kirbyson, B.A., B.ED., M.A.
Winnipeg School Division No. 1

CO-AUTHORS
Peter L. McCreath, B.A., M.A., B.ED.
Nova Scotia Teachers' Union

Alan Skeoch, B.A., M.A.
Toronto Board of Education

Prentice-Hall Canada Inc.,
Scarborough, Ontario

For
Dawn, Geoff and Jill
Marjorie, Kevin and Andrew
Jefferson and Adam

Cover Painting: "Simon Fraser" by C.W. Jefferys. Private collection, Toronto; © C.W. Jefferys Estate. Photographed by T.E. Moore.

Canadian Cataloguing in Publication Data

Kirbyson, Ronald C.,
    Discovering Canada

For use in Junior high schools.
Contents: [v. 1] Settling a land.
Includes index.
ISBN 0-13-215657-1 (v. 1)

1. Canada - History I. McCreath, Peter L. II. Skeoch, Alan. III. Title.

FC170.K47   971   C82-094164-6
F1034.2.K47

Accompanying materials

Discovering Canada: Developing a nation
Discovering Canada: Shaping an identity
Discovering Canada: Teacher's Guide

©1982 by Prentice-Hall Canada Inc., Scarborough, Ontario
ALL RIGHTS RESERVED

No part of this book may be reproduced in any form without permission in writing from the publishers
Prentice-Hall, Inc., Englewood Cliffs, New Jersey
Prentice-Hall International, Inc., London
Prentice-Hall of Australia, Pty., Ltd., Sydney
Prentice-Hall of India Pvt., Ltd., New Delhi
Prentice-Hall of Japan, Inc., Tokyo
Prentice-Hall of Southeast Asia (Pte.) Ltd., Singapore

ISBN 0-13-215657-1

4   5   6   7   **BP**   91   90   89

Printed and bound in Canada by The Bryant Press Limited

Project Editor: MaryLynne Meschino
Production Editor: Wilda Lossing
Design: John Zehethofer
Maps, charts and diagrams: James Loates
Illustrations: Jon McKee
Composition: CompuScreen Typesetting Ltd.

Policy Statement

Prentice-Hall Canada Inc., Educational Book Division, and the authors of *Discovering Canada* are committed to the publication of instructional materials that are as bias-free as possible. The student text was evaluated for bias prior to publication.

    The authors and publisher also recognize the importance of appropriate reading levels and have therefore made every effort to ensure the highest degree of readability in the student text. The content has been selected, organized, and written at a level suitable to the intended audience. Standard readability tests have been applied at several stages in the text's preparation to ensure an appropriate reading level.

    Research indicates, however, that readability is affected by much more than word or sentence length; factors such as presentation, format and design, none of which are considered in the usual readability tests, also greatly influence the ease with which students read a book. These and many additional features, such as marginal notes and glossary, have been carefully prepared to ensure maximum student comprehension.

Preface

To you, the student, we wish a successful journey in *Discovering Canada*. In the pages that follow, you are going to meet all kinds of people who have been part of Canada's history. You are going to experience a wide variety of situations and events and places. You will travel by way of stories, explanations, illustrations and photos, dramatizations, letters and diaries, maps and diagrams.

To speed you on your way, we present some of these parts in adapted form. In other words, we sometimes changed language—of a letter, say, or a speech—so that it would be more understandable to a modern student. For other parts, we used conversations or anecdotes or word-pictures to help you "picture" what was going on. We took pains, at all times, to ensure that made-up parts were based on historical fact.

A journey awaits you. May it be a good one. May you find out much about Canada and the world—and about yourself.

Acknowledgements

It would be difficult to exaggerate the amount of support the authors received from the people at Prentice-Hall of Canada. Rob Greenaway, Executive Editor, was instrumental in originating the project and keeping it on course through its years of development. His belief in its value encouraged us constantly. MaryLynne Meschino, Project Editor, through her advice and hard work, improved every part of the book. She assisted with organization, choice of content, the wording and overall pattern of questions, the general readability and style. She supervised the research for pictures and illustrations, and carried out much of the work herself. During even the most difficult times, MaryLynne's sense of humour cheered us all. Wilda Lossing, Production Editor, devoted her caring attention and considerable energy to the preparation of the final product. Her concern for quality is reflected on every page.

The authors would also like to thank all the others whose talents helped to make this book possible: librarians, typists, archivists, colleagues. Certain individuals and organizations helped us at particularly critical times: the staff of the St. James Library, Winnipeg; Dr. Jean Friesen, provost, University College, Winnipeg; Wayne Kirbyson.

Students of Argyle Alternative School in Winnipeg and Parkdale Collegiate in Toronto deserve special thanks. Various materials in this book began as ideas tried out with them.

To our families, whom we can never thank enough for their patience and comfort, we dedicate *Discovering Canada*.

1 Discovery: How important is it in our lives?

In August 1977, the spacecraft *Voyager I* was launched into space. Its destination—Jupiter and Saturn. *Voyager*'s mission was to discover as much new information about the two distant planets as possible.

Along with the scientific equipment for research, *Voyager I* also contained a gold-plated copper disc. On this disc was recorded information that describes what our world is like. Here is a list of the information on the disc:

- greetings in 60 languages;
- music from many different cultures and time periods (classical music, jazz, rock and roll, etc.);
- photographs of human beings from many cultures;
- photographs and diagrams that depict our knowledge of mathematics, chemistry, geology and biology;
- 18 recordings of "sounds of the earth": surf, wind, thunder, birds, whales and other animals;
- 18 sound essays on the evolution of the earth.

- Do you think the Voyager I mission is similar to Columbus's voyage to America? Why or why not?
- Are there still things to discover in the world today?
- Why do you think the disc with information describing our world was put on the spacecraft?
- Do you think the information gives a good picture of our world? What would you want to add to the list? Take out of the list?

Chapter overview

What questions popped into your mind when you first read the title of this chapter and saw the picture of the spacecraft? Perhaps you wondered, "This is supposed to be a Canadian history book. What is a spaceship doing in it?" or "Why is the first chapter about discovery? And what does discovery have to do with *my* life?"

Discovery is really a part of everybody's lives. When you study Canadian history, you are discovering, or finding out about people and events in the past. But this is only a small part of the discovering that goes on in your life. When you learn to play a new game or sport or when you go to a movie, you are finding out something new. Indeed, every day can bring you new discoveries. So, just like an explorer in the New World hundreds of years ago, or like the astronauts who landed on the moon, you are a discoverer.

This chapter tries to get you to think a little more about discovery, especially the kind that we are concerned with in this book—discovering the past.

Signposts

What kinds of discovery are there?

One kind of discovery: Discovering the past

Key words

discovery	artifacts	ancestors
records	culture	New World
archaeologist		

What kinds of discovery are there?

Take a pencil or pen and jot down five discoveries. Are the ones on your list mostly well-known discoveries that have affected many people? Did you include discoveries that you yourself have made?

Discoveries come in all shapes and sizes. Some are spectacular and can have a tremendous impact on people all over the world. Think, for example, about the invention of the steam engine or the discovery of penicillin [peh-nih-SIH-lihn]. In contrast, other discoveries are personal and may affect only a few people. A student looking through a microscope for the first time may feel a sense of wonder about the details of a grain of sand.

There is almost no limit to the kinds of discoveries people can make. The following pictures are about discovering. Try to figure out what kinds of discoveries are being made.

Penicillin is a drug used to fight infection.

Fig. 1-1 Making discoveries.

GETTING THE FACTS

1. Suggest what is being discovered in each picture. Write one complete sentence for each photo.

USING YOUR KNOWLEDGE

2. a) Do you think that some of the discoveries being made in the pictures are more important than others? List the discoveries in what you feel is their order of importance. Put the most important discovery at the top of your list and the least important at the bottom.

b) Look at the discovery at the top of your list. Why do you think it is the most important? Explain why the discovery at the bottom of your list is the least important.

c) Compare your list with the lists your classmates drew up. Were the lists the same or quite different? Suggest reasons why the lists were the same or why they were different.

THINKING IT THROUGH

3. Do you think it would be fair to say that every discovery can be important in its own way? Give reasons to back up your opinion.

One kind of discovery: Discovering the past

Why try to discover the past?

In question 3, you were asked whether or not all discoveries are important in some way. In every discovery, people find out something new; a new piece of information has been added to their picture of the world. This may change the way they behave, or increase their understanding of the world around them. In this way, then, every discovery—no matter what it is—can be called important.

When you study history, you are making important discoveries. History can be described very generally as the study of people and events of the past. These people—explorers, leaders, pioneers—and their actions have shaped the world you live in today. Therefore, the more you find out about them, the more you can learn about your world. These discoveries may influence the decisions you make and the way you shape the world around you.

That is one reason for trying to find out about the past. There is another reason too—discoveries about the past can be just plain interesting.

How do we discover the past?

How do we find out about people and events of the past? Unfortunately, we cannot simply go and ask Samuel de Champlain [shah^m-PLA^N] what his first meeting with the Indians of North America was like!

To find out about the past, we generally refer to **records**, which are written accounts of events. Champlain, for example, kept a journal or diary in which he described his adventures, feelings and ideas. Other records that tell us about past events include letters written by people who lived through the events, newspaper articles, maps and drawings.

Fig. 1-2 What can you learn from this early map of New France?

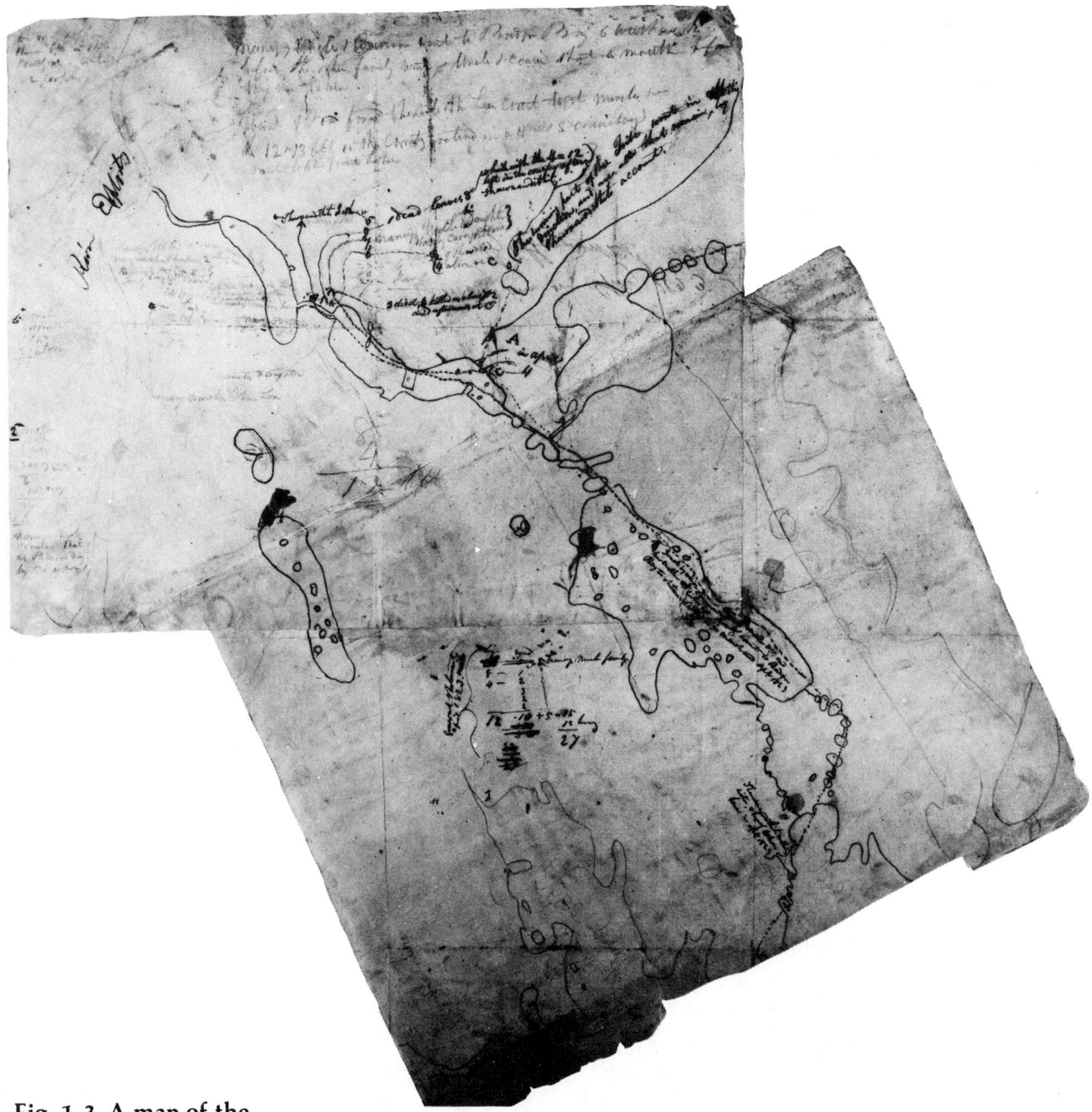

Fig. 1-3 A map of the Exploits River and Red Indian Lake in Newfoundland, drawn by Shanawdithit, the last of the Beothuk Indians. For more about Shanawdithit see chapter 5.

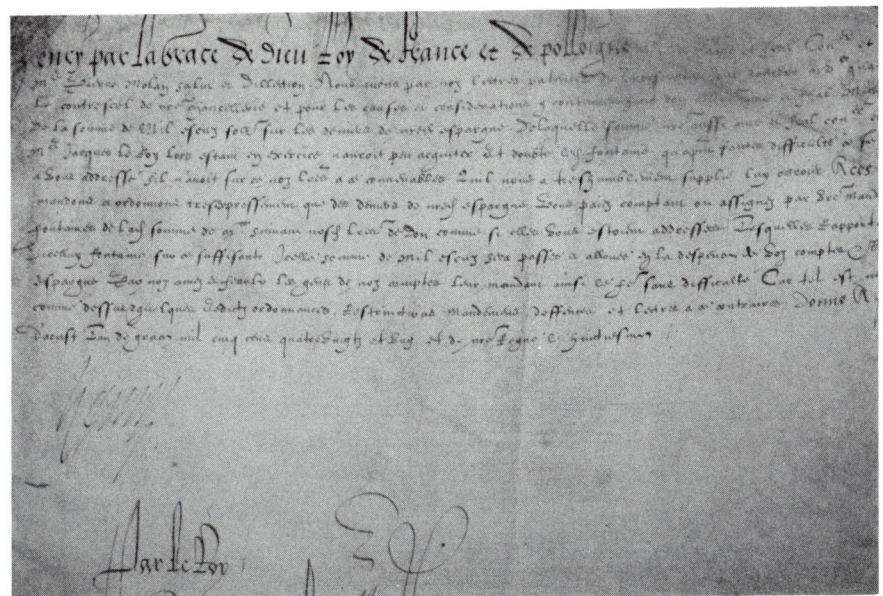

Fig. 1-4 Letters are a good source of clues about the past.

A problem arises when we try to find out about the past from records. Quite often, many of the accounts that people wrote in the past have been lost. In fact, the further back we go in history, the less complete the record becomes. For example, a great many of the letters written by Canadians in the 1800s are still around. These give us a pretty clear idea of what life in pioneer Canada was like. However, there are fewer written accounts about what the earliest explorers of North America found in their travels. We, therefore, have to rely on fragments of information from different sources to get a picture of those earliest days. Putting these fragments together is like assembling a jigsaw puzzle from which many of the pieces are missing. The gaps in the story have to be filled in by educated guesswork. In a sense, then, historians, **archaeologists** [AHR-kee-AH-loh-jihsts], or any people who study the past, are like detectives who look for clues that will lead them to the entire story.

The problem of finding out about the past gets bigger the further back in history you go. Even though written accounts may be incomplete, they at least give us some clues about the people and events that came before us. But people only learned to write about 5000 years ago. Human beings existed long before they kept written accounts; in fact, humans have been traced back as far as one million years! What do we know about

Fig. 1-5 Beothuk combs carved from bone and antler. Can artifacts such as these and the ones in Fig. 1-6 help us learn about the past?

At Old Crow in the Yukon Territory, evidence has been discovered that goes back 40 000 years.

these people? Not very much, compared to what we know about people living in the 1800s. To find out about the earliest people, we have to study the objects they left behind and guess what life was like for them. These objects, such as tools and weapons, are called **artifacts** [AHR-tih-fakts]. They are the clues that we use to piece together a picture of the earliest humans.

Our knowledge of the past is incomplete, but new discoveries are being made all the time. For historians and many other people, putting together the puzzle of human existence is an exciting challenge.

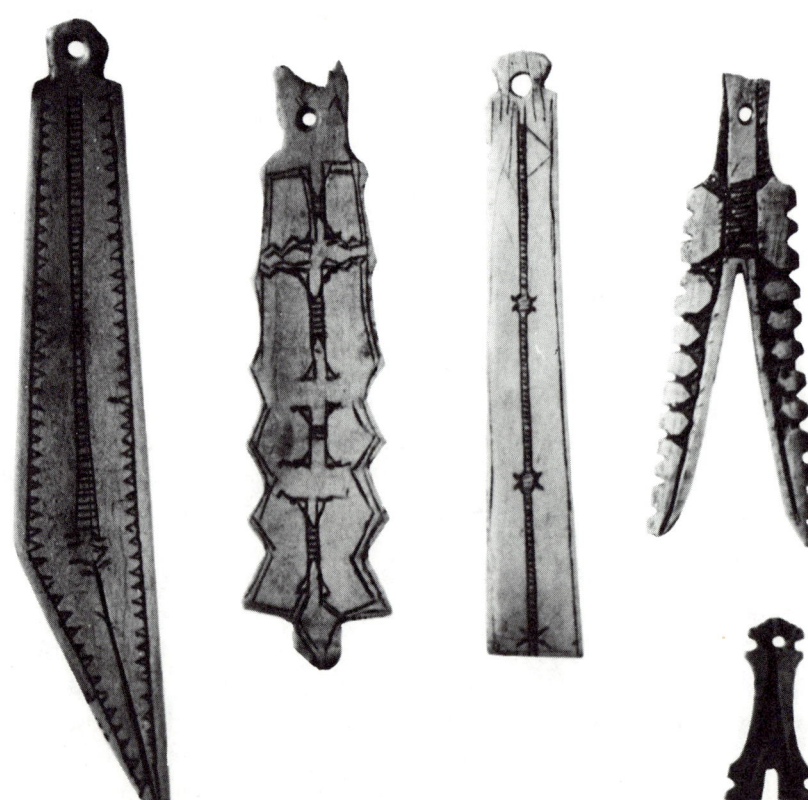

Fig. 1-6 These carved and decorated bone pieces are usually found with Beothuk burials. We are not sure what they were used for. It is thought that they may have been worn as amulets (charms) attached to clothing or strung as a necklace.

GETTING THE FACTS

4. Skim (read over quickly) the section "Why try to discover the past?" Then, in your own words, explain why it can be important to study the past.

5. Unscramble the following words. Then use each word in a sentence.

    ictfatra   uactdeed   krossuweg
         crorde   raidy

USING YOUR KNOWLEDGE

6. a) How much do you know about the history of your own family; for example, where your grandparents were born, what they did for a living, what your parents were like when they were young, what you were like when you were a child, and so on? Describe one interesting person or event in your family history. You may want to do this by writing a story or paragraph, or by drawing a picture.

   b) How did you discover whatever you do know about your family history: Through old letters? Stories that were told to you? Photographs?

THE INVESTIGATIVE REPORTER

7. Not all records have to be written by people who lived hundreds of years ago. Encyclopedias [ehn-SĪ-kloh-PEE-dee-uhs], textbooks and computers provide information about the past. This information has been gathered from old letters, diaries and other sources, and written down in one easy-to-get-at account.

   a) Would you say that "Discovering Canada" is a record? Explain why or why not.

   b) Leaf through the book and find three examples of accounts written by people in the past.

8. Look in a dictionary for the meaning of archaeologist. Write the definition in your notebook and briefly explain how an archaeologist is like a detective.

The following story is about a young girl who makes a discovery. Susan finds an object from the past that helps piece together the puzzle about the earliest human beings. (Remember, the further back you go in time, the more gaps there are in

Susan Sharp and Samuel Green are fictional people. However, the facts of their story are based on recent discoveries made by archaeologists at the Royal Ontario Museum. Their evidence shows that Stone Age people (Palaeo-Indians) were able to survive in the very shadows of the glaciers.

our picture of the way people lived.) The story also shows how some of the most important discoveries often happen just by chance.

Susan finds the point

Susan Sharp was nervous. Ever since she had made her discovery, people had been asking her questions. First, the people from the Royal Ontario Museum questioned her. Then a couple of large newspapers did features on the fluted point for their Sunday editions. And now she was being interviewed by CBC television.

The interviewer started to speak into the camera. "Ladies and gentlemen, our program today will feature two people who have made important discoveries about the earliest people to live in southwestern Ontario. With us in the studio is Susan Sharp. Susan is a grade 8 student who lives on a farm in the Alliston area. Susan is the person who found the fluted point, and she will explain how the discovery occurred. Also with us is Dr. Samuel Greene. He is an archaeologist and Curator [kyoo-RAY-ter] at the Royal Ontario Museum. Dr. Greene will discuss his own discoveries of the fluted point in the area. He will also explain why these recent discoveries help us know more about the origin and lifestyle of early Stone Age societies in North America."

The interviewer turned to Susan and asked, "Susan, exactly how did you make your discovery?"

Susan's mouth was so dry! She was afraid that she wouldn't be able to get any words out. But the interviewer gave her a kind smile, so Susan relaxed a bit and started her story.

"My friend, Sheila, and I were walking across one of the fields on our farm that had just been ploughed. There were lots of small stones on the surface of the ground, so we began whipping them at fenceposts. Then, in a big cluster of stones, I noticed one that had a strange shape—it was a lot different than the rest. It looked like a large Indian arrowhead, so I slipped it into my pocket."

"Can you describe this stone a little more, Susan?" asked the interviewer.

"Sure. It was a leaf-shaped piece of stone about 10 or 12 centimetres long. There were U-shaped grooves along each side of the stone. It actually looked like some kind of spearhead."

"And what did you do with this piece of stone?" asked the interviewer.

A fluted point is a stone arrow or spear point. It is made by shaping the point and then cutting a wide flake or chip from each side.

A curator is a person in charge of a museum or library.

Fig. 1-7 Early Palaeo-Indian fluted spear point from Middlesex County, Ontario.

Susan responded easily now; her nervousness had disappeared. "I brought it home to show my dad. He was really interested in the stone because he had found one just like it years ago, and in just about the same area. Dad contacted a man he knew who was interested in arrowheads and the whole mystery of early humans. This man got excited about the discovery and got in touch with Dr. Greene at the museum in Toronto. Dr. Greene got excited about the spearhead too, and came out to see us."

"Thank you, Susan," said the interviewer. She now turned to the man on her other side. "Dr. Greene, why were you so interested in Susan's discovery? Thousands of arrowheads have been found in Ontario. Why is this one so special?"

"It's special because it is one of the keys to the mystery of the earliest human beings living in this part of the country. You see, this fluted point is not just an Indian arrowhead. By its appearance, we know it is a spearhead used for hunting by the earliest known inhabitants of North America. These people are called early Palaeo-Indians [PAY-lee-oh- IHN-dee-uhns]. We know that they lived in other parts of the continent. We didn't know, though, whether or not they reached this part of the country. If they did, then we should find clues of their presence—weapons and other artifacts they may have used. But, until recently, no campsites had been found. This is where Susan's fluted point discovery comes in."

Susan sat up straighter in her chair. She felt proud to play a part in unravelling the mystery of early humans.

Dr. Greene continued. "Every time a fluted point is discovered, there's a chance that there will be a campsite on the spot. When I heard that two points had been found in the same area, I went right over."

"Dr. Greene," asked the interviewer, "do you have to find a campsite to be sure that the Palaeo-Indians lived in the area? Isn't the fluted point enough?"

"Oh, no," replied Dr. Greene. "A single fluted point could have been lost by a passing hunter. Or it could have been carried a great distance by a wounded animal. However, a campsite, with fluted points and other artifacts related to camping activities, would show that these people probably lived in the area."

"I see," the interviewer commented thoughtfully. "What did you do when you got to the Sharp farm?"

"Well, first I looked at the ridges of land in the field. From them I could tell that this was the kind of place that early

Fig. 1-8 Fluted points and other clues have led us to believe that early Palaeo-Indian people in Ontario may have hunted barren ground caribou.

To engrave is to cut or carve the design into the wood or bone.

humans chose for campsites in the Great Lakes region. I left the farm and returned later with a small crew. For two weeks, we studied the field very carefully, looking for more artifacts and areas where fires had burned."

"And what did you finally come up with?" asked the interviewer.

Dr. Greene responded, "We found a few more flakes, and some small tools, which were used for engraving designs in wood and bone, or for piercing skins. We also discovered some areas where fires had burned. It is hard to say, though, whether or not these were actually hearths [hahrths]. In sum, then, I'd say that we found only the barest trace of early humans. However, we did find enough material to justify going back next year and doing a longer and closer study of the area. I tend to believe that we really have found an early human campsite here, but I'll need more evidence before I can be certain."

"Thank you Dr. Greene. And thanks to you, Susan," said the interviewer. "You both have taught us quite a bit today, not only about our early ancestors [AN-sehs-ters], but about how people today go about studying the past."

Susan was thoughtful as she walked out of the studio. After listening to Dr. Greene, she was amazed that she, an ordinary person, had made a discovery so important to the study of human history. But she was even more amazed by the Palaeo-Indian people. Here was a people with its own culture and customs—and she had never known about them before! Dr. Greene made them seem so real. She decided to read more about early humans in the next few weeks.

GETTING THE FACTS

9. Put the following events in the order in which they happened.
- Dr. Greene brings a crew to the Sharp's farm to explore the field in which the fluted point was found.
- Susan shows the fluted point to her father.
- Susan and Dr. Greene are interviewed on television.
- Susan finds a fluted point in a field on her farm.
- Dr. Greene finds out about Susan's discovery.
- Dr. Greene and his crew study the field carefully and find more traces of Palaeo-Indians.

10. Dr. Greene was trying to find clues to show that Palaeo-Indians had lived in southern Ontario. Why did he think that the discovery of one fluted point would not be enough to prove that Palaeo-Indians had lived in the area?

11. When Dr. Greene examined the field on Susan's farm, he found clues that seemed to suggest that Palaeo-Indians had lived in the area. List the clues that he found.

12. What conclusion did Dr. Greene come to about whether or not Palaeo-Indians had lived in the Alliston area?

USING YOUR KNOWLEDGE

13. The records or objects left behind by people in the past can tell us a great deal about what their society was like. We can

15

learn such things as the society's customs, attitude toward nature, and entertainments.

In the Susan Sharp story, you learned that the fluted point and other objects help tell us about the way early humans lived. Think back to the story of Voyager I at the beginning of this chapter. The records it contains will perhaps tell people in the future about the way we lived.

Imagine that you are going to gather objects and put them into a time capsule. These objects are to be a record of your own life. You hope that people in the future will open the capsule and get a picture of what your world was like and what was important to you.

a) List at least five objects that you would put into the time capsule.

b) What would these objects teach people in the future about you and your world?

THINKING IT THROUGH

14. Susan's discovery of the fluted point affected many people. Interested people all over the world would know a little more about early humans. Susan also made another discovery:

a) What was it? (HINT: Reread the last paragraph of the story.)

b) Do you think it was an important discovery? Explain why or why not.

c) Have you ever made a personal discovery like Susan's? Describe it briefly.

Conclusion

Now that you have worked your way through this chapter, are you perhaps better able to answer the question asked in the chapter title?

Discovery is certainly a part of everybody's lives. There are many different kinds of discoveries—spectacular ones that permit us to land humans on the moon, and less flashy ones that nevertheless add something new to a person's life. Whatever the discovery, the result is the same. It broadens our point of view and helps us understand a little more about the world we live in.

This book will try to help you find out more about one particular area of discovery—the people and events of Canada's past. It will also help you acquire the tools of the historian—the research and study skills that will assist you in your learning.

But remember—the things you find out in your history studies are not the only discoveries you will be making. To remind yourself of this, keep a journal of discovery.

Journal of discovery

Get a special notebook and give it the title "Journal of discovery." Each week, describe one discovery that you have made. Your description can be any length you want and your discovery can be of any type. You may want to write about, or draw a picture of, something you learned at school. Or it could be about something personal—a new feeling or a different way of seeing things.

After a few months, the journal will give you an interesting record of how you and your understanding of the world may have changed. For people in the future, it will be a historical document that gives a picture of a young Canadian in the 1980s.

GETTING THE FACTS

15. Use each of the following words in a sentence. Your sentence can define the word, describe its importance or use it in some other way: archaeologist, evidence, clue, detective, discoverer, journal.

USING YOUR KNOWLEDGE

16. Is there anything left to discover? Discoveries are a part of living and will be made as long as life continues. Use your imagination to think of one discovery that could be made in each of the following areas: a) food, b) computers, c) use of the oceans, d) space travel, e) medicine.

THE INVESTIGATIVE REPORTER

17. a) Why do you think this book is called "Discovering Canada"?

b) Turn to the table of contents in the front of the book. Skim through the headings and write down five topics that you hope to find out more about.

17

2 Canada's past, present and future: What methods will we use to study Canada?

The mystery cave

I balanced my five-speed against the small birch tree. The front tire was flat, all right. At least I had made it to my cave. I called it George's Cave, named after myself, because I had discovered it. My buddies and I had been using it as a meeting-place since summer began. Nobody else seemed to know about it.

As I climbed up to the mouth of the cave, I heard a noise. It sounded like the clang of metal on rock. I crouched, then flattened myself against the sloping ground, like Spiderman. I peered into the mouth of the cave.

Two people—it looked like a man and a woman—were busy digging a hole. She was swinging a pick and he was shoveling out the gravel. Beside them was a large trunk. It looked really heavy, like the one my Aunt Gertie kept locked in her basement.

The woman appeared to be prying at a rock in the hole. Leaning on his shovel, the man began looking around. He glanced toward the cave opening. Frightened, I jumped back, and my foot sent pebbles scattering.

"What was that?" the woman snapped.

The digging stopped. I tried to hold my breath.

"I don't know," answered the man. His voice sounded mean. "I'm going out to take a look around. We can't take a chance on anybody watching us."

I looked back at my busted bike.

- When you read "The mystery cave," which of the following questions came into your mind?
  a) Why doesn't George have a ten-speed?
  b) How did he get the flat tire?
  c) Who is George?
  d) Where is the mystery cave?
  e) What is the colour of George's hair?
  f) Who might the diggers be? Robbers? Treasure hunters? Rock collectors?
  g) What might the trunk contain?
  h) Was the trunk made in Canada?
  i) Are the diggers planning to bury the trunk?
  j) Do the man and the woman seem nervous? If so, why?
  k) When did this story take place?

- Which of the questions may be helpful in solving the mystery? Which ones are not likely to be helpful?

- What other questions did you think of?

- What skills have you been using as you try to piece together the story of the mystery cave?

- Here is another "mystery" to solve: How did Canada get its name? Your teacher may ask you to write your answer in your notebook or to tell it to the class.

Chapter overview

The case of the mystery cave was an exercise in using *skills*. It required you to read, to make observations, to develop questions, to classify, to reach conclusions, to express yourself—probably through both spoken and written words.

These skills are important to your study of history. In chapter 1, you saw that people who study the past are like detectives. It is easier for you as a detective to put together the puzzle of the past if you know the skills of history and social science. In other words, skills are the tools that you use to piece together the story of people and events in Canada's history.

This chapter will involve you with a variety of skills. You will improve old skills and learn some new ones. The practice you get in this chapter is only the beginning. As you do the questions throughout the book, you will have many chances to practice these skills. This will help you improve your study methods in history and social studies. The questions are grouped under four headings: **GETTING THE FACTS, USING YOUR KNOWLEDGE, THINKING IT THROUGH,** and **THE INVESTIGATIVE REPORTER.**

Signposts

Near the beginning of each chapter, you will find "Signposts"—a list of the main topics or sections. In this chapter, the signposts are

> Getting the facts

> Using your knowledge

> Thinking it through

> The investigative reporter

Key words

skills	sources	compare/contrast
detective	chronology	cause/effect
facts/opinions		

Getting the facts

Getting the facts is the first step in learning about any topic. Detectives try to gather as many facts as they can before they start to solve a case. Facts, after all, are the pieces of the story you are trying to understand.

Getting the facts involves various skills. Throughout *Discovering Canada* you will be working with these skills, which include: observing pictures, charts, diagrams and maps; reading for main ideas; reading for details; paraphrasing (stating, naming, describing, identifying, summarizing); separating facts from opinions.

Detectives do these things. So do students of history. When you use these skills to study the history of Canada, you are playing the part of historian as detective.

Working with visuals

1. Which of the following have you seen in person?
   a) The **legislative** [LEH-jih-SLAY-tihv] buildings in the capital of your province
   b) The Pacific Ocean
   c) A polar bear in its natural Arctic surroundings
   d) The Olympic Stadium in Montreal
   e) A Newfoundland fishing village
   f) The CN Tower in Toronto
   g) The Rocky Mountains

The word "visual" is used to include photographs, paintings, drawings, charts, diagrams and maps.

Perhaps you have had a chance to see them all. Depending on where you live in Canada, you probably have seen one or two. Yet, the chances are good that you know what every one of them looks like. The reason, of course, is that you have seen pictures of them—on television, in magazines, on calendars, in newspapers, in books. Without pictures, our knowledge of the world today would be much less than it is.

The same is true of our knowledge of history. Through pictures, we can be familiar with people, places and events that we cannot observe with our own eyes.

The pictures—paintings, sketches, engravings and photographs—in *Discovering Canada* are an important part of the book. So are other visuals, such as maps, charts and diagrams. They have been included in the book to help you broaden your experience. Learn to examine them carefully.

21

Pictures

Suppose you were looking up the story of an explorer, like René-Robert Cavalier de la Salle [deu la SAL]. In a book you came across this picture:

Fig. 2-1 "The Building of the Griffon" by Fergus Kyle

2. a) As you look at this picture, what do you see?
   b) Now answer the following questions:

   i. What is the main activity in the picture?
   ii. How many people are involved? Are they all men?
   iii. Would you expect to see women and children? Why or why not?

iv. What can you tell about the people from the way they are dressed? In what century might the scene have taken place?
v. What can you tell about the location?
vi. Would knowing something about the artist help you to understand the painting?
vii. What would be a good title for the picture?

Compare your answers for a) and b). Which contains the most facts? Probably b). The reason is that you have been guided by a series of specific questions. In other words, you have looked at the picture in an organized way. Throughout *Discovering Canada* you will be encouraged to follow this method of looking at pictures. This will help you to learn more from them.

Reading

Reading is an activity that you rarely stop to think about—you just do it. Or you try to. If a story or explanation is easy, you sail along. If the reading is difficult, you struggle away, or give up. It depends on how important the results are to you.

Yet reading is a combination of skills. You can improve these skills if you understand what they are, and if you put them to use in a deliberate way. You need a method, like the detective has. A method will help you learn to read better and enjoy reading more.

Take the following brief story as a sample to work with. After you have read it, we will look at some methods of sharpening your reading skills:

> A man's car broke down on a country road. He got out to see if he could discover the problem. He looked under the hood, but the more he looked the more confused he got. He would have to get help, but he was undecided whether to start walking or to wait for somebody to come along.
>
> Suddenly a cow wandered up to the car, and took a look under the upraised hood. "Looks as though your trouble is the battery," it said.
>
> The man was startled. He took one look at the cow, then ran down the road. Soon he met a farmer, and told her the incredible story.

"Was it a black-and-white cow with one ear missing?" asked the farmer.

"As a matter of fact it was!" exclaimed the man.

"Oh, that's Matilda, eh?" said the farmer. "I wouldn't pay any attention to her. She doesn't know anything about cars."

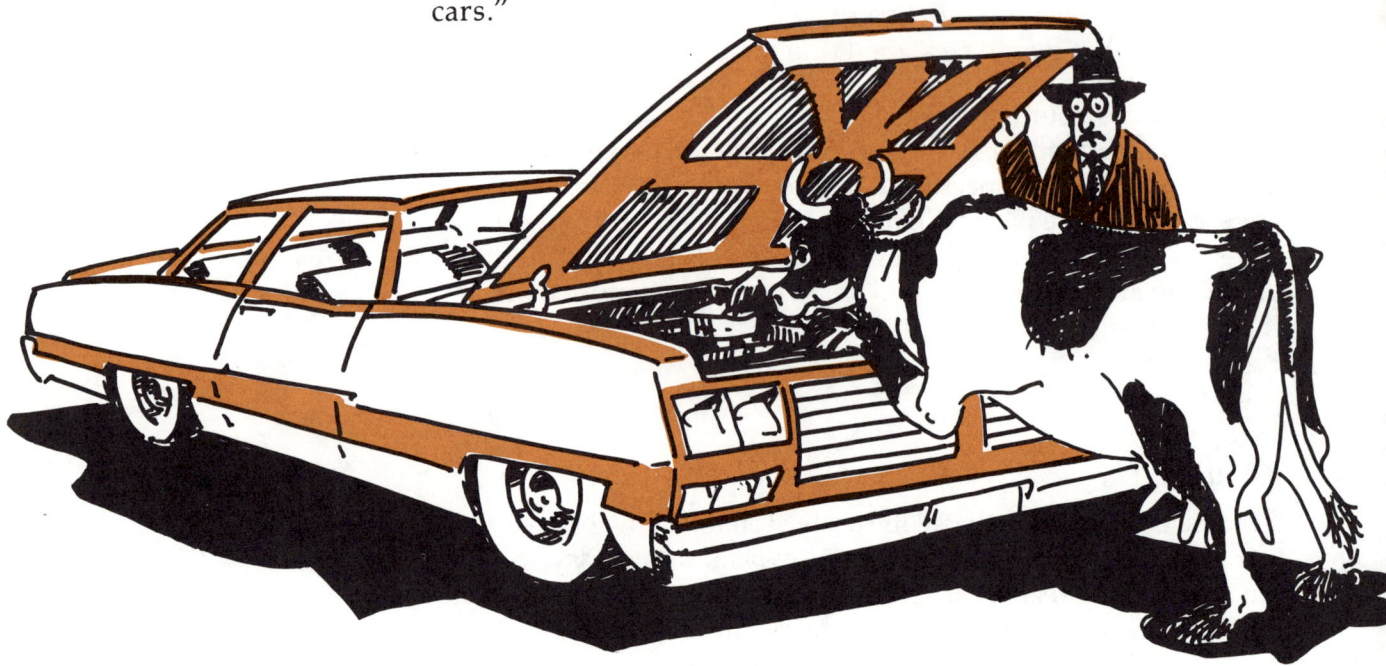

3. a) Which of the following would be a suitable title for the story?

    i. Cows say the darnedest things
    ii. A tall tale
    iii. Hearing is believing
    iv. Farmers are hard to fool

b) What is the main point in the first paragraph?

    i. The driver was unable to figure out why the car had broken down.
    ii. It is more serious for a car to break down in the country than in the city.
    iii. Traveling alone is a risky thing to do.

c) Why did the arrival of the cow startle the driver?

    i. Sheep-raising was the main kind of farming in that part of the country.
    ii. Cows are usually shy and try to avoid people.
    iii. The cow spoke.

   d) What is the most surprising thing about the ending of the story?

      i. The farmer remarked on the cow's ignorance about cars, not on its talking.
     ii. The farmer thought the driver had an overactive imagination.
    iii. The farmer knew the cow by name.

What skills did you use in answering the questions? First of all, to answer part a), you had to "skim"—that is, read quickly—the whole story. The skill of skimming is helpful in getting an overall view of the content. Remember this as one of the first steps whenever you read.

The next step was to "read for details." To answer parts b) to d), you looked at particular points, ideas, descriptions and events. Reading for details—a more thorough kind of reading—can deepen your understanding of a story or an explanation.

Another step is to "ask questions" about the content. For the above story, the questions were already given. However, you could have made up your own. Such questions often come from topic sentences, or from other clues, such as headings and pictures. When you read in a questioning way, you are using your brain more actively, digging deeper—and usually understanding better.

4. Write the following in your notebook, then complete the conversation:

   Younger student: I can never get my school work done on time. Other kids get finished before the bell, but I'm always still trying to figure out what I'm reading.
   You: Maybe you need to sharpen your reading skills.
   Younger student: How do I do that?

Facts versus opinions

"Just give me the facts" is a common expression. You can imagine it being used in any number of situations; for example, a parent questioning a son or daughter arriving home later than expected; a teacher asking Johnnie or Jane about the frog in the classroom closet; a lawyer speaking to a witness in a courtroom.

In each case, the questioner wants the facts, not opinions. What's the difference?

A *fact* may be defined as something—an event, an object, an individual—which actually exists (or has existed), can be observed, and can be shown to be real and true. An *opinion*, on the other hand, is a feeling or viewpoint a person has about something. Indeed, the word opinion is often expressed as "personal opinion."

Look at these two statements:

a) The train is one way to travel. (FACT)
b) The train is better than the bus as a way to travel. (OPINION)

Statement a) can be proven as a fact. You can experience it first-hand. You can actually see a train, watch it arrive, or depart from, the station, with travelers on board. Whether or not the train is better than the bus is, however, a matter of opinion. A person feels a preference for one or the other. Facts may be considered—such as the cost, time involved, comfort and so on—but opinions do not spring automatically from facts. A person can say, "I can't explain it exactly, but I just like trains better."

5. Write each of the following in your notebook. Beside each statement of fact, print "F." Beside each statement of opinion, print "O."

a) People eat pumpkin pie.
b) Canada celebrated its 100th birthday in 1967.
c) Pumpkin pie tastes better than rhubarb pie.
d) Tall oaks from little acorns grow.
e) Canaries require a regular diet of raw meat.
f) Wayne Gretzky is a great hockey player, known to his teammates as a leader.

Fig. 2-2 Wayne Gretzky

Using your knowledge

Once you get the facts, you have gathered some information about a topic. But what then?

Suppose you see a program on TV about junk food. The amount of it they eat is described by some young people talking to an interviewer. Then a doctor comes on to explain how junk food lacks nutrition needed for good health and leads to overweight.

"Very interesting," you say, as the program ends. It happens to be your lunchtime. You don't think very much about it, but the food choices in your kitchen could be grouped as follows: a) a granola bar, an apple and a glass of milk, and b) a bag of salted chips, a handful of sugar candy and a can of cola. If you choose b), you are ignoring the facts you have "gathered." You have not thought about the information and put it to use.

"Using your knowledge" skills are a group of skills that help you study and really understand the facts you have gathered. Think of detectives, for example. They may discover a number of facts in a case. They cannot solve the crime, however, until they *use* the information to come up with leads. In this book, "using your knowledge" skills will teach you to understand facts and put them to use. You will do things such as compare facts, look at causes and effects, and search for bias.

The next few pages will introduce you to some "using your knowledge" skills. You will use them to understand a man of mystery in Canadian history: Adam Dollard [doh-LAHR].

Adam Dollard: Unselfish hero or victim by accident?

(1) Adam Dollard died a violent death in his twenties more than 300 years ago. The place was near the Ottawa River, in what was then New France.

Why is it that some history books tell his story in great detail—while others ignore Adam Dollard completely?

There are some unanswered questions about Dollard. Was he a brave soldier who died unselfishly to save the new settlement of Montreal? Did he stumble into an ambush while trying to make money in a hurry from the fur trade? Was he just one of the hundreds who happened to be killed in the early struggle to settle Canada?

New France had been started by Samuel de Champlain. In 1605, he settled at Port Royal in what is now Nova Scotia. Then he moved to the St. Lawrence River in 1608 to start the colony at Quebec. In 1642, Montreal was established as a church centre, before becoming the headquarters of the fur trade.

The French had made bitter enemies of the Iroquois [EER-uh-kwah] Indians. The French had befriended the Algonquins [al-GAHN^G-kwihns] and the Hurons, who had been fighting the Iroquois long before the Europeans arrived. The Iroquois had attacked and destroyed Huron villages in what is now southern Ontario.

These are all facts agreed upon by historians. Certain other facts are also accepted. For example, it is known that Adam Dollard was a 25-year-old soldier at Montreal in 1660. The Iroquois attacks on Montreal were at their peak. Small war parties struck quickly, claimed a few victims, and vanished into the wilderness. Now that they had wiped out the Huron villages, the Iroquois had perhaps decided on a knock-out blow for Montreal, the western **outpost** of New France.

For one reason or another, Dollard set out from Montreal in the spring of 1660. With him were 16 French Canadian companions. They travelled up the Ottawa River to the Long Sault [soo] Rapids. A small band of perhaps 40 Hurons and Algonquins joined them. They were met by canoes carrying more than 700 Iroquois warriors. Fighting raged for seven days. At the end, Adam Dollard and his companions, including all the French Canadians and some of the Indians, lay dead.

These are the basic facts. There is more to the story, depending on which of two versions you accept. The *traditional* account has been around for hundreds of years. The *revised* account dates back a little more than 50 years.

(2) The *traditional account* adds the following information: In the late winter of 1660, a rumour reached Montreal that the Iroquois were on the warpath. A force of several hundred had wintered up the Ottawa River. They planned to hit New France with a massive attack. Montreal was the first target.

Adam Dollard and a group of young French Canadians decided there was only one thing to do—go after the Iroquois where they had been spending the winter. Strike the first blow, give the Iroquois a hard fight. Maybe they would leave Montreal alone.

Dollard and his fighting men were successful. Though defeated, they fought bravely. The Iroquois were very impressed. If a handful of French Canadians and their Indian **allies** were so tough to beat, what chance would the Iroquois have of conquering Montreal, let alone all New France? Rather than continue on the warpath, the Iroquois went home.

(Remember: You have just read the traditional, or older, view of the facts and the meaning they add up to.)

(3) The *revised account* completes the story quite differently: Dollard believed that small bands of Iroquois would be coming down the Ottawa River. They had become quite bold in recent years, since their defeat of the Hurons. Probably the Iroquois would be loaded down with beaver pelts, after a winter of

trapping and trading with northern Indians. They would not be expecting to run into any French Canadians.

Dollard and his friends planned to catch a few Iroquois by surprise. At the Long Sault they found a small fort built with rough logs. They settled in and waited. Iroquois canoes swished through the rapids and into the gunfire of the French Canadians. Unknown to Dollard, these were only the advance party of an Iroquois army. Within hours it had him trapped in the simple fort. It was a matter of time before he and the other defenders ran out of food, water and weapons.

Although the Iroquois had defeated Adam Dollard and his companions, they did not continue on to attack Montreal. The reason was probably not their fear of the French. More likely they were following their custom of returning to their villages after a battle. The people back home were always keen to hear about the results and to see the prisoners who had been captured.

Fig. 2-3 An artist's impression of Dollard at the Long Sault. What is the artist's point of view about Dollard?

Chronology

Chronology [kruh-NAH-luh-jee] is about events being in the correct order according to when they happened; that is, according to time. If an explanation or story has events in the wrong order, it is bound to be confusing. Suppose the Adam Dollard story had events in the following order:

a) Adam Dollard left Montreal for the Long Sault
b) Champlain founded Quebec
c) The Iroquois overwhelmed the fort
d) The Huron villages were destroyed by Iroquois attackers
e) Montreal was established as a centre for churches and the fur trade
f) The advance party of Iroquois arrived at the Long Sault

Confusing, isn't it? A jumble of facts does not help us to understand. In this case, the facts are about events that took place over time and in a certain sequence. We can make sense of these facts only if we organize them properly.

6. In your notebook, write the events in the correct chronological order. A helpful way of improving your skills to do with chronology is to make up a *timeline*. Here is an example of how you could show events leading up to Dollard's battle at the Long Sault:

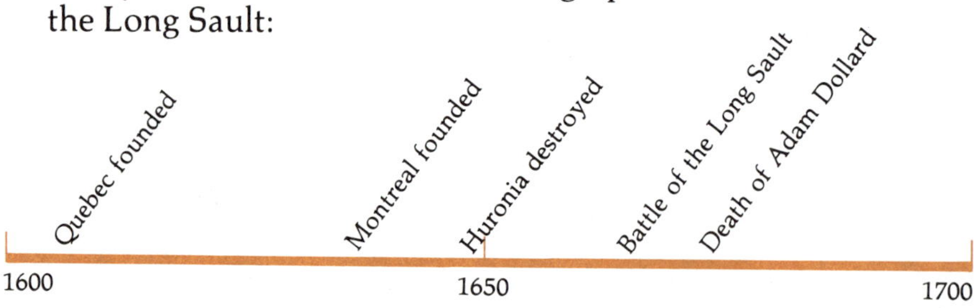

Timelines help highlight important events that take place in a certain period of time. They also help you keep the order of these events straight. Timelines appear at the beginning of many of the chapters in this book.

Fig. 2-4 Timeline

Quebec founded — Montreal founded — Huronia destroyed — Battle of the Long Sault — Death of Adam Dollard

1600 — 1650 — 1700

7. Make a timeline showing at least *five* important events in your life so far. Then add *three* or more events that you expect may be part of your life in the future.

Comparison and contrast

Comparing and contrasting can help us to understand facts and ideas more clearly. *Comparing* means finding things that are the same. *Contrasting* means finding differences.

For example, take the two accounts of the battle between Adam Dollard and the Iroquois—the traditional and the revised. The first step is to reread these and pick out the main points. One way of doing this is to make a chart.

8. Copy the following chart into your notebook and fill in the missing points.

	TRADITIONAL	REVISED
What was the situation?	Montreal was fear-struck by rumours of an Iroquois plan for a mass attack on the settlement.	Small groups of Iroquois were expected to be hauling a rich load of furs.
What action resulted?	Dollard left Montreal with some companions for the Long Sault.	
Why?		
What events took place?	Dollard and his companions fought the Iroquois, holding them off for several days.	
		Badly outnumbered, Dollard and company were eventually overcome and killed.
What was the outcome?	Amazed by the bravery of Dollard, the Iroquois decided not to attack Montreal for fear of defeat.	

Fig. 2-5 Comparison and contrast chart for Dollard at the Long Sault.

9. For the two accounts of the story of Adam Dollard, list *two* points that are the same and *two* points that are different.

Cause and effect

If something happens, people generally assume there is a reason for it. For example, if you catch a cold (*effect*), the explanation is that you went to the store during a snowfall without a hat (*cause*).

10. Suppose another fact were added to the story of Adam Dollard: He and his French companions made out their wills just before leaving for the Long Sault. Which of the following statements is the most likely *cause* of the decision to make wills?

31

a) Dollard was a pessimist, always fearing the worst.
b) Making a will was the usual thing to do in those days before a trip away from the main settlement.
c) Dollard was sure he was going to die a martyr's [MAHR-ters] death.

Did you find the question difficult to answer? Did you think of another possible cause not mentioned above? Could it be that all of those causes led to the one effect? You shouldn't be surprised if you are not sure. As we have already seen, the facts about Adam Dollard are not complete. The lack of facts makes it hard to know *what* happened, let alone *why*.

In the next section, you will be taking a more detailed look at cause and effect. It is one of the most intriguing tasks facing the historian as detective.

Thinking it through

So far, you have gotten some facts, examined them closely, and perhaps come up with some new ideas. You are now ready to put all your knowledge and ideas together. You can put the pieces together by forming opinions, by drawing conclusions, or by solving problems. The skills needed to do this belong to the "thinking it through" group of skills. The next section of this chapter will introduce you to some of these skills.

In this section, you will also use the skills you worked with in the two earlier sections. You will still be observing, reading for main ideas, comparing and so on. It's just that the emphasis will be on the next group of skills, on thinking it through. You will find out about these as you read the following scenes and complete the activities.

Analysis: The problem of finding causes

SCENE 1: *Strange behaviour*

Hiram arrived at his classroom a few minutes after 9:00. Mr. Swerdlap, the teacher, cast a sidelong glance in Hiram's direction but said nothing. Mr. Swerdlap was replacing a bulb in the filmstrip projector. He was trying to hurry so he could begin the class in Canadian history.

From across the aisle, Ferd whispered to Hiram, "You'll be lucky if you don't get sent to the office. You know how Mr. Swerdlap hates lates."

"Lay off, Ferd," snapped Hiram.

"Don't be so touchy," Ferd replied.

The projector flashed a picture on the screen. Mr. Swerdlap explained, "There's Mr. Mackenzie King, who holds the record for the most years as prime minister of Canada. His companion there is his favorite dog, Pat."

Hiram leaped up and ran out of the room.

A number of questions may spring to mind about this scene, but the most obvious one is "Why did Hiram act as he did?" What may be the *cause* (or causes) of his sudden departure from the classroom?

11. What possible causes can you think of?
12. Which of the following explanations do you think is the most likely? Why?
    Mr. Swerdlap: "I guess Hiram forgot something at his locker. He was in a rush when he arrived—late again."
    Ferd: "He's probably afraid of getting bawled out for being late."
    Max (Hiram's best friend in class): "Maybe something happened to him at home or on the way to school. Maybe he's upset."

When something happens, we assume there must have been a cause. Yet, as the case of Hiram shows, it is not easy to be sure of the cause (or causes) of a particular event.

If you found that more than one cause was needed to explain Hiram's action, you are on the right track. You cannot explain most effects by giving a single cause. When you do, you are probably oversimplifying. When you oversimplify, you may be leaving out important points or details. The result is likely to be a misunderstanding and possibly some other harmful outcomes.

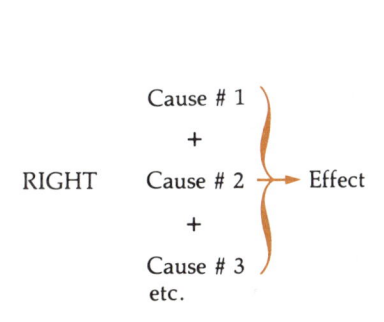

WRONG   Cause ⟶ Effect

RIGHT   Cause # 1
         +
         Cause # 2 ⟶ Effect
         +
         Cause # 3
         etc.

Fig. 2-6 An effect (action, event) usually results from two or more causes happening together. The diagram shows what is usually "wrong" and "right" in figuring out causes.

Logical thinking

SCENE 2 *(ten days earlier): Father Fludd loses an argument*

Having just finished dessert, the Fludd family are having a talk. The subject is the same as it has been for several days: whether or not to get a dog. Hiram wants one; his father does not. Father Fludd argues that tropical fish are enough pets for one household. But Hiram declares that you cannot take a goldfish for a run, nor can you teach a guppie to do tricks.

"We don't even have to go looking for a dog," Hiram says. "Let's just go over to Aunt Sara's. Her poodle, Frantic, has just had pups, and we can have one for nothing!"

Hiram's father is not convinced. "Let me put it this way," he says. "All poodles are jumpy and yappy, a real nuisance. Frantic's pup is a poodle. Therefore, Frantic's pup is bound to be a nuisance."

"No, Dad," Hiram protests. "Not all poodles are like that. Some of them may be, but I don't think all of them are."

"Well, the Corbetts down the street have one. Every time I walk by, that creature leaps and spins and somersaults and barks like crazy. Sam Gunn, at work, tells me his poodle acts like there's a demon inside her whenever a person comes to the door. That's proof enough for me."

But Hiram was not ready to give up. "So you don't want a noisy, jumpy dog. Basset hounds are easy-going, and they hardly bark at all. So a basset hound would be a good dog for us."

Mr. Fludd groaned, but he was smiling. "All right, Hiram, all right. You've got me there. But we don't have time to shop for one just now."

"No problem, Dad," Hiram announced. "See this ad in today's paper: GOOD HOME NEEDED FOR BASSET PUPS. CALL 237-4191."

13. Who do you think gave the most logical and convincing arguments, Hiram or his father? Why do you think so?

The discussion between Hiram and his father shows some clear thinking by both. You probably noted the step-by-step way each tried to prove his point.

Mr. Fludd tried two methods of ruling out a poodle as a possible pet:

(1) He took the stand that "all poodles are a nuisance." Because Frantic's pup was a poodle, that meant that it would be a nuisance.

(2) When Hiram challenged his remark about poodles, Mr. Fludd replied by giving two examples of annoying poodles. These were enough, he insisted, to make the conclusion that all poodles are the same.

Hiram saw that his father's argument made sense. He realized that his own argument would have to be logical too. Since Mr. Fludd objected to noisy, jumpy dogs, Hiram pointed out that not all dogs were annoying. He backed up his statement with the example of the easy-going basset hound. Hiram's clear thinking therefore ended up winning him the argument.

Clear thinking does not always work as smoothly as this, unfortunately. For example, you may have trouble using "logic" with the schoolyard bully. Yet clear thinking is always going to be more useful than muddled thinking.

Weighing evidence

SCENE 3: *The accident*

In the early morning rain, Hiram took his basset hound, Randy, out for its regular run. It was always a good time for both. It was so good that Hiram had been late for school three times in the week since Randy had joined the Fludd family.

Randy's leash had already come apart, so Hiram let him run alongside. The dog had always seemed to stay close to the boy anyway. All of a sudden, Randy spotted something across the street. The dog took off. The black car swerved, but the dog went under. The driver of the car managed to stop a half-block away. Randy was hurt but still alive.

The driver took the injured dog and the shocked boy back to the Fludd house. Hiram's mother drove him to school. She said not to worry. She would rush Randy to the animal clinic; they would take care of him.

Four witnesses were present at the scene of the accident: (1) Hiram (2) the driver (3) a neighbour (4) a passing motorist, who spoke to the neighbour. Here is what each of the witnesses had to say:

(1) Hiram: "I only saw Randy running, then I saw him lying on the road. I sort of had my head down, before, because of the rain. I didn't really see the car. I just hope Randy's not going to die."

(2) The driver: "I had no chance to miss the dog. It simply jumped in front of my car without warning. No warning at all. I was driving slowly, too, because of the rain, even though I was a little late for work. I'm sorry about the dog, and I know the boy's upset. Now I'm really late though. A lot of pressure at work these days. It's a busy time of year. Dogs shouldn't be running loose in the streets."

(3) The neighbour: "The car was going too fast. Rain makes these streets mighty slippery. Even on a sunny day—in other words, normal conditions—the driver wouldn't have been able to stop in time. Guys like that make me mad; they should be thrown in jail. I saw the whole thing. Hiram was running, like I've seen him do before, with the dog a couple of feet in front of him. The dog did jump onto the road, but he veered back to the boulevard. It was too late, and the car hit his hindquarters."

(4) The passing motorist: "I was a couple of blocks away when I saw the black car swerve. It took quite a while to come to a full stop. I guess the driver was going a little too fast. When the car went by me minutes before—I was at the intersection, coming off a side street—it seemed to run the red light."

14. Which witness gives the most convincing evidence? The least convincing? Give your reasons.

You have just used the skill of weighing evidence. Now you can try to improve that skill by understanding more clearly how to do it. Let's see if we can figure out the steps you may have used.

First, you skimmed through the four statements to get a first impression.

Then, you formed a hunch, a kind of educated guess: "Witness so-and-so is the most convincing."

Next, you asked yourself questions like the following:
 i. How carefully did each person seem to have observed the event?
 ii. Which witness had the least reason for distorting the truth?
 iii. Was any one witness specially qualified, or located, to give more dependable evidence than the others?
 iv. Which statements stand out as probably factual, and will therefore help you to reach a conclusion?

Perhaps your method was a little different. Probably, though, you can see the part played by critical questions in weighing evidence.

SCENE 4: *The conclusion*

15. Which of the following scenarios [seh-NAYR-ee-ohs], in your opinion, is the best conclusion to the story? Give your reasons.
    a) *Happy ending:* Hiram goes straight home from school. Mother arrives shortly after. The dog, Randy, is able to walk, thanks to the splint on its right hind leg. Frightened by the experience of being run over, Randy has lost his bark. Now much less annoying to parents of Hiram. Mr. Swerdlap phones, learns of the reasons (causes) of Hiram's leaving the classroom, says all is well.
    b) *Sad ending:* Hiram goes home, finds himself locked out. Waits on the front step in the rain. Mother arrives after two hours. No dog. Randy's life could not be saved. Phone call from school instructs Hiram to appear in the principal's office upon his return to school.
    c) *Mixed:* The dog dies, but father buys Hiram several exotic fish for his aquarium. Hiram's interest in tropical fish is renewed. He decides to study to be a marine biologist. Mr. Swerdlap is annoyed at first, but excuses Hiram's leaving class upon hearing the causes.

16. Describe how you would have ended the story.

The investigative reporter

So far in this chapter, you have been practicing a number of skills. These skills have helped you get the facts, analyze them, and form opinions or conclusions. All these activities have likely required you to search for information and to write it down or record it in some other way. So, at the same time you are a detective looking into the past, you are also a reporter who researches and presents information. The skills of researching and reporting are important. They form the last group of skills you will learn from this book, the "investigative reporter" skills. Investigative reporter skills include: learning how to get the most out of a textbook; defining a topic by developing questions for research; finding out about, and choosing, sources other than textbooks; taking notes.

As a reporter, you can do all your basic work in the classroom. Probably all your reporting activities can be carried on there. In later chapters of *Discovering Canada*, however, you will be learning more of the investigative reporter skills. You will be using the library, developing skills for interviewing, and preparing reports and other kinds of presentations. If, at some time in the future, you have the chance to do some investigating outside the history classroom or the school, you will have the skills you need.

The investigative reporter at work

In this section, you are going to join Herbie, another student like yourself, in the role of investigative reporter. His teacher, Ms. Forest, has given Herbie the following topic to research: The role of blacks in Canadian history.

Ms. Forest begins by reminding Herbie that a textbook is a handy place to start. Together they study the setup of *Discovering Canada*.

The textbook: How to use "Discovering Canada"

As a textbook, *Discovering Canada* is set up to be both a source of information and a program for using this information. In other words, you will gain knowledge about Canada and also develop a set of skills. These skills can be used to study a variety of social studies topics.

If you know how a book is organized, you will be able to make better use of it. Here are some points about the setup of *Discovering Canada*:

- **Table of contents:** lists chapter titles and the signposts, which are the main topics of each chapter.

- **Index:** lists alphabetically the topics, events, terms, names of people and other specific items found throughout the book. The page numbers where these items are found in the book are also listed

- **Chapter organization:** each chapter is organized in the same way. Each begins with a two-page spread, consisting of a visual and a brief story or situation. This introduces the main idea of the chapter. Then the chapter overview tells about the content. The signposts and the key words are listed next. Key words signal important ideas in the chapter.

- **Activities:** as you have seen from this chapter, the activities are grouped under four different headings. Each heading stands for a group of skills. As you practice these, they will become part of your approach to history and social studies.

- **Marginal notes:** in the margins you will find explanations of special terms, as well as extra bits of information and items of interest.

- **Timelines:** appearing in many chapters, timelines show where each main event fits in a certain period of time.

- **Glossary:** definitions of glossary words—which appear in **bold** type—are given in a section near the end of the book. Pronunciation guides appear with these where necessary, and with other possibly difficult words throughout the book. The key to the pronunciation guides appears in the back of the book.

When you use other books, begin by looking at how they are organized. You will save yourself a lot of time and effort.

Preparing questions for research

Herbie: I can see that this textbook is organized in a certain way. It helps to know that. It should make my research easier.

Ms. Forest: Yes, and the same is true for other books you will use. Don't just start reading from page one and hope to stumble sooner or later on the information you want. Look books over, the way we did *Discovering Canada*.

Herbie: Now, how should I begin to investigate about blacks in Canadian history? Should I start reading?

Ms. Forest: You could go through the index, but you don't really know what you are looking for yet. First, let's change the topic into the form of a question. For example: "What part have blacks played in Canadian history?" Hmmm... a big question. Let's try to stay away from the mistake so many reporters make—trying to cover too much in one report.

Herbie: How do I cut down this big question?

Ms. Forest: It's not so difficult. There are two obvious ways to narrow the question: (1) You could put a limit on the period of time to be covered and deal only with events around 1800 or 1900 or (2) you could choose a theme to focus on. For example, instead of including all the topics you can think of, zero in on a certain person, or a certain event, or life in one part of Canada, or how people made a living.

(They spend some time discussing possible topics. One is Black Loyalists in Nova Scotia. Another is people who fled to Ontario from slavery in the United States. Herbie wonders about blacks in Western Canada. Ms. Forest thinks there is probably enough information—an important point in research—to write something on each of these topics. Herbie should choose one.)

Herbie: So my research could start with a basic question like "How did blacks—or one black person—take part in the Loyalist migrations to Nova Scotia?"

Ms. Forest: Right! After you've read a bit, you may decide to change your question. However, you can only do that after you've checked to see what information is available.

Herbie: Am I ready to start reading, then?

Ms. Forest: Pretty well. With a bit of practice, you will learn to read in order to choose main ideas for an outline. This time,

I will help. Here are some specific questions to guide your reading, and to get your outline started:
—Who were the Loyalists?
—Why did they come to Nova Scotia?
—Why were blacks part of the movement of people known as the Loyalist migration?
—Is there a black person who was well-known during early Loyalist times in Nova Scotia?
—What was life like for the Loyalist blacks? How were they treated? What problems did they have? What successes?

17. As Herbie did, write some of these questions in your notebook. Choose the ones you think are important and/or interesting. Add any other questions you can think of.
    Then check *Discovering Canada* to find out a) how much of the necessary information it contains, and b) what information must be looked for in other books.

Sources of information

Herbie and Ms. Forest talked about the next step: to locate sources of information besides the textbook *Discovering Canada*. Herbie took it for granted that he would go straight to the computer. Ms. Forest was not surprised because the computer was used for so many things.

She thought about how schools had changed since she was a student. Until a few years ago, a person looking for information thought first about *books*. Possibly *magazines* and *newspapers* came to mind. But books of one kind or another were the main sources. Now, information comes in so many more forms, like computer programs, cassettes . . . .

Still, some things do stay the same, she thought. We still get a lot of our information from books, from things in print. Even if a book is listened to on a *recording* or *tape-cassette*, it is a book all the same. Though years-old copies of a magazine may be found only on *microfilm* and viewed on a TV-like monitor, the copy is still a magazine. A library may be called a media centre, but people still use it for the same reasons as before.

Ms. Forest realized that Herbie was getting a little restless.

Ms. Forest: Here is a very important fact about sources of information. They are either first-hand—called *primary* sources—or second-hand—called *secondary* sources. If the information is first-hand, it comes from the person or persons actually taking part in an event. Second-hand information comes from people who know about the event, but did not actually take part in it. For example, an author or film-maker describes, explains or shows what happened.

Herbie: What's this got to do with books?

Ms. Forest: Books, people, and any other source of information are all either primary or secondary sources. Perhaps this chart from our textbook, *Discovering Canada*, can help explain:

Fig. 2-7 Types of sources

TYPE	EXAMPLES	DESCRIPTION
Primary	letters, diaries, photos, speeches, notes of eyewitnesses, oral traditions, autobiographies	first-hand reports by, and about, the people taking part in the event being investigated
Secondary	articles and books written by authors working with primary sources, e.g. research studies, biographies, some texts	second-hand accounts presented to the reader by a middleman, i.e. by an author (or authors), an editor, a film-maker
Other	some textbooks, encyclopedias, dictionaries, bibliographies	teaching books, intended to give the reader a handy, often simple, explanation

18. Write the following list in your notebook. Put "P" beside each primary source and "S" beside each secondary source. Beside sources that are neither primary nor secondary, put "O" for "other."
    a) A letter written by the Black Loyalist, Thomas Peters
    b) *The Dictionary of Canadian Biography*
    c) A ship captain's log, showing the names of Black Loyalists
    d) A book, *The Black Loyalists: The Search for a Promised Land in Nova Scotia and Sierra Leone 1783-1870* by James W. Walker, published in 1976
    e) A sketch of Black Loyalists drawn by an artist who visited them

Fig. 2-8 What are some skills of the investigative reporter?

Taking notes

Herbie: Am I about ready to start writing—at last?
Ms. Forest: The sooner you start writing, the better. Even while reading your textbook for general information, you can start taking notes. As a result, you will have at least part of the answers to some of your research questions.
Herbie: What about this primary and secondary stuff?
Ms. Forest: Don't worry too much about it for now. In assignments later in the year, you will need to become more "choosy" in your use of sources.

For the time being, it is enough to use what I call the "textbook plus" method of research. That is, you dig out all the information you can from the text. Then you try to find the rest of what you need from one other book. If necessary, you turn to still another book.

These other books may also be textbooks. But remember that textbooks cover a great many topics. They cannot go into the detail you may find in a book written about one topic only—such as Professor Walker's book on the Black Loyalists.

For the sake of variety at least, you should consider using a book or two that is not a textbook.

Herbie: Whatever kind of books I use, I still have trouble taking notes. Any suggestions?

Ms. Forest: Note-taking is a very individual thing. What works for one person may not work for another. However, some of these tips may help:

(1) Read over the part of the book that deals with the question you are trying to answer. Use the outline you made earlier.
(2) After you understand the information as clearly as you can, write the facts and ideas down in your own style.
(3) Check the book for any details you may have missed.

19. With Herbie, you have shared the experience of going through several steps as the investigative reporter. Tell a story in which you explain what you have learned so far about doing research for a report.

Conclusion

You have now had a preview of *Discovering Canada*. The activities you have worked with are a sample of what lies ahead. The activities—questions, problems, projects and so on—throughout this book are intended to help you learn about Canada's past and present.

But you are going to do more than learn facts, important though they may be. You are going to improve some skills you may already have, and gain and develop many new ones. These skills, which cover a variety of things from reading to methods of thinking and problem-solving to investigative reporting, can make you a more successful student of Canadian history. You should find something else about these skills: they can serve you well in your everyday life.

Fig. 2-9 Practice your skills of picture analysis. Examine this picture carefully and answer the questions on page 22-23.

45

3 Before the Europeans: Who were the native peoples of Canada?

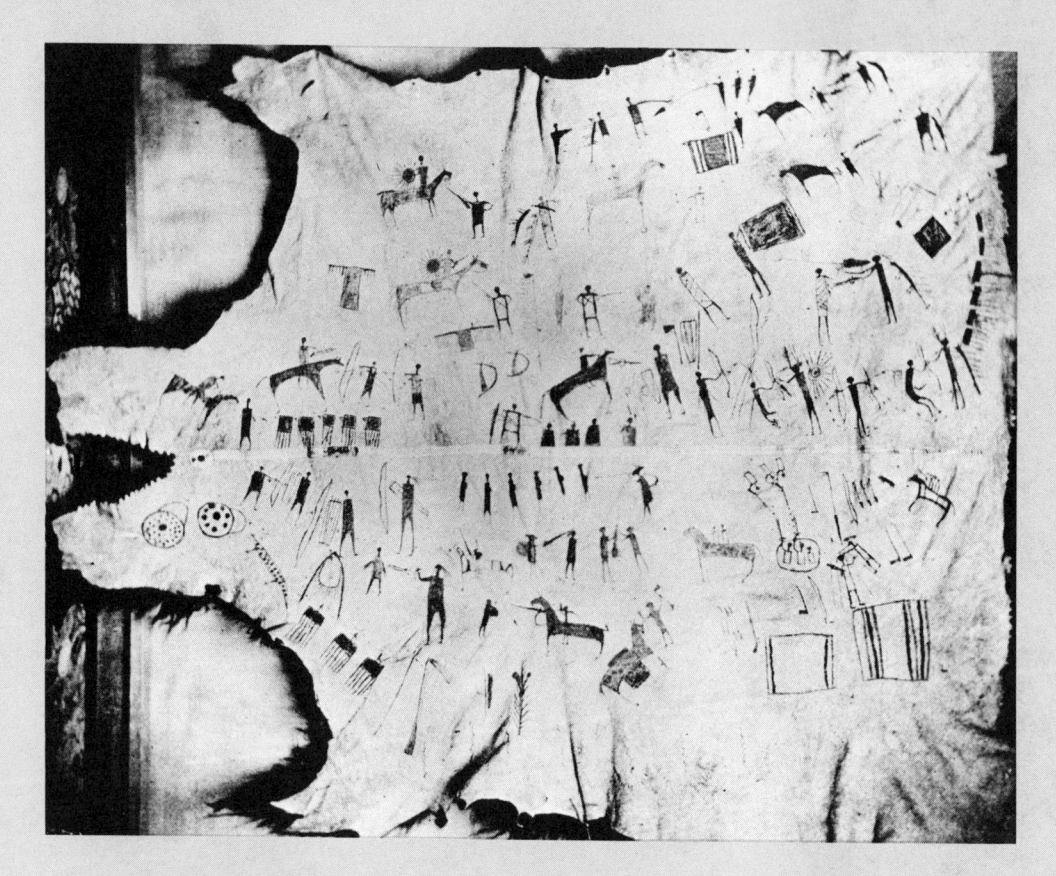

On the buffalo robe is an example of picture-writing by Blood Indians in Alberta about 100 years ago. Can you "read" the story?

- Give two reasons why this painted buffalo robe is valuable.

The story of Coyote and the salmon

Coyote could change his shape when he wanted to. One day he was crossing a creek. The water was choppy. He lost his balance and fell in. To escape drowning, he changed himself into a board. He floated downstream, into the Fraser River and on toward the Pacific Ocean. At last he was stopped by a fish-dam owned by two old women.

The women needed fuel, so they threw Coyote into their fire. Faced with death again, Coyote changed himself into a crying baby. The women were shocked. They grabbed the baby from the fire and tried to make it feel better. One of the women said, "Let's raise the baby as if it were our own child."

Time passed, and the baby grew. The women found it hard to get along with. One day they were going on a trip. Before leaving, they gave the baby—Coyote—some advice. They declared, "No matter what happens, do not open any of the boxes we are leaving with you."

"OK," said Coyote. But he was not ready to obey his parents. Besides, he could not stop wondering what the boxes contained.

Coyote had another idea also. The dam of the two women kept salmon from swimming upstream to his people. The dam, therefore, must be removed.

The two old women left. Coyote smashed the dam. Then he turned to the boxes. He could not leave them alone. He opened each one.

Out of the first box poured smoke; out of the second, hordes of angry wasps; from the third, clouds of flies; and from the fourth, an army of beetles.

Because Coyote cared for his people, they enjoyed a feast of salmon. However, because he disobeyed his parents' advice, his people are attacked by smoke, wasps, flies and beetles. When the salmon swim upstream, the bugs fly with them.

Based on *When The Morning Stars Sang Together* by John S. Morgan.

- Suppose you were asked to pick a different title for the story. Which of the following best fits the main idea of the story. Why?
  —You can't trust a coyote
  —If you want to stay out of trouble, obey your elders
  —If you change too much, people will think there's something fishy

- This story comes from Indians living along the Thompson River in British Columbia. What does it tell us about their ideas, their attitudes and the influence of nature on their way of life?

- What do you think is the purpose of stories like this?

Timeline

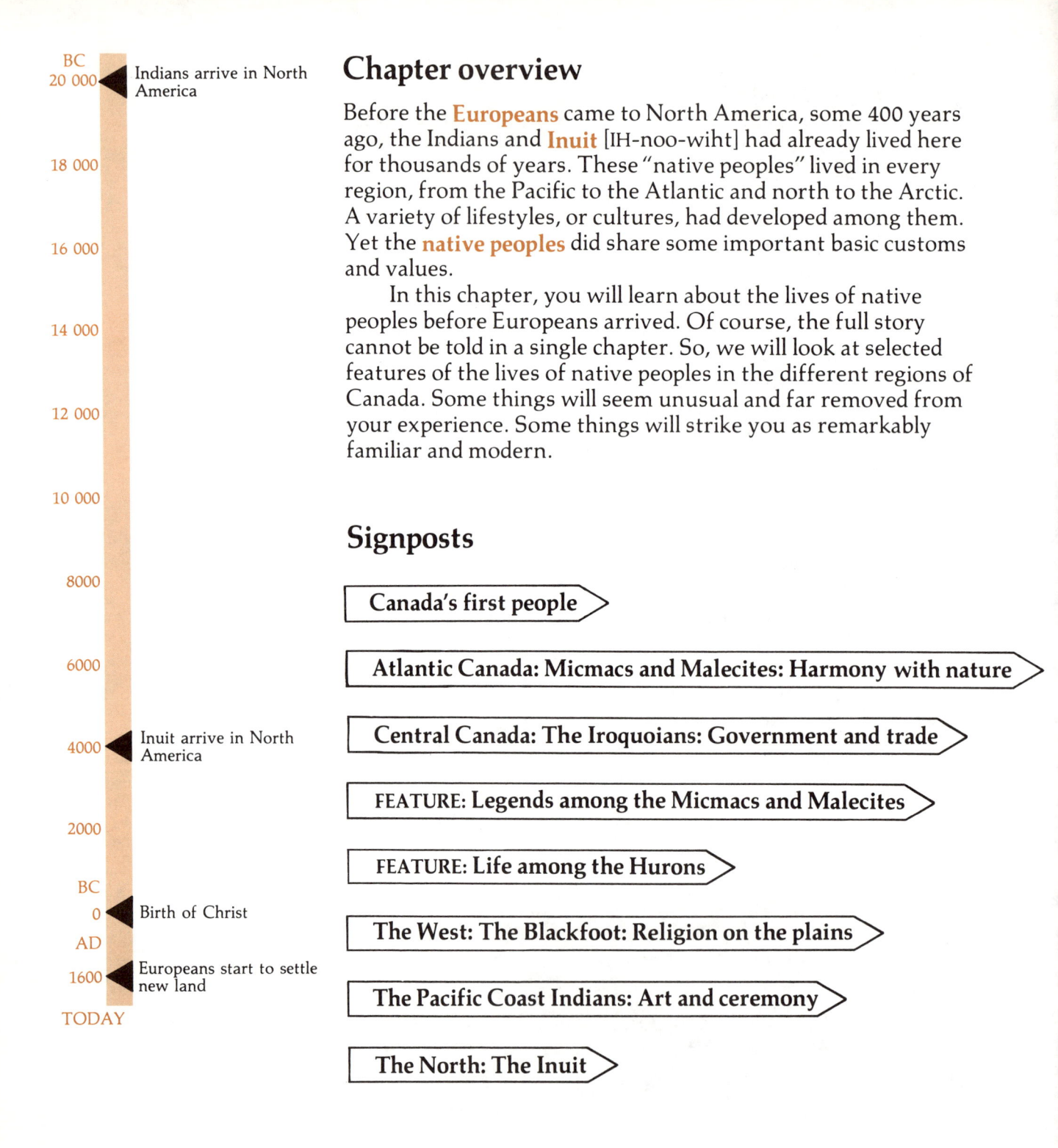

- BC 20 000 — Indians arrive in North America
- 18 000
- 16 000
- 14 000
- 12 000
- 10 000
- 8000
- 6000
- 4000 — Inuit arrive in North America
- 2000
- BC 0 / AD — Birth of Christ
- 1600 — Europeans start to settle new land
- TODAY

Chapter overview

Before the **Europeans** came to North America, some 400 years ago, the Indians and **Inuit** [IH-noo-wiht] had already lived here for thousands of years. These "native peoples" lived in every region, from the Pacific to the Atlantic and north to the Arctic. A variety of lifestyles, or cultures, had developed among them. Yet the **native peoples** did share some important basic customs and values.

In this chapter, you will learn about the lives of native peoples before Europeans arrived. Of course, the full story cannot be told in a single chapter. So, we will look at selected features of the lives of native peoples in the different regions of Canada. Some things will seem unusual and far removed from your experience. Some things will strike you as remarkably familiar and modern.

Signposts

Canada's first people >

Atlantic Canada: Micmacs and Malecites: Harmony with nature >

Central Canada: The Iroquoians: Government and trade >

FEATURE: Legends among the Micmacs and Malecites >

FEATURE: Life among the Hurons >

The West: The Blackfoot: Religion on the plains >

The Pacific Coast Indians: Art and ceremony >

The North: The Inuit >

Key words

native peoples	nation	monopoly
legend	clan	supernatural
confederacy	ceremony	tradition

Canada's first people

Legends can be interesting because they tell us stories and teach us lessons. They often have another value as well: they can start us on a study of the people who produced them. The story of Coyote and the salmon introduced us to Canada's first inhabitants, the native peoples.

According to experts in native studies, Indians came to Canada more than 20 000 years ago, during the last Ice Age. They crossed over on a land bridge from Northeastern Asia. This bridge of land now lies beneath the waters of Bering Strait.

The Inuit made a similar crossing somewhat later, perhaps 4000 years ago. Groups of them made their way across the Canadian north, some settling as far east as Greenland.

During this time—a period of thousands of years—the Indians moved gradually southward. Eventually they developed ways of life suitable to the different regions.

By the time Europeans came to settle, around the year 1600, a variety of native lifestyles existed. The Inuit had adapted to the harsh climate of the far north. Several different groupings of Indians occupied the vast territory between the Pacific Coast and Newfoundland.

In the early days, each of the groupings contained many tribes. The tribe was a loosely organized association of Indians who shared the same culture and language. A tribe was usually subdivided into bands or villages of a few families. In some cases, these bands or villages might have little or no contact with other members of the tribe. When parts of a tribe got together, it was probably to cooperate in a major event; for example, a war, a hunt, or a get-together to trade.

As time passed the tribal community began to develop a national identity. Not only did each community share the same

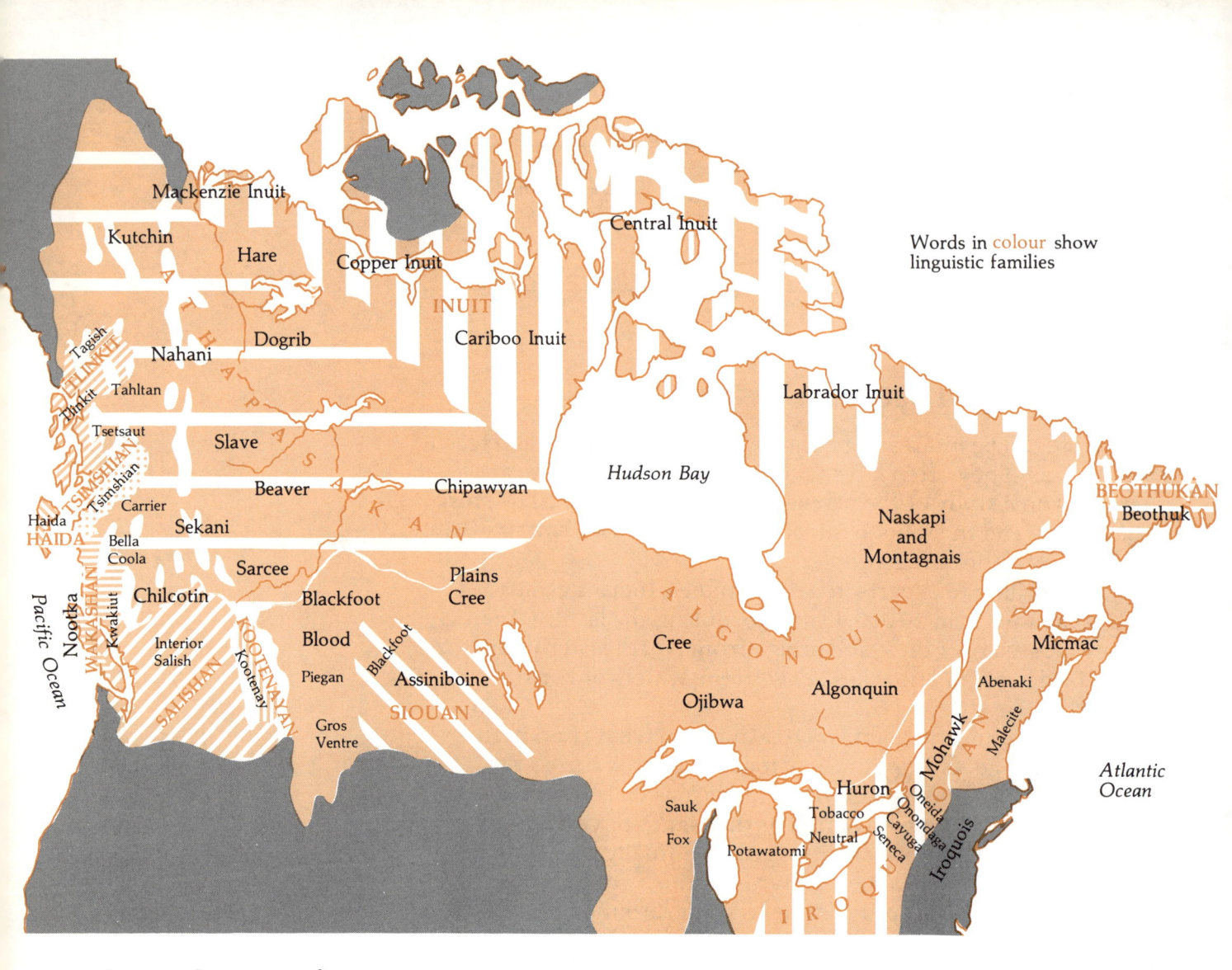

Fig. 3-1 Locations of native peoples before 1500.

A dialect is a branch of a main language; a dialect is often spoken by people living in a region apart from the larger population.

culture and language, it also developed its own political organization and power over its own territory. For this reason, the different groups of native peoples are now called **nations**.

Among the various nations of native peoples, as you shall see, there were many things the same and many things different. For example, there were at least ten different languages, and some 50 dialects [DĪ-uh-lehkts]. These languages were not written down. Therefore, spoken records, such as legends, and memory were vital in the ongoing life of native peoples.

GETTING THE FACTS

1. a) Arrange the following peoples in the order in which they arrived in Canada:
   —Inuit,
   —Europeans,
   —Indians.
   b) How many years ago did each group arrive?

2. The map shows where the different groups of native peoples lived. In your notebook, write the names of the different language groups. Then list the names of the nations that belong to each.

Atlantic Canada: Micmacs and Malecites: Harmony with nature

Waqan studied the fresh animal tracks closely, just the way his father had taught him. He could see they had been made by a young moose (tia'm), but a big one.

tia'm [teem] is the Micmac word for moose

He checked the direction of the wind. He had to be careful that his scent would not be carried to the nostrils of the hunted animal. Luck was with him; he was downwind.

A feeding ground lay just beyond. Waqan remembered the clearing near the river. The tracks were headed that way. He followed them carefully between the tall pines. At the edge of the forest, he crouched and gazed in wonder at the animal no more than 50 paces away. He had never seen so big a moose!

"This is my big chance," he thought. The moose had presented itself for death so that Waqan and his family could survive. But more than survival was at stake for Waqan. By killing his first moose, he would prove that he had become a warrior. He would leave the games of childhood behind and take his place among the men.

Waqan's hands trembled slightly as he fitted an arrow to his bow. Almost without thinking, he bellowed his imitation of a moose call. He had practiced it so many times. The animal shied, then turned its head in his direction. Waqan released the arrow. It struck the moose's chest near the shoulder. The moose stumbled, then made for the trees.

The hunt was going exactly like the hunt of his dreams. A great moose would not go down from a single arrow. He would track it farther, following the hoofprints now marked by blood.

51

The moose would plunge on, until it grew weak from fatigue [fah-TEEG] and loss of blood. Then Waqan would end the contest with his spear.

THINKING IT THROUGH

3. a) What does Waqan do that shows he has been well trained to hunt the moose?

b) Do you think hunting was important to Waqan and his people? Explain your answer.

The scene with Waqan could have happened many times 500-1000 years ago—long before Europeans came. Among the Micmacs [MIHK-maks] and the Malecites [MA-lih-seets], the moose was an important source of food. It was also important for other reasons: hide (used for clothing and wigwams); sinew (used as a kind of rope); and intestines (used for storing food and as bags for carrying). Just about every part of the animal had some use. The same was true of the caribou, bear, beaver and porcupine. Along with the moose, these were the animals on which the Micmacs and Malecites depended during the winter months.

For as much of the year as possible, however, the Micmacs and the Malecites lived by the seashore. Here the Indians had a rich supply of food to draw from. The resources included salmon, eel, lobster, clams, oysters and other shellfish, as well as seals and shorebirds. Berries—blueberries and wild strawberries—roots and seaweed were also available in summer and fall.

Migratory means moving from place to place, often according to the seasons.

The Micmacs and the Malecites were migratory [MĪ-gru-TOR-ree]; that is, they moved their campsites according to the seasons. In spring, summer and fall, they lived off what they could find at the seashore. During the winter, they moved closer to the larger, life-giving animals of the forest. Here they set up their cone-shaped wigwams.

The Micmacs and Malecites migrated according to a regular cycle. However, each group of Indians kept to its own pattern within the hunting and gathering area. For example, the Malecites did not venture beyond their part of what is now New Brunswick. The Micmacs occupied northern New Brunswick, the Gaspé region of Quebec, and all of Prince Edward Island and Nova Scotia, including Cape Breton.

Fig. 3-2 Indians of the Micmac nation, shown after European contact. What aspects of the traditional Micmac way of life can you see? How can you tell that the Micmacs pictured have had contact with Europeans?

The continuing search for food was clearly a central part of Malecite and Micmac life. The main job of the chiefs was to assign hunting and gathering territories to each family. Just as governments now collect taxes, the chiefs collected supplies of food from their people. Then they shared the supplies with individuals who could not look after their own needs.

GETTING THE FACTS

4. List at least four land animals that the Micmacs and Malecites hunted.

5. Why did the Micmacs and Malecites live by the seashore for as much of the year as possible?

USING YOUR KNOWLEDGE

6. The Micmacs and Malecites depended on nature to survive. Skim the story of Waqan and find three facts to back up this statement.

7. Many people in the Atlantic Provinces today make a living by fishing part-time and by farming or holding other jobs part-time. Describe one way in which their lives are similar to the lives of the Micmacs and the Malecites. Give one way in which their lives are different.

Central Canada: The Iroquoians: Government and trade

The Iroquoian [IH-ruh-KWOI-uhn] Indians lived in southern Ontario and upstate New York. One of the Iroquoian nations, the Hurons, controlled the area north of Lake Ontario. South of the lake lived another group of five Iroquoian nations. They belonged to the Iroquois **confederacy** [kuhn-FEH-duh-ra-see].

Unlike the Micmacs and Malecites, who were nomads [NOH-mads], the Hurons and the Iroquois lived in settled villages. They were good hunters, but they depended more on

Nomads are people who are migratory. This means they change the location of their campgrounds from time to time.

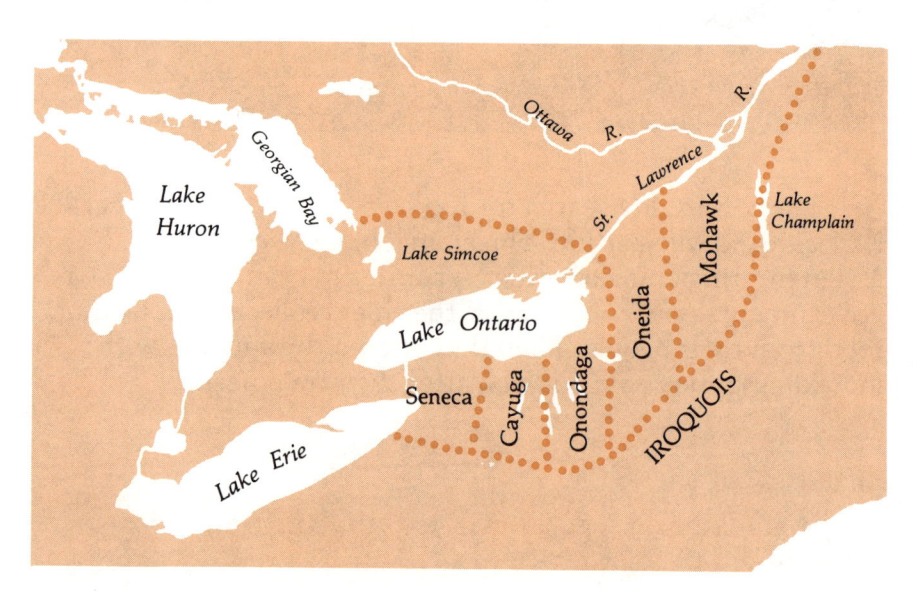

Fig. 3-3 The Five Nations of the Iroquois Confederacy.

Legends among the Micmacs and Malecites

People have always had a sense of wonder about the world around them. The Micmacs and the Malecites were no different. Long before Europeans came, the Indians had their own beliefs. Some of these beliefs are found in their legends.

In the eyes of the Micmacs and the Malecites, every rock and river, every tree and bird and animal had a spirit. Some spirits were good and some were evil. The spirits had different forms—giants, people, animals. All spirits were magical.

Indian legends grew up around these spirits. The legends were used to amuse children and teach them about life.

Glooscap is the central figure of the legends. Where he came from is a mystery. According to legend, Glooscap looked and lived like an ordinary Indian. Yet the Great Chief, as he is called, was twice as tall and twice as strong. He was never sick, never married, never grew old and never died. He had a magic belt which gave him great power, and he used this power only for good.

One Glooscap legend tells how he created people:

> Taking up his great bow, he shot arrows into the trunks of ash trees. Out of the trees stepped men and women. They were a strong and graceful people with light brown skins and shining black hair. Glooscap called them the Wabanaki [WAH-buh-NAH-kee] which means "those who live where the day breaks." In Canada in the old time, only the Micmacs and the Malecites belonged to these people of Glooscap.

Glooscap told the people he was their Great Chief and would rule them with love and fairness. He taught them how to build birchbark wigwams and canoes. He showed them ways to catch fish, and how to know which plants were useful for healing. He taught them the names of all the stars, who were his brothers.

Glooscap had a strong message for the people about the importance of nature. The following shows how the Indians felt about animals:

> He showed the men how to make bows and arrows and stone-tipped spears. He taught them how to use them. He also showed the women how to scrape hides and turn them into clothing.
>
> "Now you have power over even the largest wild creatures," he said. "Yet you must use this power gently. If you take more game than you need for food and clothing, or kill for the pleasure of killing, then you will be visited by a terrible giant called Famine. When he comes among men, they suffer and die."

Based on *Glooscap and His Magic: Legends of the Wabanaki Indians* by Kay Hill.

GETTING THE FACTS

8. In your notebook, write the letters a) to d). Put a "T" beside the following statements that are true, and an "F" beside the statements that are false.
a) Micmacs and Malecites made up legends to explain themselves to Europeans.
b) Micmacs and Malecites believed that spirits drifted through the air.
c) Native peoples used legends to teach their children about life.
d) It was believed that Glooscap came from the sea.

When the Tuscarora Indians joined about 1720, the Iroquois became the Six Nations Confederacy. See chapter 14 for more about the Iroquois and the story of Molly Brant.

The name Canada comes from the Huron-Iroquois word "kanata," which means village or community.

Every Iroquois belonged to a clan, named after an animal; for example, Bear, Turtle, Wolf, Beaver. Members of the same clan could not marry each other. In fact, a Mohawk Bear clan member could not marry someone from the Bear clan of another Iroquois nation. This was because they thought of one another as brothers and sisters.

farming. Both Hurons and Iroquois traded a lot with other nations.

Although they had much in common, the Hurons and the Iroquois were enemies. Both were part of the same Iroquoian culture, which means they shared many customs and beliefs. They spoke similar languages. Yet five Iroquois nations—Mohawks, Oneidas [oh-NI-duhs], Onondagas [AH-nuhn-DAH-guhs], Cayugas [kay-YOO-guhs] and Senecas [SEH-nih-kuhs]—joined as a confederacy. The Hurons stayed apart.

The Iroquois and government

How did Indian peoples run their affairs before the coming of Europeans? In some cases, where small numbers of people were scattered over a large area, "government" meant no more than decisions by the head of a family (or band of families). However, the Iroquois had a highly organized way of making decisions.

The Iroquois put much thought and effort into making government serve the needs of their people. They have been seen as the inventors of a new form of government—federal union. This is the kind of union eventually used by both the United States and Canada.

The diagram in Fig. 3-4 suggests how the Iroquois union, or confederacy, was set up.

The basic unit was the matrilineal [ma-trih-LIH-nee-uhl] family; that is, the combination of all the individual families descended from the oldest living woman. Under her leadership, they lived together in a dwelling known as a longhouse. If she were a member of the Bear clan, all the daughters, grandsons and grand-daughters were members of the Bear clan. Husbands belonged to other clans, possibly to other nations.

The clan was the main social unit. To celebrate an event like a wedding, for example, families of the same clan would gather. Since the clans cut across tribal lines, families of Senecas, Cayugas and Onondagas might come together for the celebration.

The clan was important to the running of the nation and to the running of the Grand Council itself. The women of the leading clan families appointed the chiefs. If the head women felt that a chief was not acting wisely, they could take away his power. In fact, if a council of chiefs could not agree on a problem, the clan mothers had the right to step in and make a decision.

Village Council

Purpose: To look after village matters. Each village in a nation had one.

Members: Council members were all men, headed by the village chief. All village council members represented various clans in a village and were appointed by their clan matrons.

Council of a Nation

Purpose: To deal with the affairs of the nation.

Members: Head chiefs from all the villages in a nation.

Confederacy or Grand Council

Purpose: To look after issues affecting all five nations in the Confederacy (for example, to help keep peace among the five nations).

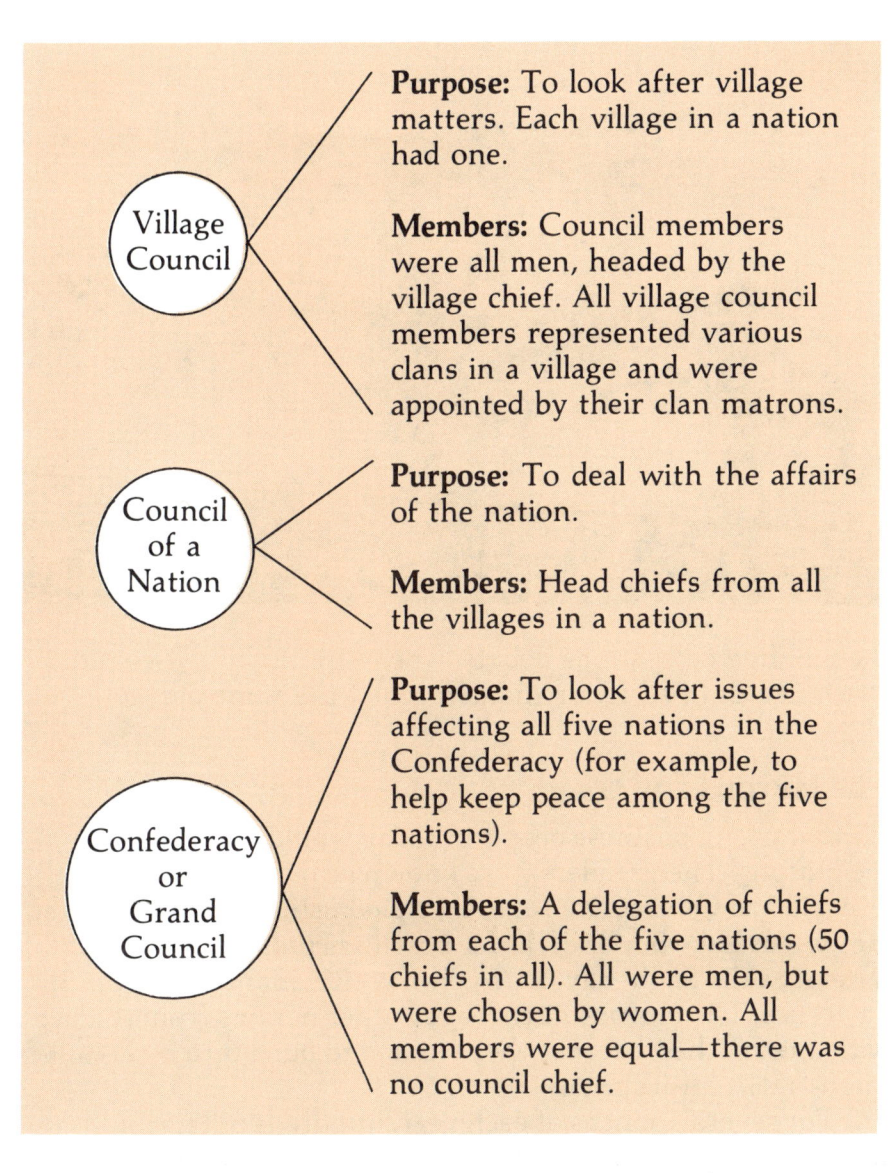

Members: A delegation of chiefs from each of the five nations (50 chiefs in all). All were men, but were chosen by women. All members were equal—there was no council chief.

Fig. 3-4 The government of the Iroquois Confederacy was highly organized. The three different councils represent three levels of government, ranging from the village council to the Grand or Confederacy Council.

Individual nations made decisions about their own affairs at the Council of their nation. However at least once a year a delegation of chiefs from each of the five nations went to a Grand Council. The purpose of the Grand Council, or Confederacy Council, was to look after matters that affected all five nations.

After opening ceremonies of prayers and songs, issues requiring discussion were suggested. An issue was first discussed separately by each of the five national delegations. Debate continued until all members agreed to the same decision. Once each national delegation reached a decision,

Grand Councils followed many procedures. For example, an issue could not be debated on the same day it was proposed, nor after nightfall.

Fig. 3-5 Model of an Iroquois longhouse made of bark, dating from the early 1600s.

As you can see in Iroquois government, it was essential to reach a unanimous decision (complete agreement) over an issue. Debates were often long and drawn out.

See the map on page 109.

then all five delegations debated the issue. Again, discussion continued until all five nations reached the same decision.

The Hurons and trade

Hard-working business people of today would have admired the Hurons. Their traders were known all over present-day Ontario and Quebec. By 1600, they did business with nations as far west as Lake Superior, as far north as Hudson Bay, and as far east as the Saguenay [SAH-geh-nay] River and the lower St. Lawrence. The Hurons discouraged other nations from trading with one another, because they wanted to build up a **monopoly** [muh-NAH-puh-lee].

For several months of each year, hundreds of Huron traders were on the move. They used their birch bark canoes to transport the produce of their farms—especially the corn and other foods so valuable to non-farming Indians.

Other trading items became even more important as time went on. From nearby nations, the Huron obtained corn (they could not grow enough themselves to supply all their customers), tobacco and hemp. They made rope and fishnets from the hemp. In exchange for their goods, the Hurons received a rich supply of dried fish, as well as furs of all kinds. These included mooseskins, and even buffalo robes.

The Hurons were very successful at trading. They met many other nations and became friendly with most of them.

Life among the Hurons

What was it like to be a young Indian 400-500 years ago? How were Indian children treated?

Suppose an interviewer from the 1980s could somehow talk to a young Huron boy from the days before the coming of the Europeans. The conversation might go something like this:

Interviewer: What are you going to do today?

Huron boy: The men are taking us hunting rabbit. Ever since my friends and I could walk, the men have been training us how to use a bow and arrow. We have been practicing over there in the meadow.

Interviewer: So now you are ready to go away from the village, in search of moving targets, in order to get food. Will you be dressed differently? The weather is very cool, yet you are wearing almost nothing.

Huron boy: My only clothing will be my loincloth and moccasins. Even in winter, we dress lightly. This toughens us and gives us healthy bodies like our mothers and fathers have.

Interviewer: What about the girls?

Huron boy: Just as we are learning to be men, they are learning to be women. Both have very important responsibilities among our people. From an early age, the girls learn to pound corn, prepare food and to work in the fields.

Interviewer: Did you say "work in the fields?"

Huron boy: Yes, we are excellent farmers. We grow many crops—corn, squash, beans. Besides food, we also grow tobacco. Our people use it in many ceremonies, and other Indians are willing to give us many furs for our extra tobacco.

Interviewer: So the women look after most of the farming. Do the men handle the trading?

Huron Boy: My father and a large group of warriors will be leaving when the moon is full. Their canoes will carry them to faraway waters. They will take much food and tobacco—and come back with loads of beaver skins.

Interviewer: It seems that your father will be away a long time. Will you miss him? Who will make sure you behave?

Huron boy: Yes, I will miss him and two of my uncles also. But many other members of our family will still be at home. Besides the women and girls, my two grandfathers, my cousins, my uncle with the injured foot.... Of course, our dogs stay with us. And we know how to behave.

Interviewer: Do you all live together?

Huron boy: We live in the same longhouse. It is a happy place. Sometimes it gets noisy, but the children try to act properly, like the adults. The adults never strike us. They show us how to behave by their example.

Interviewer: Thank you. You have been very helpful. Good luck with your hunting.

Fig. 3-6 Indians bartering. According to this picture what items are being traded?

However, they remained the rivals of their long-time enemies, the Iroquois. Before the Europeans came, the wars between them had been little more than raids by small parties of warriors. A few would be killed; the winning side would capture perhaps a dozen prisoners. Rarely did one nation (or group of nations) send a large body of men—say 400 to 500—to invade the territory of another.

But what might happen when the Europeans arrived? What if the Huron and their allies got hold of guns? Would the Iroquois find themselves under pressure to get guns as well? What other changes might threaten the apparently strong Huron way of life? Unknown to the Iroquois or the Hurons, these questions arose with the arrival of Europeans in the upper St. Lawrence-Great Lakes region.

GETTING THE FACTS

9. How were the Hurons and the Iroquois related?

10. Each of the following sentences expresses a fact or an opinion. Copy them into your notebook. Beside each sentence, write "fact" or "opinion."
a) The Hurons and Iroquois lived in settled villages.
b) The women of leading Iroquois clan families appointed the chiefs.
c) The Hurons were wise to trade all over what is now Ontario and Quebec.
d) The Hurons and Iroquois were long-time rivals.

11. Write a short explanation for each of the following terms: legend, confederacy, nomads, monopoly.

USING YOUR KNOWLEDGE

12. The basic unit of the Iroquois was the matrilineal family.
   a) Briefly explain what the matrilineal family is.
   b) Give one example of the power that women had in running the nation.
   c) In present-day society in Canada, are family units matrilineal? If not, what are they?

13. The Hurons were extremely successful traders. Skim the section "The Hurons and trade" and list at least three facts to back up this statement.

The West: The Blackfoot: Religion on the plains

The Blackfoot have lived for hundreds of years on the plains east of the Rocky Mountains, in what is now Alberta. In the past, they depended for life on the buffalo. When horses became available, they were able to travel long distances in search of their main food supply.

Like other native people in North America, the Blackfoot were very close to nature. The supernatural—or spiritual or religious matters—also played a big role in their lives. Two examples can tell us much about their religious beliefs: the medicine bundle and the Sun Dance.

The medicine bundle was believed to give protection against harm. A rawhide bag was used as a container. Wrapped

Fig. 3-7 Hunting buffalo on the plains.

inside were objects such as a medicine pipe, feathers from an eagle or owl, sweetgrass, chokecherry wood, pieces of tobacco, stones and other objects.

A young Blackfoot could become the owner of a medicine bundle in one of two ways. Sometimes he would go into the wilderness and spend many days without food or sleep. He would pray to the spirit powers for advice. Eventually he became exhausted and fell into a deep sleep. He would then have dreams in which he was told which articles had special powers for him. These articles he would collect and guard with his life. In other cases, medicine bundles were passed on to members of the nation during special ceremonies that usually included a dance.

The Sun Dance was one of the most important ceremonies among the Blackfoot. It was called a Sun Dance because it was held in early summer and to stare at the sun was part of the ceremony. Staring at the sun helped to concentrate on prayers to the spirits whose help they were seeking.

The Sun Dance was one of the many events held when the members of the nation got together after months of traveling and working in separate bands. Most of these events centred around great feasts and just having a good time, but the Sun

Dance was a very serious ritual [RIH-tyoo-uhl]. People who had suffered from bad luck during the past year, or who hoped for special help in the year ahead, took part. Most often, the Sun Dance was the result of a promise or pledge.

Much preparation was needed. They had to find a place where hundreds of people could meet, and where their horses could pasture. Nation leaders then made arrangements for the Sun Dance. These arrangements were according to tradition, an accepted way that had come to be followed over the years. A slender tree, which had a Y-shape at the top of its trunk, was chosen and cut down to make the special centre pole. The Sun Dance took place within a circle of ground around this pole. Sometimes the circle was marked off by other poles and branches, to enclose the area.

Young men who wanted to take part stayed together in a tipi for several days. They fasted; that is, they did without food,

A ritual is something that is done the same way each time. It may be a small thing, such as which sock you put on first. Usually, however, rituals are concerned with important matters.

Fig. 3-8 A shaman, or medicine man.

A shaman is a spiritual leader and healer.

and sometimes without water. Then the shaman [SHAY-muhn], or medicine man, prepared each man. In some cases, he made pairs of cuts in each person's chest or back. Under the skin he looped leather strips, which were connected by ropes to the centre pole.

Each person then danced, gazing into the sun and seeking his power there. He pulled all the while on the ropes, until the flesh gave way and he was free. The scars that formed after a few weeks were looked upon as a badge of courage.

Fig. 3-9 The making of a brave. What is happening in this picture?

Fig. 3-10 Painting of a shaman asking for success in war.

GETTING THE FACTS

14. Fig. 3-10 shows a shaman, or medicine man. He is asking help from thunder, the spirit of war, in an upcoming battle. The shaman is a member of the Blackfoot Indians, one of the Plains Indians nations.

    a) What can you tell about the Blackfoot Indians from this picture? (Think about religion, transportation, clothing, artwork and so on.)

15. Write the list under Column A in your notebook. Beside each word or phrase, write the phrase from Column B that means the same.

Column A	Column B
shaman	came with Spanish explorers
chokecherry wood	the spirit of war
tradition	used for hauling small loads
horses	an accepted way of doing things
dogs	often part of a medicine bundle
thunder	medicine man or woman

THINKING IT THROUGH

16. People taking part in the Sun Dance made many sacrifices. They did without things and often suffered pain in order to receive help from the spirits.

   a) Can you think of examples of people today who are willing to make sacrifices for something they believe in?

   b) Do you think that these people who are willing to suffer show courage? Give reasons to explain your viewpoint.

Fig. 3-11 Kitsipimi Otunna, a woman of the Sarcee nation. Examine the picture for clues and describe as much about the Sarcee way of life as you can.

Fig. 3-12 A Blackfoot travois.

The Pacific Coast Indians: Art and ceremony

The Indians of the Pacific Coast are known as "the Salmon People." They include the Nootka, the Coast Salish [SAY-lihsh], Kwakiutl [KWAH-kee-YOO-tl], Bella Coola, Haida [HĪ-duh], Tsimshian [TSIHM-shuhn] and Tlingit [TLIHNG-giht].

Before the coming of Europeans, they had a high standard of living. One reason was the large supply of salmon in the rivers running into the Pacific. The Kwakiutl knew the value of the salmon. They held a special ceremony when the first fish was caught each season:

> The first fish was treated as an honoured guest of the rank of a visiting chief. They believed that the salmon permitted itself to be harpooned or clubbed, or captured in certain definite ways . . . but it was extremely bad luck to molest [harm] a fish in any other way. . . . Since the salmon's soul was immortal [lived forever], a mistreated one might warn the others not to return to a certain stream, thus bringing tragedy to the people who had misused the privilege of eating their flesh.

From *The Salmon People* by Hugh McKervill.

The Pacific Coast Indians were blessed with an abundance of salmon and other seafood, a gentle climate, wild fruit and vegetables, and tall cedar trees. They developed a settled way of life. This made it possible to have an advanced culture, one with much variety. The totem pole and the potlatch are examples.

Totem poles were carved out of cedar trees with tools made of stone. How did the custom begin? Nobody knows for sure, but the following explanation is interesting:

> Edensaw [ee-DEHN-sah], one of the great Haida carvers, told this story about the beginning of totem poles. Many years ago, the Haida lived in cold and comfortless huts, without columns or any such things outside their dwellings. One day a chief, who seems to have been of more than ordinary intelligence, set himself to devise a more comfortable style of house.
>
> While he was thinking over a plan, a spirit appeared to him and showed him the style of a house with the measurements and every other detail complete except that there was no carved column (totem pole).
>
> The chief and his tribe set to work and gathered the material they needed. Just as they were about to build, the

Iron was not something the Pacific Coast Indians were known to make. However, they had iron tools before the recorded arrival of Europeans on the scene. This is another example of a mystery from history.

Fig. 3-13 Totem poles in Kitwanga, British Columbia, 1915. What do totem poles tell us?

From *Indiens Inuit Métis* by Hope MacLean.

spirit appeared to the chief again. The spirit showed him the same plan, but with this difference: in front of the house was placed a carved column, with his crest (a Raven) carved on top. Underneath the Raven was a second carving, the crest of his wife, an Eagle. The spirit told the chief that all the people in every village were to build houses the same, and to set up columns.

Totem poles are examples of artwork of the Pacific Coast

Indians. Yet they are much more than examples of artistic skill. Each part of a totem pole reveals something about an important person, spirit or event in a family's past history. Also, a totem pole in front of a person's house was like an announcement: "We are a family of wealth and influence in this community!"

Pacific Coast Indians thought of themselves first as members of families. A number of families, all related in some way, lived together in a village. The villages of a certain region were part of the same nation.

In many ways, the Pacific Coast Indians differed from other Canadian Indians. But there was one difference that really stood out: the community was divided into two groups—nobles and commoners. A person was born into one group or the other.

The nobles had more rights than the commoners; for example, nobles had the very important right to fish in the best locations. But within each group, the members were ranked in order of importance. Thus the lowest noble was hardly any better off than the highest-ranked commoner.

A chief or top-ranking nobleman had many advantages. While it was the custom for several related families to share the same house, he and his family could choose the part of the house they wanted. He had more possessions. On fishing trips and other projects, he was the leader. He had the best seat at special ceremonies. One such ceremony, important to a person's standing in the community, was the potlatch.

The word potlatch means "giving." It was (and still is) a ceremony usually given by a chief and his group for another chief and his group—or for several chiefs and their followers. The host chief gave presents to each of the guests. The most valuable gift went to the highest-ranking guest, and so on down the line.

A potlatch was usually held to mark a major event, such as a marriage, a birth or the naming of a new chief. The more wealthy and powerful the chief, the fancier were the meals and the presents. These could include huge amounts of food, cedar canoes and other goods. The guests receiving the gifts were like witnesses to a "contract" confirming the host chief's "step up the ladder" of success.

It may seem that to hold a potlatch was to take a quick route to the poorhouse. Not so. In a way, a potlatch was a kind of insurance. All the important guests were bound to respond by holding potlatches!

Pictures of birds, animals and monsters were carved on other objects also, such as dishes and tools. Sometimes pictures were painted on clothing and blankets.

Fig. 3-14 An Indian potlatch at Alert Bay, British Columbia.

GETTING THE FACTS

17. What was the purpose of the totem pole?

18. List the advantages of being a member of the noble class of the Pacific Coast Indians.

USING YOUR KNOWLEDGE

19. A Pacific Coast Indian could show his or her success in life with totem poles, with potlatches and in other ways. How do people today show that they are successful?

The North: The Inuit

The Inuit population is spread over the widest area of any native people in the world. A few remain in Siberia [sī-BIH-ree-uh]; the others are descendants of Inuit who migrated hundreds—even thousands—of years ago. As the map shows, they relocated across the north from Alaska to Greenland.

Their lifestyles varied from place to place. Yet Inuit everywhere had much in common before the coming of Europeans. For example, they all spoke basically the same language. "Inuit," meaning "the people," was the name they called themselves. They lived in small groups, usually made up of a few families.

Fig. 3-15 This picture appeared in a book by Henry Ellis in 1746. What does it show about Inuit life at the time?

To survive, cooperation and sharing were vital. They were nomads, constantly on the move, hunting and fishing and gathering food and the other necessities of life. The Inuit believed that spirits caused the things they did not understand. And they believed in magic as a way to deal with things they could not otherwise control.

Inuit everywhere adapted to the harsh geography of the North. They developed a **technology** [tehk-NAH-luh-jee] that wasted nothing of the scarce natural resources they had. In some regions, such as the Mackenzie Delta and Labrador, they were a little better off. But in all parts of the North, the people had to be highly inventive [ihn-VEHN-tihv] to live successfully. The following are just a few of a long list of examples of how they adapted:

SUNGLASSES: Although they had no glass, the Inuit invented "sunglasses," or goggles, that protected their eyes. Made of ivory or wood, these goggles had thin slits through which a person could look without being blinded by sun reflecting off the snow.

CHEAP ENERGY: They made lamps of stone or whalebone, with moss for a wick and seal blubber for fuel. The lamp was lit by grinding stones together to produce a spark. The lamps were then used for light, heat and cooking.

TRANSPORTATION: On land, the Inuit traveled great distances on dog sleds. The main part of the sled, the runners, was often cut from the jawbones of whales. Pieces of bone or antler from caribou connected the runners.

On water, the Inuit traveled in kayaks [KĪ-yaks]. These were slim craft (about 6 m long and 60 cm wide) made from sealskin. The kayak fit its occupant so snugly that it could keep out water even if it turned over. If it did turn over, the kayaker could get right side up with a motion of his arm or paddle.

HARPOONS: There were many different kinds of harpoons for hunting different kinds of animals. The picture shows an interesting example. The harpoon head, made from stone, was attached with walrus-hide line to a shaft of walrus tusk. The animal hunted with this harpoon was— walrus! Usually a hunter needed to drive quite a few of these through the hide of an adult walrus to kill it.

Fig. 3-16 Ready for the throw.

HOUSES: These were made from whatever materials were available; for example, snow, stones, turf, animal skins and driftwood. A house, or igloo, might be built of snow blocks. When the temperature went above freezing, the snow top of the igloo was sometimes replaced with animal skins. During the brief summer, an Inuit family might live in a tent of sealskins stretched over a frame of whale tusks.

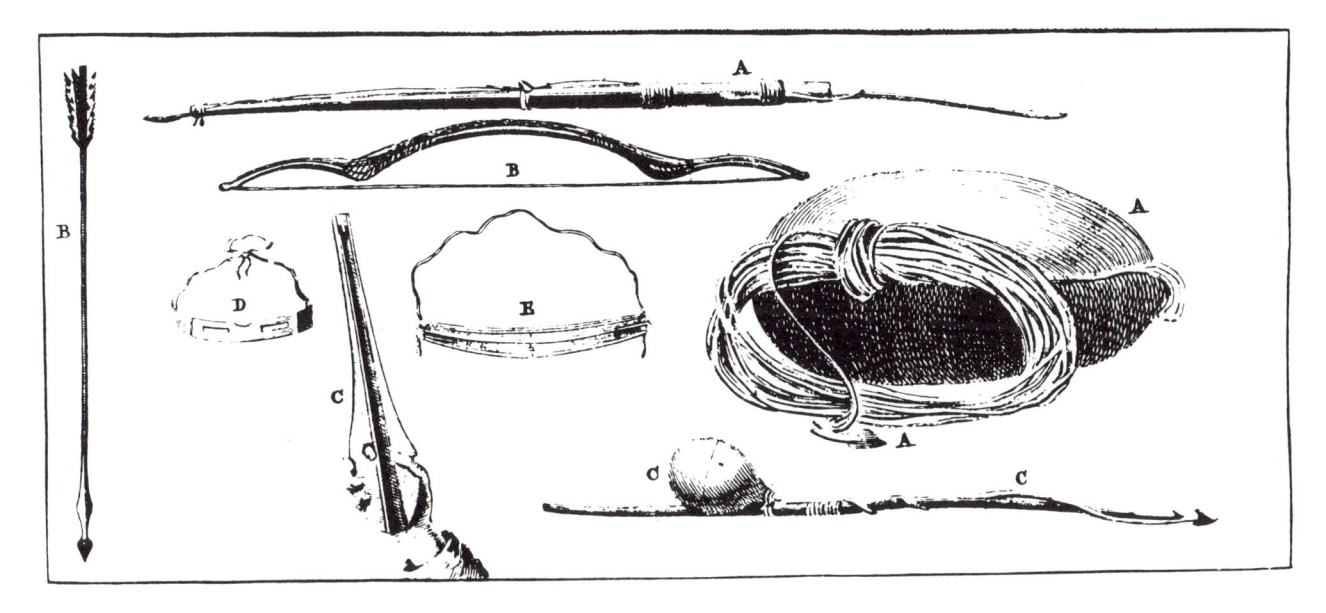

PARKAS: Clothing had to be warm and lightweight. Caribou skin or fox fur was ideal for making hooded coats or parkas. Sometimes, to keep dry as well as warm, the Inuit wore overparkas of animal intestine [ihn-TEHS-tihn] or fishskin. The Inuit were equally clever about other articles of clothing. In some cases, boots were made from the lower legs of polar bears, including the soles of the bear's feet. More often, boots were sewn from other animal skins, and worn over socks woven from grass.

USING YOUR KNOWLEDGE

20. Suppose you were part of a group on a winter camping trip in a wilderness area in your part of Canada.
    a) Make a list of items you would be sure to take with you.
    b) Which, if any, of the items could you yourself make? Why are so many of them impossible for you to make?
    c) What things could you expect to find in nature that would help you to survive?

Fig. 3-17 Drawing of tools used by the Inuit along Hudson Strait and in Northwestern Hudson Bay: A. The great harpoon for whales, with its barb coil; B. The bow and arrow; C. The small harpoon, its bladder and barb, with the instrument to dart it at the seals; D. The "snow eyes" or sunglasses; E. The breast ornament made of a sea-horse tooth. As shown in a book by Henry Ellis, 1746.

Conclusion

Now you have learned about some of Canada's earliest inhabitants. By the time Europeans arrived, more than 400 years ago, the native peoples had quite a variety of cultures. They had adapted skilfully to nature in the various regions and had developed forms of government, trade, religion, art, ceremony and technology.

The native peoples' traditional lifestyles were quite different from what they are now. That's hardly surprising. The world, not just Canada, was a very different place 400 years ago.

Perhaps this is a useful point to keep in mind, whether we are meeting new people of our own time or people of long ago. Their ways may seem strange to us at first, but we may find that we can learn from people whose cultures are different from our own.

And people from different times and places may have more in common than they realize. Take the following simple story for example:

Kids at play

Over the top of the slope and through the tall grasses, three boys romped in single file. The two others followed the zig-zag path traced by the tallest. As he did, they imitated the motion of horses. They slowed to a walk as a dog, big as a wolf but friendly, ran up to meet them. Suddenly the tall one dropped the piece of leather rope he was carrying. He sat down beside it. The others did the same. It was too hot, he had decided, to play that game.

He looked out across the quiet prairie. In the distance he could see a cluster of dark objects. Buffalo, maybe. They seemed to be moving, but only slowly. It was too hot for them also.

The tall boy turned to look at the gently sloping hill he had just come from. Suddenly, in his imagination, it was snow-covered. He remembered last winter. He and his friends had played on a hill like that. The best part was sliding down on a piece of rawhide.

Fig. 3-18 Coppermine Inuit bow drilling, Coppermine, Northwest Territories, 1915.

GETTING THE FACTS

21. A story like this one could have taken place 500 years ago. The boys were probably Plains Indians, perhaps Blackfoot or Cree. At the beginning, what game do they seem to be playing? Explain your answer.

USING YOUR KNOWLEDGE

22. How are the games—both the summer one and the winter

one—like the games played by young people today? How are they different?

THE INVESTIGATIVE REPORTER

23. As a topic for a report, choose one aspect of the life of any Indian nation; for example, hunting, family life, art or religion.

a) Make up a basic question you would like to investigate. (You may have to change it later, depending on your question and what information you are able to find.) Then make up at least five specific questions that break down the basic question.

b) Make a list of sources of information. The books you need may already be in your classroom, but let's suppose you go to the library. The library is set up to make your research easier. You may go straight to the reference section if you are looking for an atlas or an encyclopedia.

Otherwise, check the card catalogue. Often this is divided into two sections: the "Subject Index" and the "Author and Title Index."

Each book in the library is given a number. You check the subject index, looking under the N's for "Native Peoples" or perhaps the I's for "Indians." The name of your chosen Indian nation may be listed on its own.

For each book that looks useful, you write down the number, the author and the name of the book. Once you have your list, you can probably go to the shelves. If you are not sure, consult the librarian. If you are lucky, the books you want will be in.

c) Remember the guidelines in chapter 2 for sizing up a book. Also keep in mind the guidelines for note-taking (page 43-4). They can help you to locate information that relates to your research questions and to take most of the notes "in your own words."

d) From your notes you can then write a first draft of your answers. Leave enough space so that you have room to make corrections. Read over your answers. Is each one explained clearly enough? Do they follow one another in the best order for an organized report? Is the information interesting? Make whatever improvements you can. Perhaps you could add an introduction and a conclusion.

e) Rewrite your information so that you have a report to be proud of.

4 Discovery: How has it influenced the story of Canada and Canadians?

You are Sven Golfsson, a big strong man in your mid-twenties. Along with your mates, you have been at sea for many days.

"That's a good wind today," says your first mate, eyeing the full sail.

Your ship plows westward through the open sea. So far, so good. No storm has blown up to swamp your ship. Monsters have not burst upon you from the depths of the sea. Tempers have stayed calm among members of the crew.

You spend much of your time staring at the horizon, hoping to spot land. Sometimes your thoughts flash back to Greenland, the land of your birth. You hope your father hasn't killed anybódy since you left. Already he had been chased out of Norway—where your grandparents still live—and then Iceland, for killing people in quarrels. You think of how hard your family works to scratch a bare living from that rugged land.

"I'm going to be famous," you tell yourself. "If those rumours about a continent to the west prove to be true, and I discover it, I will be famous. Who knows? Maybe we will find a wealthy kingdom and conquer it and seize its riches. Or we will come upon green valleys and great forests, where we can bring our people to settle and prosper . . .

"Land ahead!" someone shouts. You peer past the dragon-head front of your ship. The fog is rising and green hills appear as if by magic. Soon you are close enough to drop anchor; you and some of the men head for shore in small boats. As you trudge up the grassy embankment, a flock of ducks flies over and a startled deer dashes toward the woods. You find wild grapes growing—or, at least, berries as big as grapes. "Grape-land," you think, may be a good name for this place.

In the next few weeks, you organize the building of a house. It's much like your house in Greenland. Then you prepare to sail home. There you will be known as "Sven the Super Sailor," and people will thrill to your story of discovery. Someday, if you are lucky, you will go back to your "new found land."

- What could you do to make people back in Greenland believe your story about a "new found land?"
- Hundreds of years after your discovery, history books still say nothing about it. Why not?

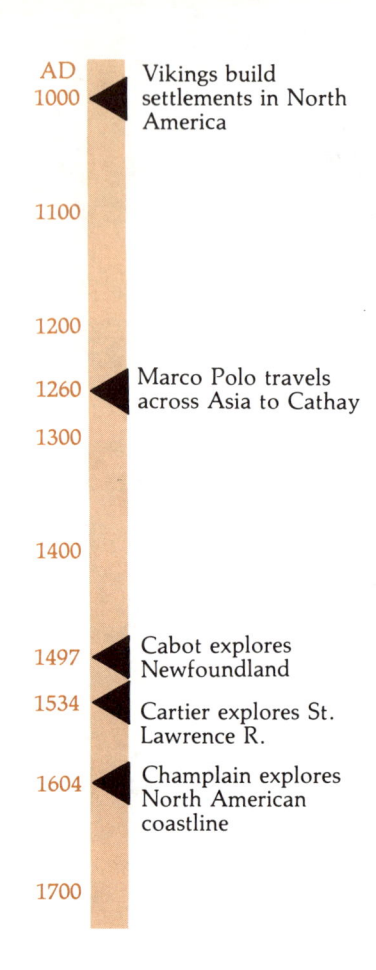

AD 1000	Vikings build settlements in North America
1100	
1200	
1260	Marco Polo travels across Asia to Cathay
1300	
1400	
1497	Cabot explores Newfoundland
1534	Cartier explores St. Lawrence R.
1604	Champlain explores North American coastline
1700	

Chapter overview

In chapter 1, you read about some different kinds of discovery and how they were important to people's lives. Next you are going to look at the influence of discovery, by Europeans, on the various regions of Canada.

Discovery has been going on, of course, throughout Canadian history. In this chapter, you will meet some of the people who traced the pathways for others to follow. We hope not only that you gain knowledge about these people—but also that you get some feeling of appreciation for their achievements.

Signposts

> The Viking puzzle

> The Age of Discovery

> Discovery in Atlantic Canada: A shot in the dark

> Facing the unknown

> FEATURE: Joe and Hannah: Heroic explorers of Canada's North

Key words

Vikings	sagas	Northwest Passage
hypothesis	Age of Discovery	explorers

The Viking puzzle

Mo: I heard on TV that tomorrow is Columbus Day in the United States. What's that all about?

Joe: Christopher Columbus was supposedly the first European to discover North America. The Americans honour his memory. It's a good excuse for a holiday.

Mo: What do you mean "supposedly?"
Joe: Because he wasn't really the first European to come here.
Mo: Well then, who was?
Joe: Some **Vikings**, probably. There may have been others, even earlier. But the Vikings arrived around 1000 A.D., some 500 years before Columbus.
Mo: Then why don't they drop the name Columbus and name the holiday after the first Viking?
Joe: I don't know exactly. Columbus is one of those names Americans have grown up with. It's easy to say and spell.
Mo: If Columbus is not "No. 1" any more, I think they should change it. Did you say who the first Viking was?
Joe: Bjarni Herjolfsson [BYAHR-nee HAYR-yohlfs-suhn], probably.

Who were the first Europeans to discover North America? The above conversation brings out two points: (1) for the longest time, it was believed that Columbus was the first and (2) we now know that the Vikings came much earlier.

It is easy to see why Columbus became recognized as "No. 1." After his voyage to the West Indies in 1492, he reported his success back in Europe. Then he made follow-up trips to prove he had crossed the Atlantic Ocean. Other explorers from many countries quickly followed. They all came to North America "after Columbus."

Centuries passed, and historians found new clues. The remains of Viking settlements were unearthed in Iceland and Greenland. If Vikings had traveled that far from Norway and their other Scandinavian [SKAN-dih-NAY-vee-uhn] homelands, maybe some had continued on to North America. Further clues appeared in written stories, called sagas. They suggested that people like Bjarni Herjolfsson and Leif [leef] the Lucky had sailed to new lands west and south of Greenland.

In one saga, the author told of the motives that inspired people like the Vikings to venture into the unknown:

> If you wish to know why people journey forth in the face of great danger, the answer lies in three qualities of human nature. One is the spirit of rivalry and the desire for fame; for taking risks is a certain way to be famous. Another is the desire for knowledge; for it is human nature to want to know and to find the truth with one's own eyes. The third

Other Vikings did try to keep up a settlement. It seems they had many fights—both with the native peoples in the area and among themselves. Those who were not killed seem to have given up and gone back to Greenland. Even in Greenland, there was no settlement left when other European explorers arrived hundreds of years later.

Based on a passage in *Explorers of the North. Volume 1: The Polar Voyagers* by Frank Rasky, which was quoted from the Norse chronicle *The King's Mirror.*

is the desire for gain; for people seek after riches wherever they may be found, even though danger awaits.

One of the key questions about the Viking puzzle not answered in the saga is: If the Vikings did come to North America, what parts did they explore? According to the sagas, they landed at a place they called Vinland or Wineland. They gave it this name because of the wild fruit they found, which they believed to be grapes. They tried to start settlements there, but all signs of them seemed to have disappeared.

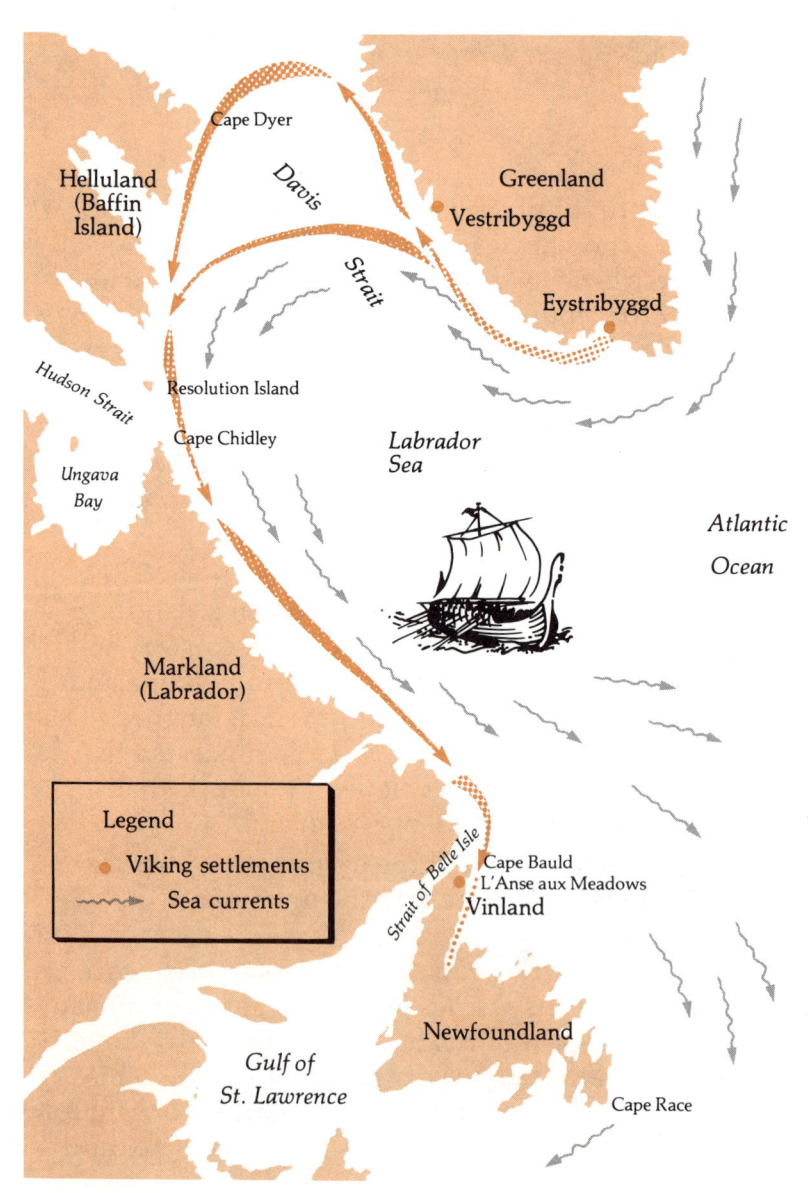

Fig. 4-1 Viking routes. The lines show the routes that Leif Erikson and other voyagers are supposed to have followed from the Norse settlements in Greenland to Newfoundland.

Definite proof of the Vikings' achievements has been hard to find. But mysteries like the ones about the Vikings make people curious. The search for clues went on. Finally, a breakthrough came in the 1960s.

Helge [HEHL-guh] and Anne Ingstad were the ones responsible. A husband and wife team from Norway, they had been studying the mystery of the Vikings for years. The Ingstads had examined old **documents** and maps, read the sagas and a countless number of books, and talked with other experts.

The Ingstads sifted through the many clues, and personally took boat trips along routes the Vikings may have followed. Then they came up with a **hypothesis** [hī-PAH-thuh-sihs] that we can summarize as follows: The Vikings discovered Newfoundland, and therefore North America, about 500 years before Columbus reached the New World. To test their hypothesis, they figured out what part of Newfoundland the Vikings had most likely visited. That part was the northeastern tip, at a place called L'Anse aux Meadows [lahⁿs oh meh-DOH].

They began a **dig**. This is an organized way, used by archaeologists, of searching the ground for clues about a settlement. The Ingstads expected to find the remains of Viking-style houses and other clues. It was time-consuming, but exciting too—like hunting for buried treasure. Their efforts were rewarded. They found the remains of houses that were like houses in Norway and Greenland in Viking times. Other "treasures" included Viking jewelry, tools—even iron nails, which were unknown in North America before Europeans came.

Since the 1960s, the Ingstads and others have continued to piece together the puzzle of the Vikings. It is still a puzzle with most of the pieces missing. The Vikings seem to have had little effect on North America. Only a few things have been found to prove that they were here. But, it is still enough to show that they came before Columbus—500 years before. And the search goes on for more about the Vikings, as well as for clues about other people who may have visited North America even earlier.

GETTING THE FACTS

1. Why was Columbus, rather than the Vikings, long thought to be the first European discoverer of North America?

2. What clues led historians to believe that the Vikings had travelled to North America before Columbus?

Fig. 4-2 Sod houses of a Viking settlement at L'Anse aux Meadows National Historical Park in Newfoundland. Archaeologists found the ruins of a settlement here and were able to reconstruct the houses as they must have been hundreds of years ago.

USING YOUR KNOWLEDGE

3. People such as the Ingstads try to solve mysteries about the past. They examine pieces of information and then come up with a theory, or hypothesis, about what may have happened. Next, they look for facts or pieces of evidence to prove that their story is valid.

   a) What was the Ingstads' hypothesis?

   b) What evidence did they find to support their hypothesis?

   c) Do you think that they found enough evidence to prove that their explanation was correct? Why or why not?

4. Do you remember the following rhyme?
"In fourteen-hundred-and-ninety-two, Columbus sailed the ocean blue"
Write a similar rhyme about the Vikings.

THINKING IT THROUGH

5. Why do you think Columbus is still honoured, even though he is no longer "No. 1"?

6. Reread the passage that tells about some motives for venturing into the unknown.

   a) List the three motives suggested in the passage.

   b) Imagine you have decided to perhaps risk your life and explore the unknown. Which of the three reasons would be your strongest motive for doing so? Give reasons for your answer.

The Age of Discovery

Suppose you could go back in time, to Europe in the year 1475. If you chose the place that was the centre of European knowledge, you would be in Italy. Or rather, in one of the Italian city-states—like Venice or Genoa [JEH-noh-uh]—because Italy was not one country like it is today.

   Of the many things that would surprise you, one would be the hot debate surrounding this question: Is the world flat or round? Actually the "round earth" people were getting the better of the argument.

   To find out why, you would want to talk with a young man named Christopher Columbus. In the true spirit of the Renaissance [REH-nuh-sah{^{n}}s], he was asking questions about long-held beliefs; for example, that the world was flat. Columbus, a sea

Renaissance means "rebirth." It is the name given to a period of European history in which there was a rebirth of interest in new knowledge and discovery. The Renaissance followed a period of ignorance and poverty known as the Dark Ages.

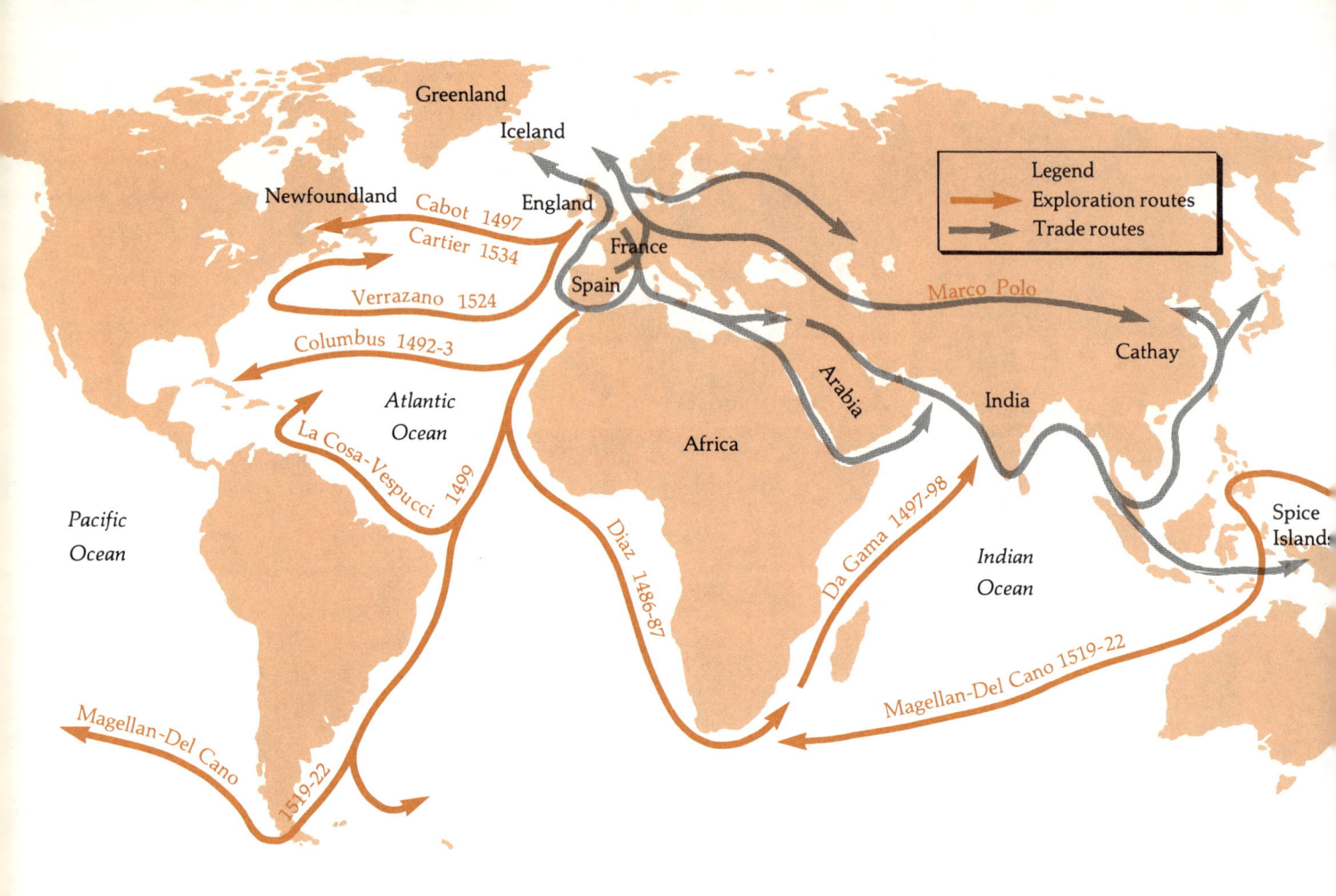

Fig. 4-3 Routes to the East.

captain, had given the matter a lot of thought. He was familiar with the latest findings of geographers and scientists. He had talked with other sailors and travelers.

A strong influence on Columbus was a book written some 200 years before by Marco Polo, a citizen of Venice. Polo had spent 20 years traveling across Asia to Cathay and back by land. Once home, he wrote about the faraway lands he had visited. He told of the things he had seen—silks, jewels, buildings decorated with gold, and spices (pepper, nutmeg, cloves).

Why were spices so important? Because Europeans, especially the kings and queens and other rich people, had become used to spices. In those days before refrigerators, they used spices to keep food from spoiling. Spices also covered up the bad taste and smell of food that had been around too long!

84

But the cost of spices had been going up incredibly. They came from the other side of the world, from the East Indies, known as the "spice islands." From there, they changed hands several times before crossing Asia and the Middle East and reaching cities in Italy.

Columbus had the problem figured out. If you traveled *east* by land, you arrived in the "Indian" islands off the coast of Asia. If you traveled *west*, you could reach "India" by water—faster, and a lot cheaper. Of course, this conclusion assumed the world was round.

So Columbus moved to Lisbon, Portugal. Lisbon was a kind of headquarters for voyages of discovery. When he failed to find supporters for his project to sail west, Columbus moved on to Spain. King Ferdinand and Queen Isabella were impressed by his idea. They gave him the money he needed for ships, sailors and supplies.

Columbus then made his famous voyage of 1492. His three ships were the Nina, the Pinta and the Santa Maria. He reached land at the island of San Salvador in the West Indies. Though he explored much of the region, he did not find the land of Marco Polo. Yet Columbus was sure he had arrived somewhere in Asia. So were the King and Queen of Spain, when he returned there to a hero's welcome.

Columbus made three more voyages across the Atlantic

Columbus did not know that the continent of North America blocked his planned westward route.

The Portuguese were already paying explorers to find an eastern sea route to India.

When Columbus went ashore on San Salvador, he thought he was in the Indies, islands off the coast of the Asian mainland. Therefore, he called the native people "Indians." Later explorers made the same mistake. Thus, the native peoples of North and South America became known as Indians.

Fig. 4-4 An artist's impression of Columbus leaving for America.

85

Ocean in the next 10 years. He never reached Cathay, though he died in 1506 believing he had. Actually, he never even set foot on the mainland of North America.

Yet the voyages of Columbus were important. The "Age of Discovery" was underway. He had opened up new routes for exploration and trade. In the capital cities of western Europe, kings and queens dreamed of expanding their power across the ocean. They hoped for riches that would increase their influence in Europe. In the seaports of Europe, explorers and their business partners scrambled to get expeditions together. They followed the routes of Columbus, but they went farther—and many made the fortunes he had hoped for.

GETTING THE FACTS

7. Choose the best completing statement and then write each sentence in your notebook:

The Renaissance was
a) an organization that backed voyages of discovery.
b) a company interested in obtaining spices.
c) a time in which questions were asked about long-held beliefs.

Christopher Columbus was
a) an explorer who sailed in the service of Spain.
b) an explorer who believed the world is flat.
c) a businessman dealing in spices.

The voyages of Columbus were important because he
a) successfully sailed to Asia.
b) became very rich.
c) opened up new routes for exploration and trade.

THINKING IT THROUGH

8. Europeans wanted spices from the East Indies. However, they knew that it took a long time to travel east by land to get to the islands. How did Columbus plan to solve this problem? What new piece of information helped him to find his solution?

9. Suppose you are Columbus. You realize that you have not reached Asia, because your route is blocked by a "new world." Draw a diagram to explain the problem to Queen Isabella. How would you plan to solve this problem?

Discovery in Atlantic Canada: A shot in the dark

The map makes it seem so straightforward. There is Western Europe on the right. European explorers sailed to the left—that is, westward—and discovered Canada. Naturally, they ended up in Atlantic Canada when they crossed the Atlantic Ocean.

But the early explorers did not expect this result. John Cabot did not even know there was a continent where Canada is today. Taking a shot in the dark, he arrived in our Atlantic waters and explored some coastlines. These must be some outer parts of Asia, he decided.

Others followed. Eventually they could not ignore the disappointing fact: North America blocked the ocean route to Asia. So explorer after explorer looked for an all-water route through or around North America—for a **Northwest Passage**.

Once the resources of North America had been discovered, however, the French and English changed their goals somewhat. They recognized the value of the plentiful codfish in the Grand Banks. The fur trade, especially the beaver, made fortunes for many. It led to the opening up of the interior, to the west, to the north and to the south. Yet, in the back of the minds of many explorers must have lurked the thought, "If only *I* could be the one to discover the Northwest Passage..."

John Cabot: A man of mystery

Homeland: Italy (Venice)

Project: A voyage to discover an all-water route to the riches (especially spices) of Asia.

Sponsor: King Henry VII gave Cabot permission to sail in the name of England. English business people put up most of the money.

Discoveries: Probably Newfoundland and/or Cape Breton Island, although Cabot reported that he had reached Asia.

Outcomes: The story of John Cabot is full of question marks. Little is known for sure about his personal life up to 1497. Historians have long been puzzled about exactly which places he discovered (voyages into the unknown are difficult to describe, and the resulting accounts are often just as difficult for people reading them to figure out!)

In 1498, Cabot set out on a second trip. He was never seen in England again. What happened to him, his crew and

Fig. 4-5 John Cabot

his ships? Nearly 500 years have passed, and few clues have been uncovered.

Cabot's crossing of the Atlantic had lasting results, however. He made England's first claim to territory in North America. English fishermen became regular visitors to the fishing areas that Cabot had described. Interest and skill in ocean travel was on the rise in England.

GETTING THE FACTS

10. What was the Northwest Passage? Why were explorers so eager to find it?

USING YOUR KNOWLEDGE

11. What do you think might have happened to Cabot's second expedition? Choose the hypothesis that you think is the most reasonable. Give reasons for your choice:
a) Cabot did not even reach the new land again. His ships were lost at sea.
b) Cabot found the Northwest Passage and reached the Spice Islands. He decided to stay there and live in comfort for the rest of his life.
c) Cabot and his crew reached the new land and started a colony. However, they all died of hunger and disease.
d) Because he failed to find the Northwest Passage, Cabot was too embarrassed to return to England. Instead, he went to live in Italy.

12. Read the following paragraphs and then answer the questions:

Why did ordinary sailors sign up for voyages of discovery? It was not for riches. If gold or other valuables were obtained, the captains and their government would get the benefit. It was not for fame. If a new land were discovered, it would not be named after an ordinary sailor. On returning to his homeland, he would not be invited to have dinner with the king. It was not for fun. The food was plain at the best of times; sometimes it was rotten. The ships were grubby. Ocean travel in those days meant hard work, and boredom mixed with danger.

On the other hand, sailors on voyages of discovery often received higher pay than other sailors. By the time of Cabot and Cartier [kahr-TYAY], long voyages were becoming more common. Life as a sailor was risky anyway. A sudden storm or attack by pirates could happen close to home as well as in faraway waters. Besides, life on land was no picnic. An "old" person was someone in his or her forties.

a) What would be a suitable title for these paragraphs?

b) Imagine you could interview a sailor from the 1500s. Prepare a list of the questions you would ask.

Jacques Cartier: Pathfinder for France

Homeland: France

Projects: To search first for an all-water passage to Asia; then to follow the St. Lawrence River in the hope of finding riches "closer to home."

Sponsor: King Francis I of France paid Cartier to explore for his country—and his king.

Discoveries: Various parts of Newfoundland, and parts of what are now Nova Scotia (Cape Breton), Prince Edward Island, New Brunswick and Quebec. In other words, much of the Gulf of St. Lawrence, as well as the St. Lawrence River itself.

Outcomes: In three voyages (1534, 1535 and 1541), Cartier had made contact with native peoples and added much to Europeans' knowledge of Canada. However, he had not discovered the riches of the East nor even a possible route to them. For the time being, French leaders lost interest. They had been after gold and diamonds, not beaver pelts.

Almost nothing is known about Cartier after 1541. His detailed accounts of his voyages were published for readers of his own time. Historians have been reading these accounts and quoting from them ever since.

About 50 years after Cartier, people in Europe became interested in North American furs. Beaver hats came into fashion. French fur traders began traveling to Canada. To cross the Atlantic was always risky, but people got more used to the idea. French fishermen also began making regular visits to the Gulf of St. Lawrence. Map-makers were making their maps more and more accurate.

The time was right for the next great discoverer—Champlain.

Fig. 4-6 Jacques Cartier as imagined by a painter some 300 years after his death. No actual picture of Cartier is known to exist.

Fig. 4-7 Samuel de Champlain

Port Mouton [MOU-TOH^N] is so called, because during Champlain's visit there a sheep jumped overboard. Mouton is the French word for sheep.

Scurvy is a disease caused by the lack of vitamin C, found in fresh vegetables and fruit.

Port Royal was more successful than Ste. Croix, but in 1607, de Monts' monopoly was cancelled. In 1608, it was renewed for one year and he decided to move to the St. Lawrence. See chapter 9 for what happened to Port Royal after de Monts and Champlain left.

Samuel de Champlain: An explorer plus

Homeland: France

Projects: To help French explorers on fur-trading voyages by acting as a map maker.

Sponsor: King Henry IV of France appointed Champlain Royal geographer.

Discovery: The St. Lawrence River as far as the Lachine Rapids in 1603; the coastline of North America, from present-day Nova Scotia to present-day Massachusetts [MA-suh-CHOO-sihts] in 1604-5.

Outcomes: In 1604, Champlain went with Sieur de Monts [deu MOH^N] to the Bay of Fundy. De Monts had been granted a monopoly of the fur trade. In return, he was to start a colony. They spent the winter on the island of Ste. Croix. Many of the men died of scurvy. In 1605, they moved across the bay to Port Royal. Champlain explored the Atlantic coast and made careful maps of what are now Nova Scotia, New Brunswick, Maine and Massachusetts. The maps were so accurate that a sailor could use them today. Many places along the coast still have the names Champlain gave them more than 350 years ago.

In 1608, Champlain moved to a location at present-day Quebec on the St. Lawrence River. He devoted the rest of his life to the development of a fur-trading colony there.

USING YOUR KNOWLEDGE

13. Draw a chart of three columns. Place the following headings at the top of each column: explorer, his aims, his achievements. Fill in this chart for Cabot, Cartier and Champlain.

14. On Champlain's map completed in 1632, the following are some of the names that appear [Champlain's spellings]: Gaspay, Baye de Chaleu(r), Anticosty, La Magdelene, Cap de Ray, Baye de la Conception, Isles St. Pierre, Cap Breton, Canceau, Port Mouton, Ste. Croix R., Menane I., Baye Ste. Marie, Cap de Sable, La R. Ste. Jean.

a) On a modern map of the Atlantic Provinces, see how many of the names you can find. Compare your "detective" work with that of your classmates. (Your teacher may have you print your discoveries, with English spelling or modern French spelling, on an outline map.)

b) Why do you think some of the names no longer appear on a present-day map?

Facing the unknown

Try to imagine what it was like to be an explorer 400 to 500 years ago. As your ship heads up the St. Lawrence, the tiny village of Quebec fades from view behind you. Ahead is a wilderness never seen by Europeans.

Where do you expect to end up? You have a hunch, based on rumours and guesswork, that the St. Lawrence will take you a long way. Maybe the St. Lawrence is the first leg of the Northwest Passage. Or perhaps you are on your way to disaster. You can only imagine what to expect in the way of native people, climate, animal life, waterfalls and other possible hazards that could wreck your ship—or endanger the lives of you and your crew.

The days pass without trouble. So far, so good. Then you come to a large island that splits the river. Sailing to one side, you look out on rapids. From shore to shore, white water tumbles over a rock-piled river bed.

Fig. 4-8 Explorers often faced the dangers of travel on narrow, roaring rivers. In this picture Simon Fraser races down the river that now bears his name.

You turn your ship around and drop anchor. You are curious about the island and its giant hill dark with forest. Some of your mates think you are crazy, but others join you in the exhausting climb to the crest. Breathless and sweat-soaked, you forget your aching limbs as you gaze at the scene below. You can see another river flowing from the north! Now what do you do?

This scene may seem unreal, but it is the kind of thing that happened to explorers of Canada. As each region was gradually opened up, discovery became less and less difficult to plan. Maps began to show certain known areas. An explorer could sometimes count on a trading post and contacts with native people.

Yet each discoverer went beyond what was known. Each faced the same kinds of fears, dangers, mental and physical stress and tough decisions. Keep these facts in mind as you learn about explorers. Try to put yourself in their place.

Fig. 4-9 Early explorers.

Henry Hudson

Samuel Hearne

Alexander Mackenzie

George Vancouver

Pierre La Vérendrye

EXPLORER	DATE	DISCOVERIES
Henry Hudson	1609-11	Hudson River, Hudson Bay
Etienne Brûlé	1609(?)-32	South of Lake Ontario
Pierre Radisson and Médard Groseilliers	1650s	Sault Ste. Marie region; north shore of Lake Superior
Louis Joliet and Father Jacques Marquette	1669-73	Lakes Ontario, Erie and Huron; Lake Michigan and upper Mississippi River
La Salle and Father Louis Hennepin	1669-82	Lakes Ontario and Erie; Niagara, Ohio and Mississippi Rivers to the Gulf of Mexico
Daniel Dulhut	1680s	Region south and west of Lake Superior
Henry Kelsey	1690-92	Buffalo country of Northern Saskatchewan and possibly Alberta
Pierre La Vérendrye	1731-43	West of Lake Superior as far as the Saskatchewan River and south to South Dakota
Anthony Henday	1754-55	First European to travel west to within sight of the Rockies
Samuel Hearne	1770-72	Overland to the mouth of the Coppermine River on the Arctic Ocean
Alexander Mackenzie	1789, 1793	Down the Mackenzie River to the Arctic Ocean; overland to the Pacific
George Vancouver	1791-95	Vancouver Island and much of the coast of British Columbia
Sir John Franklin and many other Arctic explorers	early 1800s	Canada's vast northland of coastline, waterways and islands

Fig. 4-10 Discovery in Canada. This chart is not a complete list, but it shows the leading explorers for well over two centuries after Samuel de Champlain.

Joe and Hannah: Heroic explorers of Canada's North

Have you heard of those famous explorers of Canada's North, Joe and Hannah? You haven't? Well, perhaps you know them by their Inuit names, Ipilkvik [ih-PIHLK-vihk] and Tukkolerktuk [tuh-kuh-LERK-tuhk]. No?

Do not be surprised. If you check the indexes of history books, you will find many explorers listed—Columbus, Cabot, Cartier, Drake, Hudson, Kelsey, La Vérendrye, Frobisher, Cook, Vancouver, Franklin, Peary, Stefansson and so on. You likely won't find Joe and Hannah. Many people were great explorers, but their names were never recorded (written down). Joe and Hannah belong to this group.

Take a look at the facts about Joe and Hannah—or, more correctly, Ipilkvik and Tukkolerktuk. They came from two leading Inuit families in Baffin Island. In 1858, they became known to some visiting English people and were invited to sail to England. There Ipilkvik and Tukkolerktuk were married and stayed for nearly two years. They learned to live as English people, but they chose to return to their Inuit homeland.

For the next 15-20 years, they lived lives of travel, adventure and danger. A chance meeting led to a friendship with the American explorer, Charles Francis Hall. First, he stayed with them and learned their Inuit language and ways of traveling in the Arctic. Then Ipilkvik and Tukkolerktuk were Hall's guests in the United States. They helped Hall to raise money for an Arctic expedition—the first of several in which they would act as guides, interpreters and advisers.

One object was to reach the area, somewhere around King William's Island, where the Sir John Franklin expedition had disappeared in 1846. The first attempt was marked by a year-long struggle overland to Pelly Bay. During that time, Tukkolerktuk had a baby, which became ill and died. Yet her wise advice saved the expedition from hostile native peoples, and Ipilkvik's quick action prevented tragedy at the hands of crew members from a whaling ship.

In the spring of 1869, the group that set out again included Pudnak, a little girl adopted by Ipilkvik and Tukkolerktuk. This time they reached the spot where the Franklin expedition had shipwrecked. After finding remains of the Franklin ship, the two Inuit and their daughter returned to the United States with Charles Hall.

A trip to the North Pole was then planned. In 1871, they all set out in the ship *Polaris*. They managed to reach the north coast of Greenland, but Commander Hall took ill and died. The rest were stuck for the winter, as the ship was trapped in ice. Finally the *Polaris* drifted free, only to run into a mass of floating ice. All the people abandoned ship, and found themselves adrift on an ice floe.

Fortunately Ipilkvik was able to build snowhouses. He provided food, too, by killing several seals and—just when they were on the brink of starvation—a polar bear. The ice floe and its marooned passengers drifted south. Near Newfoundland, they were picked up by a sealing ship. They had survived.

Back in the United States, however, the Inuit family was struck by tragedy. First Pudnak died. Then Tukkolerktuk, who had never really recovered from the months of hardship, died soon after. Ipilkvik left the United States, never to return, and worked with other explorers in the Far North.

GETTING THE FACTS

15. One expert on northern Canada wrote: "Neither Ipilkvik's nor Tukkolerktuk's name appears on modern maps of the Arctic, though the maps bear many names of people less courageous, patient, and intelligent, far less important in the history of Arctic exploration." In your own words, tell what the statement means.

Conclusion

The early explorers opened up routes into all the regions of Canada. Their pathways were followed by other explorers, charting more new territory, and by soldiers, pioneer farmers, priests and missionaries, business people, tradespeople and labourers. Generation after generation of "new Canadians" came to join in the struggle for a better life.

USING YOUR KNOWLEDGE

16. How was Canada "discovered"? All regions at once? Northern regions first, then southern regions? In just a few years? To answer, skim the chapter and note where and when each explorer made his discoveries. Then refer to Fig. 4-10 and examine the discoveries and their dates. It may be helpful to locate the places on a map of Canada. Use this information to write a short paragraph describing how the New World was "opened up" or discovered. Why do you think the discovery of Canada happened in this way?

THE INVESTIGATIVE REPORTER

17. Pick one of the discoverer-explorers mentioned in this chapter. Make a plan for research, collect information and prepare a brief report. Your teacher will help you decide on the length and whether or not to include maps and drawings. (HINT: You may find it helpful to reread the last section of chapter 2. That will refresh your memory about the steps to follow in getting organized.)

5 Cooperation and conflict: What happens when different cultures meet?

Strangers meet

Suppose some friends of your family come to town. They are back for a visit, 15 years after moving to another province. They arrive with their children: Sue, age 14, and Brad, age 12.

The young people are strangers to you. Feelings of shyness may get in the way for a while. Yet you speak the same language. Your clothes and general appearance are similar.

Soon you may be trading stories about school and other experiences you have in common. After all, you belong to the same "culture." It's taking a lot for granted—but the chances are you could understand one another well enough to get along, to cooperate.

The following story shows a first meeting between people of different cultures:

Scene A

You are taking a trip across one of the world's great oceans. Your ship is caught in a storm and sinks. You and two friends land on an island. You walk along the beach. You carry the only thing you managed to save—a boat paddle. Suddenly you notice three near-naked people approaching in the distance. One is carrying what looks like a spear.

Scene B

You live on an island in one of the world's great oceans. With two of your neighbours, you decide to go down to the seashore. You take your spear in case you meet some game on the way. Over the hill you climb, and scramble down to the beach. Suddenly you notice three people approaching in the distance. They are wearing more clothes than are needed in this hot climate. One of them seems to be carrying some sort of club.

- In your own words, explain the meaning of the word "culture."
- Are people of different cultures more likely to misunderstand each other—and experience "conflict"—than people of the same culture? Why or why not?
- Imagine that you are either one of the shipwrecked people, or one of the inhabitants of the island. Tell what you might have said to your friends about sighting the three strangers.
- Tell the rest of the story.
- Did you decide that "cooperation" or "conflict" was the most likely outcome? Why?

Timeline

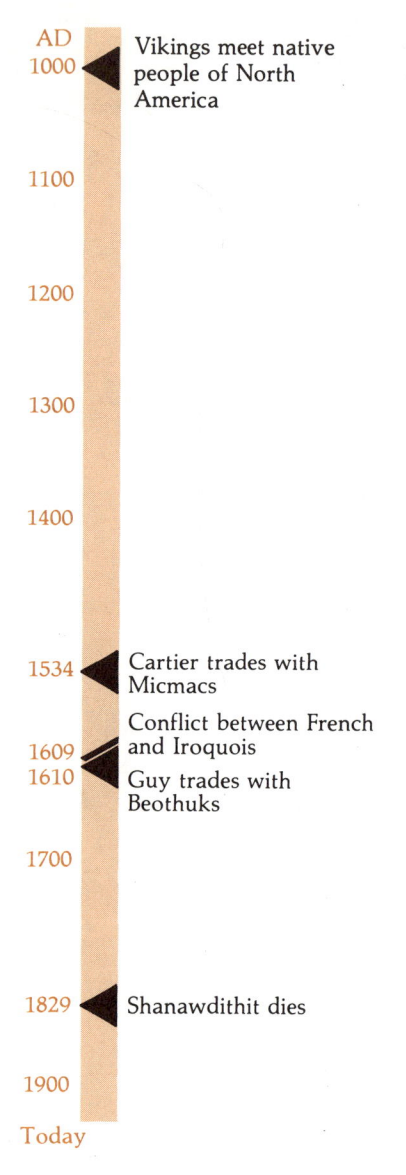

- AD 1000 — Vikings meet native people of North America
- 1100
- 1200
- 1300
- 1400
- 1534 — Cartier trades with Micmacs
- 1609 — Conflict between French and Iroquois
- 1610 — Guy trades with Beothuks
- 1700
- 1829 — Shanawdithit dies
- 1900
- Today

Chapter overview

When people of very different backgrounds meet, they often don't know what to expect of each other. What happens during the first contact, however, can be very important for future dealings between them. A friendly experience can lead to cooperation, where people help each other. An unhappy one can bring conflict, where they harm each other.

    This chapter is about early contacts in Canada. In each part of what is now our country, people from Europe met native peoples. The results were often surprising for both sides. Sometimes there was cooperation; sometimes there was conflict. In either case, both sides were affected. These first encounters led to events that influenced the history of Canada.

Signposts

> First contacts: Conflict with the Beothuks; cooperation with the Micmacs

> FEATURE: History can be one-sided

> The St. Lawrence River: Champlain meets the Hurons and the Iroquois

> FEATURE: The Jesuits in New France

Key words

cooperation	contacts	settlement
conflict	stereotype	imperial

First contacts: Conflict with the Beothuks; cooperation with the Micmacs

We do not know for sure just when Europeans first met Indians in North America. Already centuries old, the mystery will probably go on forever.

History can be one-sided

In every region of Canada, Europeans met native peoples. From coast to coast, they came in contact.

What happened? The story is only partly known. Our information comes from records—explorers' reports, letters, government files—left by Europeans. We are faced with at least two big problems. One is that the facts are slanted; that is, biased. They give only European views and feelings and ways of explaining things. The other problem is that the native peoples did not leave written records of their side of the story. What we know of their views is second-hand, as told by Europeans.

What did the Europeans tell? Sometimes they praised Indians for their bravery, their strong family ties or their hunting skills. More often, the Europeans failed to understand native ways and viewpoints.

The result was often "snap judgments" that were unfair to the Indians. Letters, diaries, reports and newspapers written by Europeans were filled with these half-truths and false impressions. Because history books and school books used these sources, they often gave a false picture of the Indians.

Indians became the victims of stereotyping [STAYR-ee-oh-TĪ-pihng]. Certain images became common; for example, Indians as hatchet-swinging collectors of scalps. Such an image is a stereotype, and may be quite misleading.

In books written before the 20th century, Indians were often called "savages." Sometimes the writer intended "savage" to mean wild or uncivilized. Other times it simply meant different. Also, by "savage" some writers meant natural, or close to nature. Still others used the word to mean people who were not Christians.

The word "savage" may have had many meanings over the years. However, it is hard to imagine nowadays that the word was ever used as a compliment. Or that it was merely a descriptive word like "tall" or "redheaded." More likely, to be called "savage" was to be "put down" and labeled as inferior.

So it helps to be watchful. Explanations of any person, group or event can be one-sided. When you read statements about Indians, remember you may be reading a one-sided view. If an explorer, a fur trader, a priest, a politician—or even a history writer—refers to Indians as savages, ask yourself the question: Is he or she revealing personal attitudes and values?

THINKING IT THROUGH

1. Think of at least three stereotypes that are common today. For example, the stereotype of a business executive may be someone who thinks about nothing but money and making deals. Are these stereotypes unfair? Are they true in any way?

Fig. 5-1 John Guy

The best hunch we have is that the first meeting happened around the year 1000. Vikings like Thorfinn Karlsefni [KAHRLS-ehf-nee] tried to start a settlement in Newfoundland. They left us clues in stories known as sagas. The sagas tell about encounters with native peoples called "Skrellings." The Skrellings could have been Inuit or Micmac Indians—or Beothuks [BAY-oh-tuhks], who are described in this chapter.

The Vikings told of two kinds of meetings with native peoples. Sometimes meetings were peaceful and they traded tools for furs. But other times they fought. Five hundred years later, around 1500, explorers told a similar story. They were never sure if they would meet with cooperation or conflict.

Up to 1500, we have only bits and pieces of information about the first contacts between native peoples and Europeans. After that, meetings between these sharply different cultures happened more and more often. Finally, a detailed story was written down. This story was the one John Guy told about meeting the Beothuk Indians.

The Beothuks of Newfoundland: Conflict

An Englishman named John Guy led an expedition to Newfoundland in 1610. He started a settlement at Cuper's Cove (now called Cupid's Cove) on Conception Bay, where he spent the winter of 1610-11. On May 16, 1611, Guy wrote a letter to his business partners in England. In the letter, he told about his experiences with the Beothuk Indians:

> On the south shore of Trinity Bay—which we called 'Savage Harbour'—we found savages' houses, no people in them. In one house we found a copper kettle . . . a furre goune of Elke-skin, some seale skins, an old saile, and a fishing reele. Orders were given that nothing should be removed. So that the savages would know that someone had been there, everything was moved into one of the cabins and laid orderly one upon the other. The kettle was hanged over them, and in it some bisket and three or four amber beads were placed.
>
> The eighth day it began to freeze, and there was thin ice over the sound. Because we heard nothing more of the savages, we came to the place where they had made a fire two days before. Things remained as we had seen them, each item attached to a separate pole. An old boat saile was

100

there, three or four chains of shells, about twelve furs of beaver, a fox skin, a sable skin, a bird skin....

We were convinced these items were brought there for the purpose of barter. Furthermore, they obviously expected us to be fair in trading with them. Because we had not supplied ourselves with fit things for to trade, we tooke only a sable skin and a bird skin. We left for them a hatchet, a knife, and foure needles threaded. Master Whittington had a pair of cizzars which he left there for a small beaver skin. All the rest we left there untouched. These savages by all likelihood were attracted to us by reason that we tooke nothing from them at Savage Bay....

John Guy's letter quoted in *The Native People of Atlantic Canada* by H.F. McGee.

GETTING THE FACTS

2. Is the John Guy letter a primary or a secondary source of information? How can you tell?

3. Many of the words in the letter are spelled differently from the correct spelling of today. Make a list of at least five of these words. How can you be sure that your list is accurate?

4. Make a list of any other words in the passage that you do not understand. Find out their meanings and write a definition for each word in your notebook.

Fig. 5-2 Meeting the Beothuks and the Micmacs.

5. Which of the following would be the best title for the story told in the letter?
a) A hunting trip
b) Trying to be friends
c) The coming of winter in Newfoundland
d) A fight over furs

USING YOUR KNOWLEDGE

6. Which of the following words describe John Guy's attitude toward the Beothuks?—respectful, suspicious, scornful, critical. Give reasons for your choices.

7. Describe your first contact with one of the following. Did it result in cooperation or conflict? a) a new teacher b) a new neighbour c) a person your own age. Explain the effects on your relationship.

The English, led by John Guy, and the Beothuks had begun friendly and trusting relations. The two groups even agreed to meet again the next year, at the same place. They were hoping for more trade with each other.

Unfortunately, disaster struck. A different shipload of Europeans arrived before John Guy and his friends. They did not know about John Guy's arrangement with the Beothuks. The Europeans saw a large, active group of natives on the shore and thought they were going to be attacked. They fired a cannon shot at the shore and the Beothuks fled into the woods.

The Beothuks probably felt double-crossed. As far as they knew, it was John Guy and his people who had fired the cannon. The Beothuks never again trusted Europeans who came to Newfoundland. The Beothuks tried to stay away from them, but if caught by surprise, they didn't wait to see if the visitors were friendly or unfriendly; they attacked.

THINKING IT THROUGH

8. When two groups meet, they often give each other signs or clues to show how friendly they are. Each group examines the signs and then decides whether or not to be cooperative.
   a) When John Guy visited the Beothuks' homes, what did he do to show that he was friendly?
   b) By what signs did the Beothuks show that they were friendly and interested in trading with the English?

9. The later group of Europeans saw the Beothuks on shore and concluded that the natives were going to attack. What signs led them to this conclusion?

10. Does a scene that looks very unfamiliar automatically seem frightening? (Look back at the story which opened the chapter.) Can you think of any examples from your own experience?

Some native North Americans learned to accept the presence of Europeans. They traded, sometimes on a regular basis. If there was trouble, it was often because of rivalry. That is, one native group and its European allies would fight another native group and its European partners. Contact between the cultures meant at least some kind of communication.

The case of the Beothuks was different. Until 1600, the bays and inlets of Newfoundland had been the summer homes of the Beothuks. Each summer they had come to the coast to collect food to last the winter. Then, during the 1600s and 1700s, many European settlers decided to make their homes on the coast of Newfoundland.

To avoid trouble, the Beothuks tried to stay away from the settlers. Now, unable to travel freely to the coast in summer, the Beothuks began to starve during the winter. Sometimes they were desperate for food and would come near the settlements. However, the Europeans thought that the Indians were trying to steal, and were ready to shoot them on sight.

The Europeans were also terrified of the Beothuks, who covered their skin with red ochre [OH-ker]. This gave them a very unusual appearance, like nothing human the Europeans had ever seen. Beothuks seemed to come out of nowhere, then vanish. When faced with these odd-looking, strange-acting people, the settlers frequently shot at them.

Each meeting of Beothuk and European seemed to lead to trouble. Misunderstanding deepened. In 1600, the Beothuk population had probably been about 1000. Since then, the numbers had been dropping.

Newfoundland became a British territory. Finally, the British government realized that, if something were not done, the Beothuks would be completely wiped out. In 1768, it made rules that forbade anyone to harm or kill Beothuks. But the government was too far away to enforce the new rules. In a desperate attempt to make contact with the Beothuks and help

Red ochre is a reddish substance obtained from clay.

them, the British government encouraged people to capture some of them.

Finally, in 1823, a group of English did capture a starving Beothuk girl named Shanawdithit [shaw-NOW-dih-tiht]. She was taken to St. John's where she worked as a servant. Meanwhile, a man named William E. Cormack became concerned about her. He had already traveled across the island of Newfoundland once, in 1822, in the hope of meeting Beothuks. Now, in 1827, he tried again. He found the remains of their last village, but as before, there was no sign of a living Beothuk.

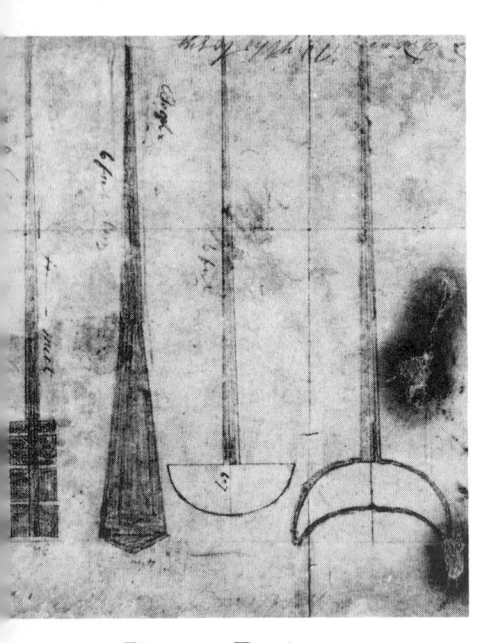

Fig. 5-3 During Shanawdithit's stay with Cormack, she revealed much about the ways of the Beothuks. These drawings by Shanawdithit are thought to be of religious or ceremonial implements.

Fig. 5-4 Shanawdithit or "Nancy" as English-speaking people named her.

Meanwhile, Shanawdithit was learning English and making drawings to explain Beothuk history and culture. She had much to tell. But she became ill with tuberculosis and died soon after, in June 1829.

Shanawdithit was the last of the Beothuks.

GETTING THE FACTS

11. In a short paragraph (five or six sentences), summarize what happened to the Beothuk population.

USING YOUR KNOWLEDGE

12. Why do you think the English gave Shanawdithit the English name "Nancy"?

13. Suppose you could have talked to Shanawdithit a few years after her arrival in St. John's. What four or five questions would you have wanted to ask her? What else might you have said to her?

THINKING IT THROUGH

14. What do you think is the most tragic fact about the contact between the different cultures, the English and the Beothuks? Explain why you think so.

Fig. 5-5 Before Europeans came, stone was used for all the tools with cutting, piercing and scraping edges. After contact, iron became available and soon replaced the stone tools.

Jacques Cartier and the Micmacs: Cooperation

During the summer of 1534, Jacques Cartier made his first voyage from France to North America. He explored the coast around the Gulf of St. Lawrence. In the ship's log, he kept a daily record of the places he saw and the people he met. In later years, the log was written in book form and published. One of the many topics people were able to read about was his first meeting with native people in the Baie de Chaleur ("Bay of Heat").

On July 4, 1534, Cartier dropped anchor in an inlet in the bay. The crew was in need of a rest, and the ship in need of repair. Cartier decided to use one of the ship's long-boats in the meantime to explore the coast more carefully. While exploring, he had his first meeting with some Micmac Indians.

On July 6, Cartier's boat entered a small harbour. Suddenly it was surrounded by 40 to 50 canoes full of natives. They were

Fig. 5-6 This picture of Micmac Indians was painted in the 1820s, after European contact. What are some things in the picture that Cartier would not have seen when he met the Micmacs?

holding up some furs on sticks and hollering and waving to the French to go ashore. Cartier decided, however, that it would be better to leave. He describes what happened next:

> And they (the Indians), seeing we were rowing away, sent two of their largest canoes in order to follow us. These were joined by five more . . . and all came after our longboat, dancing and showing many signs of joy, and of their desire to be friends. . . . But we had only one of our longboats. We decided not to trust their signs, and waved to them to go back. Instead, they surrounded our boat with their seven canoes. No matter how much we motioned to them, they would not leave. So we fired shots over their heads. They began to paddle off in very great haste.

The next day the Indians were back. This time they came in nine canoes to where Cartier's ship was anchored. Then, some Micmacs on the shore held up fur clothing. They had come to trade, Cartier concluded:

> We likewise made signs to them that we wished them no harm, and sent two men on shore. We offered them some knives and other iron goods, and a red cap to give to their chief. The two parties traded together. The Indians even bartered the clothes they were wearing.

The Micmacs and the French first met on friendly, and quite equal, terms. Their friendship grew over the next 200 years. No sudden tragedy came along to ruin it. From France came fishermen, fur traders, missionaries—and eventually settlers, the Acadians.

Each side took on some of the lifestyle of the other. The French learned to travel by canoe and began to wear clothes made from animal skins and furs. Many—at least in the early years—married Indian women, and raised their half-Micmac, half-French children as traders and farmers. The Micmacs came to prefer arrows tipped with iron rather than stone or bone. When they could, they chose guns over bows and arrows. They became accustomed to European tools, imported tobacco, new types of food and drink and, to some extent, Christian beliefs.

Based on Cartier's words in *The Voyages of Jacques Cartier* edited by H.P. Biggar.

"Exchanging beads for gold is a fantastic idea. We'll go and get our beads."

GETTING THE FACTS

15. If you have not done so already, answer the question asked in the caption for Fig. 5-6.

16. How do we know about Cartier's first meetings with the Micmacs? Are these accounts reliable?

USING YOUR KNOWLEDGE

17. In spite of an uncertain beginning, Cartier and the Micmacs eventually cooperated.
   a) Skim through the section and find evidence to show that the first contact was uncertain.
   b) Hypothesize: Why do you think Cartier and the Micmacs ended up cooperating?

18. We have Cartier's story of the meeting, but we do not have the Micmacs' story. Imagine you were one of the Micmacs who traded with Cartier. Tell your story of what happened, and what you thought of the French.

The St. Lawrence River: Champlain meets the Hurons and the Iroquois

A tough choice

In 1608, Samuel de Champlain started the settlement of Quebec. From the beginning he was in contact with the Indians of the area, the Algonquins. He traded with them for furs, which provided the money to keep his settlement in New France going. However, one big problem faced Champlain: there were not enough furs in the surrounding countryside. They would have to go farther inland. To the south lived the Iroquois, long-time enemies of the Hurons and Algonquins.

The following is a conversation that could have taken place between Champlain and his partner, Pontgravé [poh??-gra-VAY], in the late spring of 1609:

P: And now, what is to be our plan for the summer?
C: We must push farther upstream, to meet the Indians from the interior, and thus get the pick of the furs.
P: Do you have a certain place in mind?
C: The obvious place is the great rapids, where the Ottawa River meets the St. Lawrence. The trouble is that this region is threatened by the Iroquois. We don't have enough men to defend it against them. What we can do is take the offensive and make a raid into Iroquois territory. Our muskets could teach them a lesson they would remember.
P: Is it necessary, do you think, to take sides? Wouldn't it be better to remain neutral? Shouldn't we keep out of the Indians' quarrels, and buy furs from both sides?
C: No, we don't have that choice. We have been telling the Algonquins that we are their friends, that we want to help them. As far as they are concerned, help may mean joining them in war against their enemies. They believe we have made a promise. They expect people to keep promises.
   Besides, we will be helping ourselves. The Algonquins and the Hurons control the fur supply. The Iroquois, in their warmer country, have only second-rate furs.
P: Then it is in our interest to—ah—put the Iroquois out of business?
C: No. We don't want to destroy them or take over their territory. All we want is peace, so we can trade without fear. If we could make peace by a treaty, that would be the best thing. But a treaty seems out of the question. This war with

This fictional conversation is based on material in Champlain: The Life of Fortitude *by Morris Bishop.*

Champlain is being a bit of a dreamer here. In the 1600s, peace was rare in both North America and Europe.

the Iroquois was going on long before we French arrived. Our Indian allies seem rather to enjoy it. I don't think we could make any treaty that would hold. The only thing to do is to back up our own side and give the Iroquois a good scare.

P: But isn't there some danger in provoking these fighting Iroquois?

C: Possibly. Still, they are our enemies now, because they are the enemies of our friends. Never mind worrying about the Iroquois danger. What we have to fear is our friends. Suppose they get the idea that we wish to get along with

Fig. 5-7 The Huron trading empire.

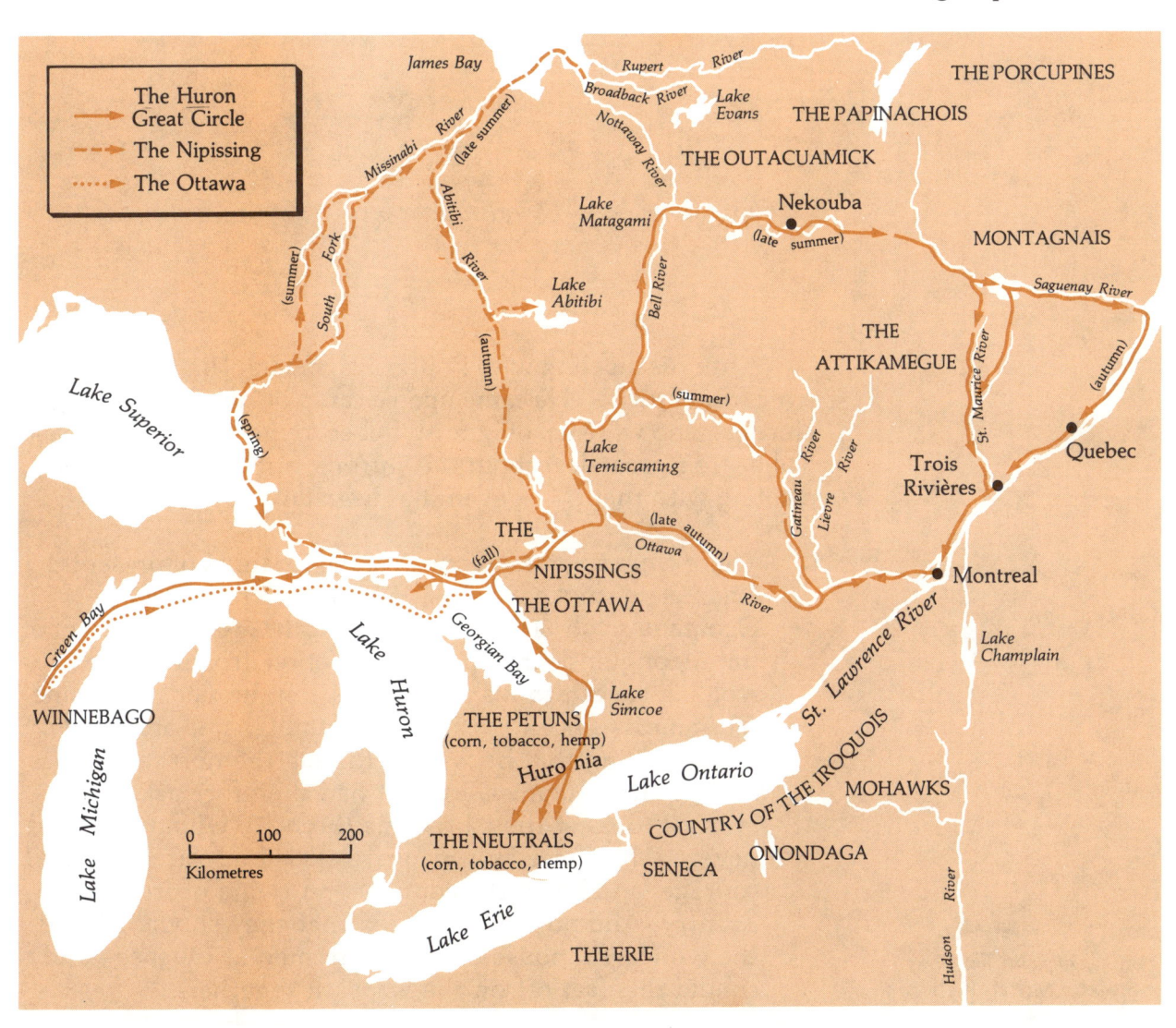

their enemies, that we don't keep our promises. Then we'll be in real trouble. No, we had better keep on the good side of our friends. If they insist we go on the warpath against the Iroquois, we had better do it.

GETTING THE FACTS

19. Give two reasons why the French were allies of the Algonquins, rather than of the Iroquois.

THINKING IT THROUGH

20. Champlain claimed he had no choice but to join the Algonquins in a fight against the Iroquois. Yet he had made a choice. What was his reasoning? (Make a chart showing the possible outcomes of: a) refusing to fight the Iroquois, b) agreeing to fight the Iroquois.)

21. Have you ever had to decide between two choices, both of which would likely have some unpleasant outcomes? If so, tell about it. Otherwise, make up an example that could happen to you.

After his meeting with Pontgravé, Champlain traveled up river from Quebec. He came upon a camp of Algonquins and Hurons, who were heading for Quebec to meet him. Champlain had heard a great deal about the Hurons, but this was his first meeting with them. The event has been described as follows:

> There were solemn greetings and exchanges of presents. Champlain smoked in ritual silence with the chiefs, Ochateguin [oh-SHAW-te-kwihn] of the Hurons, Iroquet of the Algonquins. After proper reflection, Iroquet made a scolding speech to his people. His son, he said, had come ten months since to visit Champlain. Champlain had then told him that he wished to help the northern tribes against their enemies. Iroquet had therefore asked the Hurons to meet the Christians (French), whom they had never seen. These Hurons were skilled in war and full of courage, and knew the country and rivers of Iroquois country. And now he proposed that they should all visit the wonderful house of the white men at Quebec—and should then set off on the warpath together.

From *Champlain: The Life of Fortitude* by Morris Bishop.

The war party set off in July. With Champlain were two French companions and about 60 Hurons and Algonquins. Within two weeks they had advanced up the Richelieu [reesh-LYEU] River to Lake Champlain. Soon they were deep in enemy territory. This was the land of the Mohawks who were one of the strongest Iroquois nations. The dark summer nights were perfect for travel; in daylight, the war party went ashore and hid in the deep woods.

At last, they arrived at Ticonderoga [tī-kahn-duh-ROH-guh]. There the invaders heard the shouts of Mohawk warriors. However, fighting did not begin right away. First, the Iroquois sent a small group to find out the plans of the other side. Champlain and his Indian allies announced that they had come to make war. They agreed that the battle would begin the next day at dawn. Champlain described the scene of the following morning:

> They came slowly to meet us with a gravity and calm which I admired; and at their head were three chiefs. Our Indians told me that those who had the three big plumes were the chiefs . . . and I was to do what I could to kill them. I promised to do all in my power. . . .
>
> Our Indians began to run some two hundred yards [180 m] toward their enemies. The Iroquois stood firm and had not yet noticed my white companions who went off into the woods with some Indians. . . . As soon as the enemy caught sight of me, they halted and gazed at me and I at them. When I saw them make a move to draw their bows upon us, I took aim with my arquebus [AHR-kwuh-buhs] and shot straight at one of the three chiefs, and with this shot two fell to the ground. . . . As soon as our people saw this shot so favourable for them, they began to shout so loudly that one could not have heard it thunder, and meanwhile the arrows flew thick on both sides. The Iroquois were surprised and greatly frightened. They lost courage and fled into the forest. . . .

Fig. 5-8 When conflict broke out between Europeans and native peoples, which side do you think had the advantage?

From *Champlain: The Life of Fortitude* by Morris Bishop.

An arquebus is a kind of musket, one of the first types of rifles invented. It was heavy and clumsy to use. Unlike modern rifles, the musket was loaded by stuffing the powder and shot down the barrel. When the arquebus was fired, it was rested on a stand that looked like a big slingshot with a long handle.

GETTING THE FACTS

22. Locate the following on a map of eastern North America: Quebec, Richelieu River, Lake Champlain, Ticonderoga. Draw a line to show Champlain's route into the Iroquois territory.

23. **The following words and expressions appear in the two passages from the book "Champlain: The Life of Fortitude." Look up their meanings and write short explanations for each: solemn greetings, ritual silence, harangue, gravity, halt.**

USING YOUR KNOWLEDGE

24. **Describe the battle in which Champlain took part from the point of view of either an Iroquois or a Huron. Tell how you would have felt about the event.**

A century of conflict

Under Champlain's leadership, the colony of New France gradually took root. The fur trade was the key to success. The Hurons and the Algonquins supplied the furs, in partnership with French traders. A few years after Champlain's death in 1635, New France expanded with the founding of Montreal (1642).

The Iroquois, meanwhile, found themselves caught in a squeeze. The French and their Indian partners were pressing from the north. Other native peoples occupied lands to the west and south. Finally, a chance came to improve their position. Rivals of the French—first the Dutch, then the English—proved to be willing allies.

The English had fast-growing colonies on the Atlantic coast. They were keen to trade their goods, including guns, with the Iroquois in exchange for furs. The best furs came from the north, across the St. Lawrence and the Great Lakes. However, in the way of the Iroquois stood the French and their Indian allies—especially the Hurons.

The stage was set for a showdown. The Iroquois decided to move against **Huronia**.

In 1648, a large Iroquois war party made its way unnoticed to the borders of Huronia. They found the village of St. Joseph unguarded; many of the men were away hunting. At sunrise, without warning, the Iroquois attacked. They destroyed St. Joseph, then moved on to do the same to the neighbouring village. Some 700 Hurons were killed or taken prisoner. The remaining 2300 Hurons from the two villages fled to the main settlement of Ste. Marie.

There was no relief, however. Much of the Hurons' food supplies had been destroyed and many starved during the

Fig. 5-9 Ste. Marie Village in Huronia.

winter. Spirits were already low among the survivors when the Iroquois struck again in the spring of 1649. The result: **Jesuit** [JEH-zhoo-iht] leaders such as Fathers Jean de Brébeuf and Gabriel Lalemant were killed; the villages and **missions** of Huronia lay in ruins. The Huron nation had been smashed.

New France itself remained in danger for the rest of the 1600s. The Iroquois, backed by the English, kept up the pressure. The French, along with their Algonquin allies, replied with raids of their own. As time went on, the struggle became one in which the French and the English fought for control of North America. The Indians were reduced to roles as supporting players in a story of **imperial** conflict.

The Jesuits in New France

Imagine you are a native person in Canada nearly 400 years ago. You meet your first European. Is he an explorer? Almost certainly he is, or he would not be here, so far from home. Is he a fur trader? Very likely, because the fur trade was the surest way to make some money to help pay for his exploring. Any other possibilities? There is one—he may be a missionary, hoping to convert you to Christianity.

Missionaries were present almost from the beginning of European meetings with native peoples. The best known were the Jesuits.

The Jesuits were an organization of Roman Catholic priests. They began their work in 1534. From the beginning, the Jesuits were known for their skill as teachers. Even today they operate schools and colleges.

The Jesuits came to Canada in 1625. Priests like Jean de Brébeuf and Gabriel Lalemant came to teach the native people about Christianity. In order to teach them, the Jesuits had to learn the language of the Indians. The Jesuits were some of the first Europeans to do this.

Many of the records we have that tell about early life in Canada were written by Jesuits. The records describe how the Indians looked, what they did and how they lived. They also describe the land and the Canadian wilderness. Many people in France wanted to know more about the new country and the native peoples. So, each year the Jesuit records were made into books for these people to read. The books were called the *Jesuit Relations*. Ever since, the *Jesuit Relations* have provided valuable information about early meetings between native peoples and Europeans.

For almost 20 years, the Jesuits traveled with the Indians in the wilderness. Then, during the years 1639-49, the Jesuits built permanent mission churches and schools for the Hurons.

The most important mission settlement in Huronia was Ste. Marie. Ste. Marie was the headquarters for the other missions. It was built like a village and surrounded by a wall for protection against attacks.

The Iroquois destroyed several mission villages in 1648, but Ste. Marie was the one mission that survived. However, the Huron nation had been broken by years of disease and war, and Jesuit leaders like Brébeuf and Lalemant had been killed. The Hurons and Jesuits who survived the Iroquois attacks decided to retreat from Huronia. Before they left, they burned the village of Ste. Marie. Led by Father Rageneau [razh-NOH], the survivors made their way to the safety of Quebec.

For another 100 years, the Jesuits taught the native peoples about Christianity. They even built missions for the Iroquois, the long-time enemies of the French. Christianized Iroquois actually moved into New France. Today, their descendants live at Caughnawaga [KAH-nah-WAH-guh], near Montreal and near Cornwall in Ontario.

Ste. Marie has been built again. No longer a mission, it is an interesting place to visit near Midland, Ontario.

GETTING THE FACTS

25. Make a chart showing: a) ways Europeans were influenced by Indians, b) ways Indians were influenced by Europeans.

26. a) Write a short definition of the following words: rival, ally.

b) Which Europeans were the allies of the Iroquois? Of the Hurons and Algonquins?

27. How did the warfare between the French and the Iroquois affect the Hurons?

THINKING IT THROUGH

28. If Champlain had been alive in 1650, do you think he would have regretted his decision of 1609 to attack the Iroquois? Why or why not?

THE INVESTIGATIVE REPORTER

29. Find out what happened to the Hurons who survived the destruction of Huronia
and/or
Find out how members of the Iroquois (Mohawks) came to settle at Caughnawaga, near Montreal.

Fig. 5-10 Anthony Henday and two Cree Indian guides coming into a Blackfoot Indian camp in 1754. They tried, and failed, to persuade the Blackfoot to transport furs from the prairies to Hudson Bay. Yet, Henday and the Blackfoot got along very well. Why do you suppose this was so?

Fig. 5-11 In 1788, Europeans built their first fort on the Pacific Coast at Nootka Sound. Why was this an important event?

Fig. 5-12 "Pigeon's Egg Head (The Light) Going to and Returning from Washington," by George Catlin, 1831-32.

Conclusion

Look closely at the painting in Fig. 5-12. It shows a "before" and "after" view of a Plains Indian chief painted in 1832. In the "before" side, the artist shows the chief as he appeared before contact with Europeans. In the "after" side, the artist shows changes in the chief after spending time in a city.

USING YOUR KNOWLEDGE

30. a) Examine the "before" and "after" views of the chief. List the differences you can find.

b) What do these pictures tell you about how Europeans influenced the Indians.

c) Did the Indians influence Europeans? Skim over the chapter and find examples to support your answer.

6 How did French Canada get started?

Scene 1

On the way to school one day, Pam found a wallet with $10 in it. "Finders keepers," she thought to herself.

Before she arrived at school, Pam ran into two older schoolmates, Tracy and Robin. She told them of her discovery.

"Thanks," said Robin, snatching the wallet. "We'll have this. It's not yours anyways."

Scene 2

You are an explorer in the 1600s. You have sighted the coast of North America. As far as you know, you are the first European to do so. Then you see some Indians on the shore. What do you do? Claim the land for your king? Ask their permission to come ashore?

- In Scene 1, do you think that Pam had a right to keep the $10? Did Robin have the right to take it from her?
- In Scene 2, you, as an explorer for a European empire, "discover" a new land. Do you have a right to claim it for your king?
- Is your discovery the same as Pam's? How are the situations different?
- In both cases, how would you determine who the "owner" was?

AD
1500

1534 — Roberval abandons Charlesbourg-Royal

1605
1608 — Champlain establishes Port Royal and Quebec

1650

1700

1760 — Population of New France reaches 85 000

1800

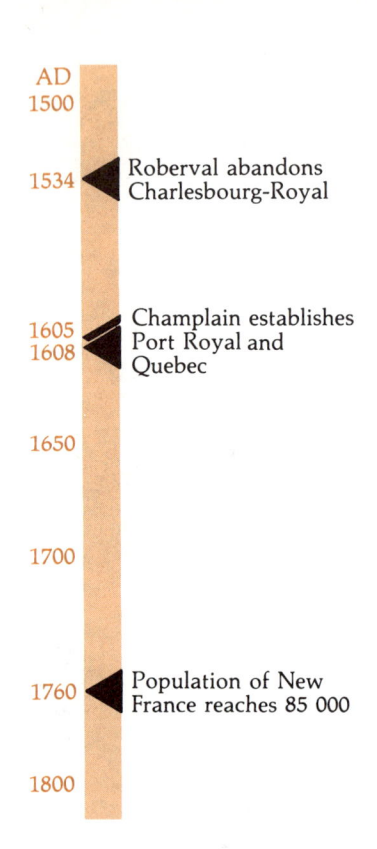

Chapter overview

The history of America during the 17th and 18th centuries can also be seen as the story of the colonies of two European countries: England and France. During the 17th century both England and France developed colonies in North America. These colonies became part of their empires. In this chapter you will study how one of these colonies—New France—got started, and how it survived.

Signposts

> The settlement of North America: By what right?

> The founding of New France

> Why did the settlers come?

> The survival of New France

> FEATURE: New France: What exactly was it?

Key words

| right of discovery | fur trade | seigneurial system |
| empires | fisheries | |

The settlement of North America: By what right?

Before the voyages of people like Columbus, Cabot and Cartier, much of the land or territory of the world was unknown to the kings and queens of Europe. They believed that any land not already ruled by one of them was owned by nobody. Therefore, whoever "found" a "new" territory had a "right" to it. In other

120

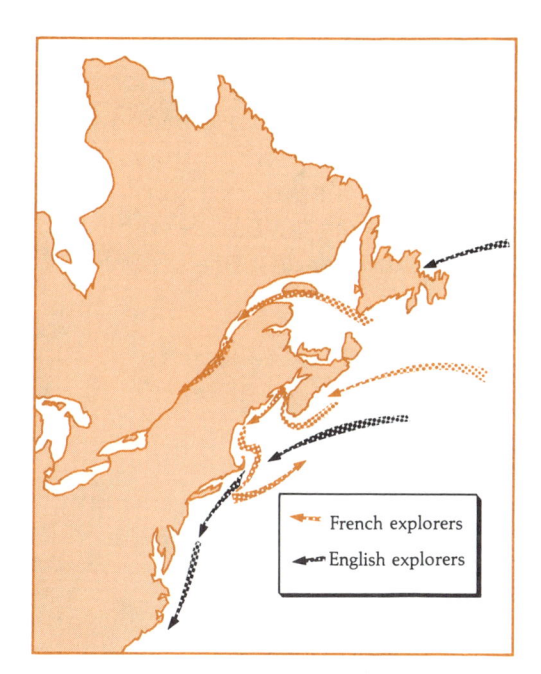

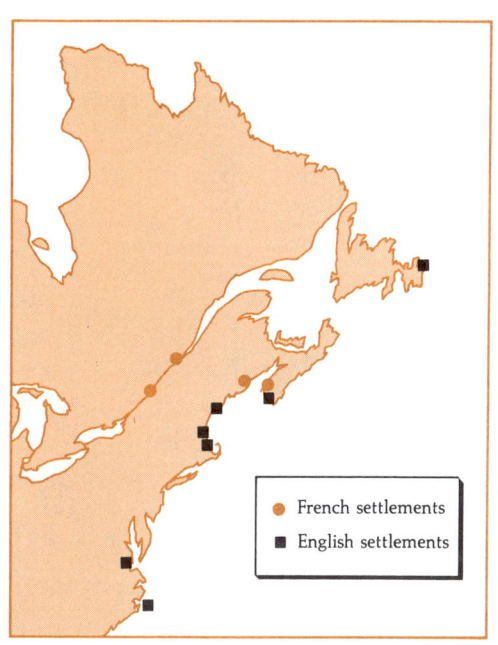

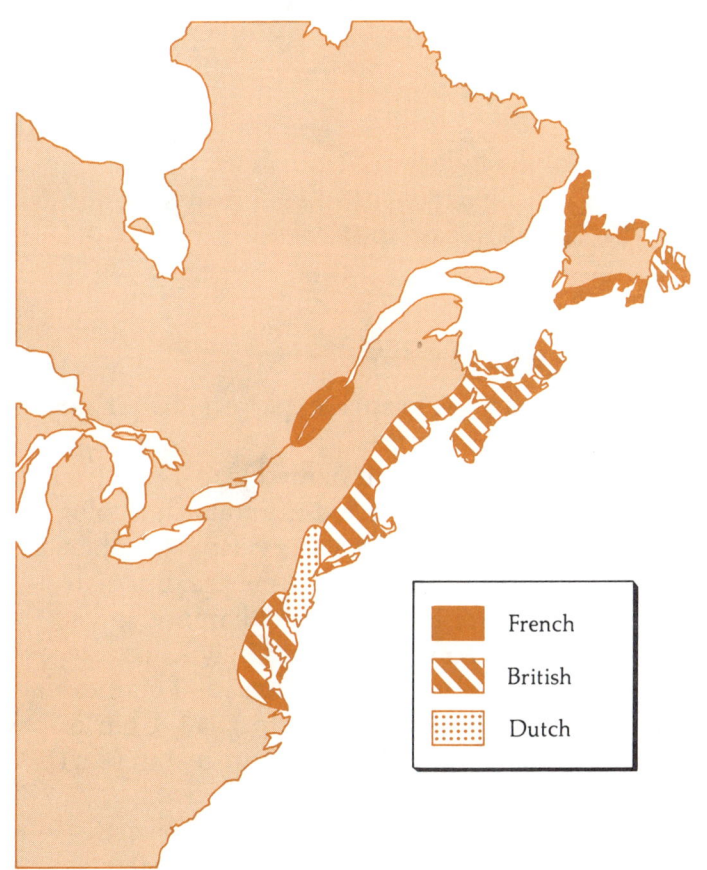

Fig. 6-1 Voyages of discovery from the 1500s to the early 1600s (left). Early settlement attempts from the 1600s on (right).

Fig. 6-2 Territories claimed by European countries. Territorial claims were firmly established during the 1690s and the 1700s.

121

words, they believed, just as Pam did, in the "finders keepers" principle.

During the 16th and 17th centuries, both England and France were acting on the "right of discovery" when they claimed different areas of North America as part of their empires. By sending people out to settle the land and establish colonies, they made their "right" to these lands more secure.

USING YOUR KNOWLEDGE

1. Examine the map on the left in Fig. 6-1 and make a list of all the places that early French explorers visited. Do the same for English explorers. Then examine the map on the right and briefly describe the areas settled by the French and the English by 1650.

   a) Is there a relationship between where French and English explorers went, and where France and England established their colonies? Explain what this relationship is.

   b) What does this settlement pattern tell you about the right of discovery?

THINKING IT THROUGH

2. What does the right of discovery tell you about the European attitude toward the native peoples of North America? Was this attitude fair or unfair? Give reasons to support your opinions.

The founding of New France

During the 16th century, various French explorers, fishermen and fur traders visited North America.

From 1541-43, a French nobleman named Jean-François la Rocque de Roberval [ROH-bayr-VAL] tried to establish a colony on the St. Lawrence River called Charlesbourg-Royal. Roberval hoped that he would find great treasure in America. Spanish explorers had brought back fabulous gold and diamond jewellery that they stole or traded from the Indians in Mexico, Central America and the West Indies. But, instead of diamonds and gold, his men found only harsh winters. In 1543, Charlesbourg-Royal was abandoned, and France lost interest in North America for the next 60 years.

It was not until 1605 that the first lasting French settlement in America was established and named Port Royal.

Fig. 6-3 Habitation at Quebec.

Champlain's drawing of the Quebec habitation. Key: A. "Storehouse" (above G). B. "Dovecote." C. "Building where we keep our arms, and the workmen live." D. "More lodgings for the workmen." E. "Sundial" with a fleur-de-lys banner on top. F. "Forge and artisans' lodgings." G. "Gallery all around the lodgings." H. "Lodging of the Sieur de Champlain." I. "Gate of the habitation, with a drawbridge." L. "Promenade around the habitation, to the edge of the moat." M. "Moat the whole way round." N. "Platforms for cannon." O. "Sieur de Champlain's garden." P. (building under letter G). "Kitchen." Q. "Space between the habitation and the river's edge." R. "The Great River of St. Lawrence." 4. The pier. (translated from French)

Port Royal was an excellent place to start a colony. Located on a protected harbour, it could be easily defended and had access to the sea. It was also located near the mouth of the fertile Annapolis Valley, and the prospects for agriculture were excellent. And nearby, there was an abundance of fish, furs, timber and game—resources that became essential to French colonization in America.

However, the founders of Port Royal, de Monts and Champlain, did not set up their permanent headquarters there. They were more interested in controlling the fur trade than in farming or fishing. They soon found that this could not be done from the Bay of Fundy because the fur trade was centred in the St. Lawrence region.

As a result, Champlain decided to establish a new headquarters at Quebec in 1608. The actual site was selected and construction of the new fort begun on July 3, 1608.

But the time ahead was difficult. Many of the men soon became unhappy with the hard life in a new settlement. In fact, before the summer was out, some of the men tried to murder Champlain.

The first winter at Quebec was cold and harsh. Soon, all the men wanted to do was survive. Twenty-eight men died of scurvy. Only eight, including Champlain himself, lived to see the flowers of spring. But somehow, Quebec survived.

Champlain recognized that the success of Quebec as a colony would depend on four things:

(1) getting along with the Indians;
(2) learning to live off the land by using the natural resources, such as timber, fish, birds, other animals, plants and fresh water;
(3) providing strong leadership in the colony;
(4) receiving the interest and support of the government in France.

Champlain believed that New France could become a very important colony to France. Therefore, he spent a lot of time making plans for New France and trying to persuade authorities back in Paris to see that they were carried out. For example, he knew that to grow the colony must have people. So in 1618, he sent a report to Paris asking the government to send 300 families out to New France. Left to themselves, most people would never have thought of going to New France to live, and few could have afforded to pay their own way out.

Always, Champlain wrote glowingly of the wealth that could come from the fisheries, wood and wood products, mines, furs, and farming of various kinds, including the raising of animals. In his report of 1618, he predicted that profits of $6\frac{1}{2}$ million livres [leevr] could come from New France each year.

A livre was a French silver coin equal in value to about $2.50 of our money today.

Even though the population remained small, the tiny settlement of Quebec survived for a quarter of a century. These first 25 years were successful because of the leadership of Champlain, the support of the Indians, the continued demand for furs in Paris and the gradual adjustment of the Europeans to the climate and environment. The colony was well-established by the time of Champlain's death in 1635. He is called "the Father of New France."

GETTING THE FACTS

3. Who was the first Frenchman to try to found a colony in North America? Why did he fail?

4. a) List three reasons why Port Royal was an excellent place to start a colony.
   b) If the location of Port Royal was so good, why didn't de Monts and Champlain set up permanent headquarters there?

USING YOUR KNOWLEDGE

5. Champlain recognized that the success of New France depended on four things.
   a) Name the four things.
   b) Were these factors important to the success of any new colony?

6. Champlain wrote letters to France in which he described the great wealth in the colony. Imagine you are Champlain. You want to convince people to come and live in New France. Write a short letter in which you describe the new land and explain why people should come there to settle.

THINKING IT THROUGH

7. The eight men who survived the first winter at Quebec suffered great hardships. They would probably say life in New France was less attractive than Champlain's descriptions in his letters.
   a) Why did Champlain make the colony seem so attractive?
   b) Do you think it was fair of him to do this? Give reasons to back up your answer.

8. DEBATE: Champlain deserves to be called "the Father of New France." Discuss what it means to be "Father" or "Mother" of a country. Then look at Champlain's life and see if he fits the description of "Father" of a country.

Why did the settlers come?

There can be no colonies and no empires without people. Some people, such as soldiers, had no choice about going to a colony like New France: they were simply following orders. But most people went to the colonies because they wanted to. They had different reasons for going, as you will see.

Here are three people who went to live in New France. As you read about them, ask yourself why each of them went to New France.

Etienne Brûlé

Etienne Brûlé [broo-LAY] went to New France for adventure. A young boy of 16, he joined Champlain's expedition of 1608 to establish the settlement at Quebec. He was one of the eight survivors of the first winter at Quebec.

But even living in a wilderness settlement like Quebec was not exciting enough for Brûlé. Two years later, with Champlain's permission, he went to live with the Huron Indians in order to learn their language. He was the first Frenchman to do this.

Champlain had taken an interest in the young Brûlé. So when Brûlé returned the next spring, Champlain was very excited to see him, and wrote:

> My French boy came dressed like an Indian. He was well pleased with the treatment received from the Indians . . .

Fig. 6-4 Champlain and Brûlé in Huronia, 1615.

and explained to me all he had seen during the winter, and what he had learned from the Indians . . . my lad . . . had learned their language very well.

With his first-hand knowledge of the Indians of the St. Lawrence region and their language, Brûlé had found his career. He became an interpreter for the French.

For the rest of his life, Brûlé lived with the Indians, just as if he was one of them. His job was to win their confidence so that they would help the French, especially in the fur trade. At the same time, he would tell the French what the concerns of the Indians were. By acting as a middleman in communications and trade, Brûlé became an important link between the French and the Indians. He helped them to understand one another.

More people began to follow Etienne Brûlé's example. They came to be called **coureurs de bois** [koo-REUR deu BWAH] (runners of the woods). Their life was one of freedom and adventure. Brûlé was the first Frenchman to travel extensively around the Great Lakes area. These travels sometimes led him into trouble and eventually cost him his life.

One time, Brûlé was captured by a band of Iroquois, the enemies of the Hurons who were Brûlé's Indian friends. Just as they began to torture him, a thunderstorm broke out. Brûlé convinced his captors that this was a sign from God telling them not to harm him. So they set him free.

In 1632, Brûlé was suddenly killed by a group of Huron Indians. He had lived with them for 20 years. Just exactly how he died remains a mystery to this day.

Marc Lescarbot

Marc Lescarbot [lay-skahr-BOH] was a very successful lawyer in Paris. But in 1606, he became very unhappy with France. He had lost a case in court and believed that it was because his opponent had bribed the judge. He was 36 and had much of his life ahead of him, but no longer wished to live in Paris. So, when his friend, Jean de Biencourt de Poutrincourt [byehⁿ-COOR deu poo-trahⁿ-COOR], invited him to join an expedition to establish a colony in America, he decided to go.

Lescarbot liked variety in his life. He was a university graduate—something quite rare at that time—and had a

See chapter 9 for the story of Poutrincourt and Port Royal.

thorough knowledge of Latin, Greek and Hebrew. One of his favourite pastimes was writing, of which he did a great deal.

The settlement to which Lescarbot went was Port Royal. There was little need for lawyers at Port Royal, so Lescarbot made himself useful by helping de Monts and Champlain with the administration or running of the colony.

Lescarbot loved the New World and spent much of his spare time writing poems about the Micmac Indians. He even wrote North America's first European-style play and had it performed at Port Royal. The play was called the Théâtre de Neptune and was a combination of Micmac and ancient Greek legends.

Lescarbot stayed only one year in America. He returned to France and took up his legal career again. He continued to write and eventually completed the first history of New France.

Fig. 6-5 Stained glass window in Notre-Dame church in memory of Jeanne Mance. What does the window tell us about her life?

Jeanne Mance

May 17 of 1642 was warm and sunny on the island of Montreal. On that day, Jeanne Mance [zhan mahns] stepped ashore from a large bark canoe and became the first European woman on the island of Montreal.

Jeanne Mance was a nurse from Langres [lahngr], France. Her family had a comfortable home there. Why did she leave? She believed that she had been called by God to serve the sick and wounded in the wilderness country called New France.

With money provided by a wealthy French woman, Jeanne Mance founded the first hospital in Montreal. For the next ten years, she ran her hospital and provided leadership to the people in their struggle for survival against the Iroquois.

In 1653, Jeanne Mance returned to France to try to convince the government to send more supplies and soldiers to Montreal.

Jeanne Mance spent a total of 30 years at Ville-Marie [veel-ma-REE], as Montreal was then called. She died in her hospital on June 28, 1673 at the age of 66. She was truly one of the pioneers of New France.

GETTING THE FACTS

9. In your own words, explain the following terms: interpreter, coureur de bois, expedition.

10. Draw the following chart in your notebook and complete it.

NAME	REASON FOR COMING TO NEW FRANCE
Etienne Brûlé	
Marc Lescarbot	
Jeanne Mance	

USING YOUR KNOWLEDGE

11. a) Explain why Brûlé was called a middleman.
    b) Why were middlemen like Brûlé so important to the colonists in New France?

12. Lescarbot wrote a lot of poems about the Micmac Indians. Imagine you are a colonist in Montreal. Describe Jeanne Mance and her work by writing a four-line poem or by drawing a picture.

Fig. 6-6 Marguerite Bourgeoys came to Montreal in 1653 and built the first church there.

13. Use books in your school or local library to find out about one of the following early colonists in New France. Write a one-page description of the person's life. If you can, focus on one interesting event or achievement in the person's life.
a) François de Laval
b) Marie-Madeleine de l'Incarnation
c) Sieur de Maisonneuve
d) Madame de la Peltrie
e) Marguerite Bourgeoys
f) Philippe de Rigaud de Vaudreuil

The survival of New France

A hundred years after Champlain built his fort at Quebec, New France was firmly established as a colony within the French empire. Quebec society was beginning to have a distinct character of its own. The population was small, but stable.

But survival was not easy for a small colony of people living in a harsh environment, far from the mother country. Such a colony could not have grown without leadership and organization. These elements were provided in New France by the Roman Catholic church and a system of land-holding called the **seigneurial** [sehn-YUR-ee-uhl] **system**

The church in New France

Nearly all the people of New France belonged to the Roman Catholic church. In fact, the French would not permit non-Roman Catholics to go to live there. To help the people, to

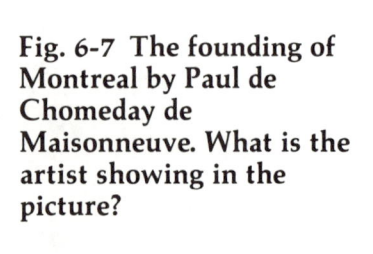

Fig. 6-7 The founding of Montreal by Paul de Chomeday de Maisonneuve. What is the artist showing in the picture?

New France: What exactly was it?

By 1700, the French empire covered much of North America. However, a lot of this territory was never seen by a French fur trader or explorer, let alone a French settler.

The term "New France" was used, generally, to refer to all France's territories in America. But, the French empire in America was actually divided into a number of administrative districts, each with its own governing official. In other words, New France was divided into sections, the way Canada is divided into provinces today. The map of New France below shows the boundaries of these sections or districts.

However, even though New France was divided into a variety of districts, about 90% of the European population of the colony lived in the St. Lawrence Valley. On the map are shown the population figures for 1750. The rest of the people lived in isolated communities. The only other clumps of population were in Acadia [a-KAY-dee-uh] and Louisiana. So, in this chapter, when we talk about New France, we are really talking about the St. Lawrence Valley region, which today is southern Quebec.

GETTING THE FACTS

14. Look at the figures in the table in Fig. 6-8. About how many people lived in New France in 1750?

15. How many of these people lived in the St. Lawrence Valley region?

USING YOUR KNOWLEDGE

16. Explain why most of the population of New France was concentrated in the St. Lawrence region.

17. What present-day province is this region a part of?

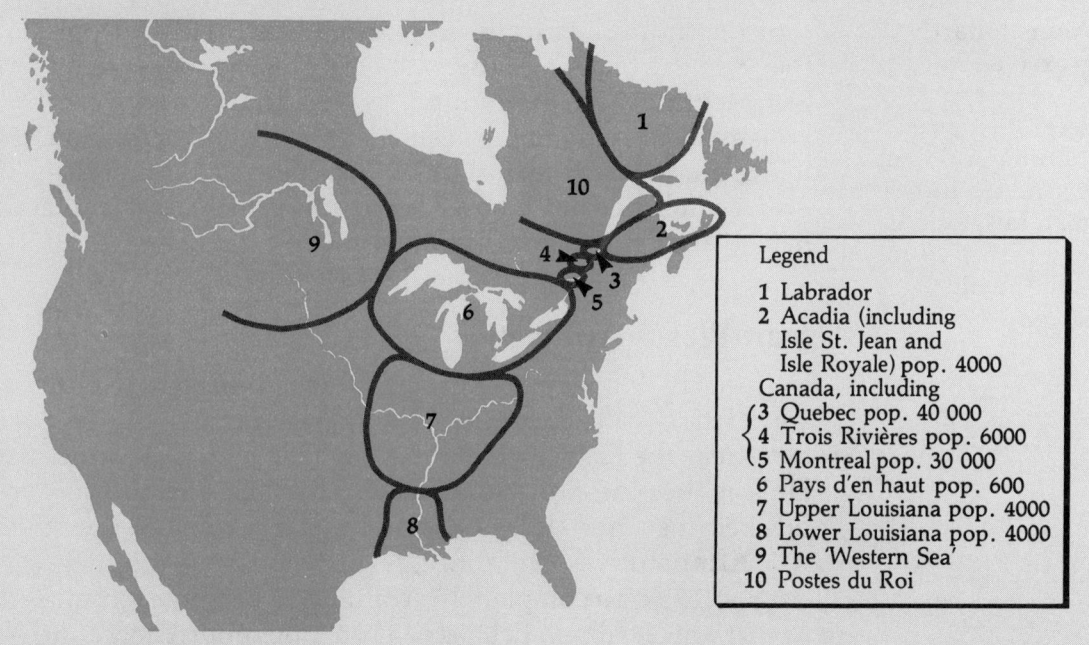

Legend
1 Labrador
2 Acadia (including Isle St. Jean and Isle Royale) pop. 4000
Canada, including
{ 3 Quebec pop. 40 000
{ 4 Trois Rivières pop. 6000
{ 5 Montreal pop. 30 000
6 Pays d'en haut pop. 600
7 Upper Louisiana pop. 4000
8 Lower Louisiana pop. 4000
9 The 'Western Sea'
10 Postes du Roi

Fig. 6-8 Regions of New France before 1763.

Fig. 6-9 Arrival of the Ursuline nuns. Shortly after they arrived in Quebec in 1639, the Ursulines set up a girls' school. Nursing sisters of orders like the Ursulines also founded hospitals in New France and cared for orphans and the old.

provide community leadership, and to see that the people followed the teachings and wishes of the church, parish priests were sent to each community. As well, to try to convert the Indians to Christianity, priests and nuns went as missionaries to live among the Indians. In 1668, a college to train priests was even established at Quebec. Today it is called Laval University, named after the Bishop of Quebec who established it.

Jean-Pierre Aulneau

Jean-Pierre Aulneau [al-NOH] was born on April 21, 1705, in a small village called Montiers-sur-le-Lay [mah^n-TYAY-su^{e}r-leu-LAY] near the French port of La Rochelle on the Atlantic coast. He was the oldest of five children. Three became priests and one became a nun. It is not known what became of the other.

After studying in France, Jean-Pierre came to Quebec in August 1734, to complete his training to become a Jesuit priest.

We meet him in February 1735, one month before he is to write his final exams at the Jesuit College in Quebec.

Reporter: Jean-Pierre, why did you choose to become a priest in New France?

Jean-Pierre: Well, that's really two questions. I chose to become a priest to serve God. I chose to come to New France because priests and missionaries are needed here. As you know, priests work in communities that are already established, while missionaries work among the Indians. The priests with whom I trained in France encouraged many of us to come here.

Reporter: Which will you be, a priest or a missionary?

Jean-Pierre: I don't know yet. But, it doesn't really matter because both have important responsibilities in New France. The parish priest is probably the most important person in the community. There is a lot more to being the parish priest than simply saying Mass on Sunday, comforting the sick and the sad, and looking after the business of the parish. As a priest you are, in some ways, like an official of the government. You must keep the register of births and deaths and draw up marriage contracts. Sometimes the parish priest is even called upon to settle arguments between the people and to give advice on legal matters.

Reporter: The church clearly has a lot of influence in people's lives.

Jean-Pierre: That's certainly true. This is a very religious society. Babies are baptized and become members of the church three or four days after they are born. Children begin learning the teachings from the Bible before they can even read. Soon they are expected to attend church and to obey the rules of the church. There are church rules to cover just about every aspect of life.

Reporter: Can you give me an example?

Jean-Pierre: Well, consider this: This is a nation of farmers, yet, for about five months of the year, the people are forbidden to eat meat, eggs or milk because of the various holy days. On top of these restrictions, the church expects each family to give part of its income to support the church. This contribution is called the tithe [tīth]. It's really a tax.

Reporter: Even though the church directs and even interferes with the people's lives, the parish priest seems to be genuinely welcome in every home.

Jean-Pierre: That's for sure. It's because he does so much for the community.

This conversation is fictional, but is based on facts and attitudes of the time.

After 1667, the tithe was at least 1/26th of the total family income. It was usually paid in threshed grain.

Reporter: What about being a missionary? Would you really want to do that?

Jean-Pierre: Why certainly. It is the job of the missionary to try to convert the Indians of North America to Christianity. This is a very important responsibility. You have to go to live with them to do this. And, let's face it, the conditions of life are rough and there is always the possibility that you will be tortured and killed. But, what better way to die than in the true service of God? After all, Christ himself suffered on the cross. . . .

GETTING THE FACTS

18. Use each of the following words in a sentence. Your sentences should show that you understand what each word means: baptize, convert, missionary, tithe.

19. a) List the duties of a parish priest in New France.
    b) List the duties of a missionary in New France.

THINKING IT THROUGH

20. Do you think the parish priests helped New France survive? Refer to the duties you listed in question 19.a) for facts to back up your answer.

Fig. 6-10 Father François-Joseph le Mercier lived among the Hurons and Iroquois for 20 years. Why do you think he is dressed in buckskins?

The seigneurial system

Now that more people were coming to New France, it was necessary to decide how to divide up and use the land. All the land of New France was considered to be owned by, or at least controlled by, the king, just as it was in Old France. But of course, the king did not actually use or farm the land himself. In fact, no French king ever even visited New France.

So, the king gave the authority to control the land to a senior official in the colony called the **intendant** [ah^n-tah^n-DA$^`$]. The intendant administered a complicated land-use system called the seigneurial system, which was modeled on the old feudal [FYOO-duhl] system of Europe.

Under this system, most of New France was divided up into long pieces of land called seigneuries. Each **seigneury** covered at least 100 square kilometres of land. To become a **seigneur**, a person had to apply to the intendant. Usually the people who applied were either wealthy or the sons of nobles in France. Once a seigneury was granted, it remained in the control of the seigneur and his offspring so long as the conditions of the grant were carried out.

In return for this grant of land, the seigneur had to agree to three conditions:
(1) to swear to be loyal to France and to obey the king or his representative;
(2) to pay certain taxes;
(3) to find people to live on and use the land.

The seigneur would then divide his seigneury into smaller sections of land. Then he would rent these sections to people who wanted to become farmers. Such farmers were called **censitaires** [seh^n-see-TAYRS]. If the seigneur could not find would-be farmers in New France, he had to pay the cost of bringing people to the colony from France.

The seigneur and the censitaire signed a contract in which each agreed to perform certain duties for the other. As a result, each became dependent upon the other to some extent. In the same way, the seigneur and the intendant were dependent upon each other. This we call interdependency, and New France could therefore be considered an interdependent society. No one individual or group of people within the colony could survive or get along without the others. Cooperation was essential to the success and survival of the colony.

In time, the seigneurial system became the centre of the organization of the society and economy of New France.

The governor, who was the king's personal representative, was officially above the intendant. However, the intendant had control of three of the four most important areas of government: justice, finance (including taxation) and the general running of the colony. The governor was in charge of the military.

Each year, the farmer had to pay a small rent to his seigneur. This rent, called the cens, was a symbol of his responsibilities to the seigneur.

Fig. 6-11 Early plan and modern aerial photograph showing the seigneurial land settlement pattern in two regions of Quebec.

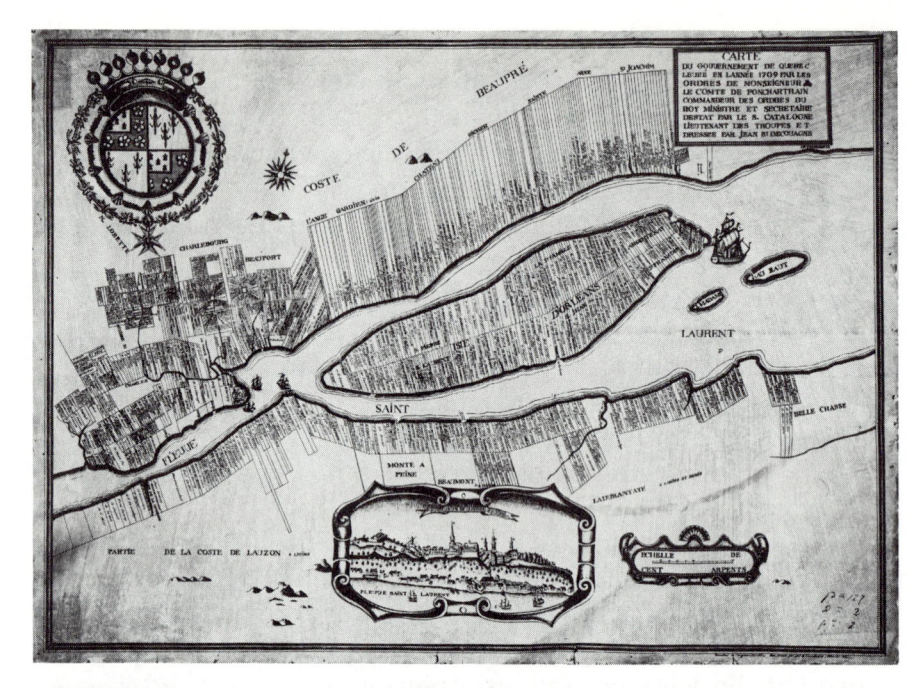

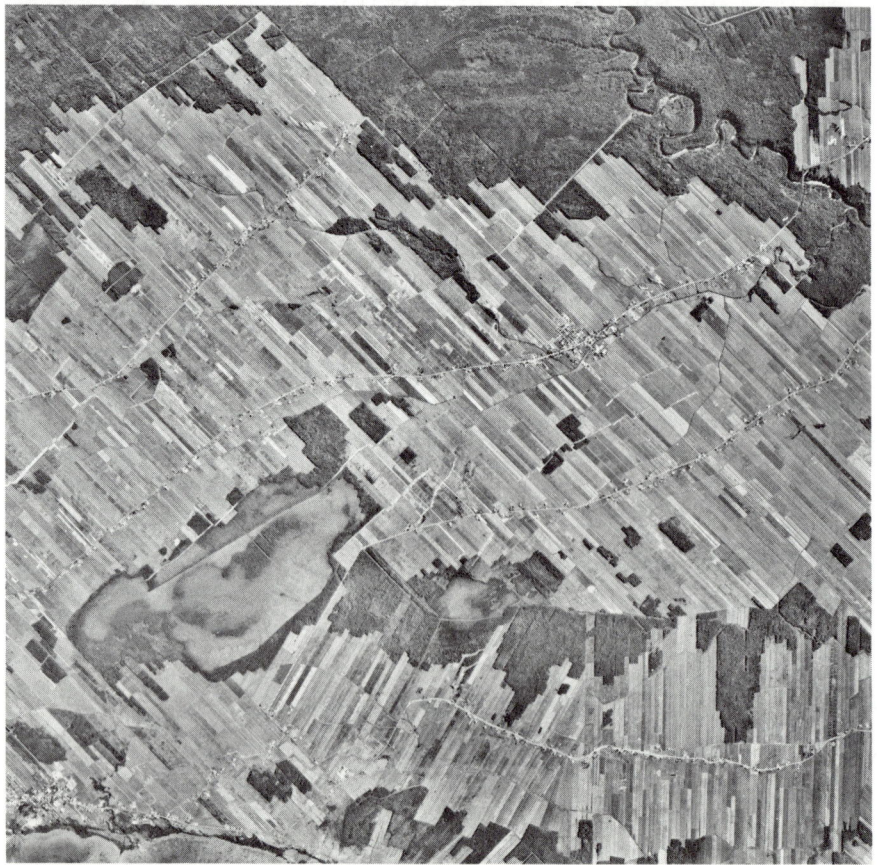

Sooner or later, most of the wealthy people of New France became seigneurs. As seigneurs, they had a direct link with the intendant, who was a chief official of the government of the colony. So, the seigneurs were connected to government. Most of the St. Lawrence Valley was farmland, so most of the censitaires were farmers. But, because most of the land was tied up in the seigneurial system, most of the natural resources of New France, such as fish, furs, and timber, were connected to the seigneurial system as well.

So, just as the church provided the social and moral leadership in New France, the seigneurial system provided the basis of organization.

GETTING THE FACTS

21. Briefly explain each of the following terms: intendant, seigneur, seigneury, censitaire.

22. Draw a two-column chart in your notebook. In one column list all the things that the intendant promised the seigneur. In the other column list the duties of the seigneur toward the intendant.

23. Look at Fig. 6-11. Why was the land divided into long strips, each bordering on the river?

USING YOUR KNOWLEDGE

24. In the settlement, why was it important to control who got the various pieces of land? What do you think might have happened to New France if there had been no system of dividing up and giving out the land?

THINKING IT THROUGH

25. a) Explain what is meant by the word "interdependence."

b) Explain how New France was an interdependent society. Suggest at least two advantages and two disadvantages to this type of society.

c) Give an example of interdependence in your own life. Do you think it is a good thing? Explain why or why not.

Government and the economy

Society in New France was organized around the seigneurial system and the social and moral leadership of the church. If the

Fig. 6-12 Jean Talon

colony was to grow, there had to be a source of wealth or a basis for the economy. In other words, a way in which the colonists could make money in order to buy goods that could not be made in New France. At the same time, there had to be a system of government. When people in a society disagree with one another on a matter that affects them all, they must find a peaceful way to solve their disagreement. This is the role of government: to help people solve their conflicts so that they can make decisions about how to run the country.

The government of New France, like that of Old France, was very much under the control of the king's officials. Also, rich and powerful businessmen could have a lot of influence in the government. Some businessmen became almost as powerful as the governor, the intendant and the bishop, who were the three most important officials in New France. During the 1660s, one such businessman was Charles Aubert de le Chesnaye [shahrl oh-BAYR deu leu shehs-NAY].

Chesnaye was one of the wealthiest men of New France. He was born in Amiens, France, in 1632. Later in life he described his parents as "worthy people," but said that he was "very poor" when he arrived in Canada in 1655. By the time he died, in 1702, Chesnaye had made a great fortune as a merchant, a fur trader and a seigneur. He was for many years the representative in America of a large French trading company, the West Indies Company.

Jean Talon was born in Champagne, France, in 1625. He served twice as intendant of New France, from 1665-68 and from 1670-72. During these brief periods as intendant, he used his great power to make the colony prosperous and successful. Among other things, he was the first to establish a brewery. He also did all that he could to encourage trade.

In 1666, these two powerful men, Talon and Chesnaye, came into conflict over the fur trade. The following conversation is based on fact, though there is no actual record of the real conversations between them. What can you learn about how the government and the economy worked in New France from the dealings between these two men?

Chesnaye: Good day, M. Talon. What can I do for you today? Have you asked me to come here today because of your plans for the fur trade?

Talon: Oh! And what might those be?

Chesnaye: Up to now the fur trade has been controlled by one company. But, it is said that you wish to open the fur trade to anyone who wishes to engage in it—including yourself!

Talon: And, does that not seem like a good idea to you?

Chesnaye: Certainly not. The West Indies Company, which has the monopoly, has done, I believe, an excellent job. We have a good working arrangement with the Indians, and we have no problem selling the furs in Paris. This, of course, means wealth to New France.

Talon: You neglect to mention that it also means profits to the West Indies Company, which you happen to represent. Don't you think that there would be much more business and much more money made and returned to New France if anyone who wished to could engage in the fur trade? Farmers, for example, might make a little extra money this way.

Chesnaye: Frankly, I don't think there are enough furs to go around. Therefore, no one would make money—except you. It is said that you plan to have your furs carried on government ships. You would therefore not have to pay freight and insurance charges, and would make money while others lost it. This you could do because of your position as intendant.

Talon: Monsieur, you may be a man of wealth and power, but you are also a seigneur. You have sworn loyalty to me and to the king I am here to serve as intendant. To accuse me of such motives could be considered treason.

But, let us not talk in such a way. Let me assure you that I only wish what is best for New France. And, it is in this regard that I have asked you to come here today. I have an idea and a business proposition for you.

As you know, our people have been fishing the waters in the Gulf of St. Lawrence since before the arrival of Champlain. But, we have never really made good use of the forests. We could be building fishing vessels from the fine timber in our forests—not to mention ships for His Majesty's navy. This could mean work for our people and for others who might wish to come. And, it would mean making money from one of the colony's best resources. I believe this shipbuilding industry would do well if it were located near the Gulf.

Chesnaye: It sounds interesting, but how does it involve me?

Talon: What I propose is to create two or three large seigneuries along the Gaspé coast. The land is good for farming and lumbering, but is also close to the sea and the fishery. I want you to accept one of these seigneuries.

Chesnaye: I do not know what to say. I am, of course, honoured that you would think of me. But, I am a man of business and must consider it as a business proposition. It is difficult to find good censitaires here and it is costly to bring them from France. And then, we cannot be sure that, once here, they will like it and stay—especially if they cannot find wives.

Talon: That's a valid point. I admit there are problems. However, the government has begun new programs that should make the task a little easier. To ensure that no man should go without a wife, we have instituted the **filles du roi** [feey due RWAH], the daughters of the king.

We also are encouraging people to have large families. Any father who has at least ten children will receive an annual pension of 300 livres from the government. Any with 12 or more will get 400 livres. It's no wonder that more babies are born in New France than Europe on a proportionate basis!

Chesnaye: It sounds good. Besides there are always soldiers who are sent out to serve here, and then decide they want to stay and become censitaires.

Talon: And, as a last resort, one can bring in slaves; Indians from the Mississippi or blacks from the West Indies.

Chesnaye: Yes, but these people rarely make good farmers. They are only useful as servants, so there is really little place for slavery in New France. But still, I can see from the government's plans that it should be possible to recruit enough people for one of these new seigneuries along the Gaspé shore.

Talon: Chesnaye, the opportunity is a great one for you. And, think what it will do for the development of New France. At least agree to give the matter some thought.

Chesnaye: That, M. l'intendant, I will do.

In 1670, Chesnaye accepted the offer. He invested over 20 000 livres in the venture, and eventually became involved in lumbering, fishing, a brickyard and, for a short time, mining. And he made a lot of money from it. But the fur trade remained his major business. Within ten years, he was easily a millionaire. He made a great contribution to Canada, as well. He opened new industries that created jobs and brought much wealth to

Fig. 6-13 Landing of the filles du roi in 1667 at Quebec. How do you think these women felt upon arriving in the colony?

the country, as well as to himself. Most of what he made, he reinvested in the country, often at considerable risk to his fortune. He died wealthy, but if he had not had the interest of the country at heart, he could have been even richer.

Talon returned to France in 1672. He went to work directly for the prime minister in Paris. He eventually received many honours and much wealth from King Louis XIV. He died a wealthy bachelor in 1694.

GETTING THE FACTS

26. Briefly describe the system of government in New France.

27. a) What is meant by the "economy" of a colony or country?
    b) Why was it important for New France to have a source of wealth?

USING YOUR KNOWLEDGE

28. Chesnaye and Talon had different points of view about the fur trade.
    a) In one sentence, explain what the two men were disagreeing about.
    b) Reread the arguments that Chesnaye gave for his viewpoint. Then reread Talon's arguments. Which man would you agree with? Give reasons for your opinion.

29. a) Explain the business proposition that Talon had for Chesnaye.
    b) Chesnaye accepted Talon's offer and, as a result, "made a great contribution to Canada." How did the Chesnaye business agreement help Canada?

30. The French government saw that the colony needed more people if it were to prosper. To solve the problem, the government created programs to encourage population growth.
    a) Describe briefly two of these programs.
    b) Do you think it was a good idea for the government to create these programs? Explain your reasons.
    c) Does our government today create programs for our country? If so, give one example.
    d) DEBATE: The government of Canada should create programs for the country.

Conclusion

During its first 150 years, New France grew slowly but survived. Only eight people in a fort at Quebec survived the harsh winter of 1608-09. But by 1750, thousands of people, most of them clustered in the St. Lawrence River Valley, had made New France their home. They were involved in many different activities, including farming, fur trading, fishing and lumbering. New France had come a long way from its shaky start!

The table below summarizes the growth of New France.

	NEW FRANCE	OTHER EUROPEAN COLONIES
1608	28	500
1641	500	40 000
1689	12 500	250 000
1760	85 000	1 200 000

From *An Introduction to New France* by M. Trudel, p. 131

Fig. 6-14 Population growth in the colonies.

USING YOUR KNOWLEDGE

31. Very few people actually went out from France to New France. Up to 1660, the average immigration was 20 people per year. This figure rose to about 350 immigrants per year during the period 1740-60. How then would you explain the population growth rate? (Note: In total, New France never received more than 10 000 immigrants.)

32. During its first 100 years, New France grew slowly, but survived. Make two lists: one of the factors that helped New France grow; and one of the factors that would have made growth difficult or slow.

33. Look at the population figures for other European colonies. Suggest reasons why the population of New France was so much smaller than the population of the English and Spanish colonies.

7 How did Canadians make a living in 1700 and 1750?

In 1960, scuba diver Don Franklin rose to the surface of the Basswood River (west of Lake Superior) with a handful of musketballs lost by fur traders nearly two centuries ago. Later dives recovered a set of 14 nested copper trade kettles, 36 wrought iron trade axes, 24 iron chisels and spears, buttons, knives, brass thimbles, trade beads, a tobacco pipe and 1000 more musket balls. All had been lost when a fur trader's canoe was upset in the rapids while trying to avoid a long portage [pohr-TAHZH].

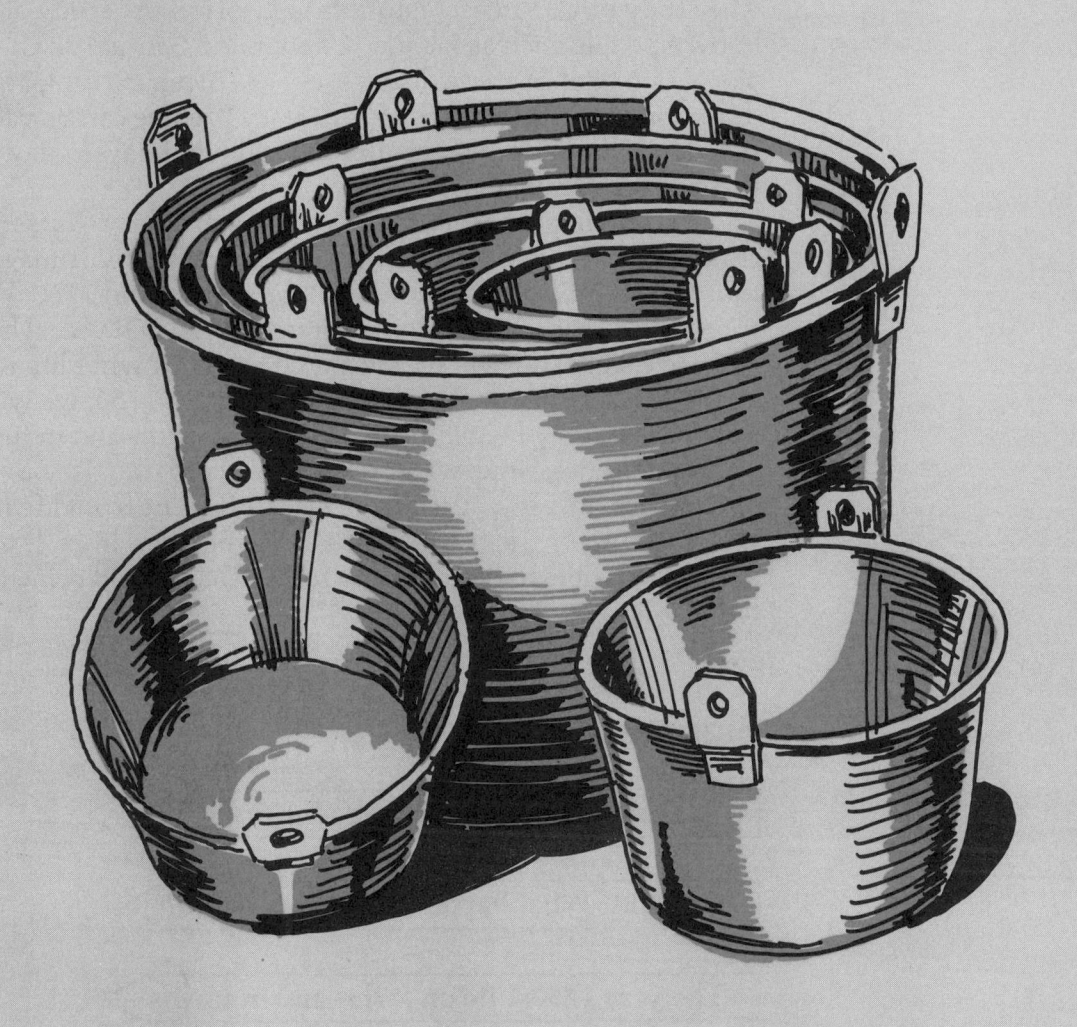

- List the items that Don Franklin found.
- Explain why the items were probably used for trade.
- These items were found because they were made of metal or some other material that the water did not destroy. What other trade goods were likely carried?
- Capsizing was one of the dangers faced by early fur traders. Can you suggest some other dangers?
- On a map, find where Don Franklin made his discovery. Which other locations might be worth exploring for similar discoveries?

Chapter overview

The study of Canadian history is very often the study of well-known people such as Jacques Cartier and Samuel de Champlain. The lives of these discoverers are often exciting and dramatic. But, the history of "ordinary" people can be valuable too. Their lives can help us understand what day-to-day life in the past was really like.

In this chapter, we will look at how ordinary Canadians made their living in New France. To do this we will imagine that time has been frozen in two years, 1700 and 1750. We can then look at the main activities of people in each year. Using our detective skills, we will search for clues about what life was like in 1700 when the fur trade was booming. In 1750, we will have a look at the way people settled down on farms and in towns.

By freezing time, we will also be able to practice our skills of comparison. How was life in 1700 different from life in 1750? We will look for the forces that shaped people's lives. It may even be possible to discover the forces that would bring changes to New France after 1750.

Signposts

The year 1700: What was the fur trade like?

FEATURE: What happened to the Griffon?

The year 1750: Life on farms and in towns

Key words

| coureurs de bois | habitants | regulations |
| Métis | speculators | |

The year 1700: What was the fur trade like?

Early explorers in North America were looking for gold, silver, spices and even silks. With the discovery of each new water route, they hoped to find a passage to China, or Cathay, where all this wealth existed. Even as late as 1730, La Vérendrye was searching along the edge of Lake Superior for the "Western Sea" that would take him to China. The explorers did not find any of the treasures they were looking for, but they did find a new treasure—furs. European interest in furs grew slowly but steadily.

Many early French explorers were very interested in furs. The money they got for them in Europe helped to pay for their search for a water route to China. As they travelled through North America, some of their time therefore was spent collecting furs from Indian trappers. As time passed, the discovery of a route to China seemed less important because so much money could be made from the fur trade. By the 1670s, nearly 80 000 beaver skins were being "harvested" in New France each year. The English were also involved in the beaver fur trade.

La Vérendrye and his sons combined exploration with the fur trade. Their adventures in Western Canada make exciting reading.

The "Western Sea" is what people in New France called the Pacific Ocean.

Fig. 7-1 The first stage in making a beaver hat. The beaver wool is being made into hoods that will later be shaped.

Fur felt was made by cleaning beaver fur and then pressing the fur so that the tiny barbs locked together, forming a material that made very attractive hats. The success of the fur trade was based on the popularity of beaver felt hats.

Why would needles be an important trade good?

Beaver was the most valuable skin because it could be made into high quality fur felt. The felt was used for hats which were in fashion in 17th century Europe.

The fur trade led to the founding of French trading centres in the interior of North America. Montreal was established in 1642 as a key trading centre. In the early part of the 17th century, furs were brought to the trading posts by Indians. The Indians trapped and killed the beavers in winter when the fur was thickest. Then they skinned them, stretched and dried the skins, baled them, and brought them by canoe flotillas [flah-TIH-luhs] to the trading posts. There they exchanged the skins for iron kettles, knives, scissors, needles and other products from Europe.

By 1700, some French people found that they could make more money if they learned how to trap animals themselves. These coureurs de bois went into the wilderness and made friends with Indians in their villages.

What was it like to be a coureur de bois? In the next story you will read about a coureur de bois in 1700. You will also get a better idea of what life was like for people in New France in 1700.

Fig. 7-2 The deadfall trap, used for mink or sable. How do you think this trap worked?

What was it like to be a coureur de bois?

Denis Riverin [REE-veu-RA^N], Montreal, April 1700

Finally our trade goods arrived and we began baling them in 90 lb. [40 kg] bundles that would be both waterproof and portable. We carefully loaded the canoe to make sure the weight was evenly spread across the fragile birchbark bottom. Our goods included three small kegs of brandy, four bolts of bright calico cloth, four muskets, 30 trade axe heads, an assortment of chisels and trade beads, two kegs of gunpowder and 100 pounds [45 kg] of musket balls. Our own food took up very little space since we planned to live off the land as much as possible. All we needed was a case of hard biscuit, some peas and a bushel of corn. Most of our food can be caught in our fishnet, which we set at night and then pull in when we are ready for breakfast. Usually we catch a trout, pike or bass. When the net fails, we shoot some small game for a meat stew. Last year, when we ran out of food, we ate reindeer moss and rock lichens. Not very tasty. On our return trip, starvation is less likely because we can choose the poorest pelts and boil them up into a thick glue-like dinner. I have even heard of some coureurs de bois who ate their moccasins.

The three of us have been working together for five years. In the beginning we thought we could make a fortune in the fur trade. It hasn't worked out that way because the price of furs is changing all the time. But the life is exciting. Our backgrounds are very different. I am the son of a noble family in France. One of my partners is a Canadian, born on a seigneury near Quebec. His parents had been tradespeople in France. The other is a **Métis** [MAY-tee]; his mother was a Huron Indian and his father a coureur de bois. He is the most important member of our crew and I am, I suppose, the least important. Being from a noble family doesn't mean as much to coureurs de bois here in New France as it does to people in Europe.

Officially, we are breaking the law. The government forbids ordinary French citizens to paddle through the wilderness in search of animal skins. Fur trading companies monopolize the fur trade. They prefer us to help establish farms and towns in New France. But, unofficially, we are encouraged. This is strange and needs explanation. Half a century ago the Indians brought their furs to Montreal in great flotillas of canoes, but the Indian wars between our Huron allies and the hostile Iroquois, who were able to control Lake Ontario and

---

Denis Riverin was a real coureur de bois who lived around 1700. This diary account is fictional, but it is based on the lives of real coureurs de bois such as Riverin. For more information on these people, see *An Introduction to New France* by M. Trudel.

Towns in New France were trading centres rather than industrial centres. Furs were packaged and shipped to France. Trade goods from France were unloaded and divided into smaller lots. Then they were shipped by canoe throughout the interior of North America. Other townspeople provided goods and services for the traders. What kinds of jobs would have been found in the towns?

Fig. 7-3 A party of voyageurs from the Hudson's Bay Company portages trade goods at a supply post along the route to the fur country. Trade goods and beaver pelts were bound in 90-pound [40 kg] bales. How many could you carry?

The Northwest Company sent voyageurs into the Indian communities to get furs. The Hudson's Bay Company set up forts and expected the Indians to bring the furs to them. What happened to each company?

even launch raids on Montreal, interfered with the fur trade. When furs stopped coming in large quantities, the trading companies were more willing to buy furs from "unlicensed" traders. At that time, people like us began going to the Indian villages and buying the furs with trade goods. It was very profitable and soon many young Frenchmen were disappearing into the bush for the summer months. It has become a serious drain of human resources from New France and has hindered farming and town construction. So the government has threatened us with flogging, fines and even death. But the threats do not work. They don't really want to stop us because we make a lot of money for Quebec. How else could the fur traders in Montreal grow wealthy? How else could the government collect tax revenue? The last time I was arrested for illegally trading in furs, the judge just fined me and turned me loose so that I could outfit another canoe for our next trip.

Our canoe was made by an Indian family on the Ottawa River. None of the French craftsmen seem able to make these canoes properly, so it was the first thing we traded for. Some canoes can carry as many as four tons [3628 kg], but ours is much smaller. The big canoes are used only by the fur trading companies who hire many men to travel great distances. On the small rivers, our canoe is much better. With a small canoe we can avoid some of the portages and thereby increase our speed. With so many coureurs de bois competing for furs, speed is very important. The first trader to arrive at the Indian villages is the one who gets the best deal. To get there first, many of us take risks in the fast water.

Occasionally, a canoe is upset and the cargo is lost. We are prepared for these risks and consider them part of the excitement of the fur trade. If a rock or submerged root punctures the birchbark bottom of the canoe, it is easy to fix. We pull the canoe out of the water, unload it, let it dry, put on a patch of birchbark and then seal it with spruce gum. If necessary, we sew the patch on with tamarack roots. Within an hour or so we are back on the river.

From Montreal, we plan to travel up the Ottawa River, across to Lake Nipissing, over to Lake Huron and then on to Sault Ste. Marie. On still water we can cover as many as 45 miles [72 km] per day. We usually paddle from dawn to dusk, only stopping for a quick lunch. When the wind is right, we are able to sail our canoe. Our tarpaulin [TAHR-pah-lihn] makes a pretty good sail. (At night the tarpaulin becomes our tent.)

Whenever we find an Indian village we begin to trade. It doesn't take very long. We show them our trade goods and they show us their furs. Then we try to strike a bargain. Each of us wants to get as much as we can, but eventually we strike a bargain. If other traders use our canoe route, the value of our trade goods drops and the value of the furs increases. When this happens, we are forced to travel farther into the wilderness. Sometimes this means going as many as 1500 miles [2414 km] from Montreal, into the country beyond Lake Superior.

After the trading is over, we relax and have a pretty good time. Most of the Indians are friendly. We have to be careful around the Iroquois, but they do not live along this northern route. In general, we mix very well with the Indians and sometimes I feel like an Indian myself.

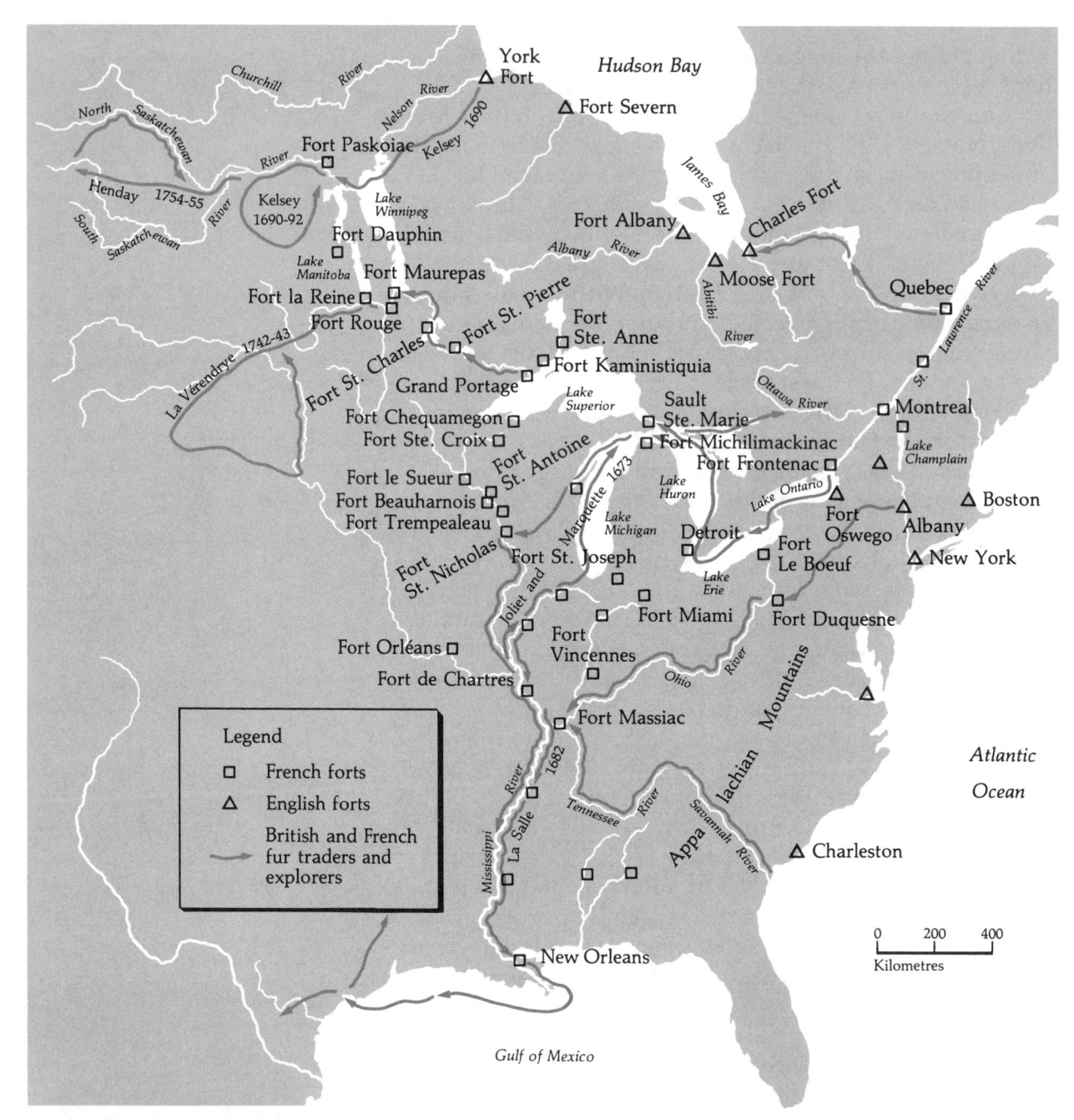

Fig. 7-4 Fur trade routes and trading posts. The fur trade route to the west started in Montreal and ended in the shadow of the Rocky Mountains.

GETTING THE FACTS

1. List the trade goods packed by Denis Riverin.
2. Why was Riverin considered an outlaw?
3. In point form, summarize how the Indians and coureurs de bois traded.

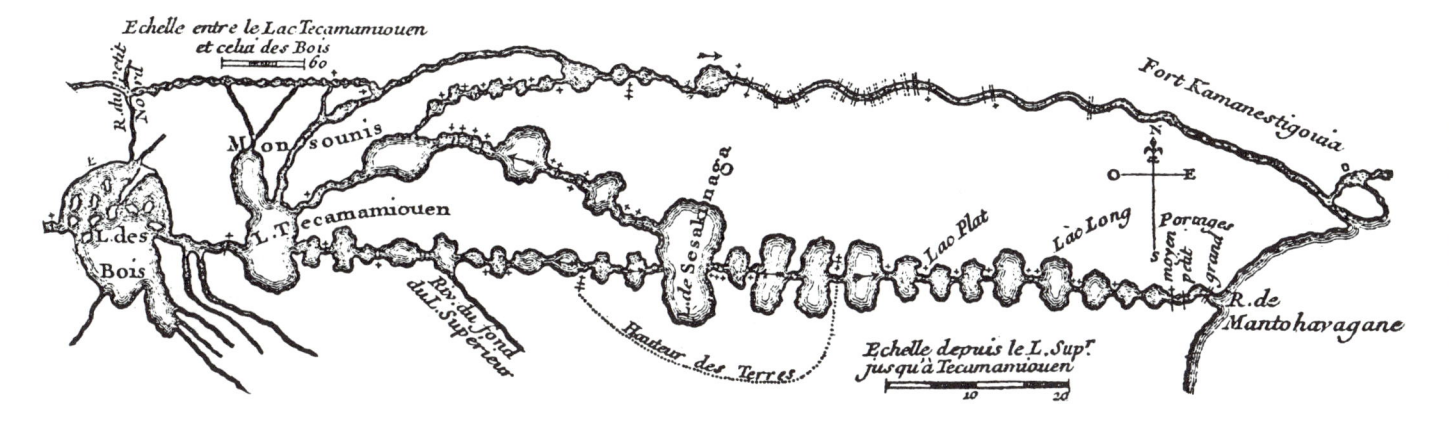

Fig. 7-5 This map was drawn by the Indian Ochagach for La Vérendrye and published in 1754. Locate the area on a modern-day map.

USING YOUR KNOWLEDGE

4. Describe two ways in which Riverin's trade would have been affected by other traders using his route.

5. The map in Fig. 7-5 drawn by Ochagach [OCH-uh-gahk] is 90% accurate when compared with the real distances between lakes. Compare this map with the one in Fig. 7-4. Which one would you prefer to use? Give reasons for your answer.

THINKING IT THROUGH

6. a) Look up the word "contradictory" in a dictionary and write its meaning in your notebook.
   b) How were the government's official and unofficial policies towards coureurs de bois contradictory?
   c) Do you approve or disapprove of the fact that the government had two policies? Give reasons for your opinion.
   d) Give examples from your own life where people have contradictory policies about something.

7. DEBATE: The life of a coureur de bois was suitable only for young men at that time.

INVESTIGATIVE REPORTER

8. One of the most interesting coureurs de bois was Pierre Radisson. He was captured by Indians and made a brother of a nation. He adapted to the lifestyle so completely that for a time he felt more Indian than French. Find out more about his life by consulting your library for references to Radisson and his biography. Then, write a one-page answer to the question "Is Pierre Radisson admirable?" Use facts from your reading to back up your answer.

Fig. 7-6 Pierre Radisson

What happened to the Griffon?

Early in 1689, a fur trader and explorer named René Robert Cavalier de la Salle built the first ship to sail on the Great Lakes above Niagara Falls. With a crew of Indians, carpenters, priests and young coureurs de bois, La Salle constructed the *Griffon* [gree-FOH^N] on the banks of the Niagara River. His idea was to build a ship that could carry a large cargo of beaver skins and thereby make more money in a single trip than could be made by other fur traders in their small canoes. The *Griffon* was successfully launched and sailed through Lake Erie, up the St. Clair River to Lake Huron and eventually left La Salle and his men at the northern end of Lake Michigan. They had traded along the way, and by this time the *Griffon* was loaded with beaver skins. La Salle ordered the crew to sail back, sell the cargo and return. The *Griffon* was never seen again.

La Salle suspected that the ship had been beached and the cargo of furs stolen. Others believed that the *Griffon* had been caught in a storm and had sunk to the bottom of Lake Huron. Whatever really happened, the people who believed in La Salle's idea lost the money they invested, which shows that the fur trade could be a very risky business.

In 1956, part of the mystery was solved when an Ontario fisherman steered his boat into a sandy lagoon on an island near Tobermory. There below him in the crystal clear water was the wreckage of a sailing ship. When experts examined one of the bolts, they found that it was held in place by an iron wedge instead of a threaded nut. This kind of bolt had been used only up to 1700. The *Griffon* was the only ship in the Great Lakes that could have had a bolt like that.

The ship had been found, but the mystery of what happened to it is still unsolved.

GETTING THE FACTS

9. Why did La Salle build the Griffon?

10. What evidence is there to show that the wreckage discovered in 1956 is part of the Griffon?

USING YOUR KNOWLEDGE

11. Hypothesize about the Griffon's fate. Imagine you are in charge of the Griffon on the return trip. Write an entry for the captain's logbook explaining what happened. There are many possibilities. Perhaps your ideas will be close to the truth.

THE INVESTIGATIVE REPORTER

12. If you are interested in the story of the Griffon, you might like to read "The Fate of the Griffon" by Harrison John MacLean.

Fig. 7-7 Route of the Griffon.

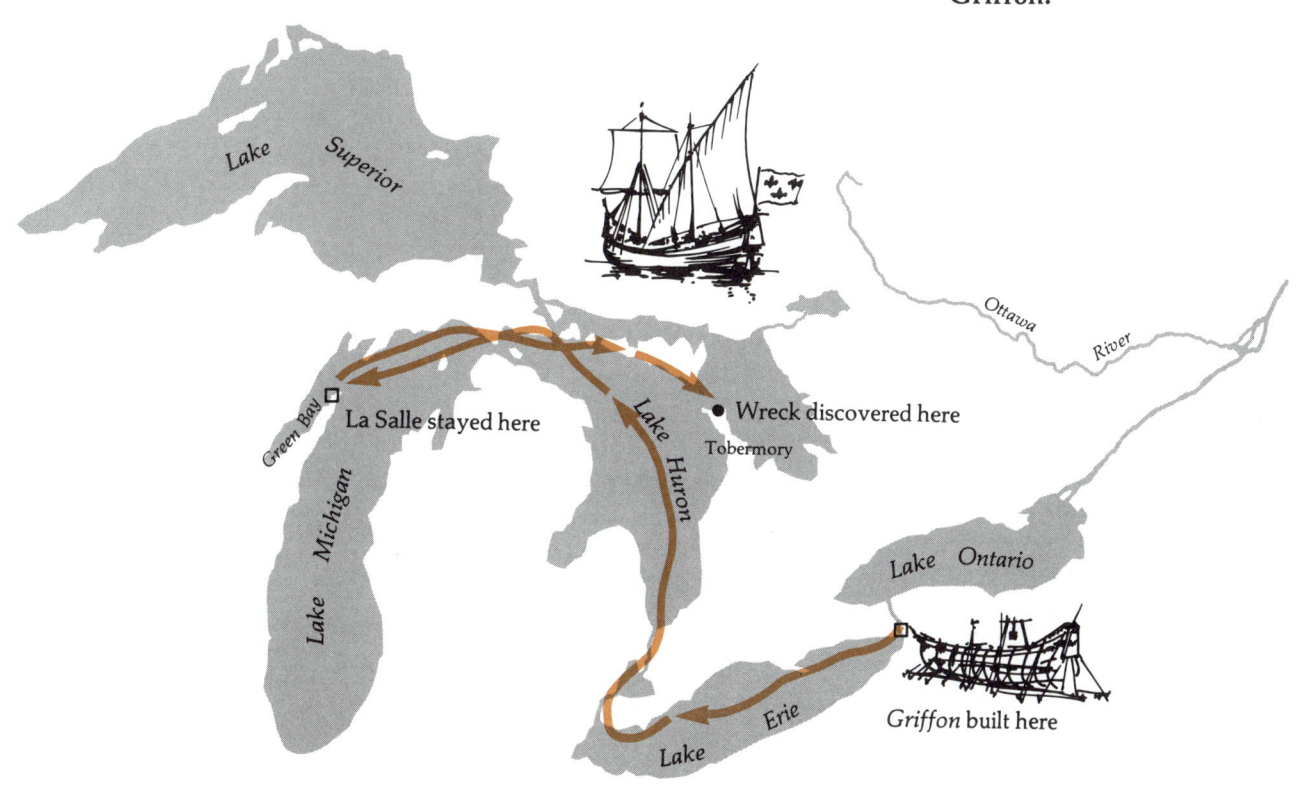

The year 1750: Life on farms and in towns

In 1700, fur trading was an important activity in New France, but the growth of permanent settlement was very slow. One reason for this was that the King of France, Louis XIII, gave control of the colony to fur-trading companies. The companies did not want people to settle.

When Louis XIV became King in 1663, he started many programs that were designed to get people to settle in the colony. He knew that a large permanent settlement in New France would make France's claim to the land secure.

Louis XIV's plans for expanding French settlement were a success. The population of New France increased from about 17 000 in 1706 to almost 43 000 in 1739. The settlers made their living on farms along the St. Lawrence River or in the growing towns.

(Opposite page) A griffon is a mythical monster with an eagle's head and wings and a lion's body. La Salle called his ship the *Griffon* to honor Count Frontenac, Governor of New France, who helped the explorer. Frontenac's coat of arms included a griffon. For what other reason might La Salle have called his ship the *Griffon*?

What was it like to be a farmer in New France?

What was the average farm like?

The following description of a typical habitant's farm is based upon historical descriptions. The name André Lamarre has been chosen because it is entered on the Seigneury of Longueuil [lohⁿ-GŒY] in the 1723 census report (see Fig. 7-11). The story itself is fictitious.

My life as a farmer

André Lamarre, 1750

I came to New France from Normandy in 1713, when it looked like there was going to be peace between England and France at last. Of course I was wrong. But that was only one of my mistakes. My biggest mistake was to believe that a city boy like me could become a wealthy fur trader in New France. The beaver trade was already filled with eager young adventurers and the market was not very good. The middleman who bought

Fig. 7-8 A farm in Château-Richer, 1787. This is likely an accurate picture of the kind of farm that André Lamarre lived on. What does it reveal about farming? What kind of activity is shown in the distance.

"Château-Richer" by Thomas Davies. National Gallery of Canada, Ottawa.

the furs from us and then sold them in Europe did not pay much. Yet they charged us high prices for their trade goods.

So I looked into farming. The seigneury at Longueuil was just being opened up near Montreal and I thought I would try to combine fur trading and farming. I was not successful, so I decided to become a full-time farmer. I didn't really have much choice—I didn't have any special skills, so farming was the only life open to me. Also, I was lucky enough to find a wife—here in New France the men far outnumber the women. Both of us would be able to make a living on a farm.

Lots of us didn't know how to farm. Louis Hébert [ay-BAYR], the first farmer in New France in 1617, started off as a druggist! I had heard that, of the 10 000 immigrants who came to the colony, 75% had no farming experience. So we have had to learn things the hard way. Take manure, for example. We had been dumping it into the river for years, but recently we were told that it is good for the land. Why weren't we told this sooner? The government has not tried to teach us about fertilizer, livestock or seed grains. The only thing they tell us is to keep our animals out of the seeded fields. So our farms are not as productive as they could be.

Even if we could produce more, where would we sell our products? France doesn't want our grain—it has more than it needs. The towns of New France don't seem to want it either. Many people prefer food shipped from Europe. And those who don't rely on imported goods have gardens and even raise animals for slaughter. Besides, it takes all our time and effort to produce what we need for ourselves.

Lately things have changed somewhat. More and more soldiers are arriving and there is an increased demand for our grain. Unfortunately, we have had a lot of bad weather, which has caused poor harvests. New France can't feed itself.

In spite of our problems, we enjoy the life on our seigneury. We have a house and several farm buildings close to the St. Lawrence River. Some farmers have small stone houses, but most buildings are made of logs notched and piled horizontally. Our roofs are thatched and sometimes cedar shingles are used. We have a stone chimney that heats the main room quite well. Our windows are covered with oiled skins that allow light in and keep some of the cold out. Most of our baking is done in a clay oven set up outside the house.

We keep all sorts of animals on the farm. Cattle are the most useful, since they provide milk, meat and power. Pigs we

This is a fictional account based on real people and events. For more information, see M. Trudel's *An Introduction to New France*.

Fig. 7-9 Louis Hébert established the first farm in Quebec. What is he wearing on his feet? Why?

The French farmers loved horses, even though they were expensive to feed and could not be worked hard. The farmers were willing to sacrifice their standard living just to keep them. In 1709, the government actually forbade them from keeping more than two horses and a colt, because horseracing was beginning to hurt farming activities. However, the law didn't work, and by 1750, there were 15 000 horses in New France.

produce in large numbers because bacon is one of our favourite foods. And of course we have horses, turkeys, chickens and sheep. We could make a lot of money from sheep if we could only find the time to build a woolen mill. Wool clothing is necessary to a comfortable life in the cold Quebec winter. Perhaps I should specialize in sheep.

Wheat is our main crop, so we eat a lot of bread. We even use wheat to pay the taxes to the seigneur and the priest. The seigneur gets one-quarter of our crop because he provides us with a mill in which we grind our grain into flour. The priest gets one-twentieth of our crop. This helps pay for the building and upkeep of a church on the seigneury. To me this isn't too bad. When there's a good year, everybody shares. When there's a bad year, everyone suffers. Bad years are common because we have barely three months in which to grow and harvest our wheat.

We grow other things too. Our crops include oats, barley, rye, peas, corn, flax and tobacco. The growing season is so short that we have to start our tender plants in hotbeds. We transplant them to the garden later when the soil gets warm enough. So far, we have not had much luck with orchards. The local maple trees provide us with sap for syrup and sugar in the early spring.

My life here in New France is good in many ways. I have lots of land and lots of firewood. I can hunt whenever and wherever I want. I can choose to work or to not work. I can spend my money on whatever I want to spend it on.

Of course, I am not a rich man. Like many other farm families, we have a one-room house and not much furniture. Our cash is usually spent as soon as we get it, so we can save very little. And then, recent crop failures have made us all quite poor. Sometimes I think about giving up farming and moving to Montreal. A lot of people are doing this. Last year, 1749, so many **habitants** [a-bee-TAH^N] moved from farms to towns that the intendant tried to stop them. I don't think he succeeded though. What can all those people do in the towns? New France has no large industry, and yet 25% of the population lives in towns.

Perhaps things will be better next year. Maybe we will have a great crop that we can sell to the soldiers coming to the colony. We can only wait and hope.

Fig. 7-10 Habitants' cottage.

GETTING THE FACTS

13. Write down a sentence from the text that shows that many settlers who took up farming in New France had never been farmers before.

14. List the advantages that Lamarre expresses about his life on the farm. List the disadvantages.

15. Why was Lamarre not upset about the taxes he has to pay to the seigneur and the priest?

USING YOUR KNOWLEDGE

16. Imagine that you are Marie Lamarre. Write a description of your life on the seigneury using André Lamarre's comments

159

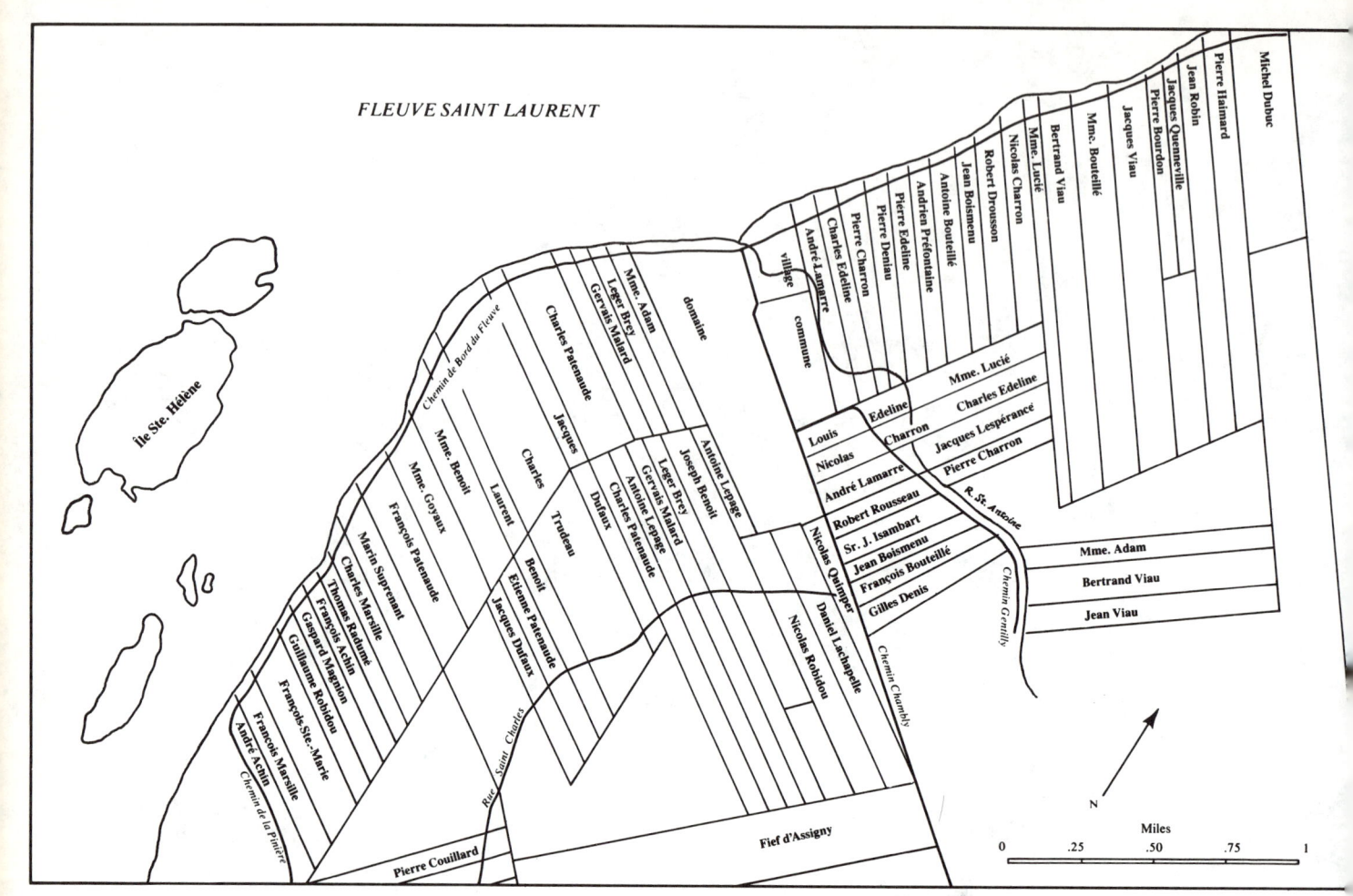

Fig. 7-11 A map showing the allotment of land in the Seigneury of Longueuil prepared from the 1723 census report. Not shown on the map are 23 landholders who leased interior lots.

as a guide. What would your role be? Would you look at farming differently than André?

17. The census of 1723 has provided historical detectives with an interesting record of what life must have been like in the past. The map of the Seigneury of Longueuil in Fig. 7-11 is particularly useful.

    a) How many farms were located on the seigneury?
    b) Why were the farms laid out in strips?
    c) Why were some farms larger than others?
    d) Group the farms according to three sizes: small, medium and large. How many of each were there?
    e) Were there any farms that may have been subdivided? Why might this happen?
    f) Which farms were the most desirable?
    g) Examine the names closely. How many farms were owned by the same person?

h) How many farms belonged to women? Why was this so?

i) Where was the main road located? Can you find any other roads?

j) Why was the village located on a stream?

k) What was the commune?

l) Where do you think the seigneur had his farm located?

m) Where would you have built the church?

n) Why were some blocks of land totally undeveloped?

In 1663, more than half the seigneurial land was held by women.

THINKING IT THROUGH

18. Make a chart in which you compare the life of a coureur de bois with the life of a farmer in New France. You may want to consider the following points:
a) type of labour involved;
b) amount of travelling;
c) dangers;
d) amount of money you would make.
Which would you choose to be? Give reasons for your answer.

19. List three problems that could arise in New France if a lot of farmers moved to the cities.

A Quebec City merchant talks about life in New France

Monique Boulanger [mohⁿ-NEEK boo-lahⁿ-ZHAY], 1750
When my husband died several years ago, the children and I took over the store without too much difficulty. There are many women in Quebec who run businesses and there are many more who have become important seigneurs. Part of the reason for this is that the women are often much younger than the men they marry. I was only 14, and my husband nearly 34, when we got married. I knew that probably I would still be a young woman when he died. I had to be prepared to run the bakery or to remarry—or both. So far I have not remarried, although several of my friends have started second families.

The bakery keeps me so busy that I have little time for anything else. It was so hard to get permission to set up the shop in the first place that I hated to give it up after my husband's death. Life in New France is strictly controlled by rules. You really feel them when you live in the town. Our lives here are very different from the free lives of coureurs de bois.

Monique Boulanger is fictional character based on real people. They are described in more detail by M. Trudel in An Introduction to New France. *Students wishing to do research on the role of women in Quebec will find many names of women in business, nursing, religion and farming in this book.*

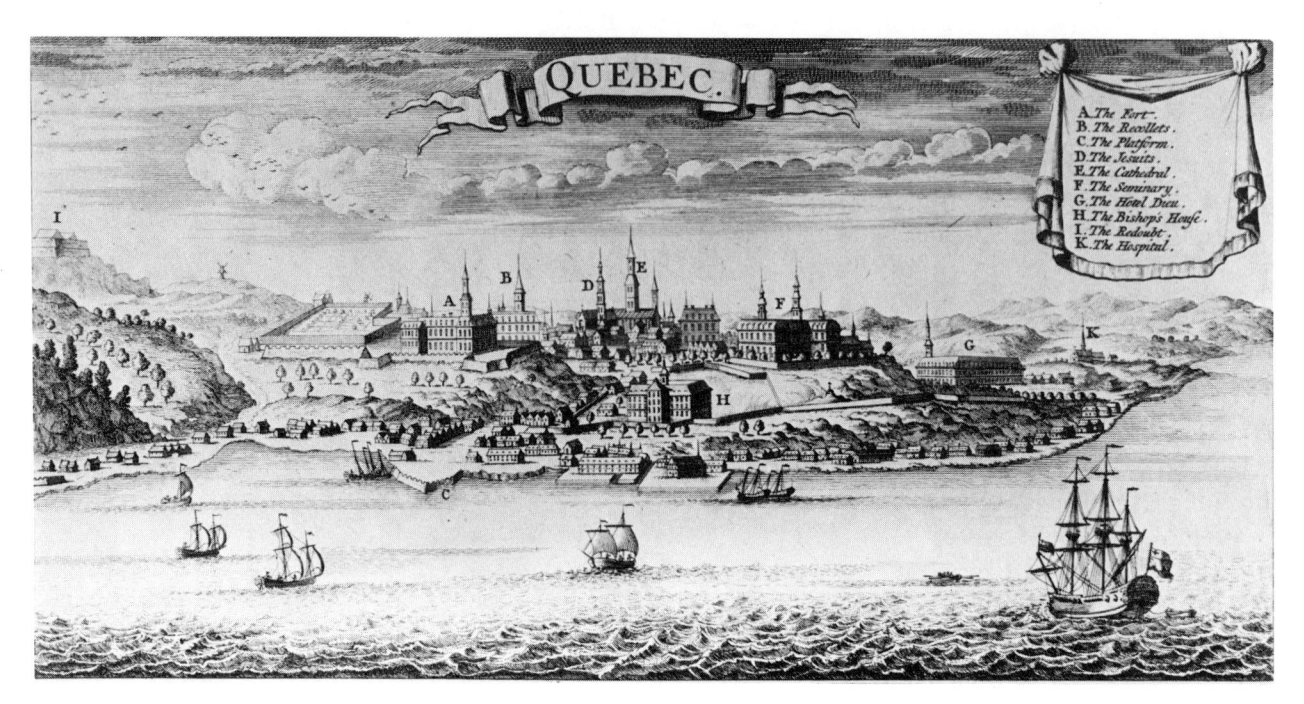

Fig. 7-12 Quebec, around 1730.

Take the price of wheat, for instance. Wheat is the basic ingredient of bread, and bread is one of our main foods. A while ago, some people tried to buy up all the surplus wheat and then sell it at very high prices. They hoped to get rich fast. The government stepped in to stop these speculators [SPEH-kyoo-LAY-ters] and bring the prices back down. Now these price regulations cover everything bought and sold in Quebec. Our bread must weigh a certain amount. And we must charge a certain price for it. Meat is regulated, and the butchers have to close their shops for 40 days during Lent when no meat is to be eaten. Alcohol is also closely regulated, especially alcohol used in the fur trade. Even firewood has to be a certain length and quality.

These regulations are not all bad. Before the regulations came in, you could never depend upon prices. Many merchants raised their prices so high that only the rich could buy things—even bread. Government controls are necessary in a society like ours, which is always short of goods. Sometimes, however, I suspect that the officials are not always honest. They seem to run the economy to their own advantage. Now that many soldiers are arriving in Quebec, I have noticed that military supplies are getting more expensive. This must mean that somebody is making higher profits.

There is one regulation that holds us back more than any

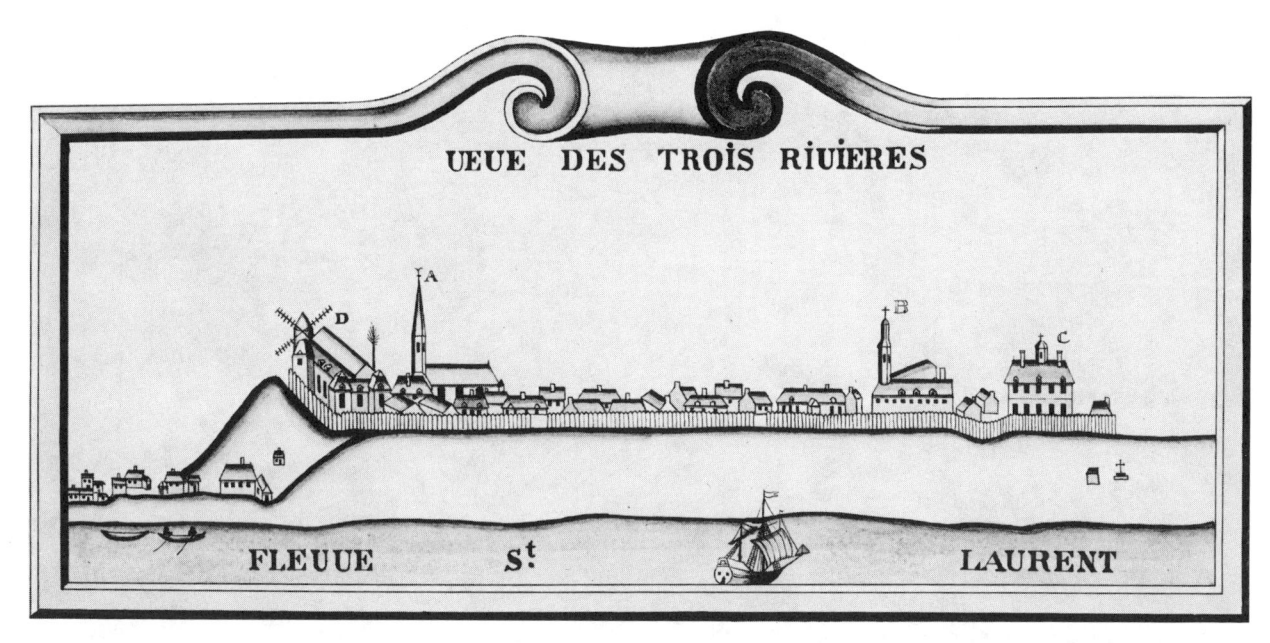

Fig. 7-13 Trois Rivières

other. France will not allow the colony to make anything that competes with French products. Almost all the manufactured goods we need must be imported from France. The colony of New France exists only to supply raw materials to France. We must not compete with French business.

For example, look what happened to the two hat makers who set up shops in Montreal and Quebec. It seemed like a good opportunity for them. They would buy beaver pelts and make them into beaver hats, instead of shipping the pelts overseas and then buying finished hats from France. Well that business had a short life. The government closed them down on orders from France.

The colony has managed to establish a small shipbuilding industry and has added some good ships to the French navy. This year, 1750, we were very proud to launch one vessel, the *Orignal* [oh-ree-NYAL]. It had space for 72 guns. Unfortunately, it leaked badly and had to be dismantled. Shipbuilding requires many specialized tradesmen that we simply don't have. Even the rope and canvas cannot be made here but must be imported from France. As a result, a Canadian-built ship from Canadian wood costs a lot more than a ship built in France from the same wood. So we usually send our wood to France and buy back our ships. It seems a shame.

We have been able to establish an iron-works near

Fig. 7-14 Playing cards were used as money in the early days of New France.

Specialized tradesmen were people who made their living doing one task, such as carpentry, tinsmithing or blacksmithing.

Fig. 7-15 Breaking Lent. Who is the man at the door? How are the people in the house acting?

A small percentage of the people were very rich. These people of the upper class enjoyed abundant food and entertainment such as balls and gambling.

Trois Rivières [trwah ree-VYAYR]. This is a real accomplishment for our small society. Now we can make our own stoves, anvils, pots and even a few cannons to guard the walls of Quebec City. In general, though, there is not much industry in the colony. So when farmers come to the city looking for work, there isn't much. There seem to be more poor and unemployed people here all the time. I really don't know what will become of them or the city.

GETTING THE FACTS

20. According to Monique Boulanger, why do so many women run businesses and seigneuries in New France?

21. Why did the government find it necessary to impose so many rules on the colony?

22. What changes seemed to be occurring in Quebec town life?

USING YOUR KNOWLEDGE

23. In 1750 Quebec City was run by rules. Give at least three examples to support this statement.

24. Imagine you were living in Quebec City in 1750. Would you support or oppose the rules proposed by the government? Draw a poster that shows your point of view and gives at least two reasons for your position.

THINKING IT THROUGH

25. The colony of Quebec existed only to supply raw materials to France.

    a) Do you think a person in France would have agreed or disagreed with this statement? How about a colonist in New France? Give reasons for your answers.

    b) Which viewpoint would you agree with? Give reasons for your answer.

Conclusion

In the 18th century, ordinary people made a living in a variety of ways in New France. The biggest source of wealth was the fur trade. Farming was the next largest and involved many people like André Lamarre. But changes were happening in 1750 and town life was attracting more people. In the towns, there were many different things for people to do to make a living. Bakers, butchers, printers, shipbuilders, ironmakers and many others worked together to produce goods for the frontier society. They were all hampered, however, by regulations from France that encouraged the fur trade but discouraged most other activities.

There were three main cities in New France by 1750: Quebec, Montreal and Trois Rivières.

USING YOUR KNOWLEDGE

26. Look through the pictures in this chapter and choose the one you like the best.

    a) Why does this picture appeal to you?

    b) Imagine you could jump back in history and put yourself in the scene. Write a short account of what you would be doing if you were taking part in the life in the picture.

8 How did the English enter the Canadian story?

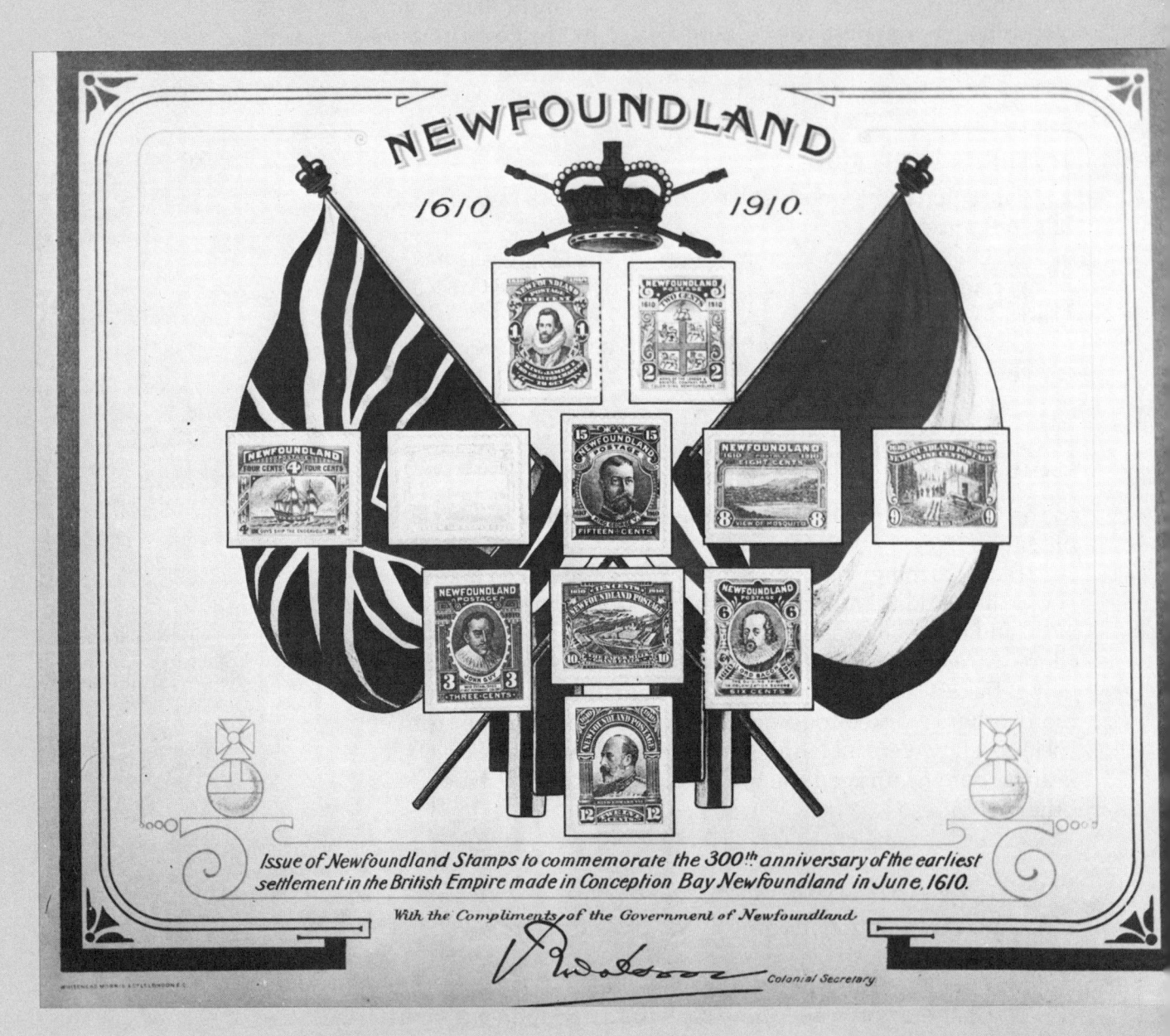

NEWFOUNDLAND

1610. 1910.

Issue of Newfoundland Stamps to commemorate the 300th anniversary of the earliest settlement in the British Empire made in Conception Bay Newfoundland in June, 1610.

With the Compliments of the Government of Newfoundland

Colonial Secretary

The Lost Colony

The year was 1587. England should have some permanent settlements in North America. Or so thought Sir Walter Raleigh [RAH-lee], close friend of Queen Elizabeth I. If far enough south, colonies could be good bases from which to attack the Spanish settlements of the Caribbean region. English people wanting to improve their fortunes could start plantations. In America they could probably grow many warm weather crops. Trade between the colonies and the mother country would lead to an increase in shipbuilding. England would gain in strength and influence in the world.

Nobody was more keen than Sir Walter Raleigh to spread English influence overseas. He had Queen Elizabeth's approval for a plan to start a colony in "Virginia." He sent an expedition of three ships carrying more than 100 men, women and children. They arrived at Roanoke [ROH-uh-nohk] Island, off the coast of what is now North Carolina.

According to reports of earlier travelers, the area was ideal for farming and the native peoples were friendly. Yet the colonists decided they needed more supplies. They insisted that the governor, John White, return to England for aid.

War broke out between England and Spain. The English navy defeated the Spanish Armada in 1588. But relief could not be sent to "Virginia" until two years had passed. It was too late. When the sailors landed at Roanoke Island, they found only the remains of an abandoned settlement. None of the people left behind three years before were ever found. They were the "Lost Colony."

- What do you think may have happened to the colony?
- In what ways were Europeans probably unprepared in their first attempts to start life in the New World?
- Would you expect one "lost colony" to discourage the English from trying again? Why or why not?

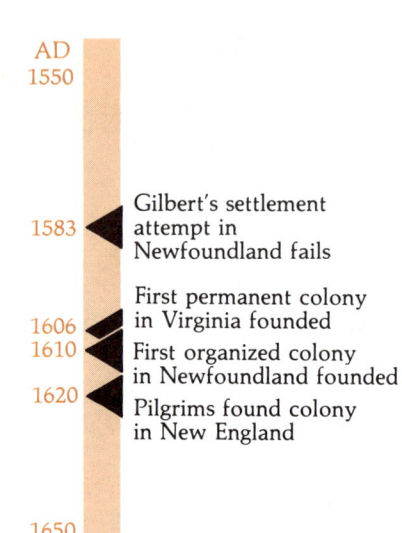

AD 1550	
1583	Gilbert's settlement attempt in Newfoundland fails
1606	First permanent colony in Virginia founded
1610	First organized colony in Newfoundland founded
1620	Pilgrims found colony in New England
1650	

Chapter overview

By the early 1600s, both France and England had started building empires in North America. Each wanted its colonies to spread over the continent. The more successful the colonies, the more wealth and power they would bring to the mother country.

As you saw in chapter 6, France gained control over much of the territory that is now eastern Canada. French settlements were established in Acadia and the St. Lawrence valley, as well as farther inland. In this chapter, you will see that the English also made successful settlements in America; for example, Virginia, Massachusetts and Newfoundland.

How did the English take root in America? Did the English colonizers have the same types of problems as the French did? Did they start colonies for the same reasons? Did they run them the same way? In this chapter, you will examine early English settlements in North America. You will find out how the English entered the Canadian story.

Signposts

> Settlement attempts: Success follows failure

> FEATURE: Scotland's first colony

> Who's in charge here? Government in America

Key words

| colony | indentured seryant | admirals' rule |
| charter | tobacco | Grand Banks |

Settlement attempts: Success follows failure

You have read about the early English settlement attempt known as the Lost Colony. It was clearly a failure. It was not, however, the only colony that failed in the years leading up to 1600. Sir Humphrey Gilbert, in 1583, sailed for the New World. He reached the harbour where St. John's, Newfoundland is now located. As expected—since European fishermen had been crossing the Atlantic for years—he met several ships. Many of them were Spanish and Portuguese [POHR-tyoo-geez], but Gilbert declared that England claimed control of Newfoundland.

The claim was based on John Cabot's discovery of Newfoundland in 1497.

    Gilbert was excited by what he saw of the land. He failed to get a colony started, but he set off for England in the hope of returning better prepared. His companion ships made it, but his was sunk by a storm.

    Sir Walter Raleigh, Gilbert's half-brother, promptly took up the challenge. In 1584, he sent two ships to explore the coast of North America. Some 2000 km south of St. John's, the captains were impressed with the climate and the land.

    The favourable reports further stirred the imagination of Raleigh. He presented a plan for settlement of Virginia, a region much larger than the state later given that name. Queen Elizabeth agreed. So, the next year, Raleigh sent another

Fig. 8-1 Sir Humphrey Gilbert

expedition. This time, the ships carried settlers—more than 100 of them.

Once again, however, the would-be colonists were not well enough prepared. They were unable to adapt to the hot, humid climate. Illness and shortages of supplies, including food, beset them. Some of the settlers made enemies of the native peoples, who could have provided help.

The first English attempts to make permanent settlements in North America ended in failure. The English colonizers knew too little about the New World. They needed to be better equipped and more strongly supported by the government and business people back home. Yet lessons had been learned. In the early 1600s, these would be put to good use in Virginia, Newfoundland and Massachusetts.

GETTING THE FACTS

1. a) In a sentence or two for each, identify Sir Humphrey Gilbert, Sir Walter Raleigh, Queen Elizabeth I.

b) State three or four reasons why the early settlements failed.

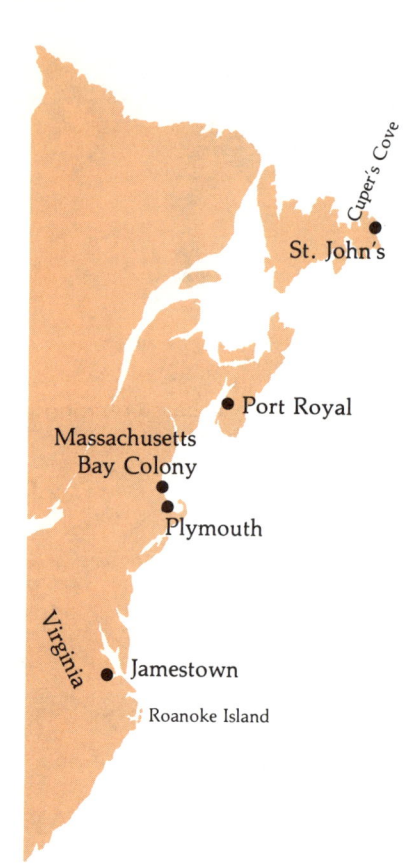

Fig. 8-2 Early British settlement

Virginia

In 1606, King James I of England granted a **charter** to a group of adventurers called the Virginia Company. They established the first permanent English colony in North America, calling it Jamestown after the king.

The first years were hard. But the popularity of tobacco, a crop the colonists learned from the native peoples how to grow, gave Virginia much needed income. When the leaders of the Company quarreled, the English government took over. Virginia became England's first royal colony.

What was it like to live in Virginia? Ideally, we would talk to someone who did. We cannot, of course. But if we look at the facts known about Virginia in the early 1600s, we can imagine a conversation. Though fictional, the following conversation with John Robson is based on real facts and attitudes. Let's suppose we could have talked with him 30 years after his arrival in Virginia in 1616:

Q. John, why did you come to Virginia?
A. I was born in London and grew up there. My father was a

carpenter. He worked long hours, six days a week. Every day was like the others. I could not see that kind of life for myself. Yet in 1616, when I was 15 years old, I was apprenticed as a carpenter under my father. At the time, I seemed to have no other choice.

Q. No other choice?
A. Not really, if I stayed in England. I would have had no opportunity to own land or to rise above the level of tradesman. Anyway, one day a friend of mine, Martin Browning, told me that he was going to Virginia, in America, as an indentured [ihn-DEHN-tyoord] servant. Once you signed on as an indentured servant, the company paid your way to America. When you got there, you had to work for the company for seven years, practically as a slave. But, once your seven years were up, you could apply for your own piece of land, which you were pretty well guaranteed. Well, the idea of someday owning my own land was what made me decide to go. Although my folks weren't too happy with the idea, I found out more about Virginia. I signed up within a month.

Q. Why didn't your mother and father want you to go?
A. Well, there were a lot of alarming stories coming back from the New World about people starving to death, or dying of diseases, or being killed by Indians. These things did happen, but I was willing to take the risk so that I would someday have my own land.

Q. You seem to have made the right choice.
A. Well, I've worked hard, and the Lord's been good to me. Also, I think I came at the right time. The market for tobacco, especially the kind we adapted to the soil here, is very big in Europe. Growing tobacco was really our key to survival. If a man is prepared to work hard, he can make a handsome profit.

    I had seven long years of indenture to serve before I could expect to own land, and hard years they were, too. But I had kind masters and I learned from them everything I know about farming.

    When I got my freedom back in 1623, I got a piece of land eight miles [12.8 km] up the James River. By the end of the first season, I had cleared enough land to plant my first crop of tobacco.

    After 1624, the government would give you an additional 50 acres [20 ha] for every settler you brought out to

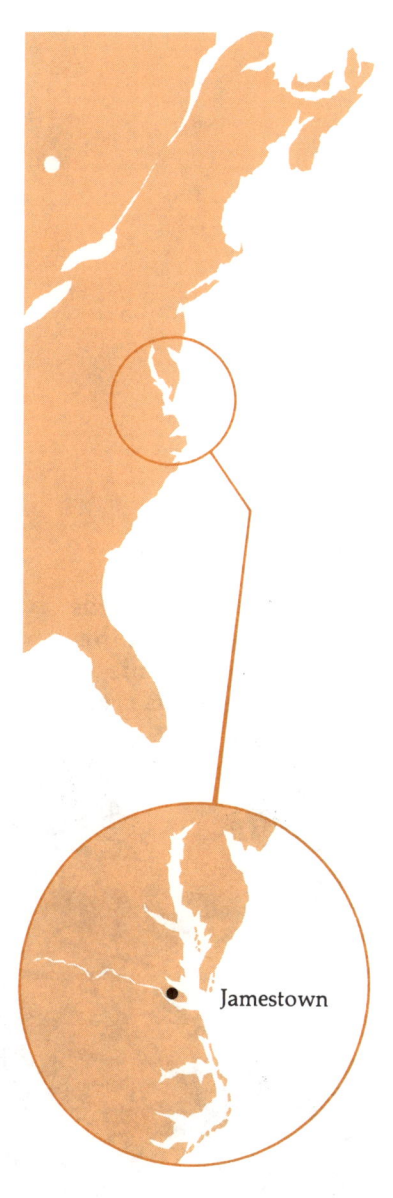

Fig. 8-3 Jamestown, 1608

the colony at your own expense. That's how I acquired more land; I've been able to bring out four people under this system. Now I have 250 acres [100 ha] to my name—not bad for an apprentice carpenter!

Q. Just what sort of government do you have here?

A. The Virginia Company used to govern here exclusively, but in 1619, a council was appointed, consisting of members from the Virginia Company as well as 22 burgesses, or representatives; two from each of the 11 areas of the colony. The House of Burgesses, I'm proud to say, was the first **representative assembly** in the New World.

Q. Where did you meet your wife? Virginia doesn't seem the sort of place an unmarried woman would want to go to.

A. The Company realized the colony couldn't grow without women. So in 1619, they started a plan whereby they recruited young girls to come out. The company would pay their passage and guarantee them a husband when they got here. Any man who wanted a wife just had to pay the

Fig. 8-4 Tobacco fields. Why do you think the survival of Virginia depended on this crop?

company 150 pounds [68 kg] of best leaf tobacco and he got himself a wife. Of course, you didn't know who you were getting—neither did the women, for that matter. But, a person can get very lonesome in this country.

I'm very happy. My Susan and I have three children. Of course, they were born here—true Virginians, you might say. I guess they'll be a new breed. I'll never forget England. But, this is their only home, their land for sure.

GETTING THE FACTS

2. What crop was the key to the growth of Virginia?

3. Explain the meaning of "indentured servant." If necessary, look up "indenture" in the dictionary.

4. Describe two plans that the Virginia Company had to make the colony grow.

USING YOUR KNOWLEDGE

5. Imagine that you are John Robson. In order to become an indentured servant to the Virginia Company you must apply in writing and explain why you want to go to Virginia. Send your letter of application to: Director, Virginia Company, London, England.

THE INVESTIGATIVE REPORTER

6. What was the Virginia Company? What did John Robson mean when he said that the government of the colony used to be the Virginia Company? What did he mean when he said the House of Burgesses was a "representative assembly"? Look in an encyclopedia for the information you need to answer the questions. Write up your answers in a report.

Newfoundland

In 1616, Captain John Mason went to Newfoundland to govern a settlement started by London and Bristol merchants. He sailed to Newfoundland and took over a settlement at Cuper's Cove on Conception Bay. During Mason's stay, other settlements were established in different areas along the island's coast. In 1619, Mason returned to England.

Fig. 8-5 A view showing the method of fishing for, curing and drying cod in Newfoundland. Describe as many of the activities as you can.

Mason thought other people should be encouraged to settle in Newfoundland. In 1620, he wrote a short book describing life there. Called *A briefe discourse of the New-found-land*, it was probably the first book ever written about Newfoundland.

At one point in the book, Mason compared life in Newfoundland with life in Virginia:

> Some say the country is barren, but they are wrong... the great abundance of woods and wild fruits which grow easily there prove the opposite. And although the soil is not as fertile and the temperature generally lower than in

Virginia, there are four main reasons why Newfoundland is at least as good, if not to be preferred:

(1) The first reason is the nearness to our home, England, to which naturally we are much attached. Newfoundland is much closer than Virginia. One can return to England from Newfoundland in as few as 12 days.

(2) For 60 years, trade has been important to us and is increasing daily. This is likely to continue. Fish is an important commodity for us; we can also sell it to other countries. Fishing provides jobs for 3000 seamen and keeps 300 ships going each year. Furthermore, the fish trade makes possible the payment of some £10 000 each year to the king in customs or taxes.

(3) Settlers can be taken to live in Newfoundland much more cheaply than to Virginia.

(4) Finally, in Newfoundland we have a better chance of being protected from our enemies. There are only a few native peoples in the northern and none in the southern parts of the country. Settlers in Newfoundland have never suffered damage from them, and worry little about building forts. Also, if any wars should take place between us and other nations, we need not fear being chased out. The ice protects us from November until April. Furthermore, with so many men and ships coming to fish, they will defend us, if only for their own sake. In the fall, the winds make it difficult to approach. . . .

What is the meaning of the symbol "£"? Find out how much it is worth today.

Adapted from *A briefe discourse of the New-found-land*.

GETTING THE FACTS

7. Explain the meaning of the following words used in the passage you just read: barren, abundance, commodity, customs.

USING YOUR KNOWLEDGE

8. Suppose John Mason were alive today and trying to convince people overseas to come to Newfoundland rather than to Virginia. Put yourself in his place, and make a poster or advertisement.

9. Bias means giving only one side of a story so that a whole, fair picture is not presented. For example, you might tell your friends only about the good parts of a movie you saw, so that the movie seems better than it really was. Is Mason's comparison of Newfoundland and Virginia biased? Give examples from the text to support your answer.

THINKING IT THROUGH

10. Many people believe that living on an island (rather than on the mainland) influences a person's life. How would living on an island affect the way people a) work, b) use their leisure time, c) travel, d) think of themselves?

11. John Mason described several advantages of settling in Newfoundland.

   a) Which advantages would most attract you to Newfoundland? Explain your answer.

   b) Suggest some disadvantages to settling in Newfoundland.

The settlement of Massachusetts

At the same time that England, France and other European countries were building empires, people in Europe were arguing about religion. For more than 1000 years, Christians had followed the religious leadership of the pope and the Roman Catholic Church.

During the 16th century, however, the Christian Church split into Catholic and Protestant. The Protestant, or "protesting," churches were started by people like Martin Luther in Germany and John Calvin in Switzerland.

Following the lead of Martin Luther, King Henry VIII of England broke with the Catholic Church. In 1534, he declared himself—in place of the pope—the head of the Church of England (Anglican). By law, people of England were required to belong to the Anglican Church. It was criticized by many, however, as too much like the Catholic Church. People who wanted to have a more "protestant" church were known as dissenters.

The Pilgrims, as one group of dissenters came to be known, wanted the right to a separate church. They were not allowed this freedom in England. Some went to live for a number of years in the Netherlands, where they were able to worship as they pleased. Unhappy living in a foreign country, they joined an expedition to the New World. In the autumn of 1620, they sailed aboard the *Mayflower*. At Plymouth, on Cape Cod Bay, they started the first permanent settlement in New England.

Plagued by bad luck, the Pilgrims endured a grim winter. The voyage to the New World had taken much longer than expected. Except for salt meat and hard biscuit, food supplies had run short. About half the settlers and ship's crew died, probably of malnutrition.

Yet the hardy survivors adapted well to their new surroundings. They learned to shoot the game and catch the fish that were plentiful enough. Native people taught the settlers how to grow corn and other farm products long known to the Indians. In the fall of 1621, the Pilgrims celebrated their first Thanksgiving Day.

The Pilgrims were well organized and united by their religious beliefs. They prayed regularly together, and worked hard. Eventually they started trading furs and lumber with business people in England. But in 1691, the Pilgrim settlements decided to join forces with the larger Massachusetts Bay Colony.

That colony had come into being because other religious

Fig. 8-6 What do you think it was like to be one of the first settlers in North America?

Malnutrition is caused by not eating enough food or the food necessary for a balanced diet.

Scotland's first colony

The person who gave Nova Scotia its name was a 17th century Scottish poet. Sir William Alexander, a friend of King James VI of Scotland, believed he could achieve fame and fortune by establishing a colony in North America. Yet he never set foot on North American soil. The settlements he attempted were short-lived.

Eventually, King James VI of Scotland also became King James I of England. In 1621, Sir William persuaded King James that there should be a New Scotland—just as there was a New England, a New France, and a New Spain. Sir William was given a charter and a grant to all the lands between the St. Croix River and the Gulf of St. Lawrence. In other words, the grant included all the land that is now the Maritime Provinces of Canada.

In each of the next two years, Sir William sent ships to Nova Scotia. The first barely got within sight of Cape Breton before turning back to winter at St. John's, Newfoundland. When a supply ship reached St. John's during the summer of 1623, it found that some of the colonists had died. Others were out to sea on fishing boats. So there were too few colonists left to attempt a settlement. After some exploring of Nova Scotia's coastline, the ship returned to England.

Sir William found himself with little to show for his venture except a large debt. King James came to his aid. The king offered to grant the title of baronet and a portion of land in New Scotland (Nova Scotia) to any Scot agreeable to certain conditions. The main condition was to pay a sum of money to Sir William! The new king, Charles I (after James died in 1625), set up a committee to look after the arrangement. His instructions included symbols which became the flag and coat-of-arms of Nova Scotia.

The scheme raised less money than expected, but a number of "baronets of Nova Scotia" had paid up by 1629. By that time, Sir William's son had started a settlement at Port Royal. It managed to last for three years.

Then, in 1632, King Charles signed a treaty with the King of France. Charles agreed to order all his subjects to leave Nova Scotia. In return, the King of France promised to pay a debt of money owed to King Charles.

Sir William lived for another ten years. He remained close to the king, who tried to make up for his losses by making Sir William the Earl of Stirling. All that remained of Sir William Alexander's colonizing efforts were a flag, a coat-of-arms and the name for one of Canada's provinces.

THE INVESTIGATIVE REPORTER

12. Solve the following mystery:

Sir William Alexander tried to establish a Scottish colony called Nova Scotia. In 1632, however, the King of England signed a treaty with the King of France and ordered British subjects to leave Nova Scotia. Yet today, about one-third of Nova Scotia's population is of Scottish descent. Why did the Scottish people return to live in Nova Scotia? To solve this mystery, look up the history of Nova Scotia in an encyclopedia. Then write a short report that answers the question.

dissenters had decided to move to New England. The largest group were known as Puritans. Unlike the Pilgrims, they were not separatists, wishing to break away from the Anglican Church. Instead, they wished to "purify" it. But many Puritans decided they were not getting anywhere in England.

The Puritans concluded that the English way of life was corrupt and evil. In 1629, a group of Puritans led by John Winthrop decided to establish a "pure" colony in America. It would be an example of an ideal society.

Compared to the small, poor band of Pilgrims, the Puritans were prosperous and well-prepared. Among them were skilled workers of all kinds—carpenters, shoemakers, tailors, blacksmiths, shipbuilders and others—and many university graduates. They arrived in the New World well supplied with food, tools and other necessities.

Within a few years, the Puritans occupied a string of villages in what is now the Boston area. By 1640, the population of Massachusetts Bay Colony had risen to 20 000. Soon after, Maine and New Hampshire developed under the control of Massachusetts. Meanwhile, settlers had moved beyond the borders of the colony to start Rhode Island and Connecticut. A British empire was growing rapidly in size and prosperity on the Atlantic coast of America.

Fig. 8-7 Sir William Alexander

GETTING THE FACTS

13. Quickly reread the section on Massachusetts. Then, construct a timeline that traces the growth of this colony. On your timeline include the following dates: 1534, 1620, 1629, 1640, 1691. Be sure your timeline contains clear statements about the events that took place at each date.

14. List four reasons why the New England area was a good place for a colony.

USING YOUR KNOWLEDGE

15. Copy the following statement into your notebook: In the 1600s, many people left England to settle in the Massachusetts area.
   a) Write a short paragraph describing why people made this move.
   b) Then, write another paragraph to explain the effects of this move on the growth of the British Empire.

THINKING IT THROUGH

16. Imagine that you are a leader in France who is trying to build up France's empire in the New World. You know how quickly the English colonies to the south of New France are growing. Write a letter to the King of France describing one problem that the growing English colonies may create for you. Be sure to explain why you are concerned and what may possibly happen to New France.

Who's in charge here? Government in America

Like France, England was anxious to have colonies during the 17th century. But, just as the English had different ways and reasons for establishing colonies, they also had different attitudes about how they should be governed. This difference of attitude is important to Canadian history because when Canada was taken over by England, the English brought their ideas with them.

Englishmen believed that the American colonies could be a source of wealth, either from the fur trade, the fishery or tobacco farming. Yet there were also financial risks involved in colonization. So, the rulers in England were happy to grant charters to individuals or private companies (which were really just a group of people joined together for a common purpose by a contract). These charters allowed the individuals or companies to establish colonies. This way the king did not have to risk losing money if the colonies failed.

Once colonies were established, they had to be governed. This situation presented problems. Many settlers expected to enjoy the same legal and political rights as they had at home. But, how could these services be provided at a distance of 4000-5000 km? In the wilderness, would it be possible to provide the same type of government that existed in England? Was one system better for governing colonies than another? Should all colonies be governed the same way?

Newfoundland: The admirals' rule

Englishmen were mainly interested in Newfoundland because of the wealth that could be made from the fisheries, particularly the cod fishing.

By 1500, English ships were sailing across the Atlantic early every spring. They spent the summer fishing off the

The Grand Banks off the coast of Newfoundland is one of the world's great fishing regions.

coast of Newfoundland, especially on the Grand Banks. French, Dutch, Spanish and Portuguese ships, as well, were there.

Gradually, more and more English fishermen decided that it would be easier to stay in Newfoundland year-round. This way, they could build wharves and fish houses, repair their boats, and be prepared to make the most of the fishing season. After a while, these people came to think of Newfoundland as their home.

The idea of people settling along the shores of Newfoundland worried the merchants and shipowners of western England. They wanted to control the fishery and gain the wealth that it offered. However, these settlers would be able to occupy the best harbours and be the first to reach the fishing grounds each year. Also, the settlers might sell their fish to Spain, Portugal or France, instead of to England. Or, they might buy their provisions from these countries, instead of from the west country merchants—who controlled the areas of England from which the fishermen came.

The merchants had a lot of power and influence in England

Fig. 8-8 Newfoundland Fishing Banks.

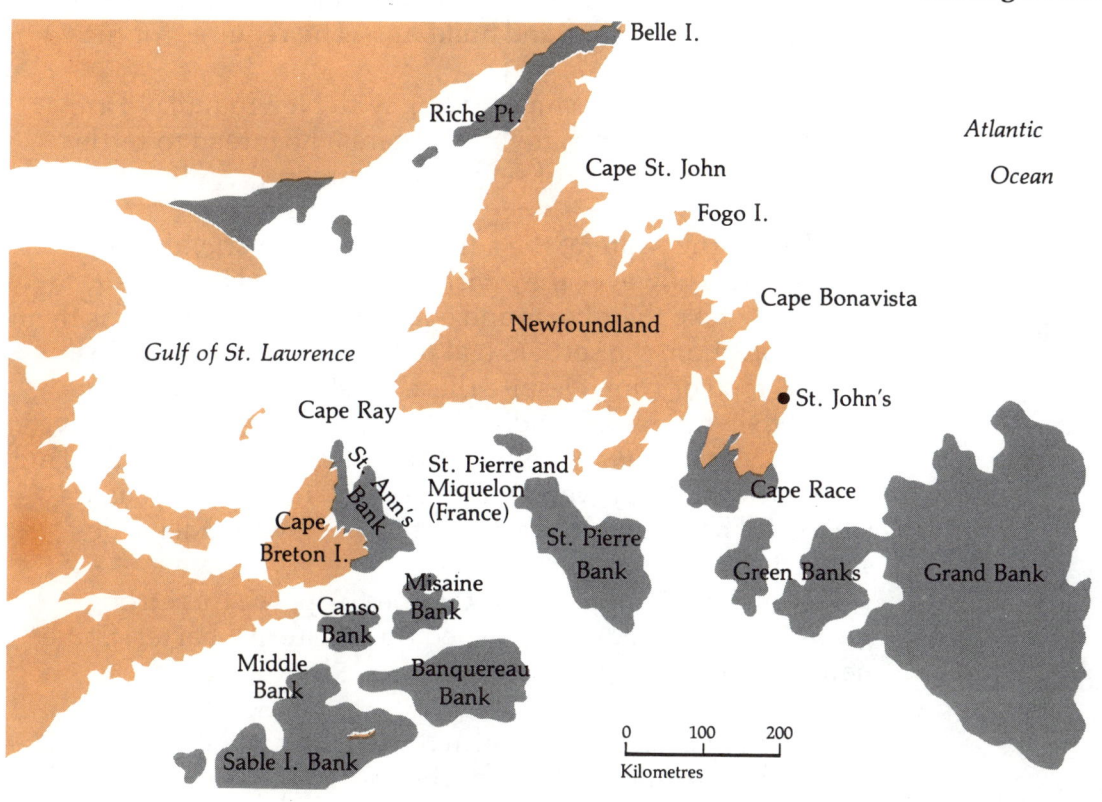

and were able to persuade the king to give them control of Newfoundland. They said it would be better for England if the fishery were conducted from England. This way a strong navy could be built. Each year, more and more young men would go to sea in large ships to participate in the fishery and be trained as sailors. These young men could be drawn upon to serve in the Royal Navy in time of war. A powerful navy would make England a powerful nation.

In 1634, King Charles I issued what has been called "The Western Charter." It gave control of Newfoundland to the English merchants and their captains and established an unusual form of government for England's oldest colony in America. People who lived year-round in Newfoundland were not allowed to engage in the fishery. That is, they could not sell their catch to merchants or other fishermen returning to England. Some of the unusual regulations of this government system were:

> ... The captain of the first ship to enter any harbour in the spring shall be the admiral of that harbour for the year. This captain shall reserve whatever and as much of the coastline, wharves and buildings as he requires for his boats and men. ...
>
> ... All owners of ships trading with Newfoundland are forbidden to carry any passengers who intend to settle there on penalties of severe punishment. ...

Under this system, the admirals and their friends could treat settlers however they wished. They could burn their houses, or take their boats and equipment. Sometimes, for their own protection, the settlers had to bribe the admirals with money, food or rum. Despite these harsh rules, settlers continued to live in Newfoundland throughout the 17th century, while this system was in effect. But, the government in England pretended that they were not there. Still, the rich merchants worried. They wanted all settlements in Newfoundland destroyed.

King Charles II had no intention to oppose this strong group. In 1676, Charles re-issued the Western Charter. Some new and harsher regulations were added:

> ... Settlers are not permitted to cut any wood or to plant within six miles [10 km] of the shore. ...

... Settlers may not use fishing wharves before the arrival of ships from England in the spring. ...

... No fisherman shall remain behind at the end of the fishing season when his vessel returns. ...

... The admiral shall take any offenders back to England for punishment. ...

Nevertheless, the Newfoundlanders remained. The King ordered these people to move back to England or to the West Indies, where England also had colonies. He gave the fishing admirals the right to destroy all settlements, to tear down every house or shack. The people suffered greatly, but they were determined. They stayed and built new houses.

Finally, in 1699, under a new king, William III, the English government gave up and passed the first Newfoundland Act. This law recognized their right to be there, though it was only a start. The law said that the settlers could use any wharf or

Fig. 8-9 St. John's, Newfoundland, 1798. What does this picture tell you about life in the settlement?

Newfoundlanders today often refer to the island affectionately as "The Rock."

fishing premise that had not been used by English ships for 15 years. It also gave any settler the right to complain to the captain of an English warship against any unfair treatment by a fishing captain. These concessions may seem small today, but they meant that the Newfoundlanders had won. The fishing admirals were still in control, but the settlers had received some rights. "The Rock" was going to be theirs.

GETTING THE FACTS

17. Define the following terms: charter, Grand Banks, Western Charter, Newfoundland Act.

18. Why was England interested in Newfoundland?

19. List three reasons why the merchants and shipowners of western England were worried about having settlers on the shores of Newfoundland.

20. Summarize the government of Newfoundland under the admirals.

USING YOUR KNOWLEDGE

21. Settlers in Newfoundland often suffered greatly under the fishing admirals. Their houses were sometimes burned and their property was destroyed.
    a) Why do you think they stayed in Newfoundland?
    b) Would you have stayed if you had been a settler there? Give reasons to support your answer.

THINKING IT THROUGH

22. DEBATE: It was unfair of England to forbid people to settle in Newfoundland.
    The following steps will help you choose and defend your position:
—Review your answer to question 19 for the English merchants' point of view.
—Skim through the section on the admirals' rule you just read for the reasons people would want to live in Newfoundland all year-round.
—Review both sides of the argument and decide which side you feel is valid.
—Think of reasons to back up your opinion.

23. Do you think the admirals' rule system of government would have helped or hurt the growth of the British Empire in North America? Give reasons for your answer.

The people participate

The government of Newfoundland during the 17th century was interesting, but was really the exception rather than the rule. Settlers in the English colonies in America generally were quite actively involved in their government. By contrast, the average person in Europe had very little influence in his or her government.

During the summer of 1619, the governor of Virginia invited each settlement in the colony to send two delegates to participate in making laws. This representative assembly, the first in North America, was called the House of Burgesses. This assembly could pass laws for the colony, provided it did not go against the laws of England and provided the governor agreed to the laws.

The New England colonies were more independent. The first settlers there, called the Pilgrims, sailed on a ship called the *Mayflower* and settled at Plymouth. Before landing, the adult males signed the "Mayflower Compact." It was an agreement to set up a system of government. The signers agreed to obey the "just and equal laws" it would pass.

The largest group to come to New England, the Puritans, established the Massachusetts Bay Colony in 1630. Before coming to America, they established their own company. Then, they brought their charter with them to America so that the headquarters of the company would be in Boston rather than in England. Soon after arriving in America, the leaders of the company decided that all the recognized free, male members of their church should have a say in government. As a result, adult males—not including indentured servants and slaves—were allowed to vote for the governor and other officials of the colony. Women in the colonies were not recognized as citizens with equal rights.

Other English colonies were eventually established, often as breakaway groups from Massachusetts or Virginia. Each established a system of government similar to those of Massachusetts or Virginia. The people of these colonies could participate in their own government, as long as they did not go

Except for a few western States, neither the United States nor Canada recognized women's rights, such as voting, until after 1900.

against the wishes of the king. Truly, it was government in which the people—the majority of adult males, at least—could participate.

GETTING THE FACTS

24. Explain the role that trading companies had in setting up the English colonies in America.

25. What was the "Mayflower Compact"?

26. Why didn't women get the vote in early New England?

USING YOUR KNOWLEDGE

27. a) Skim the section "The people participate" for information on what representative government is. Then write a paragraph in which you explain representative government and give examples from the English colonies.

   b) Describe one way that representative government in the colonies was like our system of government today.

28. Compare Newfoundland with the other English colonies by answering the following questions:
   a) Why was the colony formed?
   b) Who ran the colony?
   c) How were rules established?

Conclusion

In this chapter and in chapter 7, you saw how the English and French empires put down roots in North America. In the following years, both empires tried to increase their influence in the new land.

Stop for a moment and think of what might happen when two European countries are trying to gain more and more territory on the same continent. Now look at the events on the timeline on page 212. Were your predictions correct?

The next few chapters will fill you in on the story of what happened to the French and English colonies in North America.

USING YOUR KNOWLEDGE

29. During the 17th century, the English colonies in America grew more rapidly than the French ones did. Explain why this might have happened. In your answer, comment on a) location, b) the attitude of the people as settlers, and c) rules and regulations.

9 Acadia: The forgotten colony

Present-day reconstruction of the Port Royal Habitation, N.S.

Blessing of the Fleet, Acadian Festival, Caraquet, New Brunswick.

> I can say truthfully that I never did so much manual work ... digging and cultivating my gardens, fencing them against the greed of the hogs, making terraces, laying out straight walks, building outhouses, sowing wheat, rye, barley, oats, beans, peas, herbs, watering them, so great was my desire to have personal experience of the soil.

These words were written by a Frenchman, Marc Lescarbot. He is describing the early days of Port Royal, one of France's first settlements in the New World. The colony flourished. Over the years a strong farming culture would spread throughout the surrounding region. The area, known as Acadia, would also become a dramatic battleground for the French and English empires.

- Why do you think a colony like Acadia would become a battleground for the French and British empires (HINT: Look at the map in Fig. 9-6).
- The picture on this page shows modern-day Acadians celebrating their history. What does it tell you about the fate of the colony?

189

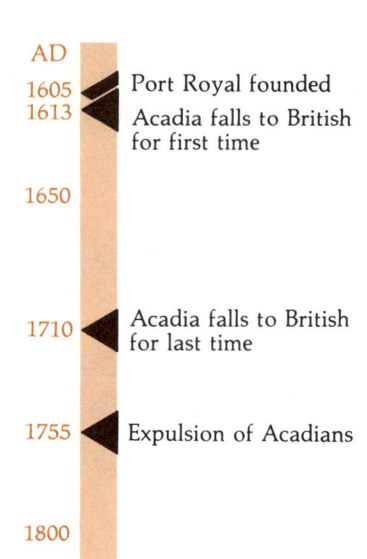

AD	
1605	Port Royal founded
1613	Acadia falls to British for first time
1650	
1710	Acadia falls to British for last time
1755	Expulsion of Acadians
1800	

Chapter overview

Often, books about Canadian history begin with the founding of Port Royal. Then, in 1608, when de Monts and Champlain move their headquarters from Port Royal to Quebec, the study of Canada also moves to Quebec with them, and the story of Port Royal in Acadia is left behind. However, the history of Acadia had just begun. European settlement, sparse though it was, remained in Acadia from then on.

The region did not grow to be politically or economically powerful, but a permanent population slowly developed into a unique people, the Acadians. Acadia was passed back and forth between the British and the French so many times that the people could not feel a part of either empire.

Acadia seems to be the forgotten colony, but its early history is full of interesting tales, adventures and fascinating personalities. In this chapter, we will examine some of that early history.

Signposts

- Poutrincourt's Port Royal
- The diary of Charles de La Tour
- FEATURE: New England's outpost
- Acadia under the English
- The expulsion of the Acadians

Key words

privateer	oath of allegiance
outpost	expulsion

Poutrincourt's Port Royal

If it hadn't been for a man named Jean de Biencourt de Poutrincourt, the history of Acadia might have been over before it really got started.

Years before the founding of Port Royal, Poutrincourt had served in the French army with de Monts. The two had respected one another and become friends. So, it was not surprising that Poutrincourt was one of the first people de Monts recruited when he set out to establish his colony in America.

You will recall from chapter 4 that de Monts had agreed to start a colony in return for a monopoly of the fur trade.

De Monts granted Poutrincourt land around the fertile Annapolis Basin. Poutrincourt returned to France and brought back skilled craftspeople and farmers—and also his son Charles Biencourt. When de Monts lost his monopoly in 1607, Poutrincourt was very disappointed. Even then, he refused to leave Port Royal until the corn had been harvested and men had been sent across the Bay of Fundy to collect furs, ducks and rock samples to take back to France to show the king. Poutrincourt, himself, went to Minas [MĪ-nuhs] Basin, to collect copper samples.

Poutrincourt wanted to show the king that Port Royal could become a very successful and self-supporting colony. It would only take a year or two more to get established. Just before sailing home, Poutrincourt even tore up the roots of some rye plants "to show France its beauty, richness and exceeding heights."

As soon as he was back in France, Poutrincourt asked for, and received, an audience with King Henry IV. He wanted to establish his claim to Port Royal. He also wanted to receive from the king the right and blessing to return. He presented the king with the produce, animals (including a couple of buzzards) and ore samples from Port Royal. He spoke of the Micmacs; what strong people they were, what good friends of the French they had become, and of the work that had begun in converting them to Christianity. And, he spoke of the rich land as a good place for settlement.

In 1609, an Englishman named Henry Hudson visited America. King Henry knew that if France did not act, England would claim all of North America for itself. And Poutrincourt had prepared his argument well. The king hoped that a colony might still be established and he therefore decided to renew de Mont's monopoly for one year. So the grant of land that de Monts had given Poutrincourt was confirmed.

De Monts and Champlain moved to the St. Lawrence because they felt that there they would have more success with the fur trade.

Fig. 9-1 Jean de Poutrincourt

Poutrincourt was determined to return to Port Royal. He had problems trying to raise enough money to buy supplies for the colony. Therefore, it was not until February 25, 1610, that Poutrincourt finally set sail for Port Royal.

Two months later, Poutrincourt and his group reached the colony. They were greeted by the local Micmac chief, Membertou [MEHM-ber-too], and his people. Except for a few leaks in the roof, the **habitation** [a-bee-ta-SYIOH^N] and other buildings were just as they had been left three years before, complete with the household goods that had been left. Even the gardens were in good condition; the Micmacs had harvested each year.

It would be nice to write that all went well and that everyone lived happily ever after. However, that was not to be the case. Poutrincourt was constantly in conflict with the Jesuit priests sent to the colony. The Jesuits had their own ideas about running Port Royal, and Poutrincourt did not agree with them. Also, he ran into money troubles again. In 1612, Poutrincourt was forced to go to France to arrange for supplies. After making the arrangements, he set sail for Port Royal on New Year's Eve, 1613. But he would not arrive in time to save his colony. The English governor of Virginia had heard about a French colony established on the coast of what is today called Maine. The governor had sent a **privateer** named Captain Samuel Argall to wipe out the colony. While doing so, Argall learned of Port Royal and decided to capture it as well.

On November 1, 1613, Argall sailed into Port Royal harbour and found it vacant. Poutrincourt was still at sea and his son, Charles Biencourt, and the rest of the men were visiting the Micmacs inland. Argall stripped the fort of all that seemed useful or valuable and burned the rest. Biencourt had no choice but to winter with the Micmacs and await his father's return in the spring.

Poutrincourt finally arrived at Port Royal on March 27, 1614. He found his fort in ruin. A broken man, he decided to give up and go home. But his son Charles Biencourt and a few followers decided to stay and rebuild the colony.

Poutrincourt returned to France, and a short time later was killed in battle while fighting for his king. It was a sad ending to the story of his courage, vision and determination.

GETTING THE FACTS

1. List at least two arguments that Poutrincourt used to interest the King of France in Port Royal.

2. Give three reasons why Poutrincourt did not return to Acadia until 1610.

3. a) True or false?
—When Poutrincourt returned to Port Royal in 1610, the habitation was in ruins.
—Poutrincourt and the Jesuits got along well together.
—A pirate named Sam Argall destroyed Port Royal in 1613.
  b) For each statement that you said was false, give a short version of the true story.

USING YOUR KNOWLEDGE

4. Explain the cause of each of the following events:
—The King renews de Monts' monopoly.
—De Monts decides to leave Port Royal.
—When Poutrincourt returns to Port Royal in 1610, the habitation is in good shape and the crops have been harvested.
—Port Royal is destroyed in 1613.

5. The King of France got interested in Port Royal because he was involved in a power struggle with England. Find evidence in the text to support this statement.

The diary of Charles de La Tour

Charles de La Tour [deu la toor] is one of the most colourful figures in Canada's history. He was the first European to spend almost all his adult life in North America.
    La Tour came to Acadia in 1606, at the age of 14, with his father, Claude. The La Tours were employed by Poutrincourt, and later his son Biencourt. When Biencourt died in 1623, La Tour found himself in charge of Port Royal. He established Cape Sable Island as headquarters for the fur trade in Acadia.
    In 1627, England and France were once again at war. La Tour remained loyal to France even though his father tried to persuade him to join the English. For his loyalty he was given the title "Lieutenant-General of the King's forces in Acadia." There are very few written records of La Tour and there are no known pictures of him. If La Tour had kept a diary, it would

Fig. 9-2 Acadia

have been fascinating reading. To help you understand La Tour and his times, we have gathered information about him and used it to write a diary for him. We join La Tour in 1632, just after he has been appointed Lieutenant-General:

November 6, 1632 It seems Acadia has a new governor, one Isaac de Razilly, whose main qualification for the job is that he is a cousin of the king's first minister, Cardinal Richelieu. He and a group of settlers have established themselves along the coast at the mouth of the La Hève River. I hear his right hand is a man called Charles de Menou, Sieur d'Aulnay Charnisay [syeur dohl-NAY shahr-nee-ZAY]. D'Aulnay's qualification is that his father is councillor to the king. Furthermore, he and Razilly are cousins. I wonder if they know about me—or about my title from the king. They are supposedly here to establish a colony, but I believe they just want in on the fur trade. A man named Nicholas Denys [deu-NEE], who has a couple of posts on the big island to the east [here, La Tour refers to Cape Breton], is also here to make money, I think. I shall have to watch them all. Thank God for the Meeg-a-maage [meeg-a-mag] who are our friends.

January 1, 1637   Razilly has died and d'Aulnay has acquired the rights to all his territory. I am upset at this news. As long as Razilly lived, I had my territory for the fur trade and d'Aulnay had his. Now, d'Aulnay will want it all, and because he has so many friends at court, headed by his father, my position here will be threatened. Let us hope that my years of groundwork in this country will not be for nothing.

April 1, 1638   I don't know how those fools in Paris can be so stupid. They don't even know the map of Acadia. They have given d'Aulnay the mainland, except for the post at Port Royal. And they have given me the peninsula, with a fort at the mouth of the St. John River. So, I have the logical centre of his empire, and he has the centre of mine. Do they want us to fight?

August 15, 1641   By using his influence at court, d'Aulnay has managed to have me declared a traitor because I trade with the English at Boston. What does the king expect me to do? I have been in this country 30 years and have never received any help or support from France; no provisions, no soldiers, no ships. I suspect that Richelieu and the king have no idea of just what an evil person d'Aulnay is. They see him as the man to bring settlement to Acadia. But he has not yet brought out any settlers. And he forces the settlers who are here to live practically like slaves at Port Royal. He is the only one allowed to trade in furs. I must survive because in the long run victory will be mine. The Meeg-a-maage are my allies and they are the key to the fur trade. I am known and respected at Quebec. Also, I have my trading outlets in Boston. The king may have issued a warrant for my arrest, but d'Aulnay can only enforce it with arms and men.

April 30, 1645   It has been a terrible month. For five years, I have fought that man. Now it seems he has won. I have not only lost my fort, but I have lost my beloved Françoise-Marie. The situation was getting desperate and so I

"Meeg-a-maage" is the name that the Indians of Acadia called themselves. Europeans found it hard to pronounce and so the name eventually became "Micmac."

Fig. 9-3 Madame La Tour defending Fort La Tour, 1645.

thought I would slip down to Boston for help and supplies. I left Marie and the family alone before without fear because the men respect her as they do me. She was such a strong force. Some traitor, one of my men, told d'Aulnay I was away. D'Aulnay captured my fort and my home. No one survived.

They say Marie was a true heroine, even fired the cannon herself. They say she died of a broken heart, but I don't believe that. I think she was murdered. Now I must escape the country. Perhaps I will go to Quebec. To my land of Acadia I say "I shall be back." As for you, Charles d'Aulnay, sleep not well, for as long as Charles de La Tour lives, your life is in danger.

May 24, 1651 It's been quite a year. One year ago today, d'Aulnay fell out of his canoe and drowned in the icy waters of the basin at Port Royal. If it is true that a man's life passes before him at the moment of death, I hope it happened to d'Aulnay. He showed no mercy or pity for any man, nor for my noble and heroic Marie.

But, more important, I am now the undisputed master of Acadia. Who would have believed that I could persuade

New England's outpost

Throughout most of the 17th century, Acadia was a colony in the French empire. The Acadians survived mainly by farming, together with some fishing, hunting, fur trading and lumbering. During the period from the death of La Tour to the final fall of Acadia in 1710, the officials of neither New nor Old France had much interest in Acadia. Some interest was shown in the Atlantic fishery and in the fur trade of what is now the Maine-New Brunswick border area.

Because of this lack of interest in Acadia on the part of France, the Acadians began to deal more and more with coastal trading merchants from New England for the goods they could not produce themselves. By French law, trade with New England was illegal. But most of the time, even French officials in Acadia conveniently overlooked it. In any case, the Acadians had no other source of manufactured goods.

Each spring, three or four ships from New England came to the settlements along the coast of Acadia. They were loaded with goods the Acadians needed. The New Englanders brought iron products (utensils, tools, firearms and machinery) and textiles, sugar, spices and other luxuries. The Acadians gave them furs, feathers, fish, grain, livestock, meat and lumber in return. The trade was to the benefit of both. France would have found it very difficult to stop this trade without a large number of ships and men.

Surprisingly, through those ships the Acadians were also able to trade with the French West Indies, because the New England merchants were illegally trading there as well!

Without the New England trade, the Acadians would have had to do without many of the articles necessary to European colonists. Any luxuries would have been out of question. It is doubtful that Acadia would have survived without it.

GETTING THE FACTS

6. List the goods that the Acadians and the New England merchants exchanged with each other.

USING YOUR KNOWLEDGE

7. Examine a map of Acadia. Does it make sense that trade should develop between New England and Acadia, rather than between New France and Acadia? Give reasons to support your answer.

8. a) Look up "outpost" in the dictionary and write its definition in your notebook.
    b) Why was Acadia called "New England's outpost"?

9. a) Why do you think it was illegal for Acadia to trade with New England? (Remember whom Acadia belonged to through most of the 17th century.)
    b) Sometimes in history, the conflict between two empires did not have much effect on the lives of ordinary people. Use the example of trade to show how this statement is true.

Fig. 9-4 D'Aulnay orders the execution of La Tour's colonists in 1645. How does the artist make you feel about d'Aulnay?

those fools in Paris that I am the only one who can properly rule Acadia. I say, let's hear it for the new King, and for his mother, the Regent.

February 24, 1653 A masterful stroke, Charles old boy, the crowning touch. I have today married the widow of my late enemy, d'Aulnay. Two years ago, I thought Acadia was mine. Little did I know that within weeks I would have three rivals. Only in Paris could they be so crazy as to give commissions to three different people to control and administer Acadia. By marrying the d'Aulnay interests, I combine the two strongest camps, and once and for all end the bitter conflict between our two families. Surely, now Acadia can really begin to grow and prosper.

August 22, 1654 Will I ever be at peace? Just as I thought I had everything under control, we are attacked from Boston. Those Puritans are strange people. They raised a force to fight the Dutch, but before they could do so, the war between England and Holland ended. So rather than disband the force, they decided to take over Acadia—again. Now I am the prisoner of Major Robert Sedgewick of Massachusetts. There has been a civil war in England. Perhaps I can work something out with this man Oliver Cromwell, the so-called Lord Protector, who now rules. After all, I am Sir Charles to the British.

La Tour did "work something out" with the English. With two English partners, Thomas Temple and William Crowne, he again returned to Acadia, this time as governor for the English. Crowne and Temple received the bulk of the profits from the Acadia fur trade. But La Tour got to live happily, peacefully and prosperously for the remaining years of his life. Things must also have worked out with the former Mme d'Aulnay, for they eventually had five children together.

La Tour died in 1666, having successfully survived the first 60 years of Acadia's unsettled history. He was buried somewhere along the banks of the St. John River.

Charles I was forced off the throne during the English Civil War of the 1640s. He was tried, found guilty of being an enemy of the country and put to death. Oliver Cromwell, leader of the anti-king forces, took over as head of the government.

GETTING THE FACTS

10. Suggest a title that best describes the life of Charles de La Tour.

11. Write a complete sentence identifying each of the following: Charles Biencourt, Isaac de Razilly, Cardinal Richelieu, Charles d'Aulnay, Robert Sedgewick, Thomas Temple, Meeg-a-maage.

**12. Construct a timeline: Draw a line down one side of a notebook page from top to bottom. Put the following dates on the line. Then beside each date, write down one important event that happened during that year.
Dates: 1632, 1637, 1638, 1641, 1645, 1651, 1653, 1654.**

USING YOUR KNOWLEDGE

13. La Tour and d'Aulnay were great rivals in early Acadia. Describe two incidents that prove this statement is true.

14. In the diary, La Tour makes d'Aulnay appear like a villain or "bad guy."
    a) Why would La Tour describe d'Aulnay in this way?
    b) Do you think this is a true picture of d'Aulnay? How could you check?

THINKING IT THROUGH

15. The Micmac Indians and La Tour: Friends or foe? Reread the diary to find out what part the Micmacs played in Charles de La Tour's story. Then write a paragraph in which you answer the above question. Be sure to give examples from the text to support your conclusion.

16. Discuss the statement: The life of Charles de La Tour would make a good movie. In your discussion, identify what you think makes a good movie story. Then consider the events in La Tour's life and decide whether or not they would make an interesting film. Which events would you concentrate on?

Fig. 9-5 Acadian life is recreated at Caraquet, the Acadian Historical Village in New Brunswick. Identify the various activities shown.

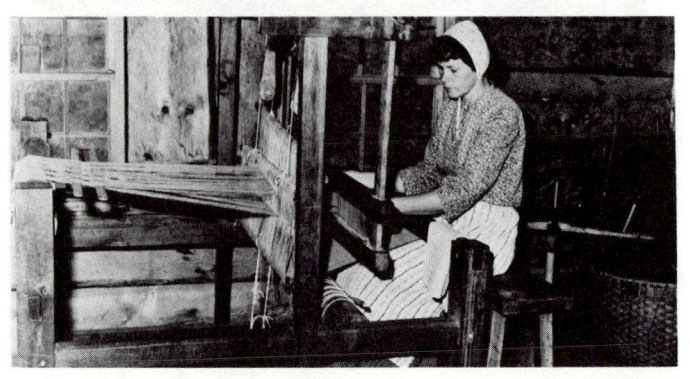

Acadia under the English

Acadia fell to the English in 1613, 1629, 1654, 1690 and 1710. The first four times, it was given back to France at the peace table. However, by the Treaty of Utrecht [YOO-trekt] in 1713, Acadia became part of the British Empire.

This meant that the English were faced with a problem: How do you control a small colony that has the language, religion and culture of your longtime enemy? Do you force the people to leave? Do you flood the colony with your own immigrants so that the French population will be in the minority? Do you station large numbers of soldiers there to keep the peace—thereby tying up a lot of your troops at great expense? Or, do you take a chance that the people of the colony will accept their fate and become loyal to their new rulers?

At first, the English did consider forcing the Acadians to leave. In fact, under the Treaty of Utrecht, the Acadians were given the option, for one year, of selling their land and leaving with all their belongings. Furthermore, French authorities from Isle Royale [eel roi-YAL] tried to encourage the Acadians to resettle on Isle St. Jean (now called Prince Edward Island).

The English soon decided that it would be difficult and costly to bring in new people to settle Nova Scotia. So, instead they decided to try to win the loyalty of the Acadians. Occasionally, British officials visited Acadian communities and asked the people to swear an oath of allegiance [a-LEE-juhns] to the King of England. Most Acadians agreed to be faithful to the king as long as they did not have to take up arms. The Acadians did not want to be drawn into an English war—especially if they would have to fight against the French. And besides, when they refused to agree to take up arms, the British did nothing about it anyway. Most felt that they had lived and survived on their own for 100 years, so why get involved in the affairs of either England or France? As it turned out, they could not avoid getting caught between the two empires. In the next section you will see what price the Acadians paid for being caught in the middle.

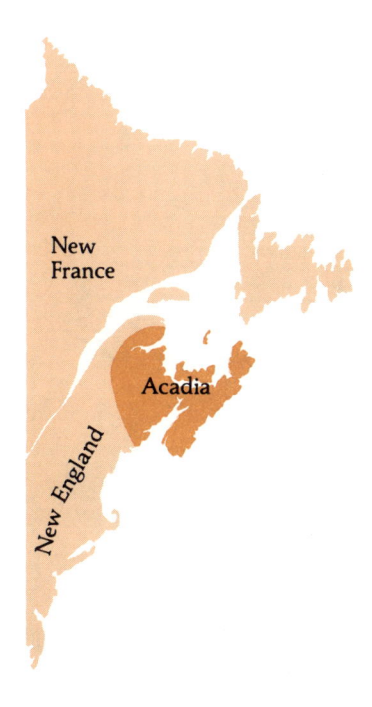

Fig. 9-6 Acadia: a land between.

GETTING THE FACTS

17. Explain what the word "oath" means.
18. By 1713, which empire did Acadia belong to for good?

19. List all the different courses of action that the British could have taken to solve their problem in Acadia.

THINKING IT THROUGH

20. What exactly was the problem, anyway? Suggest reasons why the English were worried about having the Acadians live in Nova Scotia, which was now a British colony for good.

21. Most Acadians were willing to take an oath of loyalty to Britain, but on one condition.
    a) What was that condition?
    b) Do you think the Acadians were right to refuse to take the oath because of that one condition? Give reasons to back your opinion. What would you have decided if you had been in their shoes?

The expulsion of the Acadians

It was Friday, September 5, 1755. About 400 of Acadia's leading men had crowded into the parish church at Grand Pré [grahⁿ-pray]. They had come to find out what was to become of them and the rest of the Acadians. Their fate was revealed by a British officer who spoke the following words:

> "Your land and tenements, cattle of all kinds and livestock of all sorts are forfeited to the Crown, as well as all your other effects except your money and household goods; and you yourselves to be removed from this province." He continued, "I shall do everything in my power to see that all goods be secured to you and that you are not molested in carrying them off and also that whole families shall go in the same vessel... I hope that in whatever part of the world your lot may fall, you may be faithful subjects and a peaceable and happy people."

Quoted in Canada and it's Provinces: A History of the Canadian People and Their Institutions.

What had happened? Why were the Acadians being driven out of their land?

In the last section, you saw the Acadians were willing to live under British rule as long as they did not have to fight in British wars. The British seemed to accept this for a while. However, by about 1750, the tension between Britain and France was

Fig. 9-7 Acadians hear that they are to be expelled at the parish church in Grand Pré, 1755. How are the people reacting to the announcement?

great. There was a good possibility that war would break out between the two empires in North America. In case this happened, Britain wanted to make sure that its colonies were as strong as possible and would help fight the French.

Acadia made the British nervous. There were thousands of people living there, all French and Roman Catholic. They did not take sides because they preferred to remain neutral. But were they really neutral? Britain could not be sure.

In June 1755, an English and American force captured Fort Beausejour [boh-seu-ZHOOR] in Acadia. The British decided once and for all to make sure that the Acadians would support Britain in the event of war. The British therefore asked all

Acadians to take an oath of loyalty. By this oath, the Acadians would be forced to agree to fight with Britain in the case of war. If they refused, they would be expelled from Acadia.

The Acadians were in a difficult spot. What were they to do? All they really wanted was to live their own lives peacefully and to side with neither empire. It was a painful decision to make. Finally they refused to take the oath. Look below for some possible reasons for their decision.

The British carried out their threat. On September 5, 1755, the **expulsion** was announced. More than 6000 Acadians were forced from their homes and transported to different English colonies in the south. Britain wanted to scatter the Acadians in faraway countries. That way they could not gather to fight for the French against England.

> **Why did the Acadians refuse to take the oath?**
>
> 1. We are peace-loving people. We don't want to fight anyone, especially the Indians and the French.
> 2. This isn't the first time we have refused to promise to take up arms for Britain. Nothing happened to us in the past. Why then should we expect Britain to carry out its threats this time?
> 3. Our priests have warned us that once we take the oath, Britain will try to make us into English people. They will take away our religion. If this happens then we have no hope of reaching heaven after we die.

The expulsion

Here is how one historian described the day that the Acadians were expelled:

> In all parts of the settlement, careful housewives closed the doors of their homes and turned towards the shore. From all directions the people came, the very young in their mothers' arms, the very old looking for the last time on the pleasant land that had always been their home. Some care was taken to see that families were united and placed on the same vessel, but in the confusion separation was inevitable.... Then began the work of destruction, for there was much to destroy lest Acadians who lurked in the

forest should return. For days the smoke of burning buildings rose from every part of the country. Soldiers scoured the countryside, rounding up cattle and sheep and other farm animals. These would at least help to defray the cost of transporting their former owners.

In all the Acadian land there was nothing but desolation. Blackened ruins stood in the midst of the strangely silent fields, alive till now with the busy clatter of village life. Stray animals wandered here and there and at night furtive figures stole across the countryside.

From *The History of Nova Scotia* by G.G. Campbell.

GETTING THE FACTS

22. Explain the following words: expel, expulsion.

23. What did the British threaten to do if the Acadians refused to take the oath?

24. Reread the words of the officer who announced the expulsion to the Acadians. What was going to happen to the Acadians' property?

THINKING IT THROUGH

25. Examine the three reasons that the Acadians had for not taking the oath. Which do you think is the best reason? Explain your answer.

26. Look back at the words of the officer who announced the expulsion.
    a) Describe what his attitude toward the Acadians seemed to be.
    b) When empires struggle for power, ordinary people usually get hurt. This statement is true for the Acadians in 1755. Do you think it could be true for the British too? (Do you think it was easy for the British to drive out the Acadians?) Give reasons to support your opinion.

27. Reread the description of the expulsion.
    a) Describe some of your feelings about the event.
    b) Do you feel this way because of the way the author wrote the story, or because of the events that actually happened? Or both? Explain your answer.

28. Examine the picture of the expulsion of the Acadians on page 206. Describe how the picture makes you feel about the expulsion. What do you think the artist has done to make you feel this way?

Fig. 9-8 The expulsion of the Acadians.

Was it necessary to expel the Acadians?

After reading about how the Acadians were driven from their homes, how do you feel? Was it really necessary to expel the Acadians?

This is a question that historians and other people have been arguing about for many years. Some historians feel that the expulsion was tragic and unnecessary. Others feel that, in a struggle between great empires, small groups of people sometimes get caught in the middle. Read the following arguments and decide how you feel about the expulsion.

NO, it wasn't necessary to expel the Acadians

There was no reason to fear the Acadians. They were not really concerned about politics and had no strong opinion about which empire they should give their loyalty to. After all, their colony had changed hands many times and their way of life hadn't been disrupted. Did it really matter then who ruled it? Their main concern was for Acadia, the land their ancestors had made prosperous. They just wanted to be left alone.

The Acadians therefore would not have been a threat to England if war with France had broken out. But the British used the war as an excuse. For years they hated and mistrusted the Acadians because of their language and religion. The British could not accept the idea that a group of French Roman Catholics was living and prospering in a British colony. When they saw a chance finally to get rid of the Acadians, they took it.

YES, it was necessary to expel the Acadians

There was good reason to fear the Acadians. When the British captured Fort Beausejour in 1755, they found that 300 Acadians had pledged their faith to France and were working for the French. Other Acadians were responsible for helping the Indians to revolt against the British. These were just a few of the Acadians, but after finding some of them in open revolt like this, how could they ever be trusted?

Also, Britain was a huge empire and in conflict with France. Britain needed strong colonies in North America. Acadia was especially important to the British because it could help to protect the British colonies further south. It was necessary, therefore, to make Acadia a truly British colony.

At first Britain tried to build up the colony by getting large numbers of English to move in and absorb the French. But there wasn't enough time to do this properly. The only other way to make the colony British was to remove the French and so they did. A few thousand people suffered, but a whole empire was at stake. The expulsion was just one unhappy episode in the huge struggle between the two empires.

THINKING IT THROUGH

29. a) In your notebook draw a two-column chart. In one column list reasons why it was necessary to expel the Acadians. In the other column list reasons why it was not necessary to expel them.

b) Consider all the reasons carefully and then decide if the expulsion was necessary or not. Give reasons to explain your decision.

30. Look back at your answer to question 27.a). Now that you have some more information about the expulsion, would you still give the same answer to 27.a)? If your answer is yes, explain why. If your answer is no, give your new answer.

Conclusion

The history of the Acadians is one of the most dramatic chapters in the story of Canada. The expulsion of the Acadians is an example of what happens when ordinary people get caught in the struggle between empires. In the next chapter you will discover more about what happens when empires clash.

The story of the Acadians does not end here, though. Look at the photos at the beginning of this chapter. One of them shows a modern scene—people celebrating the history of Acadia. What happened to the Acadians after 1755?

> Through the years, many found their way back; some along hundreds of kilometres of the American coast, in small decrepit boats; others on foot through countless kilometres of forest. Many returned from exile in France. They settled in remote districts of present-day Nova Scotia and New Brunswick where there was least chance of being discovered.

Today their descendants are still living in the region once named Acadia.

Adapted from *History of Nova Scotia* by G.G. Campbell.

THE INVESTIGATIVE REPORTER

31. The return of the Acadians is another dramatic story. Using books from your school or local library, find out more about the Acadians who returned. (You may want to look at

just one group of Acadians, since different groups were scattered all over the British colonies.) Look for the following information:
—Where they were sent to after the expulsion;
—Why they decided to return to Acadia;
—How they returned—the hardships and adventures they may have had;
—Where they settled.
Once you have gathered this information, use it to write a short story called "The return of the Acadians."

10 What happens when empires collide?

- What questions come to your mind when you compare the "before" and "after" paintings of Quebec?

- Examine the boundaries of the French and English empires in North America. If both empires expanded their territories, what do you think would happen?

- Identify the main river systems of North America. Why do you think the empires were interested in them?

- Explain how the fur trade could promote empire-building.

- Why does empire-building often lead to war?

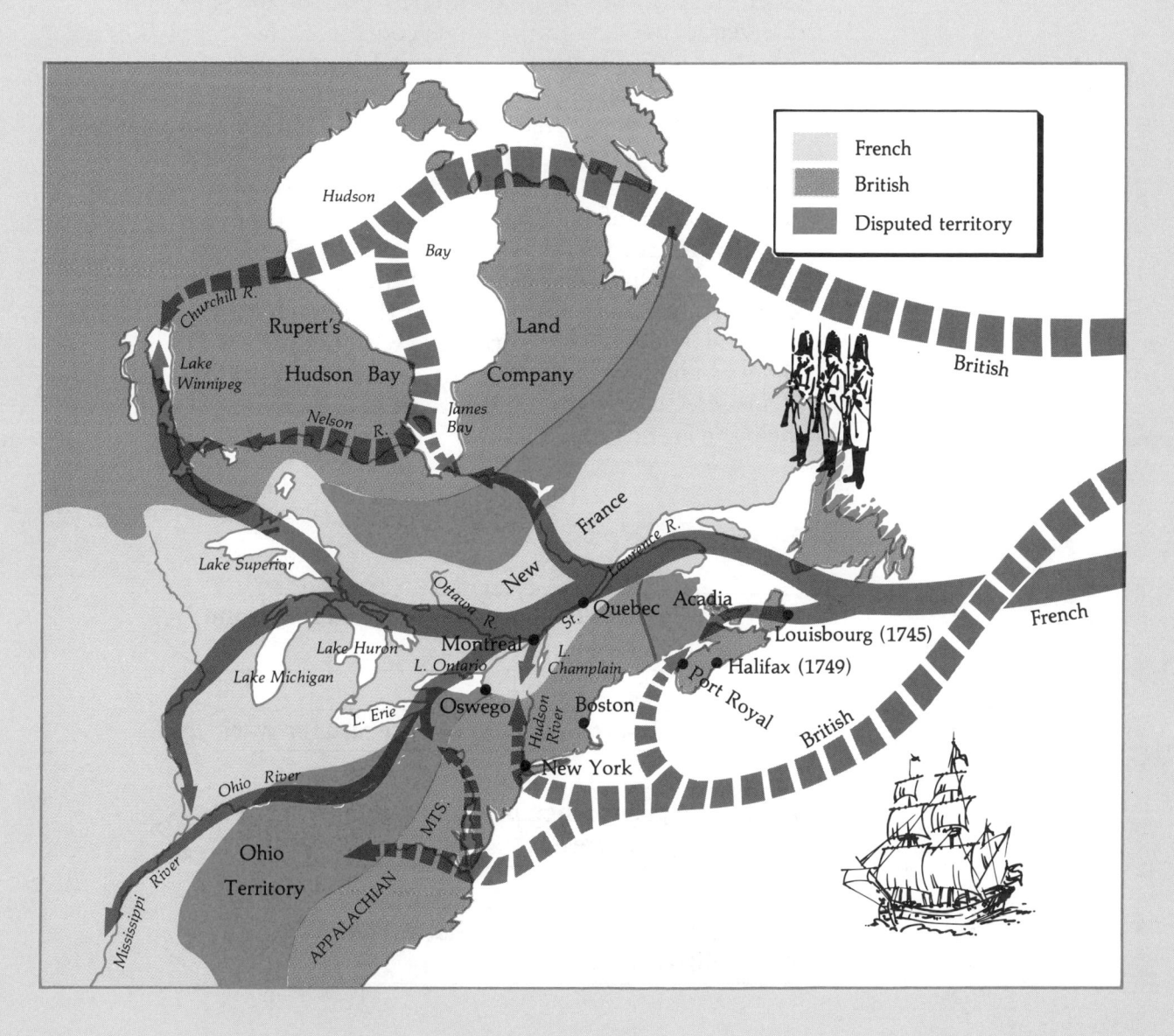

AD 1750	
1756	Seven Years' War begins
1758	British capture Louisbourg
1759	British defeat French on Plains of Abraham
1763	Treaty of Paris and Proclamation Act
1770	
1780	
1790	
1800	

Chapter overview

The nations that had control over the major river systems in North America also controlled the fur trade. Fur traders and explorers traveled mainly along these waterways, so fur-trading and empire-building were tied together. French fur traders gradually extended their fur-trading empire up the St. Lawrence, through the Great Lakes and down the gigantic Mississippi River system. Their control over this empire was threatened by English and Dutch fur traders who expanded their territory up the Hudson River to Lake Champlain and eventually arrived at Lake Ontario near the British fort of Oswego [ahs-WEE-goh]. French control of the Great Lakes was also threatened by British control of the fur trade from the Hudson Bay drainage basin. As the fur traders reached deeper into the continent, their territories overlapped more and more. The competition for furs became very strong. The rivalry was the worst in the Ohio Territory, a rich region of fur-bearing animals south of the Great Lakes along the Ohio River.

British fur traders were friends with the powerful Iroquois Indians who lived south of Lake Ontario. With the help of these Indians, they were able to disrupt the French fur trade. French fur traders, however, were allied with the western Indians. These Indians did not want the English population in the Thirteen Colonies to move into their area and were willing to help the French stop them.

Signposts

Why was there tension between the French and English empires?

How did France and England prepare for war?

What happens when people get caught between colliding empires?

FEATURE: Officers and enlisted men: What was the difference?

> The Seven Years' War: What happened to Louisbourg and Quebec?

> FEATURE: How did Wolfe find the track to the Plains of Abraham?

Key words

empires	Anglicize	
arms race	collision	blockade
forts	militia	

Why was there tension between the French and English empires?

As European countries learned of the wealth that could be found in other lands, they tried to establish colonies around the world. During the 17th and 18th centuries, both France and England were busy expanding their empires. They both founded colonies in many different places.

Both countries, for instance, set up tea plantations in India, since tea was a popular drink in Europe. Cotton and silk helped make the Indian colonies even more profitable. France and England were also drawn to the West Indies because of the sugar. And, of course, North America's furs, fish, timber and tobacco were also of great interest to both countries.

As you can see, France and England were often interested in the same lands. This was one of the reasons for conflict between the empires.

A plantation is a large farm or estate cultivated by workers living on it. Often the labour was provided by slaves or by poorly paid occasional workers.

What was the connection between the French and English empires and the fur trade?

In North America, one of the main reasons for conflict was the beaver pelt trade. Both empires wanted to control the trade. To do this, it was necessary to control the river systems in the new land. Why were the rivers so important? People in the beaver trade travelled along the rivers in search of new sources of beaver skins. Beaver ponds were located along the streams and

Fig. 10-1 The growth of the population of French and English colonies.

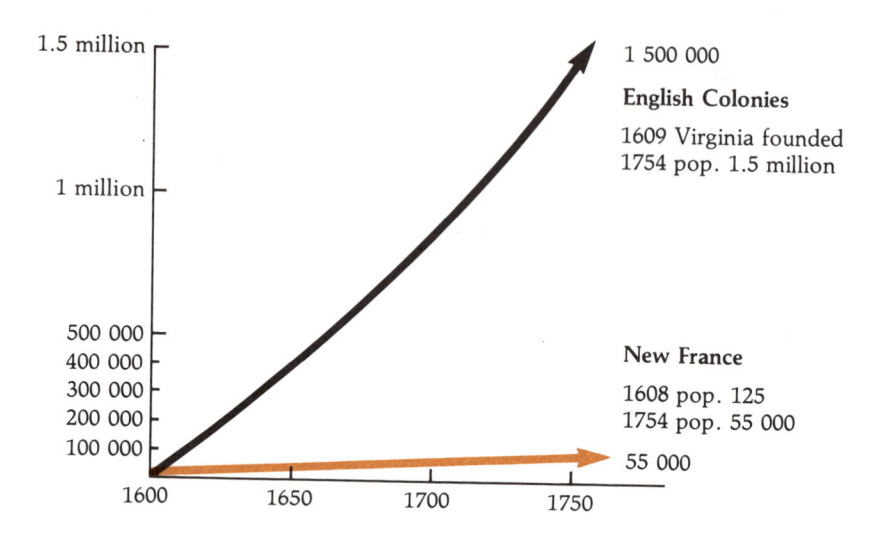

```
1.5 million ─                                    ↗ 1 500 000
                                                   English Colonies
                                                   1609 Virginia founded
                                                   1754 pop. 1.5 million
1 million ─

 500 000 ─
 400 000 ─
 300 000 ─                                         New France
 200 000 ─                                         1608 pop. 125
 100 000 ─                              →          1754 pop. 55 000
                                                   55 000
           1600    1650    1700    1750
```

rivulets that flowed together to form great rivers. If the rivers were controlled, the trappers and traders could freely find the beaver. Once the beavers were killed and skinned, they could be transported down the rivers to the trading posts.

By 1700, the French had built fur-trading forts along the Great Lakes-St. Lawrence River routes, and had begun to expand to the Mississippi Basin. The English, meanwhile, were established along the east coast of North America, south of New France. They were building fur-trading forts around Hudson Bay. The English were also interested in the fur-rich Mississippi Basin, especially the land along the banks of the Ohio River. As well, the English colonies were growing and needed more land to settle. The settlers were looking to the land west of the Appalachian [A-puh-LAY-shun] Mountains.

In this wilderness, the two empires collided.

GETTING THE FACTS

1. **List the areas of North America controlled by:**
   a) France;   b) England.
Over which areas were the two empires in conflict? (You may want to refer back to the map at the beginning of the chapter.)

USING YOUR KNOWLEDGE

2. **Examine the graph of population growth in Fig. 10-1.**
   a) In 1650, what was the population of the French colonies?

The English colonies? What was the population of each in 1750?

b) How many more people were there in the French colonies in 1750 than in 1650? How many more were there in the English colonies?

c) A major reason for the slow population growth in New France was the fur trade. How did the fur trade discourage French settlement?

d) What other reasons can you suggest for the difference in population growth?

THINKING IT THROUGH

3. Fur traders were interested in the Ohio River because it was rich in furs. English colonies were growing and the colonists wanted the land to settle in. In two columns—one for the fur traders and one for the colonists—write down the arguments that each side could give for claiming the land. Which side do you think had the stronger claim? Explain your reasons.

How did England and France prepare for war?

As tension between English and French fur traders increased after 1700, a frantic period of fort-building began. Forts were constructed along the river systems in an 18th century "**arms race**." Many of these forts stood opposite each other; for example, Fort Oswego (English) and Fort Frontenac (French). Along the important Hudson River-Lake Champlain waterway, a series of forts was constructed (see Fig. 10-2). In addition to these, two very important forts were constructed at Louisbourg [LOO-ee-burg] and Halifax.

By 1757, New France had 67 forts of which Louisbourg was the largest. Many of these forts still exist as museums. Have you ever visited one?

The building of Louisbourg

Quebec City was the centre of New France. It was the only well-designed walled and fortified city in North America. But it was located deep inside New France and depended upon supplies and reinforcements from France. French ships therefore had to be able to pass freely along the St. Lawrence River. Control of the mouth of the St. Lawrence was vitally important, so France decided to construct the fort of Louisbourg on Isle Royale (Cape Breton Island).

Louisbourg was built on a grand scale. Begun in 1720, it wasn't completed until 1745. Louisbourg covered 65 ha of land

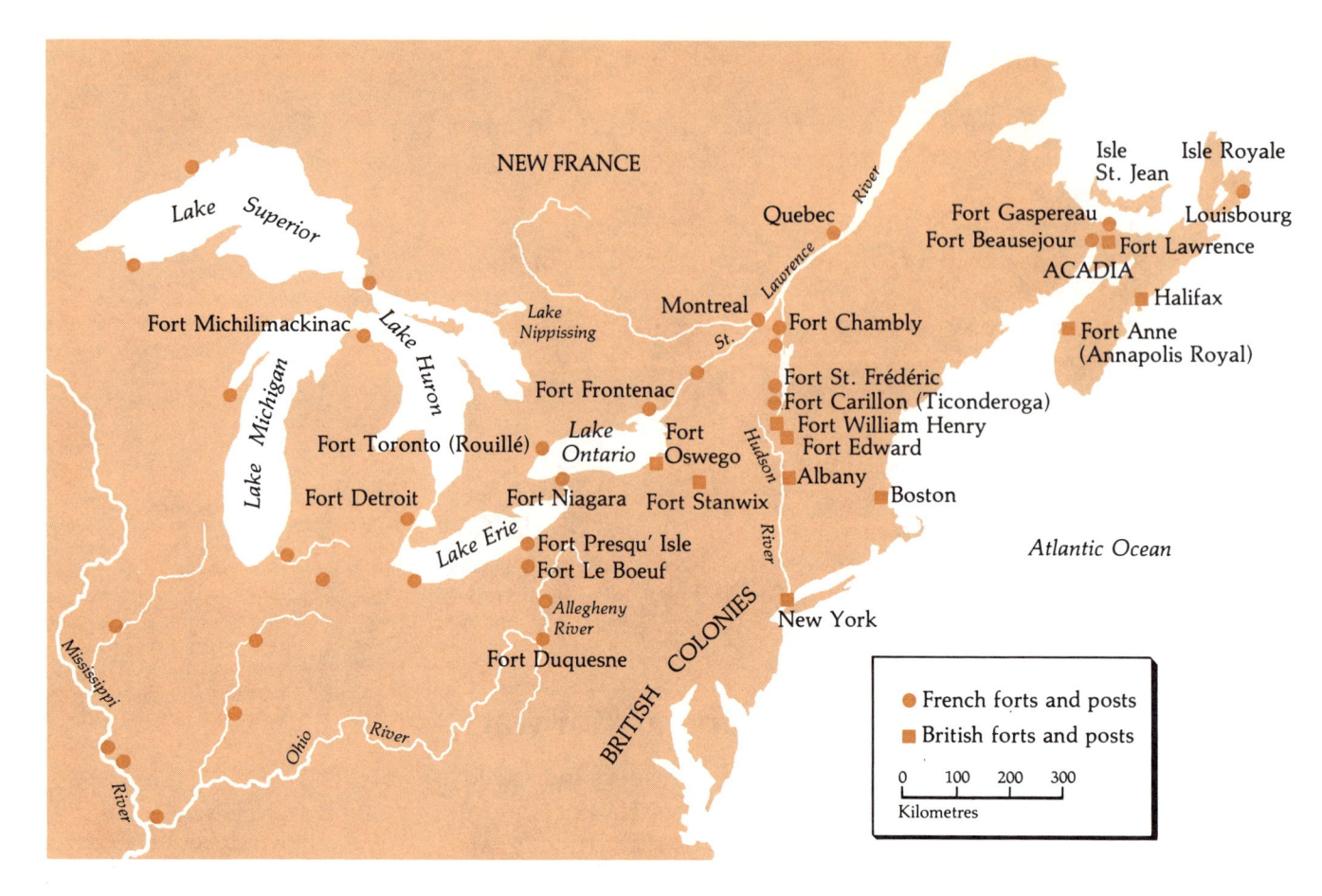

Fig. 10-2 French and British forts and trading posts.

Why is it difficult to compare money values in the past with modern money values? How could the cost of Louisbourg be determined in modern money values?

that were enclosed by walls three metres thick and nine metres high. Inside the walls were the fort and a city that housed as many as 10 000 people. The site was surrounded by water on three sides. The only land approach was a piece of swampy ground that would make the movement of enemy artillery very difficult. In front of these walls was a steep ditch, and beyond that, a flat, treeless, sloping plain that allowed all 148 cannons to fire unobstructed at any invading force.

To many French people, Louisbourg became a nightmare. For one thing, it cost a lot to build; the final bill was 30 000 000 livres, or $100 000 000. The fort was so expensive that Louis XV said he expected "to wake one morning and see the walls of Louisbourg rising over the Atlantic Ocean"!

The fort was not pleasant to live in, either. Thick fog shrouded it for most of the year, making the defenders cold and damp, even in their beds. The fort was so isolated from the rest of New France that it seemed like a prison. Everything had to be

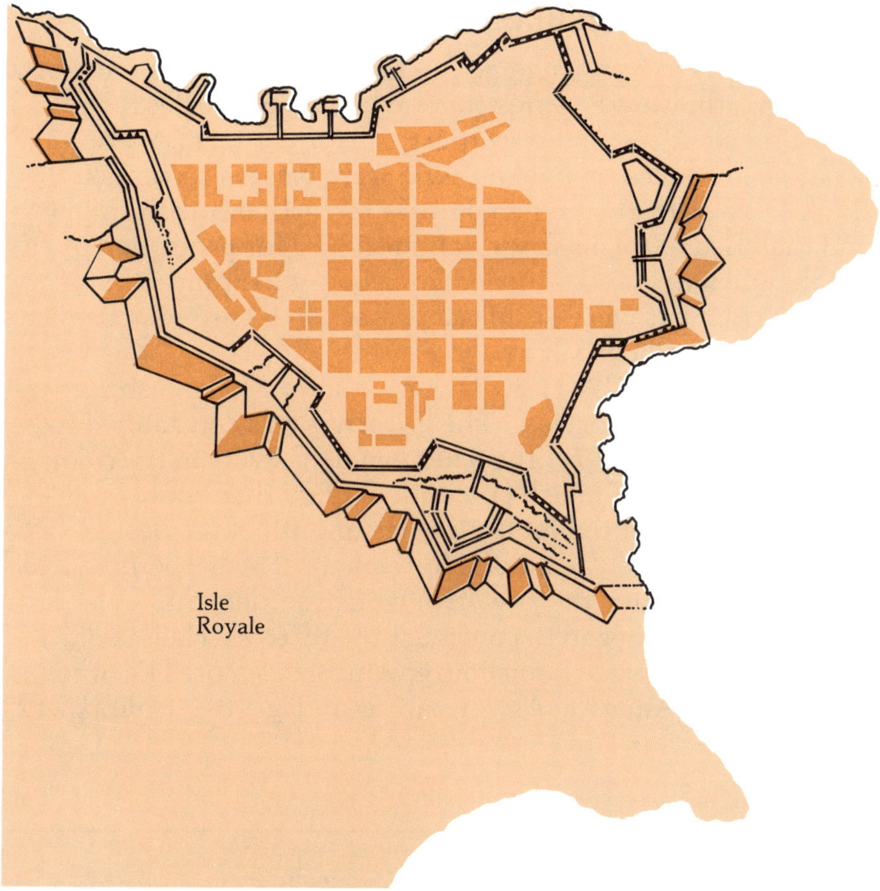

Fig. 10-3 Plan of the fortress of Louisbourg.

Isle Royale

imported—food, clothing, furniture and even entertainment. Boredom was a common complaint among the people living there.

The biggest problem with Louisbourg, though, was that it failed in its job—to defend New France. In 1745, a largely amateur army of New Englanders attacked the fort. After a two-month **siege** [seezh] the New Englanders, with the help of the British navy, conquered the fort. Louisbourg fell partly because its cannons could only aim out to sea and so were useless when the British attacked by land. Also, the walls of the fort were not kept in good shape.

The victory of the British colonists was short. England returned the fort to France in 1748. In exchange, France gave back to England one of England's colonies in India that France had captured. This exchange made the New Englanders very angry. But the lesson had been learned—Louisbourg could be conquered.

The building of Halifax

The colonists in New England felt the need for protection. For one thing, they were being attacked by raiding parties from New France. Also, English settlers on **frontier** farms were attacked and killed by Indians, who were offered rewards for English scalps by the French. Pirates terrorized British shipping and then fled to the harbour at Louisbourg for protection. As a result, when England returned Louisbourg to France, the English colonists were promised protection from a new English fortress to be called Halifax.

On July 12, 1749, a new governor and 2500 English settlers arrived at the new fortress. The governor was determined to **Anglicize** [ANG-glih-sīz] the 8200 Acadians living in the colony by building up the English population. Only then could English colonists to the south feel secure. The mouth of the best harbour was chosen as the site for Halifax. The harbour was to be the main base for the powerful British settlement.

The English began to construct the fortress. Halifax did not look anything like Louisbourg, which was more like other forts in North America. As you can see in Fig. 10-4, Halifax was

Fig. 10-4 The plan for Halifax in 1749.

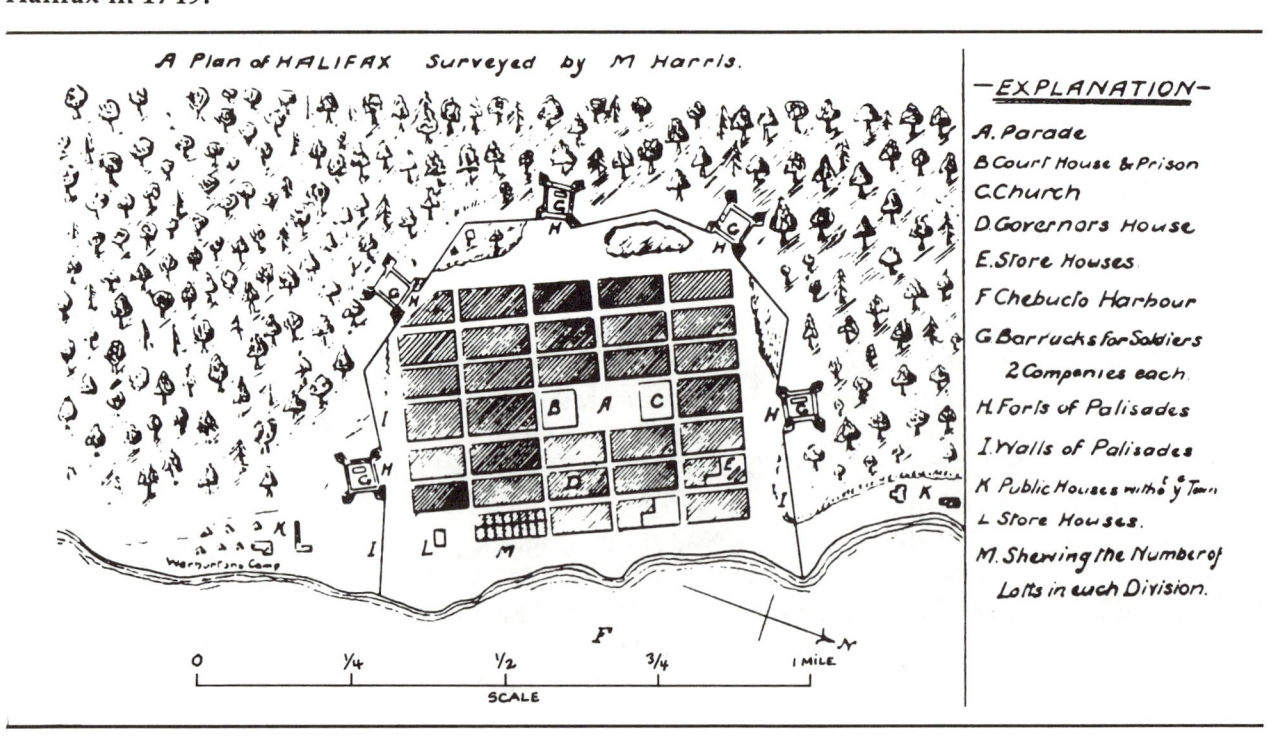

not a fortified city. Instead it was a townsite surrounded by five timber stockades [stah-KAYDS]. It did not have to be a stone fort like Louisbourg because the harbour at Halifax was 21 km from the sea, and the only entrance to it was through a narrow passage. This passage could be easily defended by a few cannons.

Halifax needed ordinary people more than it needed soldiers and sailors. Military people could be brought in by ship whenever they were necessary. Ordinary people, such as farmers to produce food, carpenters to build homes and merchants to provide military supplies, were needed to make the fort function smoothly. The early attempts to bring immigrants to Halifax had not been very successful. The first group of 2500 settlers had been attracted by an offer of free food for a year. They had been poor city people who had no skills to offer on the frontier. Many of them slipped away to the more established colonies. They were replaced by New England colonists who were experienced on the frontier and saw a chance to make money by serving in the British navy. Other settlers were attracted from Germany—farm families, fully prepared to work hard with an axe and a hoe. Work progressed slowly, but by 1752, there were 4000 people in the town.

For a more personal description of these early immigrants, read Case study 3, page 222.

Halifax faced different problems than Louisbourg did. It wasn't the possibility of a French invasion that worried the people of Halifax; it was the Indian raids. In the first year, the crew of a nearby sawmill was killed by raiding Indians. Hostile Indian bands, encouraged by a French priest and spiritual leader named Le Loutre [leu lootr], managed to keep the people of Halifax constantly alert and nervous.

Find out more about Le Loutre in your local library.

When the Seven Years' War was officially declared in 1756, Halifax was ready. By 1758, Halifax had received 23 000 soldiers and sailors who were preparing for an attack on Louisbourg, and later Quebec.

GETTING THE FACTS

4. Explain briefly why Louisbourg was built.
5. Explain why Halifax was built.
6. List the problems that each fort experienced.

USING YOUR KNOWLEDGE

7. a) How were the two forts different? Reread the descriptions of Louisbourg and Halifax, and examine the diagrams.

Fig. 10-5 English cartoonists exaggerated the differences between officers and enlisted men. What point is the cartoonist trying to make about this officer?

Scalping was a part of the North American struggle of empires. For example, two women and four children were killed and scalped by New England soldiers at the Acadian settlement of St. Anne's Point (Fredericton).

Then list the differences between the forts. Here are some points you may want to consider: locations, construction materials, types of weapons and fortifications.

    b) Why were the two forts built differently?

    c) Which fort was most effective? Give reasons for your answer.

THINKING IT THROUGH

8. The building of forts by the French and the English was an 18th century arms race.

    a) Explain the meaning of this statement.

    b) Give one example of an arms race in the 20th century.

    c) Do you think that arms races are necessary when there are two or more powerful nations in the world? Give reasons to support your opinion.

What happens when people get caught between colliding empires?

When empires like England and France collide, ordinary people are affected. The four case studies that follow show the effect of this collision:

Case study 1: English colonists

Life on frontier farms in New England had been very dangerous for many years. Raiding bands of Indians, encouraged by French leaders living in New France, had begun to kill and scalp English settlers in the 1680s. In 1704, the people of Deerfield, Massachusetts were suddenly attacked by a French and Indian war party. Forty of the villagers were killed on the spot and 111 were forced to march into the wilderness as prisoners. Throughout the first part of the century, these raids continued. Louisbourg was seen as a major danger to coastal settlements in New England. Eventually, the New Englanders raised money to pay for the first successful invasion of Louisbourg.

Case study 2: The Acadians

In 1755, the French settlers living in Acadia were deported because they were considered to be a threat to English settlers

Officers and enlisted men: What was the difference?

Officers like Wolfe and Montcalm were members of the English and the French nobility. They were the upper class. To them, war was a kind of aristocratic sport with rules of honour. They expected "gentleman-like" behaviour, even if the game caused death and destruction. When the armies of Wolfe and Montcalm fought, they faced each other on a large flat field in a formation that is very much like the way games such as checkers or chess are set up.

Privates and sailors, on the other hand, came from the opposite class—the lower class. Most were forced to join the army or the navy. Some were even kidnapped from poor areas in large cities by press-gangs. Sometimes soldiers were hired from other countries such as Germany.

One English general in 1815 was so unimpressed with his own soldiers that he called them the "scum of the earth." Wolfe did not share this opinion. He expected a lot from his troops and as a result they were very loyal to him. But, because most officers did not trust the soldiers in their command, wars were fought in a certain way. For example, officers always kept a close eye on the troops so they could not desert. Camps were never located near large forests. Night marches were considered risky. To allow sailors to go on shore leave was to invite desertion.

Most of the time, officers and enlisted men did not trust or understand each other. In fact, sometimes the behaviour of the officers seemed strange to the enlisted men. At Louisbourg, the English officers sent a basket of pineapples under a flag of truce to the wife of the French general. A young English girl who had fallen in love with a French officer was escorted into Louisbourg to say "bonjour" to him. She returned with some fresh lettuce and a tub of butter as gifts for the English officers from the French officers. Meanwhile, these same French officers were paying Indians for any English scalps they brought to Louisbourg. English officers were ordering their marines to board French ships and kill French sailors while they slept.

GETTING THE FACTS

9. Officers were constantly watching that their troops did not desert. Explain why each of the following situations was risky: camps located near large forests; night marches; shore leave.

USING YOUR KNOWLEDGE

10. There was widespread conflict between the French and English in North America. Yet in the two incidents described above, the officers behaved in a friendly manner to members of the enemy. Suggest reasons for this contradictory behaviour.

11. Artists often use cartoons to express an opinion about something. Look at Fig. 10-5, which shows an officer in uniform. What message do you think the artist is trying to present?

in Halifax and New England. It was believed that the Acadians provided food and hiding places for the raiders mentioned in Case study 1.

"I have four small children," wrote one of these Acadians. "I lived contented on my land. That did not last long, for we were forced to leave all our property and flee from under the domination of the English. The king undertakes to transport us and support us under the expectation of news from France. If Acadia is not restored to France, I hope to take my little family and bring it to Canada. I beg you to let me know the state of things in that country. I assure you that we are in poor condition, for we are like Indians in the woods."

From The Acadian Exiles: A Chronicle of the Land of Evangeline by Arthur G. Doughty.

Case study 3: Halifax immigrants

Ordinary people were attracted to Halifax in 1749 by newspaper advertisements in London papers. The ads described Halifax as safe and surrounded by rich land. This was not true. The British government needed settlers to build the fortress of Halifax under very dangerous conditions. Something of the shock these immigrants experienced when they arrived is described:

> We came to Halifax expecting to find a country known and improved by thousands of Europeans, all our own subjects, ready to provide cultivated land, rivers with fish and woods with fowl. No wild Indians to fight or unfriendly French to control. In short, no danger to encounter, no difficulties to distress or scarce any uncertainty to meet. What we found was the reverse. We are in constant danger from raiding parties financed by an agent of the King of France. He pays them for every scalp they bring him. It is not safe to stir from the forts without a good convoy and no working can be done near Halifax without covering parties of armed men.

From The Northcliffe Collection, Public Archives of Canada.

Case study 4: French villagers along the St. Lawrence

On September 4, 1758, General James Wolfe and a squadron of English raiders anchored in Gaspé Bay and his troops quickly occupied the small French town of Gaspé. There was no fighting because most of the people had run away, leaving behind all their possessions. The English troops searched the countryside and managed to round up 37 prisoners, including a woman and a child.

Then the troops began the unpleasant part of the job. They had been sent to destroy or to capture military equipment. Instead, 250 small fishing boats belonging to the French were taken to the ships. The houses were ransacked and then set afire. Barrels and racks of fish were also destroyed. Then they sailed away to find other French villages.

Fig. 10-6 Examples of military uniforms. From left to right: Regiment de Flandres, 1756; 42nd Regiment, 1757-60; Quebec Light Infantry, 1st Company, 1839.

GETTING THE FACTS

12. Locate each of the following words in the case studies. Then write short definitions for each word: domination, encounter, convoy, squadron, ransacked.

13. For each of the four case studies, summarize in one or two sentences how each group was affected by the collision of empires.

USING YOUR KNOWLEDGE

14. Choose one of the case studies. Imagine that you are one of the people caught in the situation. Write a diary entry in which you describe the hardships you suffered and your feelings about the conflict between the French and English empires.

15. The advertisements from the London papers given in Case study 3 are examples of propaganda.
   a) Imagine that you own an old house on the outskirts of

town. There is an empty lot littered with junk across the street and train tracks behind the house. You want to sell the house. Write a misleading advertisement for the house.

    b) Can this kind of false advertisement be justified? Before you answer, think about the possible reasons for the false advertising. Then think about what might happen to the people who believe the advertisement.

16. The people living in Gaspé who were forced to flee their homes clearly suffered. But what about the soldiers who took part in the raiding party? Often they disliked the jobs they were obliged to do. Imagine you are a soldier who took part in the raiding party on Gaspé. Write a diary entry in which you describe your feelings about the raid.

17. Throughout history, when empires or countries collide, ordinary people are affected. Look in newspapers or magazines for a present-day example of ordinary people whose lives are being changed by colliding countries. Write a report or design a poster that describes who the people are and how they are being affected.

The Seven Years' War: What happened to Louisbourg and Quebec?

In 1755, General Braddock, a British officer, led a force of British regulars and colonial troops into the Ohio Valley. Their objective was to attack Fort Duquesne [du^e-KEHN] and eventually drive the French out of the area. But they did not achieve their goal; they were ambushed and defeated by a party of French and Indians. Within a month, the French struck back by attacking and winning the English Fort Necessity. Open war between the two empires was not far off.

    One year later, in the summer of 1756, war was formally declared. The Seven Years' War, which would settle the conflict between the two empires in North America, had begun.

    France immediately appointed the Marquis de Montcalm [mahr-KEE deu moh^n-KALM] as Field Marshall for New France. With only 6000 regular soldiers and some 10 000 local Indians and militia, Montcalm had to defend a territory much larger than the whole of France. The task was extremely difficult. In 1757-8, Montcalm won several major battles. In one of these, he captured Fort Oswego which then gave the French control of the Great Lakes.

Fig. 10-7 General Louis Joseph Marquis de Montcalm

The area that was most important to control was the St. Lawrence River. Both sides knew that New France could only survive if supply ships from France could travel freely along the river. They knew that control of the St. Lawrence depended on control of Louisbourg. So Louisbourg became the main target of the war.

The fall of Louisbourg

In 1758, two hundred ships sailed from England, carrying 23 000 men and 1842 cannons. Their destination was Louisbourg, which the English navy had blockaded from the beginning of the war.

On June 2, 1758, French lookouts were startled by the size of the invading force. But they were prepared for an attack even though they were outnumbered. In the fort were 3000 soldiers and 3000 sailors, along with 24 companies of local

Fig. 10-8 The attack on Louisbourg, 1758. On the right, the French fleet is at anchor in the harbour, while in the distance is the British invasion fleet. In the foreground, British soldiers are drawing heavy guns into position to fire down on Louisbourg.

A company was made up of 50-60 men.

225

Battlements are low walls with open spaces for shooting, built on top of castles, towers or forts.

French militia. Cannons were aimed and ready on the battlements. The French warships, although trapped in the harbour, had 544 cannons charged and ready to fire. And if all the outlying defences failed, Louisbourg had enough food and ammunition to last a year.

Fighting went on for about seven weeks. The British army managed to land at the North Cape, which gave them control over the high ground overlooking Louisbourg. From this point they were able to bombard the town. The English navy moved in closer to the harbour and managed to destroy the French fleet. On July 26, Louisbourg surrendered.

Louisbourg was evacuated and the 5000 prisoners sent back to France. English engineers then began the job of totally demolishing the fort. They did so complete a job that the only sign left of Louisbourg was the occasional piece of brickwork along the harbour.

Why do you think the English demolished Louisbourg?

The English were now free to travel up the St. Lawrence to Quebec City—the heart of New France. If Quebec fell, New France would fall.

The siege of Louisbourg had taken a long time, and, as a result, the British were not able to attack Quebec that summer. The siege of Quebec was put off until 1759, and the British spent the rest of the summer preparing for the invasion. Small detachments were sent on raiding parties up the St. Lawrence River.

See Case study 4, p. 222 for a description of one of Wolfe's raids. These raids occurred throughout the Seven Years' War. Were they necessary?

GETTING THE FACTS

18. Why did the English attack Louisbourg?

19. Who was responsible for the defence of New France?

20. Explain why it was so difficult to defend New France.

THINKING IT THROUGH

21. a) What would the British have done if they had failed to win Louisbourg in 1758? Suggest three courses of action that the British could have taken.

b) Which plan would you choose to follow if you were an English officer? Give reasons for your choice.

The siege of Quebec, 1759

One thousand kilometres from the open Atlantic, on a broad river surrounded by heavy forests, James Wolfe and his invading force came upon Quebec. Being the only walled city in North America and perched on top of a 60 m cliff, Quebec was an unforgettable sight.

The fleet began bombarding the city from the water while Wolfe searched for a place to land. This was a very difficult task because Montcalm had placed highly mobile detachments of sharpshooters along the cliffs. The first attempt at a landing was a disaster. The landing craft got stuck in the mud offshore and the soldiers had to struggle through shallow water to the beach. French and Indian defenders were able to pick them off easily.

At the same time, English cannons were pounding Quebec into rubble. The cathedral caught fire and was gutted as winds fanned the flames. Eventually the beautiful city was heavily damaged and most of the major buildings became roofless piles of rubble. But the siege of Quebec could not be won unless the British made a landing. "We do not doubt," wrote a French defender, "that you will demolish the town, but we are determined that your army shall never get a footing within its walls." Somehow the British troops had to find a way to land so that they could surprise and overwhelm the French. For weeks, Wolfe was rowed along the bottom of the cliff looking for a landing site. Meanwhile, his men became restless and his officers grew more and more hostile.

Getting up the river was not easy because there were many dangerous shallow places. Captain James Cook, who became famous for his discoveries on the West Coast, charted a safe path for the navy.

Fig. 10-9 His Majesty's ship Vanguard entering the Gulf of St. Lawrence on the way to the battle of Quebec. The Vanguard assisted in the siege of Louisbourg in 1758 before continuing on with troops for the battle of the Plains of Abraham in 1759.

Fig. 10-10 General James Wolfe

The bilingual soldier was Captain Ronald McDonald of Fraser's Regiment.

"I will be master of Quebec," wrote Wolfe, "if I stay here until the end of November." Of course he couldn't wait that long, the fleet would have to leave as soon as the river began to freeze.

The final landing was almost an act of desperation. Near the citadel, where the cliff was the highest, Wolfe discovered a narrow goat track that led to a rolling plain on the west side of the city of Quebec. If he could get his troops up the track then he would be able to fight on open ground with massed regiments.

The track, however, could easily be defended. Wolfe's only hope of success was to surprise the French. How can a whole army be moved along the front of the city, up a 60 m cliff, then lined up in front of the walls and still retain the element of surprise? This was not an easy problem to solve.

Luck was with Wolfe. He learned from French prisoners that supplies were being sent to Quebec on the night of September 12-13. These supplies would pass by the track in small boats. He also learned that the officer guarding the track was not dependable. Putting the two pieces of information together, Wolfe ordered his troops into the landing craft.

The fleet was instructed to bombard a point on the other side of Quebec so that the French would think they were going to land there. Meanwhile, a group of English soldiers, who spoke fluent French, were ordered to capture the French supply boats. Then they were to proceed to the goat track and trick the sentries.

Everything went as planned. The challenges were answered in the darkness.

Sentry: Qui vive? (Who goes there?)
Reply: France!
Sentry: Quel régiment? (What regiment?)
Reply: De la Reine. (The Queen's)

As quietly as possible the troops rowed along the bottom of the cliff. Then another sentry challenged them.

Sentry: Qui vive? (Who goes there?)
Reply: Convoi de vivres. Ne fait pas de bruit. Les Anglais nous entendront! (Convoy of supplies. Don't make any noise. The English will hear us.)

Without a hitch, the landing craft beached at the foot of the track and the men quickly scrambled up the trail. The track was better than they expected. Even heavy guns could be hauled up.

How did Wolfe find the track to the Plains of Abraham?

Spies are an important part of successful battles. Because the information they provide is secret, it is often lost to history. Recently the activities of a British spy, Major Robert Stobo, have been discovered and help to explain why Wolfe knew he had a good chance of success in getting his army onto the Plains of Abraham.

Major Stobo was captured by French troops in 1754, while attacking Fort Duquesne. Stobo, like most captured British officers, was held prisoner until an exchange could be arranged for a captured French officer of similar rank. While waiting, Stobo was treated very well by his French captors and was able to use many opportunities to relay important information through a spy network and back to the British army. When he arrived in Quebec he was given a lot of freedom and even became the partner of a French fur trader. During his capture he sent information about the French to the British army by Indian couriers who were loyal to England. Eventually, one of these letters was found on a dead soldier's body and Stobo was arrested. He was tried by a judge and sentenced to be beheaded. The sentence was not carried out. Stobo then decided to escape in case his life were put in danger again. His usefulness as a spy had ended anyway. Along with eight other prisoners, including a woman and three children, he captured a French boat and sailed to Louisbourg in the early summer of 1759. There he met Wolfe and was immediately appointed to his staff. Later Stobo returned to Quebec with Wolfe's army and was able to give very good advice about Quebec. Some say that Stobo showed Wolfe the goat track to the Plains of Abraham.

USING YOUR KNOWLEDGE

22. When planning his attack on Quebec, Wolfe used many sources of information.

a) Suggest some information sources that he may have used. Which of these would have been most dependable?

b) Imagine you are Wolfe. The summer is coming to an end and you must find a way to stage an attack on land. Stobo comes to you with information about the track to the Plains of Abraham. You weigh both sides of the situation: On one hand you are desperate to find a way to attack the French on land; on the other hand you wonder "Can I trust the word of one spy enough to risk an army of 9000 men?" What will you do? Describe all your reactions to Stobo's information and discuss the decision you would make.

See With Wolfe to Quebec *by Oliver Warner for more information about Wolfe and Montcalm. This is a very readable book that gives a clear picture of the events of the Seven Years' War.*

In 1760, Montreal was captured, but it wasn't until 1763 that France agreed to peace terms. The last French attempt to regain its empire was the French invasion of Newfoundland in 1763. By the peace treaty, France was allowed to keep the islands of St. Pierre and Miquelon in the Gulf of St. Lawrence.

More and more men landed, and soon the track and surrounding cliff were covered with red-jacketed soldiers scrambling up to the Plains of Abraham. Wolfe was one of the first, as usual, and he began forming the soldiers into lines as the sun began to show itself on the horizon. Forty-four hundred men were landed and ready for combat. But their backs were to the cliff and they knew that the gamble was still full of risk.

When Montcalm heard of the landing, he was shocked. He mobilized as many men as he could and began lining his troops up at the opposite side of the Plains of Abraham. Men were formed into regimental rectangles with the long side facing the enemy. Guns were loaded. Final instructions were given and the attack began. Advancing at a fast pace towards the British, the French troops began firing too soon. The musket balls fell short and their formations were broken as the men stopped to reload.

Wolfe, meanwhile, began the preparation to fire. There would only be time for one volley—no reloading. Wolfe was therefore determined to make that one volley as destructive as possible.

"Make ready." (face enemy)
"Present." (aim rifle)
"FIRE!"

The volley blew great gaps in the French lines as soldiers fell wounded and dying across the plain. Then the grim work of hand-to-hand combat began. The French troops quickly retreated and fled to the city. Both Montcalm and Wolfe were wounded in the battle; Wolfe died as the French were retreating, and Montcalm died the next day.

The battle on the Plains of Abraham had lasted 15 minutes and was decided by one volley of musket fire. Although the war continued for another three years, the capture of Quebec brought about the end of the French empire in North America.

GETTING THE FACTS

23. Why was the element of surprise important in Wolfe's attack on Quebec?

24. Explain why Wolfe had so much trouble getting his troops up the goat track to Quebec. Refer to the picture of Quebec in Fig. 10-11 for information to use in your answer.

25. Describe the battle on the Plains of Abraham. Why was it over in 15 minutes?

Fig. 10-11 A view of the taking of Quebec.

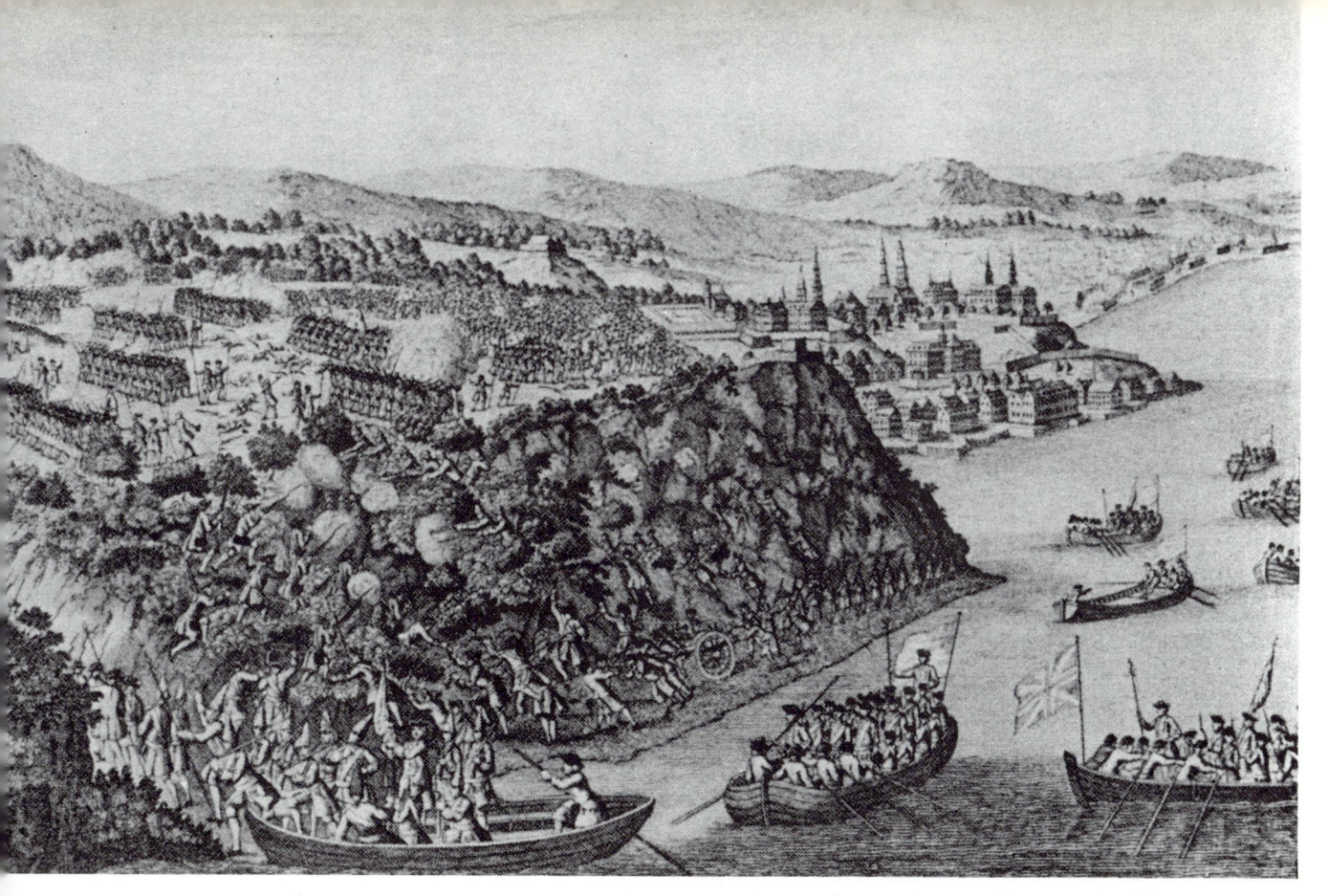

USING YOUR KNOWLEDGE

26. On March 6, 1759, the admiral in charge of Wolfe's fleet wrote a letter describing the kind of war that was to be waged:

> If... we find that Quebec is not likely to fall into our hands, I propose to set the town on fire with shells, to destroy the harvest, houses and cattle both above and below, to send off as many Canadians as possible to Europe, and to leave famine and desolation behind me... we must teach these scoundrels to make war in a more gentlemen-like manner.

Quoted in *With Wolfe to Quebec* by Oliver Warner.

a) Explain the meaning of the following words: famine, desolation, scoundrel.

b) Suggest reasons why the English would plan to "destroy the harvest, houses, and cattle," and to deport the French.

c) Would the English have been upset if this letter had been stolen by a French spy?

d) If you were in charge of defending Quebec and a French spy gave you the letter, how would you prepare for the attack?

Conclusion

Wolfe's victory was the turning point in the long struggle between the French and English empires in North America. New France was transferred to Britain by the Treaty of Paris in 1763. England now controlled a vast area of North America, including the rich fur lands of the Ohio Valley and the Great Lakes.

Yet the victory presented problems as well. What were the British to do with the French population? There were also problems with the British colonists. They no longer feared attack by the French so they wanted to move westward. The Indians living in these western lands did not want English settlers moving in. After the Indians staged a bloody uprising against the English, England guaranteed that settlement would be stopped along the Appalachian Mountains. This "Proclamation Line" angered the colonists and created tension between England and its Thirteen Colonies.

How would the French react to the new rulers of North America? How would the British colonists react? How was the story of Canada affected by the battle of the Plains of Abraham? You will discover answers to these questions in the following chapters.

THINKING IT THROUGH

27. The Canada that we live in today was shaped by events on the Plains of Abraham. Do you agree or disagree with this statement? Write an answer to this question. In your answer, you may want to start by paraphrasing the quotation (explaining what it means). Then you can give your opinion, and back up your point of view with facts you have picked up in this chapter.

28. When you have a problem to solve, begin by taking these two steps: i. identify the problem and ii. explain it briefly. When you explain a problem you show that you understand it; only then can you try to find solutions. In the last section of the chapter, you discovered that three problems faced the English after they defeated New France. These were problems with:
—the French;
—the English colonists;
—the Indians in the Ohio Valley.

a) Explain briefly what the problem was in each case.

b) Discuss in a group, or with the class, some possible solutions to the problems.

THE INVESTIGATIVE REPORTER

29. During the peace negotiations, the British government considered exchanging New France for the island of Guadeloupe [GWAH-da-LOOP] in the West Indies. This suggestion was taken seriously because Guadeloupe was a good source of sugar. Sugar was considered to be more valuable than the beaver pelts of North America. Find out more about why the British were attracted to Guadeloupe and why they chose New France instead.

Use the encyclopedia and books from your school or local library to find this information. Then answer the following question in a written report: If you were asked to advise the British at the peace negotiation, would you persuade them to take New France or Guadeloupe? Give reasons to back up your choice.

11 How did French Canadians react to the conquest?

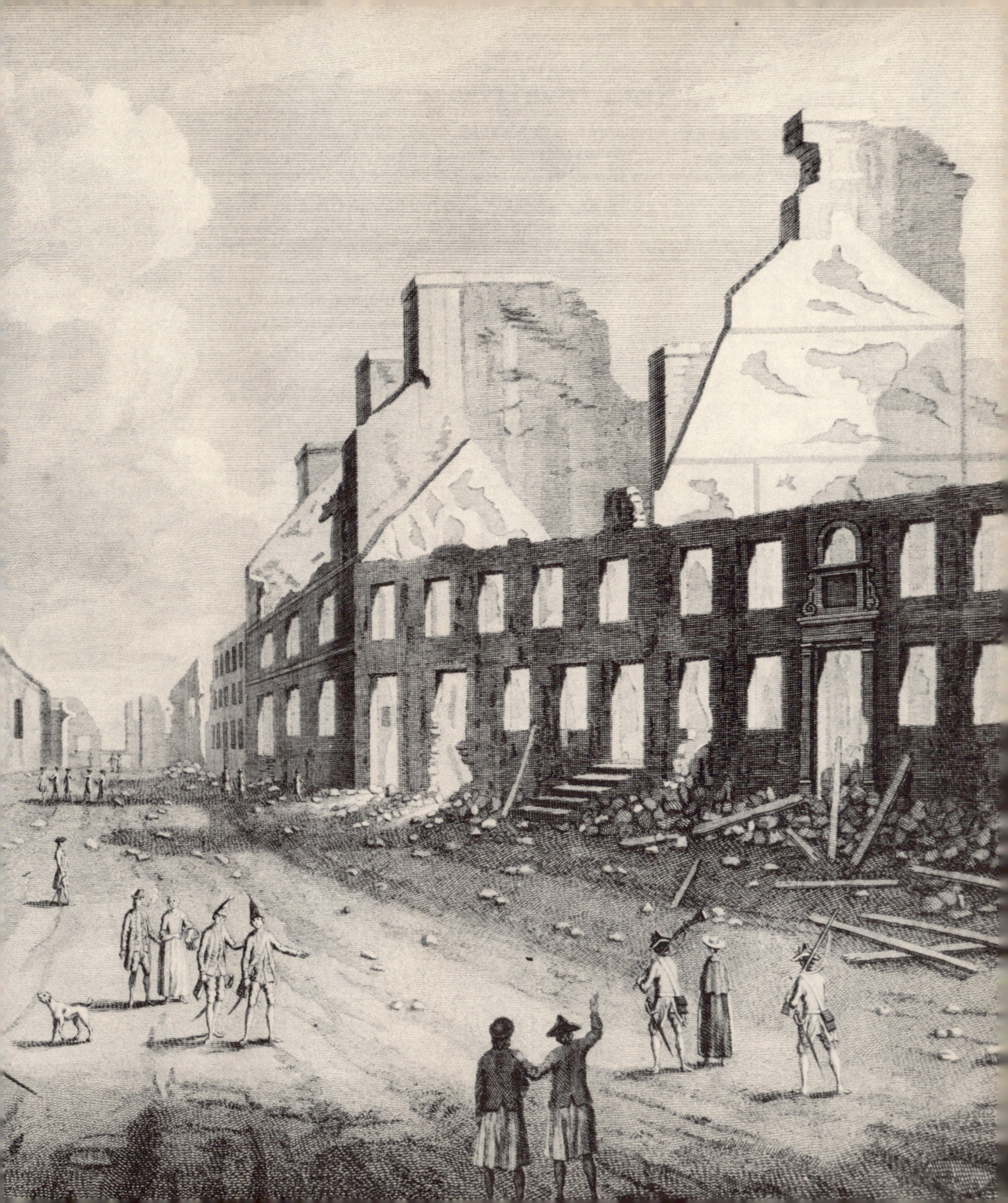

Chapter overview

On September 13, 1759, British forces led by James Wolfe defeated French forces under the Marquis de Montcalm at Quebec. One year later, Montreal surrendered to the British and 150 years of conflict between the French and English empires in America came to an end. For 150 years, the society of New France had been developing as part of the French empire. Then, all of a sudden it seemed, the colony was to be part of the British empire. This chapter will look at how the people of Quebec reacted to what historians call "the conquest."

Signposts

> September 14, 1759: A play in two acts

> FEATURE: The conquest: Did it really happen to New France?

Key word

> conquest

Introduction to the play

It is a very dramatic event to lose a war. At least, you would think so, wouldn't you? If you lived in a colony that, as a result of war, became a part of the empire of your longtime enemy, how do you think you would feel?

In 1759, there were far more French-speaking people in New France than English-speaking people. Because of the war, this large group of French suddenly found themselves under the English flag. They were worried about what the new rulers would do to them. Would the English perhaps kill them? Send them back to France or to other English colonies? Let them stay but force them to become British? Perhaps the English would leave them alone?

If you were a French-speaking person in Quebec on September 14, 1759, what questions would you ask? How would you feel? Sometimes a good way to understand the way people feel about a major event in their history is to try to put yourself in their position. Of course, not all people feel the same way about events that happen. This play will help you understand the different reactions of the people of Quebec as their colony came under British control.

The play consists of the following major characters:

Monique Robitaille [roh-bee-TĪ], age 15
Paul, her brother, age 12
Gabriel [ga-bree-EL], a 23-year-old French professional soldier
Father Frémont [fray-MOH^N], an important priest in New France
Monsieur Tremblay [trah^n-BLAY], a Quebec City merchant

As you read the play, try to imagine how you might feel in the same situation. Which of the characters might be you? If you have a chance to perform a part in the play, try to put yourself completely in the position of that person you are playing.

Notice that in the play Paul, Monique, Gabriel and the other French people speak English. In reality, of course they would speak French. The play has been written in English to help you understand it better.

September 14, 1759: A play in two acts

Act I
(Scene: September 14, 1759, 6:30 am; the morning following the defeat and surrender of Quebec at the Battle of the Plains of Abraham. Near the edge of the St. Charles River, perhaps a kilometre up from the St. Lawrence, Paul

and his sister Monique *lie huddled together, asleep under the large red coat of a British soldier. The boy awakens. He climbs out from under the coat. Cautiously looking around, he climbs onto an elevated rock and peers south toward the city.)*

Paul: *(anxiously)* Monique, wake up.... Monique, wake up! The city—it's all in smoke! Look what those English have done.

Monique: *(The girl slowly stirs. Gradually, she sits up. Still not entirely awake, she responds.)* What is it, Paul? Calm down, why are you yelling? ... Just a minute. Where are we? ... Oh, yes ... *(her voice trails off)*

Paul: *(still basically ignoring his sister)* You can see it from up here, Monique. The whole city must be on fire. *(Then, more slowly, beginning to show some terror)* You can actually see smoke rising all the way from the river to Cap Diamant ... *(there is a change in his mood from fear to anger)* ... Someday, someday these English soldiers will pay—even if I have to make them pay myself. Boy, I wish I could have been there on the Plains. I would have killed a few of those miserable redcoats.

Monique: Paul, you should not say such a thing. I'm glad you were not up there. Think of the people who did get killed, or seriously injured. You might have been one of them. Think of that woman we saw looking for her baby. I shall never forget her screams. Think of Mama and Papa. I wonder what happened to them, where they are.... Oh, I hope they are safe and we can find them. *(She slumps down on a rock, puts her head between her hands and begins to cry quietly.)*

Paul: *(a little less bravely)* Perhaps we should go back to the city and try to find them.

Monique: *(trying to become calmer)* I'm not so sure that's a good idea. How could we avoid the English soldiers?

Paul: Don't underestimate me, Monique. I'm strong and fast, and with this dagger *(which he produces)* that we got from that dead English soldier yesterday I think I can look after us. No Englishman is going to get my scalp, or yours—not without a good fight.

(At that moment there is the clink of iron from the bush. Someone is coming. Paul—dagger and all—dives for the protection of the tree under which they had been sleeping.)

Paul: Hurry up, Monique. Get down here. *(Before she can move, a rather bedraggled-looking young man appears. He is wearing the uniform of a French corporal, and has a bloodied bandage on his left upper arm)*

Soldier: *(eyeing* Monique*)* What's this? What is a young thing like you doing here? *(he notices the British coat)* And with this coat? *(Before she can respond,* Paul *jumps out from behind the tree. With dagger in hand, he seems ready to do battle.)*

Paul: That's my sister, and if you even try to lay a finger on her, I'll run you through.
Soldier: *(obviously not even to the slightest degree concerned)* Oh my, we could have used you yesterday. But, that's done now. Anyway, why would you want to kill a French soldier? We're supposed to be on the same side. But, my colours are known, what about yours? *(to* Paul*)* What are you doing with this? *(he quickly snatches the dagger from the unprepared* Paul*)* It looks unmistakably English to me. And *(to* Monique*)*— whose coat is this?
Monique: *(obviously frightened)* Please, sir, don't be offended by my brother. My name is Monique Robitaille and this is my brother Paul. We certainly mean you no harm. But, please understand that we have had a rather frightening 24 hours. Yesterday, as we were escaping the city with our parents, a bomb landed near us. We became separated from them in the rush of the crowd. Once we realized we were lost, we thought it best to head away from the river. So we came up the St. Charles River.

Soldier: And what about the coat?
Monique: Oh, as we were coming through a field just past the hospital, we came upon an English soldier. He was ... dead.
Paul: So, I figured he wouldn't need his coat again, or his dagger.
Monique: Yes, so with no blankets, we thought the coat might make good protection. Night was falling and it was beginning to get cold.
Soldier: Hmm. . . . It sounds like a good story, so I guess I'll believe you.
Paul: Have you just come from the city? What's going on there? Is it safe to go back?
Soldier: To be honest with you, when I left, my main concern was to get out alive. Dead soldiers aren't much good to the king—not to mention to themselves. I don't know if it's safe to go back. I certainly have no intention of doing so. If you *(referring to* Paul*)* could keep your mouth shut and show some manners, you might be O.K.
Monique: But, we are worried about our family. We saw our house destroyed by bombs and fire. I don't know where else to go but home—except home isn't there *(sitting down with despair on the rock)*.
Paul: Why don't you come with us? What kind of soldier would run away from the enemy anyway?
Soldier: A smart one, in this case, my friend. Once the battle is lost, a soldier serves neither God nor King by having his head cut off by the enemy. And, this head *(pointing to his head)* is probably the only one I shall ever have. So you will understand if I am not in a hurry to lose it!
Monique: Where are you going then?
Soldier: Away from Quebec.
Monique: But, why? What for? *(giving him the eye)* What are you running from ... or to?
Soldier: I'm not running away. I'm simply going to live to fight another day.
Monique: But, where will you go?
Soldier: Oh, I don't know, perhaps to Montreal. Next year, we will fight from there.
Monique: But why? Will you win next year, if you lost this year?
Soldier: To be honest with you, I don't really think so. But a soldier's job is to fight, and to live. Whether or not you win is a problem for the generals and the politicians.

Monique: So why worry now? The fighting is over, so the English won't kill you now. So, throw away your sword and come back to the city with us. You can protect us.

Soldier: *(stepping back)* By the grace of the Almighty, girl, a soldier without his head is a man of limited prospects; but a soldier without his sword doesn't deserve to be called a soldier at all.

Paul: So, what do we do? What's going to happen anyway? Since the English won the battle, does that mean we must all become English?

Soldier: That's the question on the minds of many of your fellow countrymen today, my friend. Before the battle, the lieutenant said that, if we lost, the English would show no mercy. We could all expect to be executed. That's why, once it was clear that we had lost, I decided that King Louis had no further need of me. What was the point of dying? After all, I might live to fight the English another day.

    Now that we have lost, I don't intend to become English. I've been fighting them for seven years. Why join them now? If I stick around and they don't kill me, they'll probably deport me like they did the Acadians four years ago. No, I'd rather take my chances of finding my own way to somewhere I'd like to be than leave it to King George and his ministers.

Monique: Oh, you're too pessimistic. Surely the government will send troops to save Montreal next year.

Soldier: I wouldn't count on it. They did little to save Quebec. Montreal won't likely survive, but at least next year we'll have a shot at saving it.

Voice: *(off stage)* Gabriel, you survived!

(All three turn with a start. Another soldier appears, looking much less bedraggled than the first, freshly shaved and clean.)

Gabriel: Vincent, you're a welcome sight, though you startled me. *(notices the other's appearance)* What's this, you don't look like a man who's just lost a battle, let alone a country.

Vincent: That was yesterday. Besides, didn't you hear what happened at the end? After the commander surrendered, the English allowed us to march out with arms and baggage, drums beating, flares lighted, and two cannons. We had to surrender the rest of our arms, but they promised to protect the churches, the convents and the houses. They guaranteed that, if we lay down our arms, the people can keep their property and stay in their homes—at least until the war is over and the kings and generals in Paris and London decide what to do with the country.

Paul: Then it's safe to go back.

Monique: Yes, but, we'd still like you to come with us . . . Gabriel. . . .

Gabriel: I suppose I might as well, I've nowhere else to go. Salut [sa-LU^E], Vincent.

(They then exit in the direction from which Vincent came. Vincent goes the other way.)

END OF ACT I

Act II

(Scene: September 19, 1759, 3:00 pm. The square in front of the church of Notre Dame de la Victoire [NOH-truh DAHM deu la veek-TWAHR] in Lower Town, Quebec. Civilians and soldiers of various uniforms are bustling back and forth through the square. It would seem like a typical working day in the capital city of New France if it weren't for the smouldering remnants of various buildings and houses. Two English soldiers stand before the entrance to the church which commands the square.

There is a well at the middle of the square. People regularly approach it and draw water from it. Several wooden boxes and barrels adorn the front of a store to the left of the church. Monique, Paul *and* Gabriel *enter from the opposite side of the square and proceed to the barrels.* Gabriel *carefully selects a box which places his back to a solid wall and sits down.* Monique, *too, selects a barrel and sits down.* Paul, *displaying the restlessness of a caged bull, sizes up the English soldiers with a sneer.)*

Paul: Boy, what I'd like to do to those rascals. They think they are smart. Who do they think they are standing in front of our church like that? You'd think they owned it or something.
Gabriel: Today, I'm afraid, they do. Since yesterday, it seems, God has been English.
Monique: Gabriel, please don't speak that way in front of Paul.
Gabriel: I suppose you're right. The last thing he needs is encouragement. As it is, I think it will be a miracle if we can keep him quiet long enough to stay alive and maybe even find out something about your mother and father.
   I still think it's crazy to be here. A professional soldier should know better than to return to the scene of the last battle he lost. You're bound to meet up with the enemy. Or even worse, you may see one of your own officers who may blame you for the defeat.
Monique: Oh Gabriel, don't say that. I feel so much safer because you are here.
Gabriel: Well, I'd feel much safer far away from here, but I'm not, so let's get on with it. You're sure that was where your house was, that street we passed around the corner?
Monique: *(as if in a daze)* It's a sight I'll never forget. It's like the house was never there.
Paul: Heck, the whole city's the same. It must have been some battle. I wonder what happened to all the bodies? *(He begins checking behind boxes and in nearby alleyways.)*
Monique: Your friend said that, in the terms of surrender, the English had agreed to protect us. But the English soldiers here don't seem to be paying much attention to us. And they don't seem worried that a French soldier like you is around, Gabriel.
Paul: I don't think Gabriel would frighten me either. Monique, doesn't father's friend, M. Tremblay, work around here?
Monique: Why yes, his office is over that store. Why don't you go see if he's in?
*(*Paul *goes up a nearby stairway and disappears through a door.)*

Gabriel: Who is this man?
Monique: I don't know exactly what he does, but papa has known him for years. He seems a bit strange and works at his business all the time. I have heard papa say that M. Tremblay would even work on Sunday if the church would let him.
(Paul *reappears followed by a plump, balding man with a closely-cropped moustache, who appears to be about 50 and quite in a hurry.*)
   Ah, there he is. M. Tremblay, I'm so glad to see you. Have you heard anything of our father? We became separated from him and maman yesterday and don't know where to begin looking to find them. Our house has been destroyed.
M. Tremblay: It's mid-afternoon. Wouldn't your father be in his office?
Paul: His office! It's not even there today. It was destroyed with our house.
M. Tremblay: Oh, that's too bad. It will undoubtedly hurt his business. He is such a fair man to deal with, and business is so good today.
Gabriel: Do you really think the man could be worrying about his business, when he lost his family during the battle? *(aside to* Monique*)* This guy really is a bit weird.
M. Tremblay: Well, my friend, or whoever you are, if you hope to run a profitable business, you must be prepared to take advantage of every opportunity. If your father is not working today, perhaps Father Frémont may know where he is. Let's ask these fellows *(referring to the English soldiers)* over here. . . . I say, have you seen Father Frémont? *(The soldiers do not seem to understand.)* Father Frémont . . . the priest. *(He points to his collar and folds his hands in a gesture of prayer. Finally the soldiers nod and point to the church.)*
Gabriel: I think they're saying the priest is inside.
M. Tremblay: Very well then, go and see if you can find him.
Gabriel: Who me? Yesterday, those guys were trying to kill me.
M. Tremblay: Just get on with it. *(Gingerly,* Gabriel *passes the soldiers and enters the church.)* Who is this fellow anyway? With the likes of him in uniform, it's no wonder we lost the war. At least it's over now and things can get back to normal *(rubbing his hands).* Who knows, maybe they'll improve.
Paul: *(surprised)* You almost sound like you're glad the English won.

M. Tremblay: *(seeming a bit sheepish or guilty)* Well, not exactly. But, let's face it, these wars are for politicians and soldiers. It doesn't really make much difference to us who wins, so long as they don't disrupt life or business too much.

Paul: *(highly indignant)* But, we are French and these intruders are English. What you're talking is treason.

M. Tremblay: Well hardly, my young man. I speak French, yes, and several generations ago my ancestors came from France. And I have lived all my life under the French flag. But, what good has it done me? Look how prosperous the English colonies in America are. As for me, I am Canadian. If living under an English flag opens up the trade of the British Empire to me, why should I object? Isn't a man in business to make money? What has France done for me? Send the likes of this *(referring to* Gabriel, *who is coming out of the church followed by a priest)* to protect me? And from what?

Father Frémont: Monique, Paul, how are you, my children? Gabriel has told me of your difficulty and I think I may have some good news. They say that many people from the city found shelter out by the hospital last night. So, I have sent Father Le Meur [leu-mœr] to see if there are any people from the parish. He should be back any time and may have news of your parents.

Paul: Father, M. Tremblay says it's good that the English won yesterday.

245

M. Tremblay: Well, I didn't quite put it that way. What I said was that the English colonies have prospered and perhaps, as a part of that empire, we might share in the wealth. As a matter of fact, I have been talking to certain English officers. I believe the English see us as helpless to revolt against them. They are smart businessmen and politicians; I expect they will try to win us over by treating us kindly and by leaving things much as they are.

    It's not that I am for the English. It's just that I am a realist. France has done little for us. We can benefit a great deal from having the British Empire open to us. They have won and that's the way it is. So, I say, let's not cry over spilt milk. Let's see this new situation as a new beginning for our country.

Father Frémont: Well, it seems that the English have been most ... ah ... reasonable, under the circumstances. For example, I think we should remember that our church is the soul of our society. In the terms of surrender, the English have given us the freedom to practice our religion. They've also said that we clergy may continue to do our work. This, I believe, is an important and positive sign.

Gabriel: But, with respect Father, why should the English put up with Roman Catholics here? How are you going to survive as a French priest in an English colony?

Father Frémont: Our task, Gabriel, will not be easy. But, remember, although the English have won this battle and maybe the war, we are still a French-speaking, Roman Catholic settlement. If they want peace, they will not try to change that. You have heard the view of M. Tremblay. Many of our people will think like him. Although we are French, there is no great love of France here.

    Our people have always been close to the church. They have looked to their priests for leadership. I believe we should still provide that leadership, but that it will be of a somewhat different sort. Certainly, we must avoid expressing ourselves on public issues. And, we must encourage the people to obey the English laws. But, if we do this and continue to work hard, I believe our society will remain much as it is, as I believe both God and our people would want it to be.

Gabriel: That sounds great father—again with respect, but you will be able to continue your job and also act as the agents of the English. As a French soldier *(half laughing)*, somehow I

The conquest: Did it really happen to New France?

Conquest is a pretty strong word. To be conquered, according to the dictionary, is to be completely taken over by force. Canadian historians refer to the fall of New France as "the conquest." But, were the French Canadians "conquered"? And, should we talk of a "conquest"?

Thinking back over the history of the world, when historians write about conquerors, they usually write of people like Alexander the Great, whose conquests consisted of all of the Mediterranean, the Middle East and much of Asia and Africa. Or, they talk of Napoleon, who conquered the western world from Spain to Egypt to much of Russia in 1812. But, if New France was conquered, who was its conqueror? No one British general won all the major battles. And, Prime Minister William Pitt, who masterminded the victory, never stepped foot on North American soil.

And, did the French Canadians of the day feel conquered? One noted Canadian historian, Michel Brunet [mee-SHEL broo-NAY], has written:

> French Canadians showed in general no astonishment when they learned of the Treaty of Paris. The clergy and the middle class hurried to acclaim the new king given them by the fortunes of war.
> . . .
> The people, although submitting themselves to George III, felt no obligation to serve the interest of their enemies and conquerors. Sooner or later, they thought, the "Londoners," the English, would be forced to quit the country.

From *French Canada and the Early Decades of British Rule, 1760-1791* by M. Brunet.

GETTING THE FACTS

1. In your own words, what do the words "conquest" and "conqueror" mean?

THINKING IT THROUGH

2. Based on the information presented in this section and in the play, do you think of the French Canadians as a conquered people in 1759? Give reasons for your opinion.

don't think the English will want me to continue my good work.

Father Frémont: Obviously, Gabriel, but I like to think that the clergy of New France will be doing what we have always been doing—serving God and our people. If in the future that means that we must also serve our new English rulers, then so be it! Our position will be delicate, trying to satisfy God, the English and our people. But, our leadership will be even more critical than before.

M. Tremblay: And, if I can profit from the English as well, then that's O.K., too, right Father?

Father Frémont: So long as you remember to serve God, as well as yourself, M. Tremblay.

Gabriel: I'm not so sure whom he would serve first, if there had to be a choice.

Father Frémont: Ah, here comes Father LeMeur. *(Another priest enters.)* Hello, Father. Did you have any luck? And, did you by any chance see M. and Mme Robitaille? These are their children.

LeMeur: Hello Father. Yes, many of our people made it to the hospital. I did not see Jacques Robitaille, but he had sent word that two of his children had become separated from him. He has apparently gone to take his wife and younger son to the home of his brother in Ste. Foy [sa^{n}t fwah]. He left word that he would return to the city tonight. He will come first to the church to see if there is any news.

Monique: So, papa will be coming here tonight?

LeMeur: Yes.

Monique: Oh Paul, isn't that wonderful.

M. Tremblay: Well, I must be off. Good-bye.

Others: Good-bye.

Gabriel: Well, I guess you have no further need of me. I don't feel too comfortable with all these English soldiers around.

Monique: Must you go, Gabriel? Why don't you stay and meet papa? He will want to thank you for helping us.

Paul: Besides, where will you go?

Gabriel: Thanks, Monique. But, I'm not ready to become English just yet. I think I'll head for Montreal. Maybe if we take a stand, we'll do better next year.

Paul: *(coming close to* Gabriel *and trying to be manly)* Take care of yourself, friend. And, take this *(carefully hands him the English dagger)*.

Gabriel: I will do my best, and hope to come back and tell you about it some day *(turns to leave)*. So long for now.
Others: Good-bye.
Monique: And take care of yourself.
Father Frémont: May God go with you my son. *(after Gabriel leaves)* Well, children. How about something to eat and a wash up before your father comes?
Paul: Great idea, Father. *(all exit)*

THE END

GETTING THE FACTS

3. On what date does the action of the play take place? What major event had happened the day before?

4. Explain why Monique and Paul are outside Quebec City, and separated from their parents.

5. Why did Gabriel leave Quebec City?

6. Write a short description (two or three sentences) of each of the following characters. You may want to include age, physical appearance, and character traits:

Monique   M. Tremblay
Paul   Father Frémont
Gabriel

7. Skim through the play and list four different ways that the English might treat the defeated French Canadians.

8. Below are four attitudes towards the war and the English. Each attitude is expressed by a different character in the play. In each case, identify the character in the play who would likely say these words.
   a) "Wars are for politicians and soldiers. It doesn't matter who wins as long as our life and business aren't disrupted."
   b) "I want to make these English pay for what they have done."
   c) "There is nothing to worry about. If we obey English laws, then the English will let us keep our language and religion."
   d) "A soldier's job is to fight and to live. Whether you win or not is a problem for the generals and the politicians."

USING YOUR KNOWLEDGE

9. A soldier's duty is to fight to the death for his country.
   a) Do you think that Gabriel would agree with this statement?
   b) Briefly explain Gabriel's opinion of what a soldier's duties are. Would he die for his country?
   c) Why do you think he feels this way? (You may want to turn back to chapter 10, page 221 for some ideas.)
   d) Do you agree or disagree with Gabriel's feeling about a soldier's duties? Give reasons to back up your opinion.

10. When M. Tremblay was explaining how he felt about the English takeover he said, "I am a realist."
    a) Explain briefly Mr. Tremblay's feelings about the British takeover.
    b) What seems to be most important in life to Mr. Tremblay? (What are his values?)
    c) Explain why M. Tremblay would call himself a "realist." Do you agree with his feelings? Give reasons to back up your opinion.

THINKING IT THROUGH

11. Gabriel tells Father Frémont that the priests will become the "agents of the English."
    a) In a short paragraph explain what Gabriel means.
    b) DEBATE: Father Frémont encouraged the French to obey the English because he wanted to protect the French language and religion. But he was really selling out to the English. In your debate, be sure to give reasons for your opinions.

12. In this play, you saw how differently people reacted when their country was taken over by another empire. Imagine that your community has suddenly been taken over by an outside empire. Write a letter to a friend in another city expressing how you feel about the takeover. In your letter be sure to mention your fears, what is important to you in life and how you hope the new rulers will treat you.

Conclusion

After the defeat, the people of New France were concerned about their future. The play tried to help you understand how the French felt.

There is of course another side to the story. How did the English feel about the defeat of New France? They most probably were glad to see an end to the French empire in North America. But they were also faced with many problems. How were they to deal with the large number of French people that they now ruled? The story of what England decided to do with New France is told in chapter 12. Before you look at it, though, do the following exercise.

THINKING IT THROUGH

13. Imagine you are an English government leader just after the fall of New France. You must decide how to deal with the French people who are now under British rule.

a) Make a list of all the problems that could possibly arise in a French colony that is suddenly under British rule. Consider such elements as language, religion, ways of making a living, attitude toward the English.

b) Make a list of all the possible courses of action you can take.

c) Which plan for running New France do you think would be best? Give reasons for your choice.

12 Government: How did it evolve in bicultural Quebec?

Act I
(Scene: The clubhouse in Geoff's backyard. Present are Geoff, Andy, Jill, Dave, Sara, Matthew and Patrick. Geoff kicks aside a used shingle. Either it was an extra one, or it had not been tacked down well enough. The friends all enter the clubhouse.)

Andy: *(laughing)* Some clubhouse, eh? The roof is falling down, the door has one hinge, and we've got nothing to sit on. My bottom's already cold from this dirt floor.

Patrick: So we've got a couple of things to do yet. The floor's no big problem. Mr. Murphy down the street will give us more leftover boards from the garage he tore down. I'll ask around for some pieces of carpet.

Geoff: OK, Pat. You're still in charge of getting stuff to build with. But we came here today to meet about other things. Like Dave was saying at school, we need a name for the club. I've been thinking about it, and I'd like to call us "The Adventurers."

Sara: Naw, that's dumb, Geoff. "The Tigers" is better.

Dave: Sara, you have no imagination. Just leave it to me. I will come up with a name that has class, like . . . "The Seven Musketeers"!

Matthew: *(shouting above "boos" and laughter)* Hey, I have to be home for supper in 15 minutes. All I want to know is, when's the next meeting?

Geoff: For now I guess we'll just have to call ourselves "The Club." We can always change the name later. Let's meet again tomorrow, after school. Then we can decide who is president. I'll volunteer. *(Geoff deftly ducks a baseball glove hurled by Andy. Amid shouts of "I'll volunteer" and good-natured insults back and forth, the friends exit and go their separate ways.)*

- List three decisions the group realizes they have to make.

- Here are some different ways the friends could use to pick a name for their club:
    —keep putting forward names until all members can agree on one;
    —have each member put a name on a piece of paper, place all names in Andy's baseball cap, and have someone draw one name out;
    —have a vote on a number of names suggested;
    —elect a committee of two to pick a name.
  If you were a member of the club, which way would you prefer? Explain why you think it is the best way.

1750

1763 ◄ Proclamation Act

1774 ◄ Quebec Act
1776 ◄ American Revolution

1791 ◄ Constitutional Act

1800

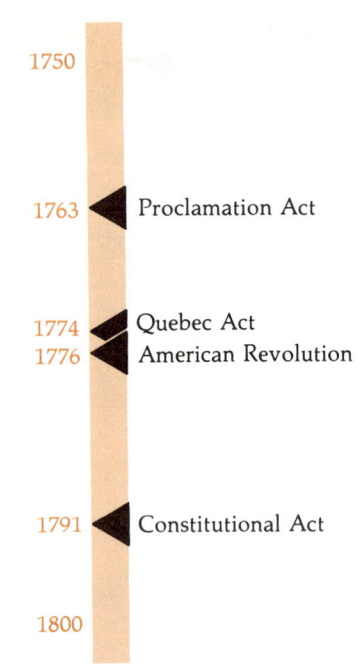

Chapter overview

A government exists to make decisions, to look after people's needs, and to keep order. The example you saw in the opening story is just about the simplest kind of government imaginable. It involves only a small group of people; all the members can meet face-to-face, and they can work things out by give-and-take. The young people have much in common. They live in the same area, speak the same language and enjoy the same activities.

This chapter, however, is about differences. The British have just taken over New France, as a result of the Seven Years' War. They bring with them their own ideas about government. Yet most of the people to be governed are of French background. In this chapter you will see how both sides, the British and the French, try to overcome differences—how they try to create a government that will work in spite of differences. In fact, you will see three different systems of government tried in less than 30 years.

Signposts

> Three scenes of 1763

> The first try: The Royal Proclamation of 1763: Anglicization

> The second try: The Quebec Act favours the French way of life

> The third try: Representative government introduced

> FEATURE: Democracy in Nova Scotia

Key words

council	constitution
elected assembly	representative government
democracy	consensus

Three scenes of 1763

In the history of every country, certain years can be seen as "turning points." The year 1763 is an example of a turning point for Canada. Big changes were underway. The future of the colonies was going to be affected. The three scenes that follow are fictional. However, they are based on real situations and will help you understand what was happening:

Scene 1: In the wilderness, south of the Great Lakes

The children were gathering firewood. The women were preparing the venison, fresh from the morning's kill. There were many mouths to feed, for bands of the Ottawa Indians had gathered in a council of war.

The great chief, Pontiac, had called the meeting. Word had reached him that their allies, the French, had been defeated. Now the British were in control of New France, in addition to their colonies stretching all the way to Florida.

The Indian way of life was in great danger. The French were only interested in the fur trade. They treated the Indian as a partner; they were not interested in his land. The British were different. Many of them had come as settlers and had changed the hunting grounds to farms.

The Ottawa warriors gathered in a vast circle to hear

Fig. 12-1 Pontiac in council.

Pontiac's message. His voice shaking with anger, he spoke:

"Why do you allow the white man to live among you? Why do you forget the ways of your ancestors? Why do you not become true Indians once more?

"You have bought guns, knives, kettles and blankets from the white men. Now you think you cannot do without them. What is worse, you have drunk the poison firewater that turns you into fools.

"Fling all these things away. Clothe yourselves in skins, and use the bows and arrows, like your ancestors did.

"As for these English, you must lift the hatchet against them!"

Based on *The Ordeal of New France* by W.J. Eccles.

Fig. 12-2 Selling Canadian homespun cloth, Montreal. How could business in Quebec be affected by the British takeover?

GETTING THE FACTS

1. In what way did Pontiac blame his own followers for the problems the Indians faced?

2. What two actions did he urge them to take in order to solve their problems?

Scene 2: On a farm on the shore of the St. Lawrence River

Pierre finished milking the cow, and lugged the wooden bucket toward the house. His father came running up from the riverbank where he had left the family boat, and raced into the house. Pierre kept the milk from spilling as he backed through the door. He heard his parents talking excitedly:

"Annette, our hopes have been dashed. The French have abandoned us to the English!"

"What do you mean, Jerome? Why do you look so alarmed?"

"Annette, I have just come from the village. Everyone tells the same news. The governments of France and Britain signed the Treaty of Paris. By this deal, New France has been turned over to the British Empire."

"Oh, how we have prayed that this would not happen. We knew that the British had won the war on the St. Lawrence. But we kept hoping that we would get our country back. What do they want with us?"

"I do not know, Annette. But I fear that our lives will never be the same. Perhaps they will not drive us out, as they did the Acadians. For years, though, we have been told that the British see our way of life as inferior. They see our customs as backward. They dislike our Roman Catholic religion. In their eyes, our laws are strange."

"I understand what you are telling me, Jerome. We have fallen under the power of the English. They will try to force us to speak their language, to accept their laws, even to think and act as they do."

"Perhaps the English will not be so terrible as our fears have led us to believe."

GETTING THE FACTS

3. Why was the Treaty of Paris a shock to the French in Quebec?

4. What fears did the French colonists have about the British takeover in 1763?

Scene 3: The office of the British governor, James Murray

James Murray is working in his headquarters in the town of Quebec. As a soldier, Murray took part in the British capture of Quebec. Now he is the governor, responsible for running the affairs of the colony.

The table in front of him is covered with maps and official papers. Murray and the members of his council have been working hard to keep things working smoothly in Quebec (called New France before the conquest).

Three years have passed since the British army and navy took over New France. During those three years, the army was responsible for running the colony. Then, in 1763, the Treaty of Paris transferred New France from the French to the British Empire. Now the time was near when a non-military government would be set up.

What changes were likely? What would stay the same? Murray is waiting for his instructions to arrive from England. The British have as many as four basic plans from which to choose. If Murray had made a chart of these choices, it might have looked something like this:

Fig. 12-3 Governor Murray

Fig. 12-4 Some possible plans for governing New France.

CHOICE	PURPOSE	POSSIBLE ADVANTAGES	POSSIBLE DRAWBACKS
Expulsion	Remove all French settlers from Quebec.		
Anglicization	Change the way of life of the French so they would think, talk and act like English people		
"French" system	Keep Quebec much as it had been under French control. Hope the French would accept British rule.		
Separation	Divide Quebec into separate parts—one for French (already present), one for English (willing to move in.)		

Murray is not alone in wondering what to expect. French Canadians—clergy, seigneurs, habitants, fur traders—have been waiting anxiously since the British takeover in 1760. English traders and other business people have been moving in from the English colonies to the south. But, the Indians to the west, such as the Ottawas, Senecas, and Shawnees, have stopped waiting. From Niagara through Indian territory to Michilimackinac [mih-KIH-lih-MA-kih-nak], they have seen the English arriving. Led by Chief Pontiac, they have launched a wave of attacks in which hundreds have been killed.

The council was the group of advisers to the governor. At this time, they included army officers and some English-speaking citizens appointed by Murray.

USING YOUR KNOWLEDGE

5. Copy the chart (Fig. 12-4) into your notebook. Complete the chart by writing in all the possible advantages and drawbacks you can think of.

THINKING IT THROUGH

6. Before you read on to discover which plan the British chose, make your own choice. Study the information on your chart and decide which plan you feel is best. (Your opinion may change after you complete this chapter.) Be sure to give reasons to support your choice.

The first try: The Royal Proclamation of 1763: Anglicization

What would the British decide? The answer came with the Royal Proclamation of 1763. The British had chosen to try Anglicization. The colony of Quebec was to be given an English lifestyle. Governor Murray was ordered to begin the changeover to English laws, language, schools, churches—and government. Quebec was to be like Britain's other colonies in North America.

The diagrams in Fig. 12-5 show the form of government before and after the British took over.

Another important change made by the Royal Proclamation was to the boundary. The western limit of Quebec was set near the Ottawa River. Furthermore, a Proclamation Line was to mark the western limit of all the other British colonies. English settlers were forbidden to claim land beyond the line,

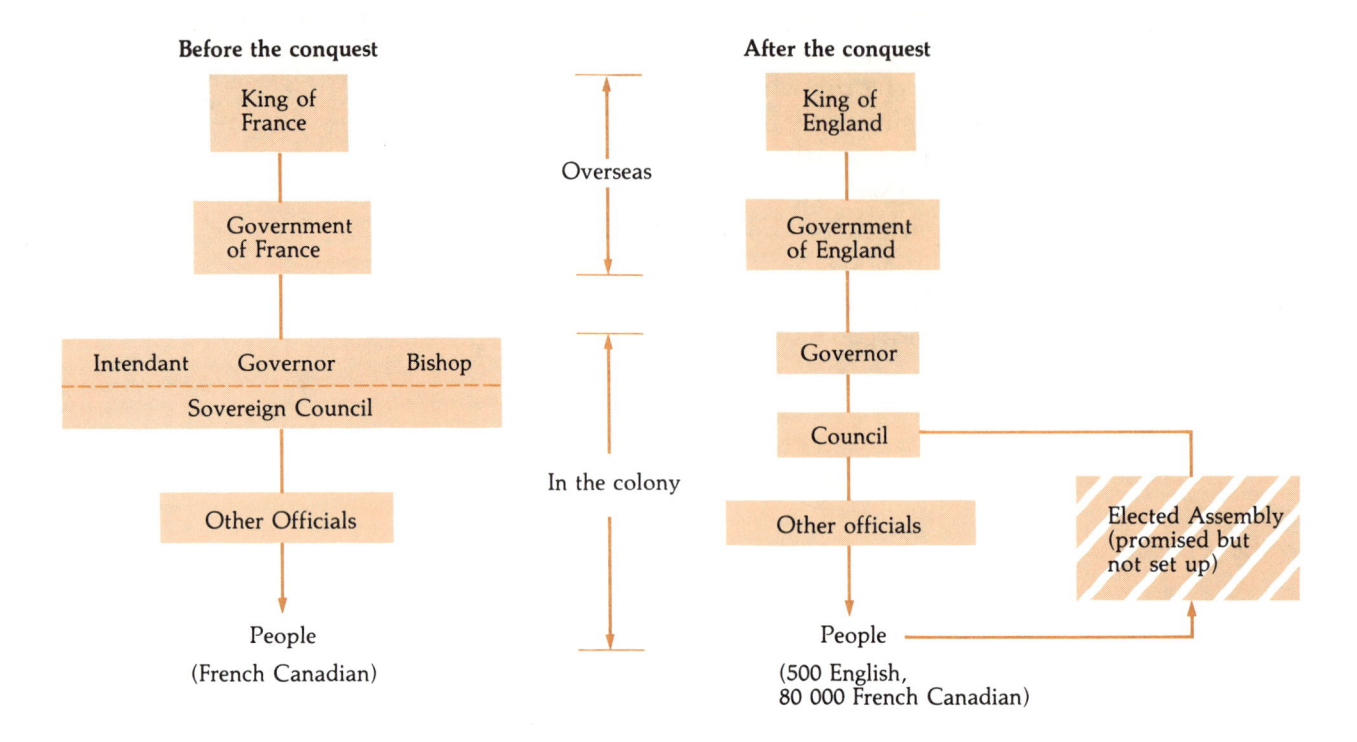

Fig. 12-5 Government in bicultural Quebec before and after the conquest.

and fur traders had to have licenses before going into Indian territory. The British hoped that a clear new boundary would keep Europeans and native peoples apart. Perhaps it would prevent a renewal of the bitter fighting of the past summer.

USING YOUR KNOWLEDGE

7. Examine Fig. 12-5 closely.
   a) State at least two differences in the government after the British took over.
   b) State at least two things that remained the same.

8. In which system did the governor seem to have more power?

9. English residents would see an elected assembly as a big improvement in the government. Why? French residents would probably disagree. Why?

10. Do you think that the native peoples were happy with the Proclamation Line? Give reasons for your answer.

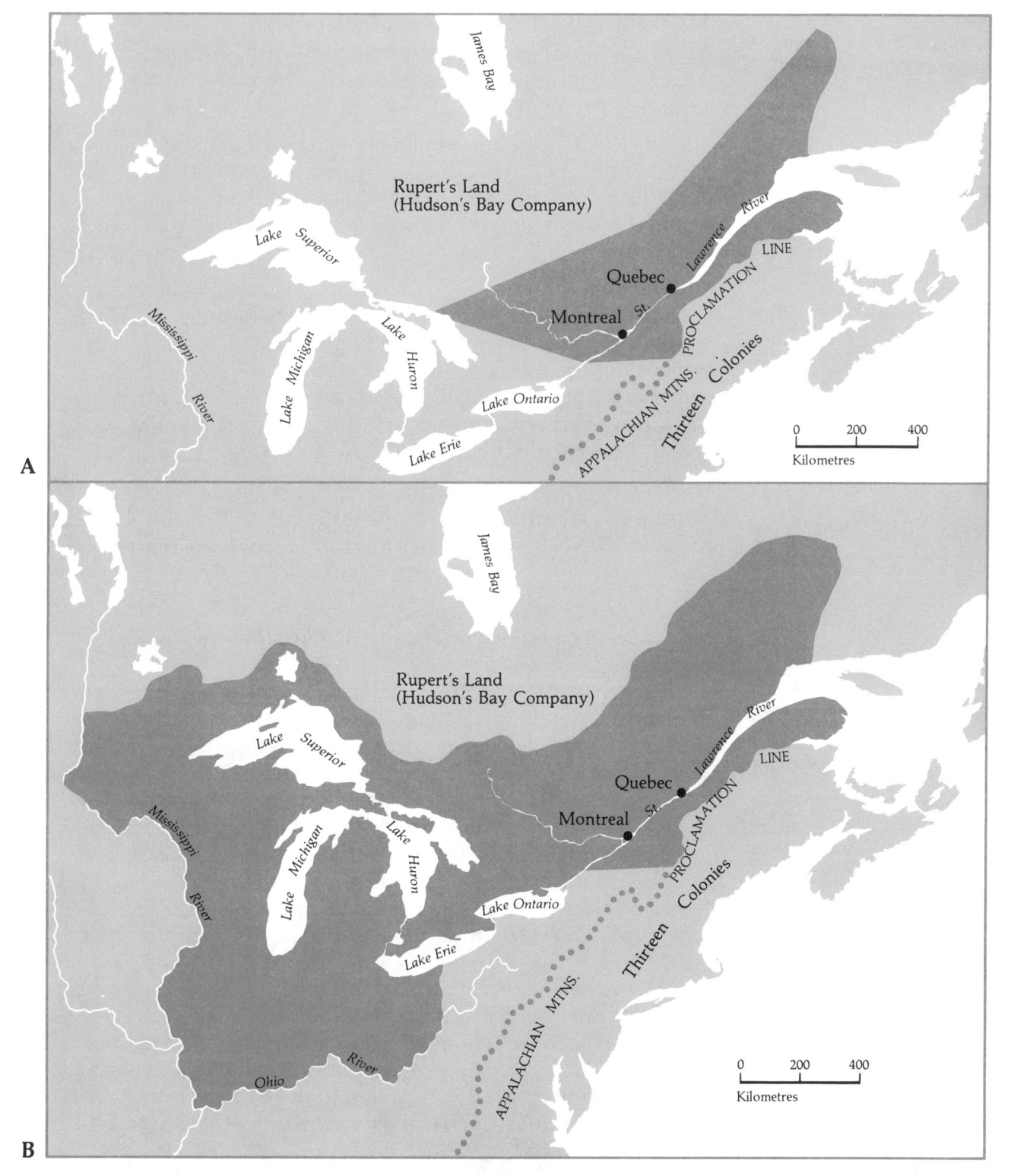

Fig. 12-6 Boundaries of Quebec — A. Royal Proclamation, 1763. B. Quebec Act, 1774.

> A dilemma is a situation where a person faces tough choices.

> Fewer than 500 English-speaking people lived in Quebec so far (compared to about 70 000 French-speaking people.)

The dilemma of Governor James Murray

About Governor Murray, one historian wrote, "Probably no British governor has ever been thrust into a more impossible position." Murray was in a tight spot for several reasons:

(1) The Royal Proclamation was not clear about many things. For example, it said that the governor *could* arrange for an elected assembly *when the colony was ready for it*. Just when this time would come was anybody's guess, but Murray was stuck with a heavy responsibility.

(2) The English in the colony were causing him trouble from the beginning. They were a small minority, but they spoke their minds. Other than the army, the English were mainly traders and business people. They had come up from New England or one of the other Thirteen Colonies, where an elected assembly was always part of the government. An elected assembly was one of "the rights of Englishmen," they insisted.

(3) The army was no longer under his control. He did not get along very well with the new officer in charge. Trouble between the soldiers and other English added to the tension in the colony.

(4) The French were nervous. It was strange to be ruled by foreigners. The French feared the changes that the English might bring.

French Catholic Church leaders were uneasy. Catholics in England did not have the same rights as other people; perhaps the same would be true here. Freedom of religion was still allowed, but the laws favoured the English Protestant churches.

The seigneurs, the other leading group, were worried too. English laws could mean the end of the seigneurial system.

Under English law, Roman Catholics could not be elected to a place in government. Therefore, all the French in Quebec feared an elected assembly. It could be used by the English to pass pro-English laws and to squeeze taxes from French Canadians.

Murray struggled along with his impossible job. He did his best to assure the French that they would get a fair deal. As for the English, some of whom he called "Fanaticks," he had little patience. The English, in turn, saw the governor as a roadblock. They complained bitterly about him to the British government. Eventually, in 1766, the British government decided to replace Murray, Quebec's first British governor.

During his term as governor, Murray had only begun to introduce an English system of law. Much of the French law, as well as the seigneurial system, remained. The Catholic church had been permitted to appoint a bishop. No elected assembly had been granted. In other words, very little start had been made on the Anglicization of the French Canadians.

GETTING THE FACTS

11. Explain each of the following:
a) Anglicization;
b) the basic idea behind the Royal Proclamation;
c) elected assembly;
d) why French Canadians were nervous;
e) why James Murray left the job of governor.

THINKING IT THROUGH

12. Write the following statements in your notebook. After each one that is a statement of FACT, print "F." After each one that is a VALUE statement, print "V":
a) The Royal Proclamation was the best of the choices open to the British when they began governing Quebec.
b) In 1763, there were far more French than English in Canada.
c) The French in Quebec were worried that the seigneurial system might disappear.
d) James Murray took his job as governor very seriously.
e) James Murray was a very successful governor.

13. Does the quotation—"Probably no British governor has ever been thrust into a more impossible position"—express a fact or a value judgement? If it is a value statement, do you think it is a valid one? Give reasons for your answer.

14. Reread the dilemma of Governor Murray carefully. Then, decide how well you think Murray handled this "impossible position" by rating him on a scale of 1 to 10 (10 is best). Give reasons for your rating.

Fig. 12-7 Guy Carleton

Remember the choices shown on page 258.

The second try: The Quebec Act favours the French way of life

A new man took over. His name was Sir Guy Carleton. Because of the criticisms of Murray, Carleton arrived from England thinking that Murray had been doing a poor job. The English residents welcomed the new governor. When he fired some of the people Murray had appointed to the council, they were hopeful. The English believed that Carleton was going to give them what they wanted.

They were soon disappointed. It was only a matter of time before Carleton's point of view was the same as Murray's. Once he was on the job, Carleton decided: My job is to make sure that Quebec is a colony loyal to Britain.

If Quebec was to be loyal, the majority of its people would have to be satisfied with the government. Carleton liked the French and their way of life. He admired the way the seigneurs and clergy seemed to keep order among the people. He found the English hard to get along with. They would be even more troublesome, no doubt, if they got the elected assembly they were demanding.

An assembly would be a step toward **democracy**. It would give the people more of a say in the running of government. The power and the control of the governor and council would be reduced.

This would be a mistake, Carleton believed. He had his eye on events in the Thirteen Colonies. Their assemblies had become meeting-places for anti-British leaders. In some cities, such as Boston, riots had already broken out—and more violence was expected. Quebec must be protected against such trouble.

Therefore, Carleton went to work to replace the Royal Proclamation. Partly through his efforts, a new act was passed in 1774—the Quebec Act. It was clearly different from the choices Britain had thought of for governing Quebec. The goal was to win the loyalty of the French—and especially their leaders, the clergy and the seigneurs.

By the Quebec Act, the idea of an elected assembly was put aside. The appointed council was increased in numbers, and the French were included. Roman Catholics were now allowed to be councillors, civil servants, judges and so on. Much of the law was to remain French. The seigneurial system was secure.

Anglicization, the basic idea behind the Royal Proclamation, seemed to be dead.

The Quebec Act increased the size of the colony considerably. On the surface, this was a move to extend law and order over the region between the Ohio and Mississippi Rivers. The fur trade was expanding, and relations with the Indian peoples was becoming more complicated. On the other hand, some of the Thirteen Colonies were claiming parts of the Indian territory. The enlarged Quebec was a kind of barrier in the way of their westward expansion.

See chapter 13 for the influence of the Quebec Act on the American Revolution.

GETTING THE FACTS

15. Governor Carleton was convinced that an elected assembly would be a mistake. Explain his viewpoint.

USING YOUR KNOWLEDGE

16. Make a chart that will help you compare and contrast the Proclamation of 1763 and the Quebec Act. Include headings for government, laws, religion, language, boundaries.

17. For each of the following people, write one sentence that expresses the way he or she probably felt about the Quebec Act: Guy Carleton, James Murray, a woman living in New France at the time.

18. Imagine that your task is to write a newspaper story about the Quebec Act.
   a) Make up a headline that suggests the basic idea behind the Act.
   b) Write an opening paragraph of two or three sentences.

19. Imagine that James Murray and Guy Carleton met one year after the Quebec Act was passed. Create a conversation that the two might have had.

The third try: Representative government introduced

The purpose of the Quebec Act was clear. It laid out a **constitution** for a colony expected to be forever French in population. That is, unless something very unexpected happened.

Then the unexpected did happen. A startling chain of events unfolded during 1774-84. In Britain's Thirteen Colonies, anti-British protests became the American Revolution. When the revolution was a success, the United States was formed. On the losing British side were many people from the Thirteen Colonies who had stayed loyal to Britain. Thousands of these Loyalists moved out. Many chose to seek new homes in the nearest British colony—Quebec.

Quebec had so recently been made a more comfortable place for the French. Now it had, almost overnight, a new population of English settlers. They had shown their loyalty to Britain. They hoped, in return, to enjoy the rights of British subjects. These rights included the English language, laws, customs—and system of government.

Fig. 12-8 The Constitutional Act, 1791.

..... Indefinite boundary
—— Definite boundary

Democracy in Nova Scotia

In October 1758, the first elected assembly in Canada met in Halifax. Fewer than ten years had passed since Halifax had been founded, in 1749, as the capital of Nova Scotia. Yet the assembly was overdue. Included in the instructions to the first governor was a paragraph saying: "And we do hereby give and grant unto you power to summon and call General Assemblies according to the usage of the rest of our colonies and plantations in America."

The British government believed an assembly in Nova Scotia was unavoidable. Most of the settlers were coming in from other British colonies to the south. An assembly was necessary to the kind of self-government they had been used to.

Governor Lawrence was an army man. He wanted to keep as much control as possible over the government. This was especially true after the Seven Years' War began in 1756.

However, the British government put pressure on the governor. He was told that English settlers would insist on a certain amount of democracy. The assembly was the least they would expect.

So Governor Lawrence finally went ahead and called the first elected assembly in 1758. He took comfort from the fact that the assembly had little power. Lawrence believed that he could keep most of the power of government in the hands of the governor and his appointed council.

Members of the assembly saw things differently. They believed that the elected assembly was another step toward more and more government by the people.

Suppose large numbers of English-speaking people moved into Quebec and into what is now New Brunswick? Could more elected assemblies be far behind?

Fig. 12-9 View of Halifax, Nova Scotia, from the Red Mill, Dartmouth.

What was to be done? The answer: Divide Quebec into two colonies and introduce **representative government** West of the Ottawa River, where the Loyalists were settling, was to be Upper Canada (Ontario today). It would be an English-style colony, complete with an assembly elected by qualified voters.

East of the Ottawa River was Lower Canada (Quebec today). Life would continue much as it had under the Quebec Act. One big difference: Like Upper Canada, Lower Canada would have an elected assembly. Representative government had first been granted in Nova Scotia in 1758. New Brunswick had had representative government ever since the creation of the colony in 1784. Now, by the Constitutional Act of 1791, it had become an accepted part of government in the British North American colonies.

In each of the new colonies—Upper Canada and Lower Canada—government was set up in the same way. It was a representative form of government (see Fig. 12-10).

A British political leader might have stated the following hopes for the Constitutional Act:

> We have given to Upper and Lower Canada a constitution as much as possible like the one in Britain.
>
> The elected assembly provides the people with a voice

British Government —makes the "big" decisions, appoints the Governor and gives him jobs to carry out

appoints ↓

Governor in the Colony —tries to carry out British Government's wishes; often depends a lot on his appointed Councils

appoints ↙   appoints ↘

Legislative Council   work together   Executive Council
—proposes laws   —advises Governor
—can block suggestions from the Assembly

—The Councils consist of a handful of leading citizens

↑

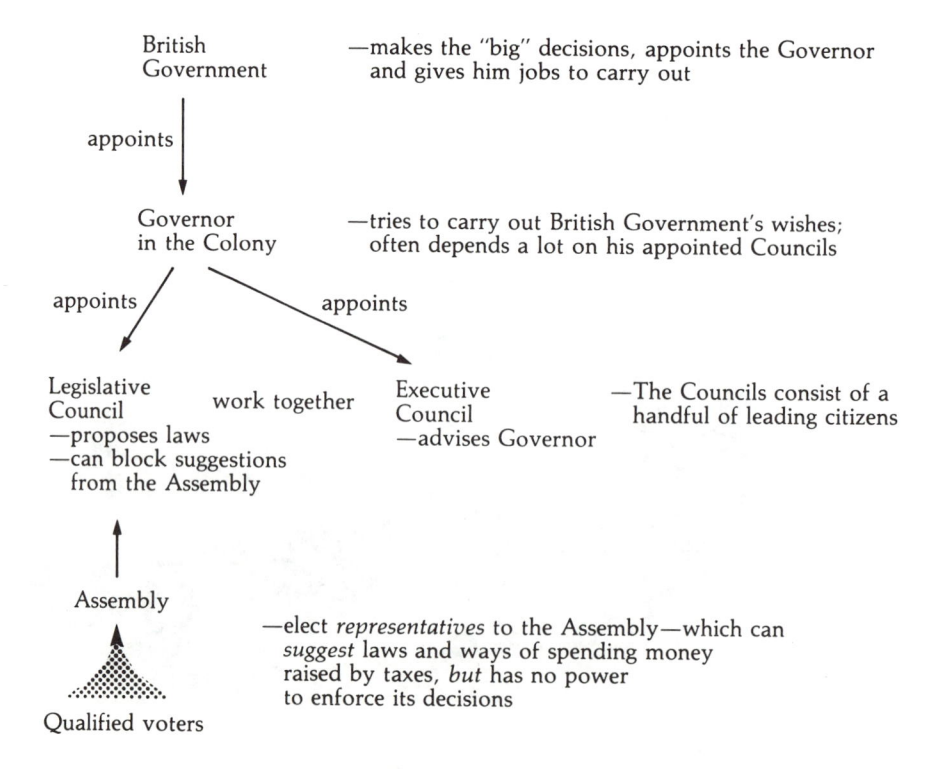

Assembly

Qualified voters —elect *representatives* to the Assembly—which can *suggest* laws and ways of spending money raised by taxes, *but* has no power to enforce its decisions

Fig. 12-10 System of government in Upper and Lower Canada, 1791.

Fig. 12-11 The first Parliament of Lower Canada, 1792.

in government. Through their representatives, people can make their wishes known to the officials in charge.

Yet we have prevented the rowdy kind of democracy that has been let loose in the United States. In the Canadas, the councils hold the real power.

The councils are appointed from among the successful and respected persons in the colonies—lawyers, owners of large businesses and the like. They will be 'true blue' in their love for the British way of life. The governors will find them trusting allies.

Upper Canada will become thoroughly British, and therefore be very well off. Naturally the French in Lower Canada will be impressed. I expect they will soon give up their French ways. They will want to become as British as possible as soon as possible.

Based on a summary of William Pitt's arguments in *The Constitution of Canada, 1534-1937* by W.P.M. Kennedy.

GETTING THE FACTS

20. In your own words, define "constitution."

21. What was the unexpected event that made the Quebec Act no longer suitable as a constitution?

USING YOUR KNOWLEDGE

22. Reread the statement by "a British political leader."
    a) What attitudes does it reveal?
    b) What might you have thought of the statement if you had been a:
—Loyalist in Upper Canada;
—seigneur in Lower Canada;
—pioneer farmer who moved from the United States to Upper Canada in the 1790s.

THINKING IT THROUGH

23. Do you agree with the "British leader" that the Constitutional Act was a good solution to the problem of keeping peace in Quebec? Give reasons to back up your opinion.

Conclusion

In this chapter you have seen a very complicated period in Canadian history. In less than 30 years, three tries were made at giving Quebec a workable government. You have seen how difficult it can be to make a government fit a situation and suit the people involved.

Sometimes you may have thought: This has nothing to do with me. Yet look at the topics with which the changes in government were concerned: How can English-speaking and French-speaking people find ways to get along in the same country? How can the native peoples deal with pressures on their lifestyle from quite different cultures? How can Canada and the United States share, as neighbours, the North American continent? These questions are important ones in Canada today!

As for the governments themselves, each had basic characteristics found in all governments—including the ones we have today. And the changes between 1763 and 1791 were like stepping-stones toward modern Canadian government.

Perhaps we can sharpen our understanding of facts about government by returning to the situation which began the chapter. Reread Act I, then continue with the story that follows:

Act II

(Scene: We return to the story of "The Club" by looking in on a Saturday morning meeting. From the conversation, we learn that Geoff *had been chosen president by* **consensus***; that is, all the friends agreed. The choice had*

been easy enough. Geoff *had volunteered, and although some protested jokingly, nobody else really wanted the job.*

Another problem has come up, however. Matthew *complains that the clubhouse is already a mess. He accuses* Andy *of always leaving junk lying around.)*

Matthew: Why do you throw your chocolate bar wrappers and apple cores on the floor, Andy? Because you're a slob, eh?

Andy: Watch it, Matthew. It's no big deal to have a little trash in a kids' clubhouse. Why don't you complain about Sara's dumb dog? Now there's a problem. It's always barking and jumping around.

David: *(doing his imitation of a politician)* Friends, Romans, countrymen, what we need around here are some *rules*!

Jill: Very funny, David, but what's with this countrymen stuff? It's countrypersons.

Patrick: Jill, can you stop punching Dave for a minute? He's right, you know. I thought the seven of us were the only ones allowed in the clubhouse. So how come you brought those Martians here yesterday, eh Dave?

(Everyone starts talking at once. After a minute or so of pleading and threatening, Geoff *gets things quiet again. He starts to make a statement, when* Patrick *interrupts him.)*

Patrick: I am the clubhouse manager. We are meeting in the clubhouse. I want to be in charge right now, if we are going to make up a list of rules.

Geoff: It's OK by me, Pat. Just remember that I'm still the president.

THINKING IT THROUGH

24. Make a list of at least four rules you think the kids probably agreed upon.

25. Who do you think stands out as the real leader—Geoff or Patrick? Why? Do you foresee any problems that may arise in the future?

Act III
(Scene: The other club members arrive to find Dave *and* Geoff *in the clubhouse. The two fall silent as the others find places to sit or stand.)*

Andy: So what are you two guys up to?

Geoff: Dave wants us to let the Martians join "The Club." Let's put it this way. His mom says we have to, and she's the spokesperson for our parents.

Patrick: Whose club is this anyway? It's ours, not our parents', right?

Jill: It's our club, but we had to have our parents' permission to start it. We agreed at the beginning that our parents would make any big decisions. Letting the Martians in is a big decision.

Patrick: Look at the list of rules we made up. You voted for them, just like everyone else, Jill. Rule #4 says, "No outsiders allowed."

Sara: Maybe we didn't realize it, but we did not have the right to make Rule #4. If the parents say so, we must let the Martians join.

Andy: Boy, we'll sure have to make a lot of changes.

Jill: But it's only fair. Many Martians have moved into our neighbourhood. We can't pretend they don't exist.

GETTING THE FACTS

26. "The Club" has developed a kind of government. For each of the following characteristics, give at least one example:
a) meeting people's needs;
b) giving leadership;
c) making decisions;
d) making rules;
e) reaching a consensus;
f) voting.

THINKING IT THROUGH

27. When the Martians join "The Club," what changes may have to be made in the way it is run?

28. Suppose that the number of club members increased to 50 and included two or more different groups. The clubhouse would be too small, of course. What further new problems might there be in running the club? (List them in order of importance.) How might each of these problems be handled?

THE INVESTIGATIVE REPORTER

29. Interview a member of some level of government (student council, school board, municipal [myoo-NIH-sih-pul] or city government, a member of the provincial government, a member of parliament [PAHR-luh-mehnt]). Make up a list of questions that you would ask the member. Tell about the answers you received.

13 The American Revolution

The Boston Massacre, March 5, 1770

On the walk, in front of the Boston Customs House, British Private Hugh White walked back and forth. He was relaxed. His captain, Thomas Preston, was having a pleasant late dinner nearby.

Then two men approached—Edward Garrick and Bartholomew Borader. They began to tease sentry White. White got angry and swung his musket, hitting Garrick on the side of the head. A crowd soon began to assemble. Insults were yelled. "Lousy rascal," "Lobster!" (British soldiers were sometimes called "Lobsterbacks" because of their red uniforms.) Then snowballs and chunks of ice were thrown at White. White cried for help but nobody opened the door of the Customs House. A bell began to ring somewhere nearby and more men joined the mob. Crispus Attucks, an ex-slave, got up from his dinner and grabbed a wooden club as he headed for the Customs House. White was getting more and more desperate as it seemed his life was in danger.

Captain Preston gathered seven soldiers together and broke through the crowd to join White. Preston ordered the crowd to disperse. The mob continued to yell insults and dared the soldiers to shoot. One Private Hugh Montgomery was knocked down by a club-swinging townsman. Getting back to his feet he picked up his musket and fired on the crowd. As the crowd began to move backwards, the other soldiers raised their guns and began firing. Within seconds, five members of the crowd were dead or dying. Crispus Attucks was one of the dead.

Three weeks later, silversmith Paul Revere [ruh-VEER] completed an engraving of this incident and called it the Boston Massacre. The engraving was copied and sent throughout the Thirteen Colonies.

The Boston Massacre was one of the first violent clashes between the British and the colonists. The engraving and the written account present the massacre from two different viewpoints. The Paul Revere engraving is often described as a piece of propaganda [proh-puh-GAN-duh]. It was designed to stir up the colonists' anger toward the British.

Based on *In the Minds and Hearts of the People* by Lillian B. Millar.

- Who seems to be responsible for the massacre in the story? In the engraving?

- Do you think the engraving would succeed in its aim? Explain your answer.

- What effect do you think the engraving would have had on the whole American Revolution?

1750	
1760	
1770	
1775	Shots fired at Lexington
1776	Declaration of Independence
1781	British surrender at Yorktown
1783	Treaty of Paris
1790	
1800	

Chapter overview

By 1763, the collision between the French and English empires in North America had ended; Britain had defeated France in the Seven Years' War. As a result, Britain now had claim to all the North American colonies.

Britain's troubles in North America were not over, however. A new collision was taking shape, not between empires but between an empire and its colonies. No longer threatened by the French, the settlers in the Thirteen Colonies now began to challenge some of Britain's authority over them. Britain, on the other hand, decided to tighten up its authority. It had discovered that the colonies were expensive to maintain. Therefore, to make more money from its empire, Britain started to increase taxes in the colonies.

The colonists did not like the increase in taxes, and also disagreed with Britain about other things. These disagreements led to conflict that increased over the years. Finally in 1776, a full-scale war between the British Empire and the Thirteen Colonies developed. This war and its results brought some lasting changes to the northern colonies that would later become Canada.

Signposts

> Tension between Britain and the Thirteen Colonies: What were they arguing about?

> Tension grows ... and explodes

> What was the difference between the Patriots and the Loyalists?

> FEATURE: The midnight ride of Paul Revere

> FEATURE: What happened when the Continental Army invaded Quebec in 1775?

> The revolution ends: Patriot victory and the Treaty of Paris

Key words

| propaganda | rebels | Patriots |
| taxation | revolution | Proclamation Line |

Tension between Britain and the Thirteen Colonies: What were they arguing about?

Tension between Britain and the Thirteen Colonies did not appear suddenly. Trouble began with the founding of the colonies in the 17th century and gradually reached a peak with the American Revolution. The colonies did not band together against Britain right from the start. Instead, unity among them grew as the tension with Britain grew.

Why did the tension develop? There were many complex reasons, but we can get a simple picture of the situation by looking at the following arguments. As you read them, try to decide which argument is most convincing. Are any of the arguments serious enough to cause a revolution?

Argument 1   Trade regulations: The Navigation Acts

Thirteen Colonies:

> The Navigation Acts of 1660 and 1663 make three main points:
> (1) Only English or colonial ships can carry goods to the Thirteen Colonies.
> (2) Most colonial products are to be shipped to England.
> (3) Colonies cannot import products from Europe unless they are shipped to England first.
> What right does the British government have to tell us that we can trade with England only, and not with other countries? We are free people and we should be allowed to trade with whomever we like.

Britain:

> You must not forget that the colonies were founded by Britain and belong to Britain. They are not independent states. Their purpose is to provide raw materials for the industries of England and a market for British goods. In other words, the colonies are to help build up Britain's economy, not the economies of other countries.

Fig. 13-1 George III was the king of England during the British Empire's conflict with the Thirteen Colonies.

Argument 2   Taxation

Thirteen Colonies:

> The power to tax should belong to our own assemblies and not to the British **parliament**. If we cannot have any representatives in the English parliament, and therefore no say in British government, why should we pay taxes to support Britain?

Britain:

> We find it expensive to maintain the colonies. At the very least, the colonies should pay for their own protection. We have sent 6000 soldiers to make you feel safe from enemies. We have every right to tax you to pay for these troops. Because North America is so far away from England, it is not possible to have colonial representatives in the British parliament. You must remember that the members of parliament represent *all* British subjects and always have the interests of the colonies in mind.

Argument 3   Treatment of the French

Thirteen Colonies:

> In 1745, we raised an army and successfully captured Louisbourg. You gave the fort back to the French in 1748. In 1758, we had to attack it again, along with British troops. French raids on New England killed many colonists. New France has been conquered, but is being treated better than we are. The French still have control of much of the interior of North America even though they have a population of only about 80 000. This is unfair.

Britain:

> Quebec is unique. It has a population of about 80 000 French citizens who have become part of the British Empire. They must be treated carefully. They must be encouraged to feel loyal to a new king. In time, they will be absorbed into the English population. But, for the time being, they must be granted special privileges, and so we allow the Roman Catholic church and the seigneurial system to remain. Also, if we cut off the fur trade, we would destroy the economy of Quebec. Because Quebec now belongs to us, we would be damaging our own economy as well.

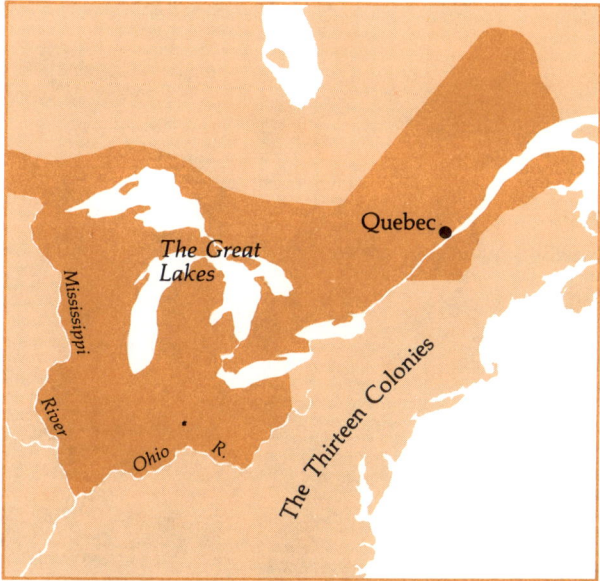

Fig. 13-2 Quebec before and after 1774.

Argument 4 Ohio Valley Territory

Thirteen Colonies:

> Our population is expanding and we need more room. Many of us fought in the last war in order to get more land from New France. In 1763, the British government put down a Proclamation Line across the Appalachians and we are not allowed to settle west of the line. Some of our colonial governments were given this land in their charter, so the land is already ours.

Britain:

> In order to win peace on the frontier, we have agreed to protect the Indian land rights in the Ohio Territory. That was our agreement with Pontiac in 1763. There is still plenty of room in the Thirteen Colonies. If people want to settle west of the Appalachians, they will have to arrange it peacefully by making a treaty with the Indians. Because we don't want another Indian war, all settlers must move back east. Also, much of the fur trade takes place west of the Appalachians. This is one of the few activities that makes money for the British government. If people settle there, the fur-bearing animals will be driven away.

After the Seven Years' War, the Indians in the Ohio Valley feared that Britain would take over their land. They therefore attacked English settlers on the frontier in 1753. Pontiac eventually surrendered and a peace treaty was drawn up.

GETTING THE FACTS

1. To summarize the main arguments between the British and the colonists, complete the following chart:

ARGUMENT	BRITISH VIEWPOINT	COLONIES' VIEWPOINT

THINKING IT THROUGH

2. Which argument do you think was most serious and would be an important step toward revolution? Give reasons for your opinion.

3. Reread the arguments presented by each side carefully. In your opinion, which side had the stronger case: the rebels in the colonies or the government of England? Be sure to use facts to back up your opinion.

INVESTIGATIVE REPORTER

4. Consult your school or local library for information about the Indian chief Pontiac, then answer the following questions:
   a) Who was he?
   b) What role did he play in the conflict between the Indians and the British colonists?
   c) How did his actions affect future relations between the colonists and the Indians?

Make sure that your answers give a clear and complete picture of Pontiac and the relations between the colonists and the Indians.

Tension grows . . . and explodes

In the last section, you learned that Britain and the Thirteen Colonies disagreed over many issues. By 1763, there was much tension between the two parties. In the years that followed, both sides did things that increased the conflict. Britain passed a number of Acts that upset the colonists. The colonists, in turn, reacted with growing anger. The tension between Britain and the Thirteen Colonies finally exploded into scenes of violence, and then revolution.

British actions

Here are some of the Acts passed by the British after 1763 that angered the colonies:

Stamp Act, 1765

All legal documents and papers in the colonies had to carry a stamp; the cost varied according to the importance of the document. The money raised went to cover the cost of British troops in North America.

Townshend Acts, 1767

Small taxes were placed on glass, tea, silk, paper, paint and lead. The money was used to pay the expenses of running the colonies.

The Tea Act, 1773

The East India Company had a surplus of tea. To help out the company, Britain allowed it to sell the tea directly to North Americans. (Normally, the tea would go to England first, as provided in the Navigation Acts.) Once the tea arrived at port, a tax was applied.

The Coercive Acts, 1774

Nicknamed the Intolerable Acts by the colonists, these Acts affected the colonies in many ways. One Act closed the port of Boston to shipping. In another Act, military rule replaced the Massachusetts government. The Acts were designed to force the colonists to obey British laws.

The Quebec Act, 1774

To secure the loyalty of the French in Quebec, Britain granted them freedom to practice their Catholic faith. The border of Quebec was also extended to include the Ohio Territory, a vast tract of land on the western side of the Appalachians to the Mississippi River.

Fig. 13-3 Replica of the original stamp used on insurance policies. Why is this a good example of a royal stamp?

Fig. 13-4 The Boston Tea Party. During the night of December 16, 1773, angry colonials disguised as Indians boarded the tea ship Dartmouth in Boston harbour. They began dumping the cargo overboard. In three hours, 342 chests of tea had been thrown into the sea.

The colonies react

Many colonists were angry. They felt that Britain was trying to have too much control of their lives. They therefore reacted to the Acts passed by Britain in a number of ways. Here are some of the colonies' reactions:

(1) *Smuggling*—Through the Navigation Acts, Britain controlled the colonies' trade. Sometimes merchants couldn't get enough of a certain product. They therefore smuggled in goods from other places. For example, sugar from the West Indies was smuggled into the colonies and used for making rum.

(2) *Boycotting*—Many colonies began boycotting high-priced British goods. They began making and buying their own goods. For example, a protest group of women, the Daughters of Liberty, encouraged people to wear colonial-made clothing rather than the high quality British-made clothes.

(3) *Incidents of violence*—Sometimes the tension between Britain and the colonies erupted into violence (see the story of the Boston Massacre at the beginning of this chapter). Some colonists felt that violence was the best way to show Britain their anger. The Sons of Liberty, a group formed by Sam Adams, reacted to British taxes by threatening to tar and feather royal officials. When the Tea Act was passed, this group showed its anger by dumping a cargo of tea into Boston harbour.

(4) *Banding together against Britain*—As time went on, the Thirteen Colonies united their efforts to oppose Britain. Committees of Correspondence were organized. These committees were set up to inform people throughout the colonies of the British government's "crimes." In 1774, the First Continental Congress was held. This was a meeting of the colonies to discuss their grievances with Britain. All the Thirteen Colonies except Georgia attended. Quebec, Nova Scotia, and Prince Edward Island were also invited, but they didn't go. The colonies were not yet talking about independence from Britain. They were just trying to find ways of obtaining their rights as free English people.

(5) *Revolution!*—You can see that tension between Britain and the colonies was growing. Violent clashes took place more and more often. Finally the conflict erupted into full-scale war.

The first military clash between the colonies and Britain took place at Lexington and Concord, near Boston on April 19, 1775. In this battle, British forces were faced with an army of **rebels** who called themselves **Minutemen**.

More skirmishes soon followed. The colonies decided to organize better their military efforts against Britain. In the summer of 1775, the Second Continental Congress formed a Continental Army of 20 000 men. Led by George Washington, this was to be the official army of the colonies. In September of the same year, the rebels launched an attack on Quebec. They thought that if Quebec could be conquered, then all the North American colonies could be

Fig. 13-5 After the Boston Tea Party, the British reacted by blockading Boston. The cartoon above is a satire. It shows the population of Boston locked up in a cage by members of the British navy who are teasing them with fish as food. What do you think the point of the cartoon is?

For a more complete description of the Boston Tea Party read *In the Minds and Hearts of the People* by Lillian B. Millar.

(Top of page) A boycott occurs when a group of people refuses to buy certain products.

pitted against Britain. The campaign against Quebec failed, however. The attack made Britain even angrier at the colonies.

The final break between Britain and the colonies came in July 1776. On July 2, a committee of the Continental Congress, headed by Thomas Jefferson, drew up the Declaration of Independence. In this statement, the colonies stated that they were free and independent of British control. Two days later, Congress approved this declaration of independence. The colonists would no longer be fighting for their rights as English citizens—they would be fighting for their freedom as citizens of a separate country.

Fig. 13-6 The Declaration of Independence was printed and distributed through the colonies. Since not all the colonists could read, the Declaration was also read to people from the steps of town meeting houses.

Fig. 13-7 Examine the cartoon and explain its message.

GETTING THE FACTS

5. Write a short explanation for each of the following: Daughters of Liberty, Committees of Correspondence, First Continental Congress, Sons of Liberty, Minutemen.

6. Explain why the Declaration of Independence was so important in the conflict between Britain and the colonists.

USING YOUR KNOWLEDGE

7. Earlier you learned about five issues that the British and the colonists were arguing over. The Acts passed by the British after 1763 further increased the tension between the two sides. Examine each Act and determine which of the five issues it was related to. In each case, explain your choice.

8. Choose one of the Acts. Imagine you are a colonist and write a letter to the British government. In your letter, explain why the Act upsets you, and suggest a plan of action that would be more acceptable to the colonists.

9. The colonies were eager to have Quebec, Nova Scotia and Isle St. Jean (Prince Edward Island) join them in the revolt against Britain. The three colonies, however, did not want to be involved, so they didn't go to the First Continental Congress. The rebels later tried to take the three colonies by force, but failed. Why do you think the Thirteen Colonies wanted the other three to join them in rebelling against Britain?

THINKING IT THROUGH

10. The colonists reacted to the British in two ways: peaceful protest and violent protest.
    a) Give one example of each kind of protest.

b) Do you think that violent protest and revolution was the only way that the colonists could have solved their problems with Britain? Give reasons for your opinion.

What was the difference between the Patriots and the Loyalists?

The American Revolution was a collision between Britain and the Thirteen Colonies. However, people in the colonies collided with each other too. Once the Declaration of Independence was circulated, the colonists had to choose sides. They had to decide either to stay loyal to Britain or to support the move for independence. Most became Patriots—people who supported the Continental Congress and the revolution. But many became Loyalists—people who supported the king and opposed the revolution. Others tried to remain neutral.

Who were the Patriots?

The Patriots started off as a relatively small group of radicals, such as Sam Adams and John Hancock. They resented the way Britain interfered in their lives. Some Patriots, such as the Sons of Liberty, caused many violent clashes with the British. The Boston Tea Party was an example.

Other less violent Patriots supported the Continental Congress. The Congress tried to avoid violence and only became committed to revolution after the battles of Lexington and Concord. When the Continental Congress appointed George Washington commander in chief, moderate colonists began to join the Patriot cause.

The Patriots came from every level of colonial society. George Washington and Thomas Jefferson were two of the wealthiest men in North America. Paul Revere was a silversmith; John Hancock was a rich merchant. The Minutemen were ordinary people who objected to taxation because most of them were poor.

It is hard for us to know how many colonists were actually Patriots. John Adams, a Patriot, estimated that one-third of Americans were Patriots, one-third were Loyalists and the other third didn't care one way or the other. Some historians think the Patriots were the largest group and the Loyalists were the smallest.

Fig. 13-8 George Washington, commander in chief of the American forces during the War of Independence and first president of the United States.

The Minutemen were the first group of organized American rebels prepared to oppose the British government by force. As the revolution grew, they began to call themselves Patriots. Thus the Patriots supported the revolution while the Tories opposed it. Americans who were loyal to King George III preferred to call themselves Loyalists.

Opposed to King George III
Minutemen or
Patriots

Supporting King George III
Tories or
Loyalists

Who were the Loyalists?

The Loyalists (sometimes called **Tories**) can be divided into two groups—active and inactive. The active Loyalists were those who were not scared by the tarring and feathering that was going on in many communities throughout the colonies. They were the targets of persecution since they openly supported the king. Many were officials of the British government, such as customs officers who had to collect the Tea Tax. The inactive Loyalists were those who continued to support the king, but did not get involved in the violence that followed.

Loyalists tended to be recent immigrants to North America. Some of them were not British. Small groups of Germans and Dutch felt more comfortable under British authority than under the Patriots. These groups feared that the revolution would threaten their language, religion and distinctive customs. The Patriots wanted a democratic government. But, because democracies are ruled by majority vote, the Germans and Dutch were afraid that minority groups such as theirs would be ignored. The Loyalists, like the Patriots, came from all parts of American society.

The revolution forced people to choose sides. Sometimes even families were split. Benjamin Franklin was a Patriot but his own son remained a Loyalist. The Governor of South Carolina was a Loyalist but all three of his sons were Patriots. The American Revolution was clearly a war that split American society into groups.

Who remained neutral?

"Those who aren't for me, are against me" is an old saying that was especially true during the American Revolution. But many people did not want to take sides—they preferred to remain neutral.

Being neutral was a difficult position to hold. A number of religious groups that opposed war had settled in North America. For example, Quakers [KWAY-kers] and Mennonites [MEH-nuh-nīts] did not believe in fighting or in taking oaths, so they were excused from military duty. However, they had to pay special taxes for this privilege.

Most of the neutrals didn't really care who won the war as long as they were left in peace. Many free blacks were part of this group. Other blacks were enlisted by British or Patriot regiments, and, as a result, blacks fought on both sides of the

The midnight ride of Paul Revere

Paul Revere stood beside his horse and stared through the night blackness towards the Old North Church in Boston. He was nervously waiting for the signal that the British army was crossing the river to march on Concord. Revere's horse was rested and ready for one of the most famous rides in history.

Revere was a Patriot [PAY-tree-uht]. He was resentful towards the British and believed that armed conflict was inevitable. All through the winter of 1775, Patriots had been organizing into groups of Minutemen prepared to use weapons on the British army if provoked. Minutemen in all the communities around Boston were kept in constant touch by means of riders like Revere, who carried letters from one Committee of Correspondence to another.

Spies had informed Revere that tonight was the night. Two lanterns in the spire of the church meant that 1000 British troops were coming across the river. At eleven o'clock there was a flicker of light in the spire. Then, *two* lanterns appeared.

Revere shoved his foot in the stirrup and was off on the road to Lexington and Concord. As he thundered through the village he cried, "The British are coming! To arms!" And all along the route, sleepy Minutemen began to assemble in small groups. (They had dressed quickly and some were even barefoot.)

Revere carried on at breakneck speed. His horse, covered with lather, kicked up small showers of gravel as it galloped along the gravel road. He passed through Lexington, warning the leaders John Hancock and Sam Adams.

On the way to Concord, Revere was stopped by a British patrol. He was not arrested because there was no evidence that he was doing anything illegal.

Meanwhile, back at Lexington, 70 Minutemen lined up to face the British. They were not taken very seriously by the much more numerous redcoats who asked them to disperse. In the confusion, someone misinterpreted the order not to fire. All that was heard was the word FIRE! No one knows who fired first. When the smoke cleared, five Minutemen were dead and ten wounded. Only one British soldier was wounded. The victory was clearly British.

Then the redcoats proceeded on to Concord, where they seized a small collection of military supplies. At Concord the firing broke out again. This time the situation looked serious, so the British officer in charge ordered a withdrawal.

By that time, however, many more Minutemen had arrived at various points along the route. One hundred, 200, eventually as many as 3000 Minutemen lined both sides of the road that the British had to use for their withdrawal to Boston. Seventy-three British soldiers were killed and 200 were wounded before they reached the safety of Boston.

GETTING THE FACTS

11. Why did firing break out between the redcoats and the Minutemen at Lexington? Who won the fight at Lexington?

12. What did the British do at Concord?

13. What happened to the British as they returned to Boston?

14. Suggest another title for the story.

What happened when the Continental Army invaded Quebec in 1775?

In 1775, the rebels in the Thirteen Colonies launched an attack on the British colonies to the north. They thought that if these colonies could be captured, then the whole continent would be united against the British.

General Washington sent an army of 4000 men to invade Quebec. He planned two attack routes. Part of the army, led by Major General Richard Montgomery, moved north from Fort Ticonderoga to Montreal. The other part, led by Benedict Arnold, trekked overland through the difficult Maine wilderness to Quebec City.

If Quebec could be captured, the British would not be able to launch an invasion from the St. Lawrence. Washington felt that he could win. He knew that Quebec had fewer than 1000 British troops. He also thought that the French population would rise against the British once the Continental Army appeared.

Montgomery captured Montreal and nearly captured the English General Guy Carleton. But Carleton disguised himself as a French trapper and escaped. Montgomery followed Carleton to Quebec.

Arnold's part of the American army suffered terribly trying to get through the bogs, rapids and rocky terrain of the forest between the Atlantic and Quebec. The troops ran out of food and had to eat candles and roasted moccasins. Only 600 of the 1200 men who had set out reached Quebec. By the time the two armies joined up, winter had arrived. Conditions got worse and smallpox raged in the camp.

Finally, Montgomery decided to attack while they still had some strength left. On New Year's Eve 1775, he and Arnold launched a desperate night attack on the walls of Quebec. The sick and poorly-dressed soldiers ploughed their way through metre-high snowdrifts in a driving snowstorm. Snow got into their weapons and made them useless. And, to make matters worse, a spy had warned the British garrison of the attack. Carleton's artillery opened fire at pointblank range. Two hundred of the American army were killed, including Montgomery, and Arnold was wounded. The British lost only six men. For the rest of the winter, the Continental Army lived in their disease-ridden camp. In May, British reinforcements under General Burgoyne [ber-GOIN] arrived at Quebec and Arnold retreated to Fort Ticonderoga. The attack on Quebec had failed.

How was the unsuccessful attack on Quebec important to the story of Canada? The fact that the Americans had been resisted showed that the northern colonies did not agree with the Thirteen Colonies. They were not interested in joining with the Thirteen Colonies and preferred to remain as they were. The American dream of one country united against Britain was not to come true.

THINKING IT THROUGH

15. If Washington and the colonial armies had won, Quebec and the other colonies would have become part of the Thirteen Colonies. Canada today might therefore have been very different. How do you think the defeat of Quebec would have changed Canada's history? Would your own life be different?

conflict. Blacks had to consider which group supported slavery less. There was no clear answer to this question because slavery was still legal in North America.

The other large neutral group was the French Canadians. The French could see no advantage to joining either the British or the Patriot cause. Some did fight for the British when Quebec was invaded, but others joined the Patriots. Most joined neither group and remained neutral throughout the war.

GETTING THE FACTS

16. List three points that describe the Patriots.

17. List three points that describe the Loyalists.

18. Name three groups that remained neutral. Briefly explain why each group chose to be neutral.

USING YOUR KNOWLEDGE

19. Imagine that you are a parent and a Loyalist in 1776. You have just discovered that one of your teenaged children has taken up the Patriot cause. Write a conversation that might take place between you and your son or daughter.

THINKING IT THROUGH

20. DEBATE the following statement: The French in Quebec were right to remain neutral in the conflict between the

Slavery was not abolished in the United States until 1865. It was abolished in Britain and Canada in 1833. During the period when slavery was legal, a slaveowner could free his slaves. As a result, two kinds of blacks lived in North America—freemen and slaves. Freed slaves were recruited in both armies later in the war.

French-Canadian sharpshooters were part of the militia that defended Quebec. They helped account for the victory.

(Opposite page) Smallpox is a contagious disease with fever and pustules, often fatal or disfiguring.

Fig. 13-9 The invasion of Quebec by Arnold and Montgomery, 1775.

Fig. 13-10 Major battles in the American Revolution.

Thirteen Colonies and Britain. Before you take a stand, review what you know about the French in Quebec—their way of life, attitudes, relations with the English. Be sure to back up your viewpoint.

There were many non-American troops fighting on the side of the Patriots. Britain used over 20 000 German mercenaries (hired soldiers) and France had 5 000 men fighting at Yorktown alone. The Loyalist forces numbered nearly 50 000 soldiers.

THE INVESTIGATIVE REPORTER

21. "Whose bread I eat his song I sing," is an old German saying.
    a) Explain the meaning of this saying.
    b) What methods did the British and Continental armies use to attract recruits? (Consult library books on the American Revolution by looking in the subject card catalogue under "recruitment.")

The revolution ends: Patriot victory and the Treaty of Paris

In 1776, during the first few months of war, the Patriots had an army of 18 000 poorly armed and trained men. They faced a British force of 30 000. Yet, when the peace treaty was signed in 1783, the Patriots were the victors. How did this happen?

One important reason for the Patriots' victory was the way the war was fought. The British could easily conquer cities like Boston or New York. However, they had trouble in the countryside. Patriots shot at them from behind trees, and used other hit-and-run tactics. This "**guerilla** [guh-RIH-luh] **warfare**" wore down the British army. In the meantime, the Patriot army was gaining more experience in fighting. As the war went on, the Patriots began to win more and more battles.

In 1778, France signed an alliance with the Patriots. It agreed to help the Patriots in their fight against Britain. This was another factor that helped lead the Patriots to victory.

Fighting continued until 1781. At Yorktown, Virginia, the British army surrendered to George Washington's army.

The Treaty of Paris

The peace treaty went into effect in 1783, two years after the battle of Yorktown. In the treaty, Britain agreed to do the following:
—recognize American independence;
—turn over to the United States all the land from the Mississippi River to the Atlantic coast between the Great Lakes and Florida;
—give the Americans fishing rights off the coast of Newfoundland.

In return, Britain wanted the Loyalists paid back for the losses they suffered during the war. The Congress agreed, but the Loyalists were never paid.

GETTING THE FACTS

22. List three factors that led to victory for the Patriots.

USING YOUR KNOWLEDGE

23. Examine the map in Fig. 13-12.
   a) How did the Treaty of Paris in 1783 change the boundaries of the Thirteen Colonies?

Fig. 13-11 The last boatload of British soldiers leaving New York.

At the important battle of Yorktown in 1781, twenty-four large French warships with over 18 000 sailors and marines successfully prevented the British navy from rescuing Lord Cornwallis and his 8000-man army (see Fig. 13-13). Five thousand French soldiers joined Washington in a combined force of 17 000 men. The British were forced to surrender and the war ended. The importance of the French role was underlined when the peace negotiations took place in Paris in 1783.

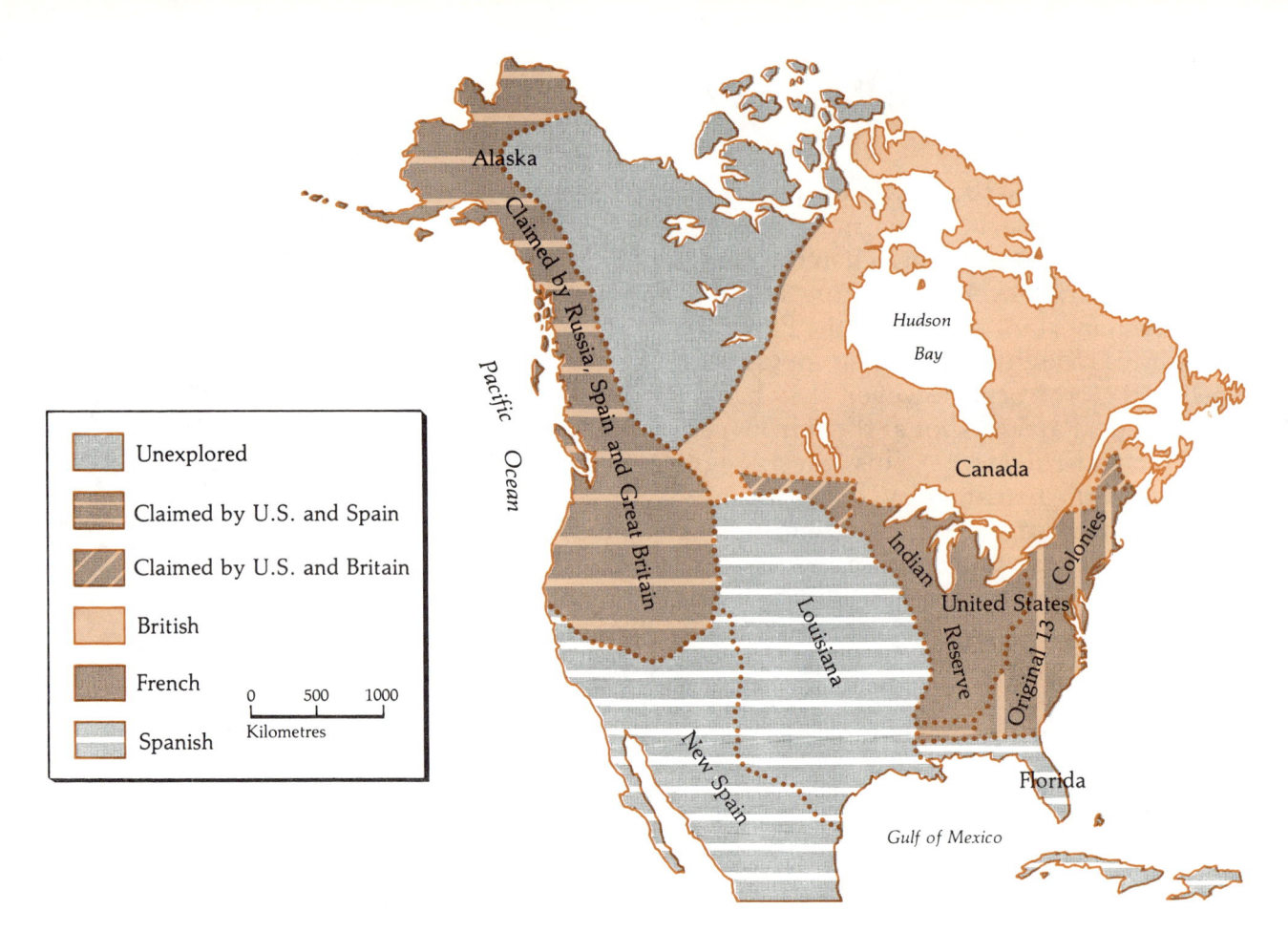

Fig. 13-12 Territories established by the Treaty of Paris, 1783.

b) Where could future border conflicts develop? What other world powers might become involved?

INVESTIGATIVE REPORTER

24. There were many battles in the American Revolution. A number of major battles are shown on the map in Fig. 13-10. Choose one, research what happened in the fighting and prepare a map of the battle. Then, explain the battle to the class. For sources of information, look in a library card catalogue under the heading "American Revolution."

Conclusion

How was the American Revolution important to the story of Canada? Even though most of the fighting took place in the Thirteen Colonies, the war greatly influenced the British colonies that would one day become Canada.

First, out of the revolution a new country, the United States of America, was born. The Americans had fought hard for their land and were proud of their victory. Over the years, they would work to build their country into a world power. The other British colonies in North America were always aware of their powerful neighbour to the south. They were influenced by American ideas, an influence that continues to this day. How often do you hear Canadians today speak about how "Americanized" Canada is?

The revolution affected the story of Canada in another way, too. Thousands of Loyalists fled to present-day Ontario, Quebec, Nova Scotia, New Brunswick and Prince Edward Island. The British population of these colonies was therefore greatly increased in the space of a few years. The Loyalists who came to the northern colonies cleared and settled new land. Their settlements eventually grew into thriving towns and communities. As a result, the Loyalists helped to open up and develop the land that would one day become Canada.

Fig. 13-13 In a disastrous move in the fall of 1781, Lord Cornwallis and his British troops retreated to the Yorktown peninsula. Cut off by land and sea by American and French forces, the British held out for three weeks. Finally on October 17, Cornwallis surrendered his entire army.

Fig. 13-14 Major-General John Graves Simcoe, first Lieutenant-Governor of Upper Canada, 1792-96.

GETTING THE FACTS

25. The entire conflict between the colonists and Britain took place in a fairly small area of North America.

    a) Locate the following on a map of North America:

Boston	Quebec
Lexington	St. Lawrence River
Concord	Yorktown
Ohio River	Appalachian Mountains
Philadelphia	Mississippi River
Montreal	

    b) In one sentence for each, describe how each was important in the American Revolution.

USING YOUR KNOWLEDGE

26. If Washington and the Continental Army had not defeated the British, North America might be a very different place today. Describe what North America might be like if the British had won the American Revolution.

THINKING IT THROUGH

27. a) In chapter 2, you learned that before you can solve a problem, you must be able to explain what it is. Explain the problems that people loyal to Britain faced throughout the revolution.

    b) Once you have explained a problem, then you can go on to the next step—to think of as many different solutions as possible. What were the choices facing the Loyalists?

    c) In your opinion, which choice was best? (You will discover what actually happened to the Loyalists in the next chapter.)

THE INVESTIGATIVE REPORTER

28. Choose two of the following people, one man and one woman. Consult the card catalogue in your library for material on them. The encyclopedia is always a good starting point. Write a short three-paragraph essay answering the following questions:

a) Who was he or she?

b) What did he or she do during the revolution?

c) How did his or her actions affect the outcome of the revolution?

Sam Adams
John Adams
John Hancock
Charles Cornwallis
Thomas Jefferson
Patrick Henry

John Graves Simcoe
Betsy Ross
Molly Pitcher
Sara Franklin Bache
Sally St. Clair
Deborah Sampson

14 The United Empire Loyalists

TEUCRO DUCE NIL DESPERANDUM.

Firſt Battalion of PENNSYLVANIA LOYALISTS, commanded by His Excellency Sir WILLIAM HOWE, K. B.

ALL INTREPID ABLE-BODIED

HEROES.

WHO are willing to ſerve His MAJESTY KING GEORGE the Third, in Defence of their Country, Laws and Conſtitution, againſt the arbitrary Uſurpations of a tyrannical Congreſs, have now not only an Opportunity of manifeſting their Spirit, by aſſiſting in reducing to Obedience their too-long deluded Countrymen, but alſo of acquiring the polite Accompliſhments of a Soldier, by ſerving only two Years, or during the preſent Rebellion in America.

Such ſpirited Fellows, who are willing to engage, will be rewarded at the End of the War, beſides their Laurels, with 50 Acres of Land, where every gallant Hero may retire, and enjoy his Bottle and Laſs.

Each Volunteer will receive as a Bounty, FIVE DOLLARS, beſides Arms, Cloathing and Accoutrements, and every other Requiſite proper to accommodate a Gentleman Soldier, by applying to Lieutenant Colonel ALLEN, or at Captain KEARNY's Rendezvous, at PATRICK TONRY's, three Doors above Market-ſtreet, in Second-ſtreet.

Loyalist regiments were raised all over North America and the West Indies. Their uniforms were as different as their points of origin.

- Would this have created difficulties for the Loyalist forces? Explain.

To build up their forces, Loyalist recruiters often advertised for volunteers. Advertisements, such as the one on the opposite page, appeared in local papers.

- What is there in the advertisement that would make people want to join the Loyalist forces?
- Look carefully at the main headline. Would it make men want to join? Explain your answer.
- Would this advertisement persuade you to join? Why or why not?
- You have decided to raise money for a charity by holding a car wash. You need people to help you out. Write an advertisement that will encourage people to come out and help you wash cars.

Emmerich Chasseurs, 1776    **Royal Highland Emigrants**    **43rd Regiment of Foot, 1775**

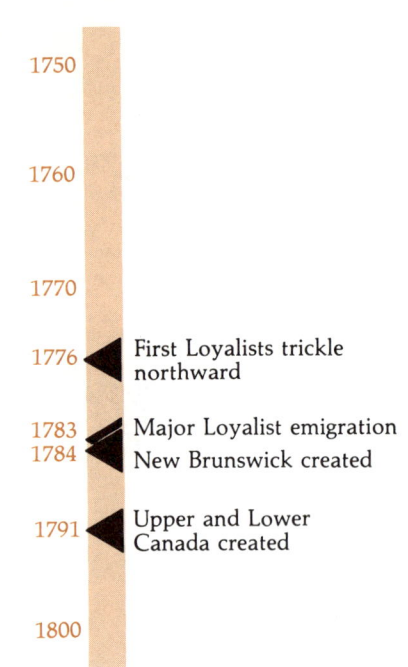

Timeline:
- 1750
- 1760
- 1770
- 1776 — First Loyalists trickle northward
- 1783 — Major Loyalist emigration
- 1784 — New Brunswick created
- 1791 — Upper and Lower Canada created
- 1800

Chapter overview

Who were the Loyalists? They were a mixed group; many were well-to-do merchants, lawyers and doctors, and many were farmers. While most Loyalists were British, some were German, French, Dutch, Jewish, black and Indian. All these people had chosen to reject the idea of revolt against Britain and to remain loyal to the King.

As the tension in the colonies increased, Patriots often threatened, and sometimes harmed, the Loyalists. How did the Loyalists react? Some decided to stay in the Thirteen Colonies—either to live life as quietly as possible or to fight the Patriots. Many went back to their native lands. By 1784, about 40 000 Loyalists had arrived in British North America (the name for Canada after 1783). British North America consisted of the colonies of Newfoundland, Nova Scotia, New Brunswick, Prince Edward Island and Quebec (including present-day Ontario and Quebec).

This chapter will help you discover the story of the Loyalists. As you work through the chapter, keep this question in mind: How did the Loyalists' story affect the story of Canada?

Signposts

> What was it like to be a Loyalist on the frontier? The case of Molly Brant

> How did the Loyalists fight back?

> What happened to Loyalists from the Atlantic coast?

> After the war: Debts and duties

> FEATURE: Who were the Black Loyalists?

Key words

| Loyalists | land granting | heritage |

What was it like to be a Loyalist on the frontier? The case of Molly Brant

"Our people have been allies of the English King for many years and our loyalty will continue for many more." These words were spoken by Molly Brant, a Mohawk Indian. She was born when the Mohawk Valley in modern New York State belonged to her nation. Molly became a leader of her people and one of the most important Loyalists.

Molly became a leader of the Loyalists for several reasons. First, she was married to Sir William Johnson, the Superintendent of Indians in British North America. Johnson had won the respect of the Indians in the Mohawk Valley. He had helped to establish the Proclamation Line, which ensured that no settlers could take Mohawk land without the Indians' permission.

Molly also had influence because she headed an organization called The Society of Six Nations Matrons. Among the Mohawks, and indeed all the Iroquois nations, women had very high status. Their advice was listened to in all matters, including peace and war. Molly's advice about the conflict between Britain and the colonies was always the same: Remain loyal to Britain. When Sir William died in 1774, Molly continued to advise his successor, Colonel Guy Johnson.

Over the years, there had been several clashes between colonists and Indians when settlers moved onto Indian land. By 1774, Iroquois chiefs were ready for war against the Patriots, who were paying no attention to the Proclamation Line. Most of the Iroquois Six Nations chose to remain loyal to Britain during the American Revolution. Some nations, however, did not.

Molly urged her people to stand up with the British against the Patriots. Instead of fleeing north, as did many Loyalists from the Thirteen Colonies, Molly stayed and prepared to defend her home. Her brother, Joseph Brant, who was highly respected by the Iroquois, began recruiting warriors for the Loyalist forces.

In the spring of 1777, Molly was forced to move from the Mohawk Valley. Her home had been attacked by the Patriots and wrecked before her eyes. The lives of her children and brother had been threatened.

Molly and her family first moved west to join the Cayuga Indians, who were part of the Iroquois Confederacy. Soon after, she was asked by Colonel John Butler to settle at Fort

Fig. 14-1 Joseph Brant, Molly's brother, persuaded most of his people to support King George III in the revolution and conducted raids on revolutionary settlements throughout the war. After the defeat at Yorktown, Brant led his people north to established Iroquois reserves at Deseronto and Brantford in Southern Ontario.

Molly Brant did not change her name when she married Sir William Johnson. If she had become Mrs. Johnson, she would have lost her Mohawk identity because the Mohawks were matrilineal. (Children took the names of their mothers rather than their fathers).

Fig. 14-2 Molly Brant lived at Fort Johnson at the beginning of the revolutionary period. Why would Johnson Hall be an effective fort? What is the building in the foreground?

Sir William Johnson owned 100 000 acres [40 468 ha] of land in the Mohawk Valley. On this land he settled Scottish Highlanders who remained loyal when the revolution broke out. The land and property was confiscated and sold to Patriots.

Niagara. Colonel Butler was Commander of Butler's Rangers, a Loyalist regiment stationed at Fort Niagara. He knew that Molly would be able to convince the Iroquois to fight with the British. It was said that "one word from Molly Brant is more taken notice of by the Six Nations than a thousand words from the white man."

As the revolution went on, violence against the Indian people increased. The Iroquois abandoned their villages, and many moved to the Niagara area. Molly continued to help rally Indian support for the Loyalist regiments. It was of no use. In October 1781, word arrived that the British had been defeated at Yorktown. Two years later the Treaty of Paris was signed.

Molly and the Iroquois were shocked by the terms of the peace treaty. The British king had given away Indian lands to the Patriots. General Haldimand offered Molly a pension of £100 a year for her help during the war. He also offered the Iroquois Loyalists new land near the Bay of Quinte [KWIHN-tee] and along the banks of the Grand River. Still grieved by the loss of their homeland, Mohawks and other Iroquois began to settle these areas. Other Indians chose to return to the Mohawk Valley.

Molly returned to the Mohawk Valley for one last, brief

visit. She returned because the new government asked her to. At her home, Fort Johnson, all that was left of the mill and the stockades was rubble. Johnson Hall, the manor house, still stood but it was badly damaged. Everything of value had been stolen or smashed. The new government offered Molly money to return to the valley. They wanted her to help control the Indians who had already returned and whose lands were being taken by new settlers. Molly Brant looked on the offer as a bribe. She returned to Quebec and declared that she would never set foot on American soil again. She would make a life for herself in her new home. There, Indian Loyalists would at least have the security of their land titles.

If you want to learn more about Molly Brant, read *Mistress Molly, The Brown Lady* by Helen Robinson.

GETTING THE FACTS

1. Give two reasons why Molly Brant was looked on as a leader of her people.

2. How were women treated in Iroquois society?

3. Why were there clashes between the Indians and the settlers?

THINKING IT THROUGH

4. Loyalists such as Molly Brant believed that it was important to be loyal to Britain. They suffered persecution and even moved away rather than take up the Patriot cause.

Fig. 14-3 The Mohawk village on the Grand River in Brantford, 1793, showing the Council House and the church.

If you had been a Loyalist in the Thirteen Colonies at the time, would you have risked your family's safety by announcing your loyalty to Britain? What would have been most important to you? Describe what you would have done in this situation.

5. The new government offered Molly money to return to the valley, but she refused.
   a) Why did Molly look on the offer as a bribe?
   b) Do you think Molly made the right choice when she decided never to return to the United States? Should she have taken the opportunity to return to the homeland of her people? Give reasons to support your opinion.

THE INVESTIGATIVE REPORTER

6. Find out what happened to the Indians who moved from the Mohawk Valley to areas in present-day Ontario. Do these Indian nations still live in the area today? Have their land titles been respected? Consult books in your school or local library. Be sure to write out at least four questions that you want to find answers for in your research.

How did the Loyalists fight back?

Most stories about the Loyalists describe how they were driven off their land and threatened with tarring and feathering. How did the Loyalists react to these Patriot threats? Many left the colonies. Others stayed and fought back. Many Loyalist regiments were formed to fight with the British against the Patriots.

At the beginning of the war, the British saw no need to form Loyalist regiments. Britain was confident that the rebels would flee at the first sight of King George's redcoated soldiers. The strength of the Patriot resistance soon shattered this belief. Loyalist regiments began to form without help from Britain. The Scottish Highlanders of North Carolina, for example, organized their own regiment. Historians estimate that the size of the Loyalist forces during the war ranged from 30 000 to 50 000 men.

Once it was decided to form a Loyalist regiment, the officers were chosen. The officers then proceeded to recruit soldiers wherever they could find them. Men often joined because of the money; forty shillings was given to each man who enlisted and was accepted.

At first, Loyalists troops were dressed in green coats to distinguish them from the red-coated regular soldiers. Some took this to mean that the Loyalists were inferior. Later in the war, Britain decided to grant them the right to wear red. However, one regiment—the Queen's Rangers, led by Colonel John Graves Simcoe—insisted in keeping the green. Simcoe felt that green was safer because it blended in with the forests where the fighting often took place.

Loyalist regiments faced more dangers than the regular British soldiers. The Patriots looked on the Loyalists as traitors, so they were harder on them than on the British. For instance, a captured member of Jessup's Rangers had been seriously wounded with a musket ball in the eye. In spite of this, he was placed astride a wounded horse and paraded before the rebel soldiers. Other Loyalist prisoners were tied in pairs and dragged behind horses. When the war ended at Yorktown, the defeated Loyalists were in serious danger. They dared not surrender and be taken as prisoners of war. Instead they had to escape through the forest.

Fig. 14-4 Tarring and feathering was used by Patriots to terrorize Loyalists. Suspected Loyalists were stripped to the waist and hot tar was poured over them. They were then often covered with feathers and paraded around town straddling a fence rail carried by Patriots. Actual cases of tarring and feathering were not common. However, the threat became the most effective weapon against Loyalists. Loyalists were handed a ball of tar with a few feathers in it. This was a warning. Many people who were threatened this way quickly packed up and moved away.

After the peace treaty was signed, Loyalist soldiers often found that they could not return home. Two privates in the New Jersey Volunteers went home to Sussex County and were badly beaten by their own neighbours. Another soldier in the same regiment was killed when he returned to visit his parents in Morris County.

In general, Loyalist forces were rewarded for their role in the war. Many of the Loyalist regiments were transported to Nova Scotia and the other British colonies. There they received special land grants in recognition of their service.

Fig. 14-5 Something of the hatred between the Loyalists and Patriots can be seen in this exaggerated engraving of the burning of New York by the Patriots. Was the engraving done by a Loyalist or a Patriot engraver?

USING YOUR KNOWLEDGE

7. Describe the cause of each of the following events:
a) Soon after the war began, the British started recruiting Loyalist regiments.
b) Loyalist regiments faced more dangers than regular British soldiers.

c) Loyalist soldiers found they could not return home after the peace treaty was signed.
d) After the war, many Loyalist soldiers received land grants in Quebec and Nova Scotia.

THE INVESTIGATIVE REPORTER

8. John Coffin, a member of the King's American Dragoons, distinguished himself in many battles during the war. One of the stories told about him describes how Coffin slipped across enemy lines to visit his fiancée. A rebel guard saw him enter the house, so he searched the house. Coffin was not to be found. When the guard left, Coffin came out from his hiding place. He had been concealed—all 6′2″ [1.8 m] of him—under his fiancée's hoop skirt. In later years, Coffin became a prosperous settler in New Brunswick. His life makes interesting reading.

What happened to the Loyalists from the Atlantic coast?

William Frost was a soldier in the Loyalist forces. When his home and property were seized by the Patriots, he and his family fled from Stamford, Connecticut to Staten Island. William was 34 and Sara 29. They had two children and Sara was expecting a third child when they boarded the *Two Sisters* in 1783.

The family joined thousands of other Loyalists in refugee camps in New York City. These Loyalists had fled to New York because of persecution in their home communities. They were waiting for ships to carry them to a new home in other British North American colonies. Hostility towards these Loyalists was great. Guy Carleton, who was head of the British forces in New York, knew this. He therefore refused to withdraw the British troops from New York until all the Loyalists had left.

The evacuation of the Loyalists was not easy. There were not enough ships to carry the people to their new homelands and the convoys had to make several trips. Carleton's main concern was to get the Loyalists out of New York. As a result, they were often set ashore in the wilderness with only what they could carry. Communities such as Shelburne (Nova Scotia) and Saint John (New Brunswick) were established in this way.

Throughout the trip, Sara kept a journal. This record gives

Fig. 14-6 Early Loyalists in the Mohawk Valley decided to move to Canada after 1776. However, Molly Brant and the Mohawks continued to feel secure because they believed they owned the land. Should they have left with these Loyalists? Why would later Loyalists be unable to take their possessions? Would you want to meet this dog in a dark alley?

Diary quoted in *Pioneer Profiles of New Brunswick Settlers* by Charlotte Gourlay Robinson.

a clear picture of what happened to the Loyalists who moved from the Thirteen Colonies after the American Revolution. The following section is based on Sara's account:

From the diary of Sara Frost, Loyalist

Sunday, May 25, 1783: "I left Lloyd's Neck with my family and went on board the *Two Sisters* commanded by Captain Brown. We were sailing to Nova Scotia with the rest of the Loyalist sufferers. This evening the Captain drank tea with us and appeared to be a very agreeable gentleman. He expects to sail as soon as wind shall favour. We have very fair accommodation in the cabin, although it contains six families besides my own. There are 250 passengers on board."

The *Two Sisters* was one of a convoy of 13 ships that carried Loyalists out of New York. The ship was protected by two British naval vessels.

Sara Frost had to wait 22 days for the convoy to get ready for the final trip north. When the convoy finally set sail, the weather turned bad and the wind almost blew the *Two Sisters* over. As the ship staggered its way through the high seas, the passengers and their baggage were thrown about mercilessly. Rain came down in a torrent and then turned to hailstones "as big as balls." When things calmed a bit at sunset, Sara went on deck. She was surprised to see the hailstones rolling about. She had her husband gather as many as he could. "Billy went out and gathered a mug full of hailstones and made a bowl of punch. And the ice was in it till we had drunk the whole of it." It was a pleasant change from the foul-tasting water stored on board ship.

In three days, the *Two Sisters* was 240 km from New York and the passengers were very seasick. And to make matters worse, there was an outbreak of measles among the children. "We bear it pretty well, but at night one child cries in one place and one in another until I think sometimes I will go crazy."

The next day a rebel warship was sighted. This caused much excitement because privateers had captured a number of Loyalist transports that were travelling alone. The warship hoisted more sail and began to crowd the *Two Sisters*. Sara wrote, "but our frigate knew how to speak to her. She gave the stranger a shot across the bow, which caused her to shorten sail and lie to."

The day after that, a heavy fog set in and remained for three days and nights. When the sun finally broke through, the convoy was drifting off the coast of dangerous Sable Island, where many ships had been destroyed. Rounded up by the naval escort, they proceeded under full sail to the mouth of the St. John River. "How I long to see that place even tho' it is a strange land. I am so tired of being on board ship, though we have as clever a Captain as ever need live."

Saturday, June 28, 1783: Sara "got up in the morning with renewed hopes to find land on both sides." They were anchored at the mouth of the St. John River. "People went ashore and brought on board pea vines with blossoms on them, also some wild gooseberries, spruce and grass, all of which grow wild. They say this is to be our city. Our land is to be five and twenty miles [40 km] up the river. We have only a building place forty feet [12 m] wide and one hundred feet [30 m] back. Billy has gone on shore in his whaleboat to see how it looks. He returns soon bringing a fine salmon." The Loyalists crowded the deck both excited and disturbed. They were excited by the prospects of a new land but disturbed by the total wilderness before them. Most of those aboard had been city people. They felt unprepared for the task of clearing land and building a city where only rocks and trees existed.

Privateers captured several Loyalist ships, escorted them to American harbours and then sold the ships and contents. In one incident, Mrs. Charity Newton, a passenger, hid all the ship's silver under her hooped skirt and then used the money to buy the ship back from the pirates, once they were safely in port.

"To shorten sail and lie to" means to take in the sails and lie still, facing the wind.

Fig. 14-7 Loyalists landing at Saint John, May 18, 1783.

Sunday, June 29, 1783: "This morning is very pleasant. I am just going ashore with my children to see how I like it." Later she recorded her disappointment. "It is afternoon now and I have been on shore. It is I think the roughest land I have ever seen. It is to be the city they say. We are to have our land up the river. We are all ordered to land tomorrow and not a shelter to go under." Then Sara closed her journal forever.

Wednesday, July 30, 1783: In a discarded army tent on the rocks above the settlement that would later become Saint John, Sara Frost had a daughter, Hannah. She was the second child born in the new and largest Loyalist community in North America.

GETTING THE FACTS

9. How did the Loyalists get from the refugee camp in New York to their new homeland?

10. Name at least two dangers that the Frosts faced during their voyage on the Two Sisters.

11. What did the Frosts find when their ship landed at the mouth of the St. John River?

12. Suggest a title for the account of the Frosts' journey.

USING YOUR KNOWLEDGE

13. Imagine that you are Sara Frost and have just gone ashore to look at your new land. Write a journal entry that expresses your hopes, fears and dreams. Start your entry off with Sara's own words: "It is I think the roughest land I have ever seen."

Fig. 14-8 Annapolis Royal in the 1770s. This agricultural settlement, made vacant by the expulsion of the Acadians, was the scene of Loyalist settlement in the 1780s.

Fig. 14-9 Many Blacks fought in the Loyalist forces during the revolution. In the years after the war, about 3000 blacks migrated to Nova Scotia.

When the free food was stopped, many loyalist families faced starvation and some even died.

THINKING IT THROUGH

14. Thousands of Loyalists arrived in Nova Scotia to make new lives for themselves. Tension developed between the old Nova Scotians and the new Loyalists. Suggest reasons for this tension, and then suggest one way of easing the tension.

THE INVESTIGATIVE REPORTER

15. Find out more about one of the following Loyalist settlements:
   a) Saint John (formerly Parrtown and Carleton)
   b) Fredericton (formerly St. Anne's)
   c) Kingston
   d) Bellevue
   e) Shelburne

16. Loyalists who tried to settle on Prince Edward Island had great problems. Many ended up leaving. Using books in your school or local library, find out more about the settlement in P.E.I. The following questions may help you research the topic:
   —Who owned land in P.E.I.?
   —To whom did they rent the land?
   —Why did the Loyalists have trouble getting land to settle on?
   —What did the Loyalists end up doing?

After the war: Debts and duties

As you learned from the stories of Molly Brant and Sara Frost, Loyalists were often forced to flee their homes. They had to leave most of their possessions behind and try to start a new life in a new place. As a reward for their loyalty, the British government gave each Loyalist family or individual a piece of land and some supplies to help them get started. Often, the land was wild, uncleared and not good for farming. Also, the supplies given to them did not meet all their needs. As a result, life for Loyalists after the revolution was very hard.

In the following sections you will see what happened to Loyalist property, and how the British paid their debts to these people.

What happened to the Loyalists' possessions?

Loyalists who tried to return home after the war found that they had nothing to return to. Their homes and belongings had often been seized by the rebel governments. Loyalist property

Who were the Black Loyalists?

The first shipload of black people to reach North America landed at Jamestown, Virginia in 1619. By the 1770s, black slaves could be found in every British colony and also among the former French colonies. As early as 1751, there was an active slave market operating between Halifax and Boston. These slaves were often skilled craftsmen, as shown in the following advertisement from the Boston *Evening Post*:

> Just received from Halifax, and to be sold, 10 strong hearty, negro men, mostly tradesmen, such as caulkers, carpenters, sailmakers and ropemakers.

Slaves were not uncommon in the British colonies of Nova Scotia and Quebec before the American Revolution, but their numbers were small. After the American Revolution, many more blacks moved into Quebec and Nova Scotia. Most of these blacks came with their owners. They could not really be called Black Loyalists, because the decision to move north was made by their owners. There were, however, a number of freed blacks who had joined British regiments after having been promised their freedom if they would fight the Americans. The result of this promise was a sudden increase in blacks running away from their owners. Virginia is estimated to have lost 30 000 slaves, while South Carolina lost 25 000, and Georgia 12 000. Many of these escaped blacks were caught by slave patrols and returned to their owners. Others did join black regiments, but were formed into non-fighting units who were used to construct roads and build camps. A few became part of fighting units, but the presence of armed blacks was not very acceptable to white soldiers, whether Loyalist or Patriot.

When the war ended, almost 500 Black Loyalists were given land grants in Nova Scotia. These were free blacks and most settled in the Annapolis Valley on small farms. As well, many Blacks were brought to Nova Scotia by their loyalist masters.

Another large group of blacks sent to Nova Scotia from New York immediately after the revolution were ex-slaves. These people had run away from their owners and were in danger of being severely persecuted after British troops had left. They were transported to Halifax. Many settled and formed a large black community that still exists in the suburbs of modern Halifax.

Life for Loyalist blacks was difficult. Not only were the conditions of life tough, they had to face discrimination from the white majority. Eventually, some decided to move to New Brunswick and some even boarded ships for Quebec. A significant number accepted the British government's offer of free transportation back to the African colony of Sierra Leone [see-AYR-ruh lee-OH-nee].

USING YOUR KNOWLEDGE

17. Black Loyalists often had a harder time during the war and afterwards in their new homes than white Loyalists did. Discuss whether this statement is true or false. Use facts from the text to back up your argument.

was then sold to Patriots at a fraction of its real value. The Law of Forfeiture [FOHR-feh-cher] in New York province allowed rebel agents to evict the wives and children of Loyalists who belonged to British regiments. The government then quickly sold the property to raise money to help pay for the war.

Loyalists who returned to their homes in the Thirteen Colonies were often persecuted, just as they had been during the war. Tarring and feathering did not end with the peace treaty.

As a result, many Loyalists had to sell whatever possessions they still had and hope to get passage on a ship to Nova Scotia. Some of the wealthier Loyalists were able to return to England. Most people, however, did not have such a choice.

Auction sales were therefore common and expensive goods sold for give-away prices. In 1783, the following two advertisements appeared in a New York newspaper.

AUCTION SALE

Mahogany Dining and Card tables, Japanned Tea Tables, Elegant Silver Candlesticks of the newest style, Table and Tea Spoons, Silver-handled Knives and Forks, Watches, very neat Elegant Silver, Mounted Small Swords and Hangers, Very Neat Tea Sets of China, Large Beer Glasses, Elegant Wilton Carpets, Small Looking Glasses and Pictures, Large Assortment of Decanters, Tumblers, Goblets and Wine Glasses. A Variety of Copper Kettles and Pots, Sauce Pans, etc., a very large Kitchen Grate fit for a Tavern or Mess House.

Other auction sales were less elegant. They perhaps revealed how different the lives of average people had been from the wealthier Loyalists:

AUCTION SALE

Eleven Milk cows, twenty four cows old and young, some fit for killing. Three very fine horses.

Auction announcements from *Pioneer Profiles of New Brunswick Settlers* by C.G. Robinson.

Fig. 14-10 Loyalist settlements.

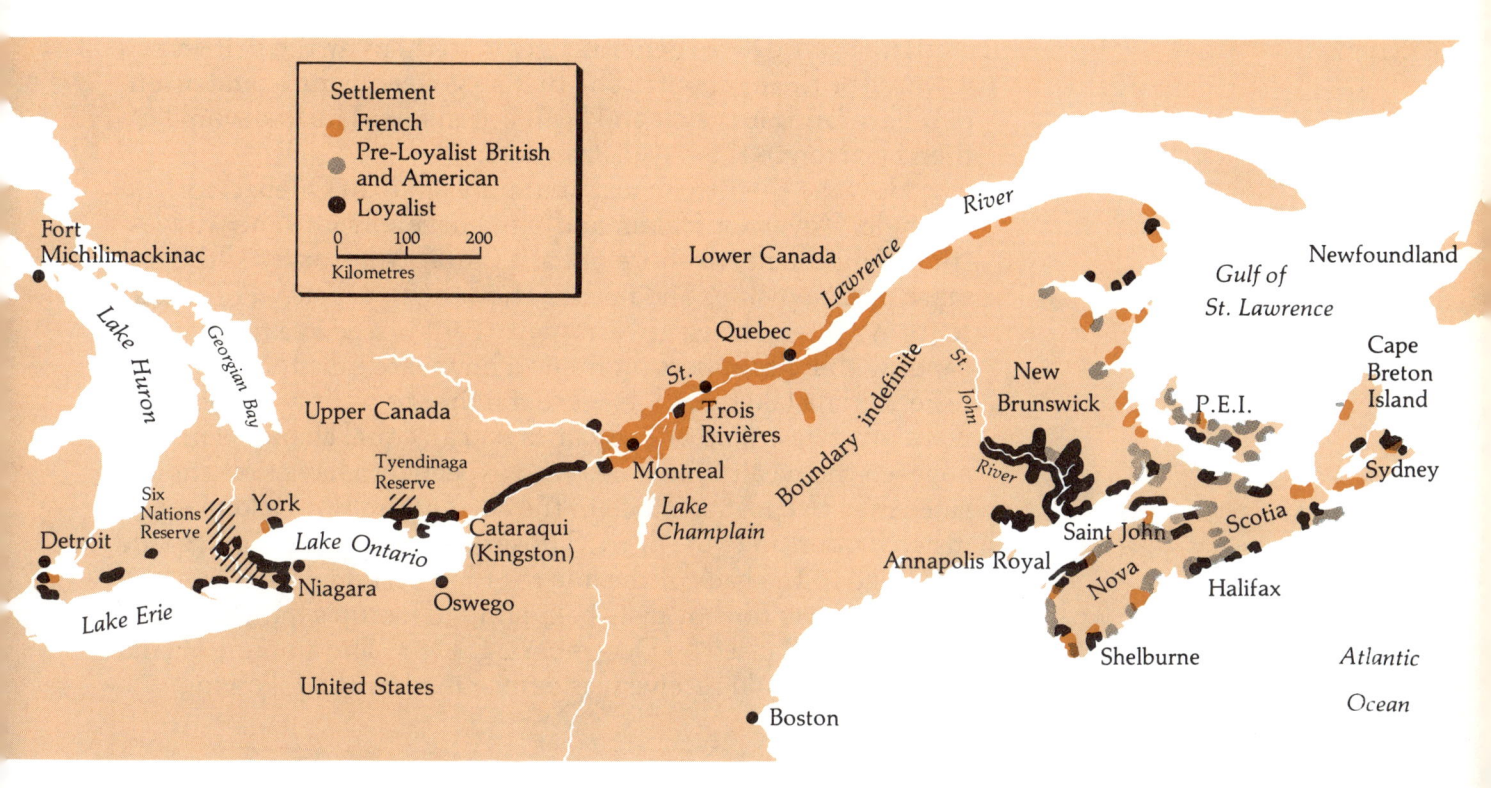

GETTING THE FACTS

18. Define the following words: auction, mahogany, japanned, decanter, goblet.

19. Give two reasons to explain why Loyalists often became poverty-stricken.

20. Why were auction sales common after the war?

USING YOUR KNOWLEDGE

21. The items up for sale at an auction often told a lot about the owners.
   a) Examine the advertisements for the two auction sales. Which owner belonged to a higher social class?
   b) Try to picture what the life of each owner was like. What kind of house did each live in? What kind of job would each owner have had?

How was land distributed to the Loyalists?

Loyalists settled in present-day Quebec, Ontario, Nova Scotia, New Brunswick and Prince Edward Island (see Fig. 14-10). The land they settled was generally given to them by the British as a reward for their support. The British government would often purchase land, survey it and lay it out in lots. The lots would then be given to the Loyalist settlers.

How did the British distribute the land? In Quebec, for example, Governor Haldimand sent surveyors into the wild land along the north shore of Lake Ontario. He ordered them to mark out townships and farms. Then the Loyalists were asked to form a line, while a government agent placed in a hat slips of paper with lot numbers on them. They were called "location tickets." The lakefront lots were the first to be drawn since they were most desirable. All Loyalists had an equal chance. This angered the wealthy families who expected to have first choice, since they had lost so much in the revolution. But Haldimand insisted upon an equal draw. Those who qualified for more land had to go to the back of the line for their second draw.

The draw for Loyalists belonging to Jessup's Rangers, for example, took place on December 24, 1783. The amount of land each person could receive was determined by the following formula:

The Formula:

To every master of a family	100 acres	[40.4 ha]
To every member of a family	50 acres	[20.2 ha]
To every single man	50 acres	
To every sargeant	200 acres	[80.9 ha]
To every private	100 acres	
To every member of their families	50 acres	
To every officer above captain	1000 acres	[404.6 ha]
To every captain	700 acres	[283.2 ha]
To every other officer	500 acres	[202.3 ha]
To every member of their families	50 acres	

For the 5251 Loyalists settled with Jessup's Rangers, Haldimand calculated that he needed 477 450 acres [193 217 ha] of land.

GETTING THE FACTS

22. How were location tickets distributed?

23. Which lots were the most valuable?

24. How much land could a family of two adults and two children receive?

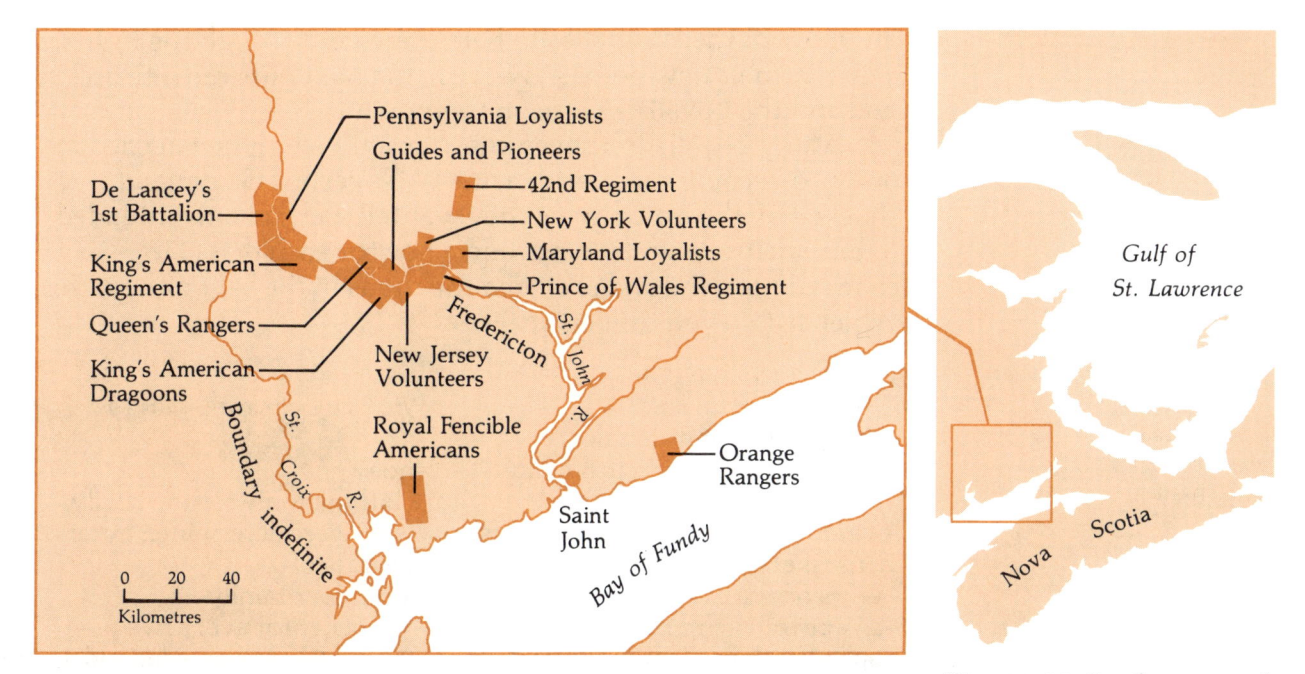

Fig. 14-11 Settlements of Loyalist regiments in New Brunswick.

THINKING IT THROUGH

25. Much of the land that a Loyalist family drew was useless to it. Why? What problems can you find in this system of land granting? What changes would you make in the system?

THE INVESTIGATIVE REPORTER

26. The system of land granting you have just read about was the most common. There were other systems, though. In the systems used around the St. John River, each boatload of Loyalists got less than the boatload before. Some settlers received lots that were only one-sixth the size of lots given earlier settlers. Can you suggest why this happened? Find out more about this system of land granting.

What supplies did the Loyalists want? What did they get?

When the Loyalists arrived at their new homes—usually uncleared lots of land—they often had nothing. They needed food and tools with which to clear the land and build homes.

After the revolution, the British had supplies for their troops left over. These supplies included salted meat, biscuits, flour, tools, guns and tents. The British gave the Loyalists small amounts of these supplies to help them get through the first years in their new homes. By 1787, the handouts came to an end and the Loyalists were on their own.

Many Loyalist refugees knew exactly what they needed in order to become successful farmers. Governor Haldimand was shocked by the list of items they wanted. He had only intended to provide them with an axe and a hoe for each man. He changed his mind and provided the items in the list on the right. Which list do you think is realistic?

Lists from *The Settlement of the United Empire Loyalists on the Upper St. Lawrence and Bay of Quinte in 1784* by E.A. Cruikshank.

What is a froe?

What the Cataraqui [KA-tuh-RAH-kwee] Loyalists wanted:
- boards, nails and shingles for each family to erect such buildings as they need
- window glass for these buildings
- a musket for each male over 14 years of age
- an axe for each male over 14
- one plough per family
- leather for horse collars
- two spades
- three iron wedges
- iron harrow teeth
- 3 hoes
- 1 auger [AH-ger] (drill for cutting holes for pegging timbers together)
- 3 chisels
- 1 gauge
- 1 hand saw
- files
- hammer
- draw knife
- froe
- 2 scythes and 1 sickle
- broad axe
- one grindstone for every three families
- 1 year's free clothing for each family
- 2 years' free food per family
- 2 horses, 2 cows, 6 sheep per family
- seeds—wheat, corn, peas, oats, flax and potatoes
- 1 blacksmith per township, with tools and iron

What the Cataraqui Loyalists got:
- axe
- hoe
- clothing (only for the needy, who were determined by appearance)
- 1 tent per family
- 1 musket for every five men
- 2 lbs. [.9 kg] of powder and 4 lbs. [1.8 kg] of lead balls
- food for three years (flour, beef and salt pork)
- seeds for each community consisting of 4 lbs. of onion seed; 11 lbs. [4.9 kg] of Norfolk turnip; 9 lbs. [4 kg] of early Dutch turnip; 12 lbs. [5.4 kg] of large Dutch cabbage; 4 lbs. of short top radish; 3 lbs. [1.3 kg] parsley; one bushel peas

USING YOUR KNOWLEDGE

27. a) List the items on the "wanted" list that do not appear on the list of items they received.

b) Do you think it was reasonable for the Loyalists to ask for these extra items? Were any items unnecessary?

c) Would you expect the two lists to be different? Explain your answer.

Conclusion

With few supplies and often little knowledge about farming, the Loyalists made new lives for themselves. The homes they carved out of the wilderness became thriving settlements.

The arrival of the Loyalists had profound effects on the colonies that were later to become Canada. For example, Loyalists who arrived in the colony of Nova Scotia built up a thriving settlement in the St. John River Valley. Many of these Loyalists were well-educated. They had their own ideas about how the colony should be run. However, the capital of the

Fig. 14-12 Traveling on the St. John River in New Brunswick, 1817.

Exact figures for the number of Loyalists who settled in present-day Canada are difficult to figure out since Loyalist immigration was not steady. Some settled and then returned to the United States. Others came to Halifax or Saint John and then moved to England.

colony, Halifax, seemed far away and unconcerned about the Loyalists. The St. John Loyalists therefore wanted their settlement to become a separate colony. In 1784, the British government created the new colony of New Brunswick.

The Loyalists brought other changes to the British North American colonies. Huge areas of wilderness in Nova Scotia and Quebec were cleared. Prosperous communities soon developed.

Perhaps the most important change of all was that the British population in the colonies suddenly increased. The communities they built up therefore had a strong British flavour. The nature of the British North American colonies was changed: they were part French and now strongly part British, too.

USING YOUR KNOWLEDGE

28. Loyalists left the Thirteen Colonies in two main waves. One group left at the beginning of the American Revolution, when conflict between the Loyalists and Patriots first arose. Another group, the late Loyalists, left after the war, when the British were defeated. Imagine that you were a Loyalist who was going to leave the Thirteen Colonies. When would you have left? Give reasons for your decision.

29. In this chapter, and in chapter 10, we saw how collisions between empires or between empires and their colonies can affect ordinary people. The Loyalists suffered; so did the Acadians.

a) Compare and contrast the Loyalists and the Acadians in a chart. Here are some points to use for your comparison; add at least three more points of your own:
—reasons for their suffering,
—type of persecution,
—effect on their way of life.

b) The French in the colony of Quebec were also affected by the collision of empires that ended in the Battle of the Plains of Abraham. How were the French treated by the British after the Seven Years' War? In a short paragraph, compare the treatment the French received with the way the Loyalists and Acadians were treated.

THINKING IT THROUGH

30. Canada today has a dual nature; it is part French and part British. The arrival of the Loyalists gave Canada much of its British heritage. Do you agree or disagree with this statement? Explain, making sure that you back up your opinions.

15 The War of 1812

The soldier boy

(It has been said that wars are often started by old men but fought by young men—and boys. This story is about one such boy, during one of Canada's early wars. Though René is imaginary, there were many real ones like him.)

René Drummond [druh-MOH^N] buttoned up his grey homespun jacket. It was part of the uniform he would wear as a member of Colonel Charles de Salaberry's "Voltigeurs" [VAHL-tee-ZHOER]. René was excited, as a 17-year-old was bound to be. He was going to be a soldier!

René did not know exactly why. The seigneur, M. Dubay, had asked him to join along with other young men of the district. They had heard the news that American armies had already been fighting on Canadian soil, far to the west of Montreal. Volunteers were needed to keep them out of Lower Canada.

René was already imagining himself in battle. His grandfather had told him stories about wars long ago. Once, when René's grandfather was a boy, the British had been the enemy. A few years later, the British and the French were on the same side. The enemy this time—the Americans. They had actually captured and held Montreal for awhile. They were trying to force the French to join them against Britain.

What was the United States trying to do now? It was hard to figure out why they were at war with the British again. Anyway, the name "United States" was just words to René. Even Montreal was a long way from his world. It seemed odd to him that strangers would come from far away to attack his part of the world.

In the next few weeks, M. Dubay said, René would be learning to be a soldier. The officers would show him what to do. They were Frenchmen, sons of seigneurs, trained by the British. When the Americans came, the French Canadian militia would be ready.

René was excited all right. He was nervous too. He had never really been away from home before. Certainly nobody had ever taken a shot at him. What would it be like?

- According to René, why was he preparing to go to war?
- Why was he excited?
- Imagine yourself to be in René's place. Tell how you might have felt.
- What do you think about a young person going to fight in a war he knows nothing about? Is loyalty to your country more important than any other responsibility; for example, to one's family?

- 1800
- 1811 ◀ Indians defeated at Tippecanoe
- 1812 ◀ U.S. declares war on Britain
- 1814 ◀ Britain and U.S. end war
- 1817 ◀ Rush-Bagot Agreement
- 1820

Chapter overview

In 1812, a war broke out between the U.S. and Great Britain. But the colonists in British North America were caught in the middle. The colonies were part of Britain's empire. Bordering on the U.S., they were the obvious target for American attack.

In this chapter, you will learn about the difficult spot the colonists found themselves in. You will also learn about the people who took part in the war, and some of the main events. You will see the way in which some of the problems were solved, and look at the effects of the war on the colonists and their attitudes.

Signposts

> Why did the British North American colonies and the U.S. fight the War of 1812?

> How did the War of 1812 begin?

> How did the war unfold?

> The War of 1812 in the Atlantic colonies

> FEATURE: The people and everyday life during the war

Key words

| right of search | War Hawks | stalemate |

Why did the British North American colonies and the U.S. fight the War of 1812?

The United States had been formed in 1783, after fighting a war of independence to break away from that empire. Anti-British feelings lingered long after in the hearts of many Americans. What if the British did something that made a lot of Americans angry? Britain was far away, across the Atlantic Ocean. Canada, a British colony, was close by, just across the border. Besides, Canada looked easy. Rich land, small population, few soldiers to protect it—and many of the settlers were former Americans!

The European background

By 1812, Britain and France had been fighting, on and off, for nearly 20 years. The ruler of France was Napoleon Bonaparte. Most of Western Europe had fallen under his control. But he could not get his armies over to invade Britain. The British navy was too strong.

Napoleon, therefore, tried to weaken Britain in other ways. He tried to cut off its trade with other countries. The idea backfired. The British used this idea against France. Because Britain had a bigger and stronger navy, they could stop ships from other countries much more effectively. Many of the ships stopped by the British came from the United States.

Besides preventing Americans from trading, the British had a second reason for stopping ships from the United States. The British insisted on the "**right of search**." That is, they would board a ship to search for sailors deserting a hard life in the British navy. Sometimes American sailors were seized and forced to be crew members on British ships.

People in the United States were angry. How dare the British treat Americans this way! Something must be done to make the British respect the young but proud country! Newspaper editorials and some politicians called for war against Britain. If war broke out, one thing was certain: the British North American colonies would be invaded.

For ordinary sailors, life in the British navy could be miserable. Sometimes sea captains had to fill out their crews with convicts.

Fig. 15-1 Tecumseh. The name means "a panther springing upon its prey."

The North American background

American settlers were moving farther and farther west. As they did so, they intruded on the territory of Indian peoples such as the Shawnee. The Indians felt their land was being taken from them. They decided to resist. The result was fighting, in which both Indians and Americans sometimes died. The Americans had guns, but so did the native peoples.

Where did the Indians get their guns? From the British colonies, thought many Americans. After all, Canadian fur traders were still active south of the border as agreed upon by the Treaty of Paris in 1783.

The event which brought things to a head was the Battle of Tippecanoe [TIH-pee-kuh-NOO], in Indiana in 1811. The Indian people, led by the great Shawnee chief, Tecumseh [tih-KUHM-seh], took a stand against the westward movement of the United States. The Indians were defeated by an American army, and many fled to Canada. If they could get the help of the British and Canadians, the Indians hoped to be able to keep alive their way of life.

A number of American politicians, from states such as Kentucky and South Carolina, believed that they could break the Indians' resistance to the westward expansion—if they could invade British North America. A successful invasion of British North America would eliminate the colonists there as possible allies of the native peoples. Because they wanted war, these Americans were nicknamed the "War Hawks."

The War Hawks claimed that Upper and Lower Canada would be easy to conquer. The claim seemed reasonable. The Canadian border was long, and defended by a small number of British soldiers and Canadian volunteers. The Canadian population was small. Because many were former Americans, invaders from the United States might be welcomed. Britain was too busy fighting Napoleon in Europe to send many soldiers to defend British North America.

An American takeover of British North America would be a big boost to the young United States. Britain might be taught a lesson, perhaps driven from the North American continent. The American settlers could move to the rich farmland of Canada.

GETTING THE FACTS

1. In a sentence or two, tell about each of the following: Napoleon Bonaparte, right of search, Shawnees, War Hawks.

USING YOUR KNOWLEDGE

2. Imagine you are an Indian who took part in the Battle of Tippecanoe. Tell how you feel about the outcome. Include such ideas as:
—your feelings about the American settlers moving westward;
—your dream of an Indian nation;
—the possibility of help from the British.

THINKING IT THROUGH

3. The following are comments on the causes of the War of 1812:

A. British actions caused the war. Britain had been fighting with France for years. Now Britain needed more sailors for its warships. The British began stopping American ships to see if there were sailors on board who had run away from the British navy. Sometimes British sea captains took American soldiers and made them work for low wages. This made the Americans angry, and the United States' government declared war.

B. The causes of the War of 1812 were numerous. A combination of problems, not just one problem, led to the outbreak of fighting. Clashes between British and American ships raised tempers on both sides. Some Americans blamed British and Canadian fur traders for stirring up Indian attacks on their settlements. War Hawks in the United States thought British North America could be taken over easily. Americans would then feel proud about increasing the size of their country. Even these reasons are only part of the explanation.

C. "Mr. Madison's War" is a good name for the War of 1812. James Madison had been president of the United States since 1809. He put down the idea of war for most of his four-year term. The British and anti-war Americans thought that the problems between the two countries could be solved peacefully. Madison seemed to have the same view. When the time for the next election—autumn 1812—drew near, Madison showed his true colours. Thinking he would get more votes, he convinced his government to start a war.

 a) Which of the three comments is most helpful in understanding the causes of the War of 1812? Give your reasons.

 b) What weaknesses can you detect in the other two comments? Give examples. (HINT: Remember about bias, faulty logic, oversimplifying, etc.)

How did the War of 1812 begin?

By June of 1812, President James Madison of the United States believed that war with Britain could not be avoided. He outlined his reasons to the rest of the government. The result was the decision to declare war.

In what was then "the West"—the Great Lakes region—the United States had a number of forts near the Canadian border. At one of these, Fort Detroit, news of the war arrived. On July 12, an army of more than 1000 Americans marched into Canada. The commander, General William Hull, made an announcement to the people of the colony of Upper Canada:

INHABITANTS OF CANADA

The army under my command has invaded your country. Do not be afraid. As long as you behave in a friendly way, you will not be harmed. Just continue with your normal, everyday lives.

I come to rescue you from the British. I am sure to succeed, so I do not even need your help. My army is powerful, and others like it are on the way.

If you choose to fight against us, we will have to treat you as enemies. Then you will discover how horrible war really can be.

The United States offers you peace, liberty and security. You must choose between these and war, slavery and destruction.

As quoted in *The Defended Border* by Morris Zaslow.

USING YOUR KNOWLEDGE

4. Put yourself in the place of an Upper Canadian hearing the announcement. What feelings and thoughts would it have aroused in you? (For example, would you have been afraid? Angry? Ready to do as the general said? Determined to join with others to drive out the invaders?) Explain why you would have reacted that way.

5. Is the announcement an example of propaganda? In your answer, refer to the definition of "propaganda" and show how the announcement does or does not fit the definition.

How did the war unfold?

In the War of 1812, British North America could be thought of as a tree. The Atlantic colonies were the roots, Upper and Lower Canada the trunk and the Great Lakes the branches.

In trying to conquer the British colonies, the United States could not really attack the roots. The Atlantic colonies were too well protected by the British navy. The branches were too widespread to be easily chopped. The trunk was the logical place to attack. The capture of Montreal or Quebec would cut British North America in two. Lines of supply and communication would be broken. Much of Canada's population would be left with little choice but to surrender.

Fig. 15-2 The War of 1812.

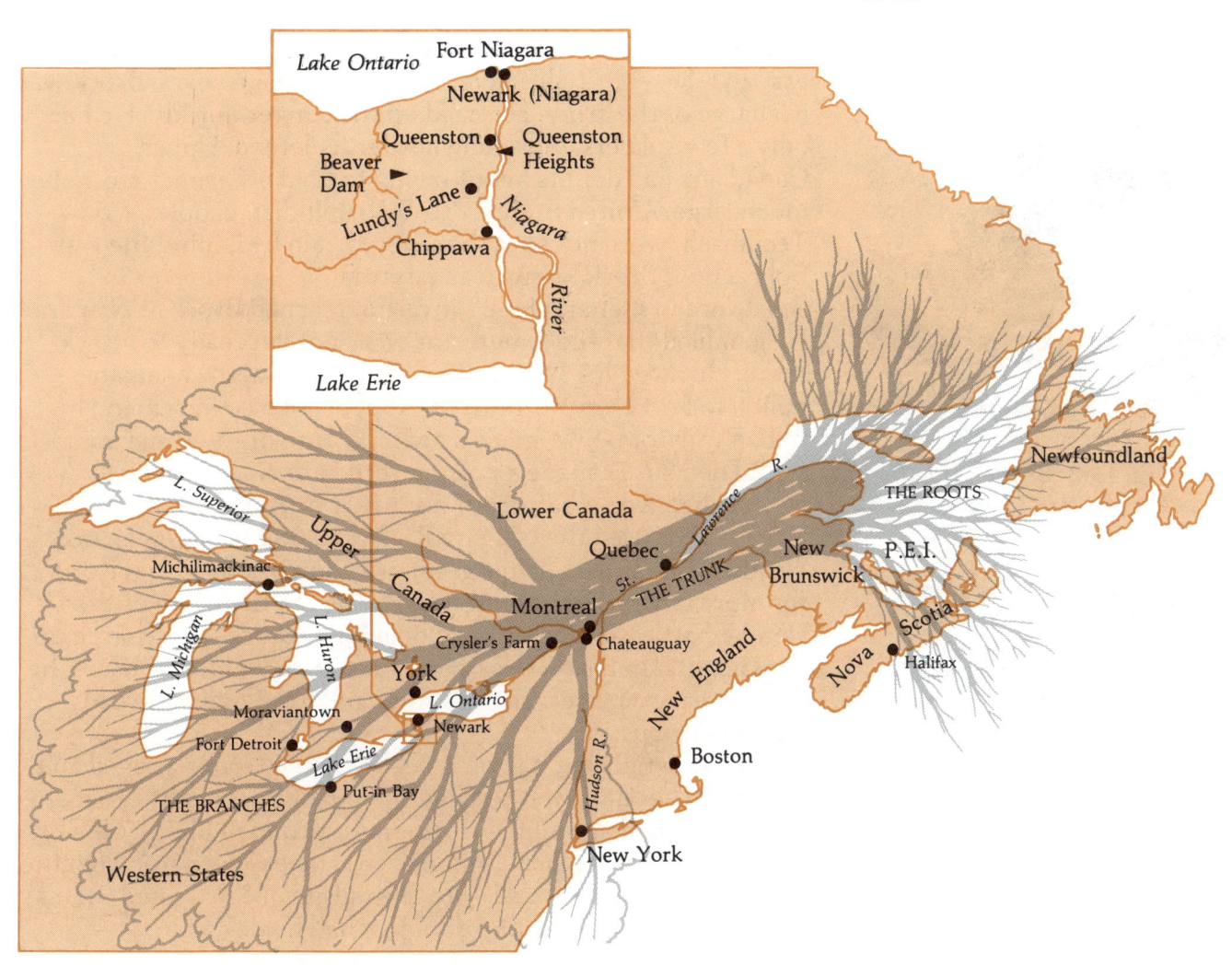

The American invasion began with the branches, however, under generals like Hull. Why? Several reasons have been given. Because many Americans did not support a war, their government went into it half-heartedly. An overall plan was not ready at the beginning.

On the other hand, the War Hawks came from the western states, near the branches. They thought that Upper Canada would make a nice addition to their region. With much of its population formerly from the United States, the War Hawks thought it would be easy to take.

Sir Isaac Brock: Man of action

Without Isaac Brock, in fact, Upper Canada might have been easy to take. A British soldier since his teenage years, Brock was in charge of the army. He sized up the danger quickly. He had only a few soldiers and a long border to defend. Upper Canadians had doubts about trying to hold off armies from the much larger United States. Pro-British Indian peoples, led by Tecumseh, were not sure they would gain by joining the war. Bold action, Brock knew, was essential.

Word of General Hull's invasion reached Brock at Niagara. He gambled that the Americans were not yet ready to attack there. He raced his army of British regulars and Canadian militia to Fort Detroit. With the support of Tecumseh and his Indian warriors, they made a swift capture of the American fort. Then Brock made a prompt return to Niagara.

He had won a battle but not the war. Another American army had crossed the Niagara River and occupied Queenston Heights. Brock, astride his great grey horse, Alfred, gave orders for more troops. Horse and rider dashed to the scene of the coming battle. On foot, sword held high, Brock led a charge up the Heights. In his officer's hat, red coat and white trousers, he was too easy a target. He was shot, and fell dying before his stunned troops.

Yet the fighting had only begun. Fresh troops arrived and, by a roundabout route, reached the top of the Heights. British soldiers, Canadian militia—including a group of black volunteers—and Indian allies combined to retake Queenston Heights.

The year 1812 ended with the failure of the United States' invasions. So far, Canada's defences had held.

Fig. 15-3 Brock's ride to Queenston, October 13, 1812.

Unlike many other people, Brock saw that Tecumseh's support was very important to the defence of Canada.

Fig. 15-4 The Battle of Queenston, October 13, 1812. This painting combines various stages of the battle. Examine it closely and identify as many stages as possible.

GETTING THE FACTS

6. In your notebook, draw an outline map of British North America from the Great Lakes to the east coast. (See Fig. 15-2 for the area that you should present on your map.) On your map, sketch the "tree" that is described in the text. For each of the main sections (roots, trunk, branches) label a few important places.

7. Why was the trunk the logical place for the U.S. to attack?

8. Why did the U.S. not attack the trunk?

THINKING IT THROUGH

9. Examine Fig. 15-3.
   a) In your opinion, does Brock look like a hero? Why or why not?
   b) Suppose the artist had wanted to show Brock as a coward and/or fool. What differences would there have been in the sketch?

329

10. Read the following lines from the poem, "The Bold Canadian."

> At length our brave commander
>   Sir Isaac Brock by name,
> Took shipping at Niagara,
>   And unto York he came.
>
> Says he, ye valiant heroes,
>   Will ye go along with me
> To fight those proud Yankees
>   In the west of Canada?
>
> And thus we replied,
>   We'll go along with you,
> Our knapsacks upon our backs,
>   Without further adieu.

From *Life and Times of Sir Isaac Brock* by D.B. Read.

a) Explain the following words and terms: took shipping, ye; valiant, adieu.

b) What do these lines tell you about Brock? About the people he invited to join him?

c) It has often been said that Canadians have no use for heroes and heroines. What do you think? Discuss this idea in class, and refer to Brock and other figures in Canadian history.

Laura Secord: A lady of legend

In the summer of 1813, the United States made another attempt to invade Canada. Once again, the main blows were aimed at the branches, from Niagara westward, rather than at the trunk.

In the Niagara region, at Queenston, lived Laura Secord. Like her husband, James, and their young family, she had become used to the sight of marching troops. Sometimes they were the blue-jacketed Americans, sometimes the British redcoats. Neither one side nor the other had control. The area was a "no man's land."

One day in June, a group of American soldiers stopped at Laura Secord's home. She overheard them talking. They spoke of a surprise attack on the British and Canadian force at Beaver Dam.

Fig. 15-5 Laura Secord at the headquarters of Commander FitzGibbon.

James was still recovering from wounds suffered at the Battle of Queenston Heights. Laura decided, however, that a warning must get through. She set off on a walk of 23 km, mainly across fields and through forests. In less than a day, she arrived with her message at the headquarters of the British commander, James FitzGibbon.

A surprise attack followed, but the approaching American army was the victim. Caught in a crossfire set up by Canadian Iroquois, it gladly surrendered to FitzGibbon. Had Laura Secord's warning made the difference? Or had FitzGibbon's Iroquois scouts already informed him the enemy was coming? Strange as it may seem, we do not know for sure.

When Laura got home, she described her adventure to her family and friends. A few officers, and probably some government people, knew about it. Otherwise, Laura's story was unknown for 40 years.

Then a magazine published an article about Laura Secord. It described her as the heroine of the War of 1812. Other writers and poets joined in praising her. She became a legend even before her death at the age of 93.

Is it possible that other women performed similar acts of courage, without getting any credit? Why or why not?

GETTING THE FACTS

11. What information did Laura Secord overhear?

12. What did she decide to do after overhearing the American soldiers?

USING YOUR KNOWLEDGE

13. Imagine you are Laura Secord or her husband. Write short diary entries for two important days in your life in June 1813.

THINKING IT THROUGH

14. Suppose the British already knew before Laura Secord arrived about the American plans to attack. Do you think she was a heroine anyway? Why or why not?

Tecumseh: The tragic warrior

As the year 1813 passed, American attacks on Upper Canada continued. Not much had changed for either the United States or Canada. But, for the Indian peoples led by Tecumseh, a lot had changed.

In the minds of the Indians, the branches of Canada and the land to the south were home. For the last 20 years, they had fought many battles to try to keep their home. Yet settlers kept coming. American armies, the "Long Knives," had defeated the Indians time after time.

Tecumseh, chief of the Shawnee, stuck to his dream of a separate Indian country. For much of his life of 44 years, he had been on the warpath. He was a leader respected by many Indian nations. He had even united them in an effort to stop the expanding United States. The enemy, however, had been too strong.

When the War of 1812 broke out, the Indians seemed to have a chance. If they joined the British and Canadians, they could perhaps turn the tables on the United States. Tecumseh's hopes were raised when he helped Isaac Brock capture Fort Detroit.

But Brock's death at Queenston Heights in October 1812 was a serious blow. In the year that followed, British control at the western end of Lake Erie grew weaker. Meanwhile, the United States used the time to build up its navy. As a result, having the upper hand on Lake Erie, the Americans were able to bring in fresh troops and supplies. As the months went by,

Fig. 15-6 The Battle of Lake Erie, September 10, 1813. Nine American vessels were pitted against a British fleet of six. The British fought with valour but suffered from a lack of sailors. The entire British fleet was captured in the end.

they regained control of Detroit and the surrounding area.

By October 1813, the British had fallen back well into Canadian territory. Their Indian allies had no choice but to do the same. Finally, Tecumseh was able to persuade the British commander to take a stand, not far from present-day Chatham, Ontario. The result: a bloody battle, American victory and the death of Tecumseh.

All hopes of a separate Indian country were gone. The leader was dead. So was Sir Isaac Brock, Tecumseh's partner early in the war. Back in England, the British government was giving almost its full attention to its main war—against Napoleon. The British view of the war with the United States was clear: get it stopped. What chance was there that British politicians would give thought to Indian rights?

GETTING THE FACTS

15. Give at least two reasons why Tecumseh chose to fight on the side of the British.

16. Why, during 1813, were the Americans successful in getting the upper hand on Lake Erie and the surrounding area?

USING YOUR KNOWLEDGE

17. What effect did the War of 1812 have on the future of the Indians of the Great Lakes region?

Colonel Charles de Salaberry: Defender of Quebec

Late in 1813, the United States was still putting much of its war effort into attacking Canada's branches. It was only a matter of time, however, before the American armies decided to attack the trunk. It was no great surprise when, in October 1813, an American force appeared to be headed for Montreal.

Colonel Charles de Salaberry was ready. With 800 volunteers—known as the Voltigeurs—and a number of Indian allies, he was waiting at Chateauguay [sha-toh-GAY], south of Montreal. On the morning of October 26, just as the sun rose, the American army of 4000 arrived and was met by rounds of heavy gunfire. The air was filled with the sounds of war whoops and bugle calls.

The Canadian plan worked as intended. The Americans believed that they were up against a much bigger army than they had expected. Their commander ordered them back across

Do you think René Drummond, "The soldier boy" from page 320, would have felt confident serving under Colonel de Salaberry's leadership? Why or why not?

Fig. 15-7 The Battle of Chateauguay, October 25, 1813. The artist has erred in his uniforms and arms, which are more of the style of 1820 than of 1813.

the border into the United States. Another invading army, advancing toward Montreal from the west along the St. Lawrence, suffered a bloody defeat at Crysler's Farm.

Montreal was out of danger. Having been threatened at last, the trunk of Canada held firm. So the year of 1813 ended. After 18 months of on-again, off-again fighting, the United States had little to show for its actions against Canada.

THINKING IT THROUGH

18. Which of the following statements do you most agree with?

a) War is always wrong.
b) War is right if your country is being invaded.
c) War is right if it helps people of a country feel united.

Give reasons for your point of view. Also refer to past wars such as the War of 1812, as well as to wars in the 20th century.

The War of 1812 in the Atlantic colonies

The cargo of one captured American ship consisted entirely of champagne [sham-PAYN]. It was carefully stored in the warehouse of a shipping company in St. John's, Newfoundland. As a Sunday pastime, three of the firm's employees took to using champagne bottles for pistol contests out on the wharf. The winner received a case of the bubbly stuff, while the loser paid for it.

The champagne prize was one of more than 200 captured by Atlantic privateers during the War of 1812. Privateers were privately owned, fast-sailing ships used for trade in peacetime. During the war, they were licensed by the British to attack enemy shipping. It was a risky business, but the possible rewards were great. One schooner, the *Liverpool Packet*, seized the cargoes of nearly 50 American ships and made a fortune for its owners and crew.

Not just the privateers but the Atlantic colonies in general enjoyed a "boom time" during the War of 1812. Britain's main naval base in North America was Halifax, a town of some 10 000 people. At times, it had nearly that many sailors, soldiers and prisoners of war in its midst. Saint John, New Brunswick and St. John's, Newfoundland were also important ports of call for the British navy. Never before had there been such demand for timber, farm products, foodstuffs and social life. Never before had so much money poured into the Atlantic region.

Another thing going for the Atlantic colonies was the attitude of the neighbouring New England states. People in this part of the United States were against the war. Trade with Britain had long been important to them. They even kept trading with the British colonies during the war. Along the New Brunswick-Maine border, people remained friendly with the "other side."

Meanwhile, the coasts of the Atlantic colonies were safe from attack by the small American navy. The British navy set up a blockade of American ports. In 1814, Napoleon was defeated and the war in Europe was coming to an end. Britain was then able to send many more ships to North American waters. Sailing out of Halifax and ports in the British West Indies, British ships tightened the blockade. One action after another was taken against United States territory.

One example was the takeover of towns on the coast of Maine. A region of the state was run by the British for several

Adapted from The Atlantic Privateers *by John Leefe.*

The people and everyday life during the war

War naturally makes us think about soldiers and generals, about guns and battles and killing; that is, about *military* facts and images. Sometimes we forget about the rest of the people and the effects of war on their everyday lives. The following quotations reveal something of the more "human side" of the war:

Farming in Upper Canada

Every family saw its able-bodied men go off to fight in the militia. As the entire colony of Upper Canada was mainly agricultural, most of the volunteers came from farms. They were constantly worried about their crops and livestock back home. While the men were away, the women had to manage the farms on their own. Besides the farm work, they had to deal with raids by soldiers, with visits from Indians who demanded food and accommodation for the night, and with any other unexpected troubles.

Whenever there was a lull between battles, the militiamen were allowed to go home to their farms. Many went home without permission to plant and harvest their crops. Food was important to the war effort, so who could blame them?

Based on *Laura Secord: The Lady and the Legend* by Ruth MacKenzie.

Halifax: Rich and rowdy

Halifax at this time was firmly under the influence of the British navy. For one thing, the town was well-protected against attacks from the United States. Besides, the navy spent a great deal of money in Halifax. Leading business people made fortunes, built expensive homes and enjoyed active lives. Farmers, fishermen, woodsmen and skilled craftspeople from all over the province sold their products in this prosperous town.

But there was another side to life in Halifax. Because the navy wanted complete control of the town, Haligonians [HA-lih-GOH-nee-uns] were not allowed to have their own police force. Day and night, drunken sailors and soldiers reeled about the streets. Townspeople took their lives in their hands if they ventured into certain parts of town. A section of Barrack Street was known as "Knock Him Down Street" because of the fights, and even murders, that were common there. The press-gangs, looking for able-bodied men for the navy, added to the danger.

Halifax was indeed a town of contrasts at the time of the War of 1812. Ugly slums sprawled a bottle's-throw away from mansions and fancy flower gardens. Taverns—which already looked as if they should be torn down—stood not far from Province House, built to last for centuries.

Based on *Halifax: Warden of the North* by Thomas Raddall.

USING YOUR KNOWLEDGE

19. Life in both Upper Canada and Halifax was affected by the War of 1812. However, they were affected in different ways.

a) Describe how the War of 1812 brought changes to each place.

b) In which of the two places do you think that the lives of ordinary people were changed most by the war? Give reasons for your answer.

An American eyewitness, Francis Scott Key, was inspired to write "The Star Spangled Banner" which became the anthem of the United States.

months. At the port of Castine [ka-STEEN], the British collected customs duties on all goods entering that part of the state. The conquered region was eventually restored to the United States at the end of the war. But the "Castine fund" of money was turned over to the governor of Nova Scotia. A few years later, the money was used to help start Dalhousie [dal-HOW-see] University.

A more spectacular action was the attack, in mid-summer of 1814, on Washington, D.C.. British troops overran the American capital city just after the President and other residents had fled to the countryside.

What followed was a British campaign of revenge. The previous spring, Americans had landed at York (Toronto), then the capital of Upper Canada. They met little opposition, but a British ammunition supply exploded, killing several of the invaders. Angrily they raided the provincial Parliament Buildings, then burned them down. Now the shoe was on the other foot. Several government buildings, including the White House, were set on fire. Sixty kilometres away, Fort McHenry (Baltimore) was bombarded by British guns.

Success on the Atlantic coast was not enough, however, to tip the balance in the war overall. The United States still had the upper hand on the Great Lakes. Just like the naval part of the war, the struggle on land had reached a **stalemate** [STAYL-mayt].

USING YOUR KNOWLEDGE

20. What does the story of the Liverpool Packet tell us about the War of 1812 in the Atlantic region?

21. How was the War of 1812 different in the Atlantic colonies from what it was in Upper and Lower Canada?

THINKING IT THROUGH

22. Wars always create bad feelings between the people of the nations in conflict.

a) Give one example from the War of 1812 in the Atlantic colonies that disproves this statement.

b) Do you think it was right for the two sides to keep on trading? Examine the pros and cons and then take a stand. Give reasons for your opinion.

Conclusion

By the fall of 1814, both sides were tired of the war. The governments of Britain and the United States agreed to stop fighting. They decided to hold meetings about the problems between them.

One important result was the Rush-Bagot [ruhsh-BA-guht] Agreement of 1817. The United States and Britain agreed not to put gunboats on the Great Lakes. Each side was allowed to keep one armed ship on Lake Champlain and Lake Ontario and two on the other Great Lakes.

In 1818, some big decisions were made about the border between the United States and British North America. At the end of the war, Britain held some territory south of the Great Lakes and in Maine. Britain might have expected to keep some of it. The United States seemed likely to put up a fight, however. Britain was not willing to argue, let alone fight. Their main worry was Napoleon, not the Americans. As a result, all captured lands were given back. The New Brunswick-Maine boundary was left unclear, and would not be settled until 1842.

The boundary through the Great Lakes was left as before the war. Beyond the Lake of the Woods, the 49th parallel was to be the dividing line all the way to the Oregon Territory, which was to be shared.

Fishing rights were another difficult problem. Britain finally agreed to allow Americans to continue fishing in the coastal waters of British North America. American fishermen also were given the right to dry their fish on the shores of Newfoundland and Nova Scotia.

The War of 1812 has sometimes been called "the war that nobody won." Neither side gained any land from the other. The British were unable to persuade the United States to agree to a separate territory for Indian peoples. The causes of the war seemed to have been forgotten when the post-war meetings were held.

The war did, however, have long-term effects. For years after, fears of another war remained. The United States built roads to the Canadian border for the use of armies on the march. On the Canadian side, the Rideau [REE-doh] Canal was constructed between Kingston and Bytown (Ottawa). This provided a second route between the St. Lawrence and the Great Lakes, in case the Americans did gain control of part of the Canadian "trunk." Fort Henry was built to guard the Kingston area of the canal route.

Both countries needed some way of stopping smuggling, which is the unlawful movement of goods across the border.

The Fenians, an Irish-American group, briefly occupied some Canadian territory in the Niagara region.

Fortunately, these preparations for war have never been needed. Small anti-British groups did launch raids into Canada as late as 1866; however, they never seriously threatened to cause a war between Canada and the United States. Gradually the memories of conflict faded. In the 20th century, the two countries can truly boast of having the "longest undefended border in the world."

Perhaps the most lasting effects of the War of 1812 were the traditions that followed from it. For many Americans, it was their second war of independence from Britain. It was proof that the United States was truly a country on its own. For Canadians, the war could be seen as proof of their determination to resist invasion. Moreover, it was a step toward a Canadian identity, as Canadians of different backgrounds and regions cooperated under pressure.

THINKING IT THROUGH

23. Write the following statements in your notebook. After each statement of FACT, print "F." After each VALUE statement, print "V":

a) The War of 1812 was the last war fought between Britain and the United States.
b) Canadian soldiers fought more bravely than the American ones.
c) The British thought they would be better off if the United States were defeated.
d) Many Indians thought they would be better off if the United States were defeated.
e) Women should get more credit for their brave actions in the war.
f) Once reservations were set aside for them, Indians were better off.
g) In the Atlantic colonies, the war was very different from what it was in Upper and Lower Canada.
h) Canada won the War of 1812.

24. The War of 1812 has been called "the war that nobody won." Yet, both the British colonies and the U.S. seemed to "win" or gain something, other than land, from the war.

a) How did each country benefit from the war? (Think of the "identity" of the country.)

b) Do you think these benefits are worth fighting a war over? Are there other ways of getting these benefits? If so, suggest some.

INVESTIGATIVE REPORTER

25. Use the encyclopedia and other books to find out more information about one of the following topics:
—The role of Upper Canadian women in the War of 1812
—Halifax in 1812: A town of contrasts

Present your information in a written report or in a poster or drawing. If you choose to do the poster or drawing, make sure your artwork presents as much information as possible.

16 Pioneer life

"I have a farm hard by—in the bush here."
"How large is it?"
"One hundred and forty acres [56.6 ha]."
"How much cleared?"
"Five or six acres [2 ha]—thereabout."
"How long have you been on it?"
"Five years."
"And only five acres cleared? That is very little in five years. I have seen people who had cleared twice that quantity of land in half the time." He replied almost with fierceness, "Then they had money, or friends . . . to help them; I have neither. I have in this wide world only myself! And set a man with only a pair of hands at one of them big trees there! See what he'll make of it! You may swing the axe here from morning to night for a week before you let the daylight upon you."

Anna Jamieson was a pioneer who described what life was like in Upper Canada in the 1840s in her book *Winter Studies and Summer Rambles in Canada*. This conversation is recorded in Vol. 2.

- Examine the painting closely. How many different farm activities can you identify? (HINT: Some of the activities are obvious, but others are not. Look closely at the objects in the picture—ladder, gun, axe, pot. They will give you clues to the other activities.)

- The passage above gives you a picture of early pioneer life. Write down as many adjectives as you can to describe pioneer life, based on your impressions from the passage.

- The passage describes the very first stage of farming. The painting reveals what pioneer farming was like after many years in the bush. In what ways would farm life change from the very early days to the later ones?

Chapter overview

The short passage you have just read gives you some idea about what it must have been like to be a **pioneer** around 1800. Pioneers who arrived in British North America between 1800 and 1850 faced a huge task. They had to cut down forests and try to establish farms. Often, if the soil was poor, they had to move to better land and start new farms.

What tools did the pioneers have to work with? They had the forest, the soil, some simple farm implements and their hands. The pioneers worked as best they could with these tools. By 1850, large areas of wilderness had been changed into thriving farm communities. There was a market for grain in England and other agricultural products and the timber trade flourished. Would you say that the pioneers were successful?

Signposts

> Making a living in the forest: The timber trade

> Making a living on the farm: Agriculture

> FEATURE: A little free advice to immigrants

> Making life enjoyable: Leisure

Key words

| pioneer | timber trade | bees |
| tools | agriculture | |

Making a living in the forest: The timber trade

Pioneer life began with the cutting of trees. No matter where the settlers landed, there were forests. Sometimes the trees were gigantic, and their outstretched branches kept the light from penetrating to the forest floor. This lack of light was a

Fig. 16-1 Clearing the land. Describe the various activities shown in this picture.

problem. Without light no crops would grow. The farmers had to have sunlight if they were going to produce enough food to live on. So the trees had to be cut down. At first, pioneers saw the trees as obstacles that kept them from making a living. Therefore, they cut and burned the trees. The pioneers wanted to clear the land as quickly as possible so they could plant wheat and produce food. This was urgent because, for example, the aid that the British government gave to the Loyalists had ended by 1788. Around the same time, there was also a famine that made it even more necessary to produce food.

In general then, the pioneers did not at first use trees as a way of making a living. However, from 1800 to 1850, trees became more and more important to the pioneer economy. The gradual development of products led to the growth of the timber trade.

(1) *Potash:* Potash [PAH-tash] was made from the ashes of trees. It was in demand in Europe, where it was used for making glass. The pioneers, therefore, could make a little extra money by selling their potash. Eventually, asheries were set up in the

Fig. 16-2 St. John and Portland, New Brunswick. Why do you think shipbuilding thrived here?

The crew on a timber raft might have as many as 50 or 60 men. They built their own shelters on the rafts. Often they had a fire for cooking, burning on a sandy hearth.

Loyalist farm communities. These asheries refined the potash, and then it was exported to Europe.

(2) *Masts:* Until 1815, Britain was involved in European wars. These wars created a new market for the pioneers. Great quantities of masts were needed for the Royal Navy. As early as 1774, the British knew they would need trees for masts. At that time, Britain did a survey of the forests of Nova Scotia. The best trees were identified and reserved for the navy. This survey was extended to Upper Canada when the supply of good white pine masts was used up in the Maritimes.

(3) *Square timber:* Europe needed wood for building, and this need was growing larger all the time. Also, the pioneer communities in North America needed timber, so the pioneer timber trade became important. Trees were felled, the limbs cut off and the trunks squared with an adze [adz] and a broad-axe. These timbers were then lashed together into monstrous wooden rafts (so big that houses were built on top of them).

The timber rafts floated downstream to the ports of Quebec and Saint John. There the timbers were loaded onto specially designed timber ships and transported to Europe. Frequently, these timber rafts were also used to carry produce from the farms along the Great Lakes for shipment to British markets.
(4) *Lumber cut in sawmills:* The next step in the growth of the timber trade was the establishment of sawmills. Sawmills produced boards for the expanding farms of the British colonies and also for the foreign market. Settlers used the boards to replace their log houses and barns with frame buildings. The structures made of boards were easier to build and could be made larger than log buildings. Log houses were often used as pig pens when Loyalist families moved into new frame buildings. The sawmill was therefore an essential step in the growth of pioneer communities. By 1854, there were 1618 sawmills in Upper Canada alone.

Fig. 16-3 Timber Cove, Quebec. How do you think the cove got its name?

Fig. 16-4 The corduroy road between York and Burlington. How do you think this kind of road got its name?

A shipwright is a person who knows how to build and repair ships.

In 1853, one hundred and twenty-two ships were built in New Brunswick alone.

(5) *Ships:* In the Maritimes, wood was necessary for the growing shipbuilding industry. As early as 1606, ships had been built at Port Royal. A schooner was built at Saint John in 1770, before the arrival of the Loyalists. But shipbuilding really became important when the Loyalists arrived. Many Loyalists had shipbuilding skills and this led to the construction of a large number of wooden ships. These early shipbuilders didn't need sophisticated factories; just a sawmill, a blacksmith shop, a group of men who were good with an axe, adze and auger, and a foreman who knew how to build a ship. The foreman, or shipwright, made the shipyard successful. North American oak was not as durable as European oak, so shipbuilders turned to tamarack, pine and spruce. The finished ships were often loaded with timber and dried fish from the Grand Banks. They then sailed to Europe on a one-way trip where both the cargo and the ship were sold. By 1800, British North America supplied more vessels of all kinds to Britain than any other country. In 1875, the peak year, nearly 500 ships were built. Most of these ships came from New Brunswick and Quebec. There was also shipbuilding in Nova Scotia, but these ships were not built for sale in Europe. They were built to be used in the colonies. The ports of Nova Scotia gradually filled up with fishing schooners built in the colonies.

Potash, masts, square timber, sawn lumber and ships: over

the years, the pioneers developed and sold these products made from trees. Wood products became an important part of the early pioneer economy.

GETTING THE FACTS

1. Examine each of the pictures on pages 346-50 carefully. In your notebook write answers to all the questions asked in the captions.

USING YOUR KNOWLEDGE

2. Trees were at first a hindrance then later a help to the pioneers.
    a) Look up the word "hindrance" in the dictionary and write the definition in your notebook.
    b) In a paragraph, explain why the above statement is true. In your answer, describe the different ways that the pioneers used trees.

3. Choose one of the pictures on pages 345-50 and put yourself in the scene. In a short paragraph, describe what you would do, how you would feel, and the people you might meet.

Making a living on the farm: Agriculture

What crops grew on pioneer farms?

Soon after they started farming, the settlers had patches of wheat, rye, oats, buckwheat and peas growing on the little fields that were studded with the stumps of trees. Indian corn, squash, melons, pumpkins and gourds [GOOR-dz] were also planted. These crops show the influence of Indian agriculture on the new farmers. Flax, used for clothing, was also important.

    Some people even planted orchards in this early period. In 1794, a traveler in Upper Canada noted that "Peaches, cherries and currants are plenty among the first settlers." Within the next decade, the slower-growing apple orchards were in full production and small cider factories were beginning to appear.

Were pioneers able to survive on these crops?

At first these farmers produced only enough food and fibres for their own use. But no matter how independent the farmers tried to be, they needed some manufactured goods. To buy iron tools or cotton clothing, it was necessary to have money. While

Fig. 16-5 Do you think these settlers look like experienced farmers?

"The working oxen of this country are very docile and easily managed. They are extremely useful in the new settlement; indeed, I do not know what could be done without them. It is next to an impossibility to plough among the green stumps and roots with horses—the plough being continually checked by roots and stones."—Samuel Strickland, *Twenty-Seven Years in Canada West*, Vol. 1.

The pigs were so ugly and so ferocious that some farmers called them "alligators," although the term "razor back" was more common.

the forests remained, farmers could sell wood products for extra money. Furs from the decreasing supply of wild animals also provided some cash (and food in time of famine). But animals and forests were slowly disappearing, so pioneers needed a more reliable source of extra money. They turned to their own farms for new ways of increasing their income.

Oxen, cows, pigs, sheep and even a few horses were soon part of the frontier farms. Pigs ran loose in the woods if there were no barns. In the fall they were hunted and killed like wild animals. All these animals, along with surplus grain grown on the farm, provided farmers with extra cash.

Farmers found they had a good market for their products at the garrisons of British soldiers protecting the Canadian border. Bread and salt pork were the staples of army life. In 1793-94, farmers on the Bay of Quinte were able to sell 480 barrels of pork to local garrisons. Breweries and distilleries soon appeared, providing another market for local grain.

As more and more farms became established, the amount of grain grown steadily increased. Wheat became the most profitable product of farms. Wheat production led to the building of flour mills all over the colonies. In 1801, Upper Canada had exported 13 963 barrels of flour to Montreal. There it was loaded aboard ocean-going ships and taken to the British market.

Fig. 16-6 The early grist mills were powered by constructing a dam across a small river; the falling water was used to turn a wheel which, in turn, moved a series of wheels. In this way the power was transferred to the millstones that ground the grain into flour.

Fig. 16-7 Flax was a very useful crop in the 19th century. The stalk provided linen thread, the seeds were used for animal and human food, and the linseed oil was used as a preservative for leather. Yet, flax was never a popular crop among Ontario farmers. Does the picture above suggest why this is so?

Hessian soldiers came from Hesse, a region in present-day West Germany.

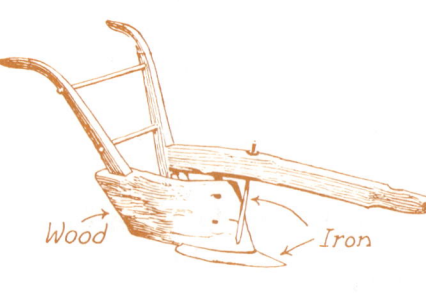

Fig. 16-8 Wooden plough

What problems did farmers have with the wheat crop?

Constant wheat-growing soon drained nutrients from the soils all over eastern North America. Farmers, pressed by the need to survive, gave little thought to crop rotation. Fertilizers did not really exist. But the biggest threat to the wheat crops was the Hessian fly. This small fly had come to North America in the straw mattresses of Hessian soldiers hired by the British to fight during the American Revolution. The flies fed on grain growing on the eastern coast of North America and spread deeper into the interior each year. By 1800, the Hessian fly was so destructive that large areas of Upper Canada could no longer grow wheat.

Farmers had to look to some other agricultural product for a cash income. Increasingly they turned to mixed farming.

This didn't mean that wheat disappeared as a product. It just meant that resourceful farmers grew other crops as well as wheat. Tobacco, possibly introduced by Black Loyalists, became a new cash crop in Upper Canada. But tobacco required too much labour. Flax also had its limitations. Flax threads were useful for linen grain-bags, towels and coarse clothing, but beyond home use there was no market.

After 1815, increasing waves of immigrants left the British Isles to settle in British North America. Many of these were Scottish weavers and small farmers who had been pushed out of Scotland. They travelled across the Atlantic on the timber ships. These ships therefore carried cargo both ways: square timber over to England and immigrants back to the colonies. As more and more immigrants came, they established farms. Their farms turned out even more agricultural products for sale.

What farm tools were used?

Up until 1850, farmers used simple hand tools. The tools were made of wood with the scarce, hence valuable, pieces of iron placed along the cutting edges only.

Ploughs were needed to cut and turn over the soil around the great pine and oak tree stumps on the farm fields. Power was provided by a yoke of oxen, as horses were prone to break their legs on the rough ground. These early ploughs were homemade. By 1850, cast iron ploughs were becoming more and more common.

Once the land was ploughed, it had to be harrowed, or leveled (made flat). This was done by using iron harrow "teeth" driven through a wooden frame. Next the grain was sown by hand. Then the harrow was dragged back across the field to bury the seed.

Harvesting was much more difficult. Once the grain was ripe, there was only a ten-day period in which it could be collected. So farmers could plant as many crops as they could harvest in the ten days. A farmer with a big family could harvest a big crop. Perhaps the most important implement next to the plough was the cradle scythe [sīth]. This machine allowed skilled cradlers to harvest about one hectare a day. It was backbreaking work. After cradling, the bundles of cut grain then had to be bound into sheaves, loaded onto wagons and stored away in barns for the fall and winter threshing.

Threshing was the process of separating the seeds of the wheat from the straw. It was done with a flail, which was made of two pieces of wood with a leather strap between. Using a flail, the farmer pounded the grain sheaves to separate the wheat from the straw. Later, the straw was raked away and the grain was winnowed [WIH-nohd] by throwing it into the air and letting the wind blow away the chaff, leaving the clean kernels of wheat on the barn floor.

Agriculture between 1791 and 1850 was therefore fairly simple. All the necessary equipment—a plough, a harrow, two

Fig. 16-9 The cradle scythe was a North American invention. Can you figure out how it worked from the photograph? Why would a cradle scythe be more efficient than the scythe or the sickle?

Fig. 16-10 Grain was threshed with swiveled flails. Find out how they worked.

Fig. 16-11 Around 1800, most farms were located in present-day Ontario, Quebec and the Atlantic provinces. However, settlement in the west was also beginning. In 1811, a Scotsman, Lord Selkirk, brought settlers to areas located in present-day Manitoba. This is a picture of the settlement on the Red River. What do you think the windmill was used for?

Chores that young people did on the farm:
Gathering firewood
Helping round up cattle
Helping in the fields
Carrying water
Spinning
Weaving
Grating salt
Cleaning candlesticks
Knitting
Looking after younger brothers and sisters
Helping to feed and care for the animals

Other jobs on the pioneer farm:
Churning butter
Making soap and candles
Butchering animals and preserving meat
Spinning thread
Weaving cloth
Making furniture

oxen, a couple of cradle scythes and a couple of flails—could be kept in one small building or even a lean-to attached to the log cabin. It wasn't until 1850 that this system changed very much.

GETTING THE FACTS

4. Name at least five crops found on pioneer farms.
5. a) Why did pioneers have to find new ways to make money?
   b) What did they do to make extra money?
6. What became the most profitable product of Loyalist farms?

USING YOUR KNOWLEDGE

7. Imagine you are a pioneer with family back in England. Write a letter to your relatives in which you explain why you are now having trouble growing wheat. Explain the problems this is causing you (you have a large family—seven children to feed and clothe!). Also mention what you can do about the problem.

8. Choose one of the farm implements described in the chapter.
   a) Draw a picture of it in your notebook and explain how it works.
   b) What tool or machine is used today for the same job?

9. The pictures in the chapter represent the early years of pioneer life, when the land and the farming community was not very developed. Describe at least four pieces of evidence in the pictures to support this statement.

A little free advice to immigrants

Immigrants are often anxious to purchase a farm partially cleared, and for those who can afford it, this is a very good plan. But you must not let your English prejudices against stumps lead you to give an extravagant price for a farm where stumps have disappeared; for from the slovenly [SLAH-vehn-lee] mode of farming pursued in this country, these farms are exhausted—that is to say, crop after crop of wheat has been taken off them until they will yield nothing; and then, when they will not return the seed that is sown in them, the wily proprietor finds a greenhorn who wants a fine cleared farm, and next autumn the poor man discovers too late, that it will cost him more money than would have bought and cleared a wild farm. To such an extent is this system carried, of growing wheat without relieving the land by a rotation of crops, or a single cart-load of manure, that I have known 27 crops of wheat taken off a field consecutively, and then, if it cannot be sold, it is allowed to grow up with briars and brambles, and the owner sets himself to clear new land. Persons wishing to buy a cleared farm would do well to rent a farm for a year or so, until they have acquired sufficient knowledge of the country to be able to judge for themselves.

From *Louisa Clarke's Annual, 1843*. Louisa Clarke was a pioneer settler who wrote a journal giving advice to other settlers.

GETTING THE FACTS

10. Explain the meaning of the following words: extravagant, slovenly, wily, proprietor, greenhorn, consecutively.

11. In the passage, Louisa Clarke says that it is better to buy a wild farm than a cleared one. Explain why.

12. According to Louisa Clarke, why was the soil exhausted?

USING YOUR KNOWLEDGE

13. Often, Loyalist farmers were called "land butchers" by later immigrants.
    a) What do they mean by this term? Is it a compliment or an insult?
    b) Do you think Louisa Clarke would refer to the farmers as "land butchers"? Explain your answer.

14. Writers in the early 19th century often came from wealthy families in England. They were quick to criticize Canadian pioneer farmers for their untidy farms and unscientific farming methods. If you were a farmer how would you respond to this attack?

Making life enjoyable: Leisure

Work was important to pioneer farmers and so they spent most of their time working. But their lives were not as lonely as you might think. Pioneer farmers often got together to help a neighbour clear land, harvest grain, or raise a new barn. These work gatherings were called "**bees**." When people got together for a bee they did more than work. They exchanged ideas, told jokes, tested tools and provided opportunities for their young people to find mates. Bees were organized for all kinds of activities, such as logging, corn-husking, apple-coring, harvesting, quilting and butchering. Samuel Strickland described a logging bee in 1826:

The story of the bee found in *Twenty-Seven Years in Canada West*, Vol. 1, by Samuel Strickland.

> As soon as the ground was cool enough, I made a logging bee, at which I had five yokes of oxen and twenty men, four men to each team. The teamster selects a good place to commence a heap, generally against some large log which the cattle would be unable to move. They draw all the logs within a reasonable distance in front of the large log. The men with the hand-spikes roll the logs one upon the top of the other, until the heap is seven or eight feet [about 2 m] high, and ten or twelve [3 or 4 m] broad. All the chips, sticks and rubbish are then picked up and thrown on the top of the heap. A team and four good men should log and pick an acre [.4 ha] a day when the burn has been good.
>
> My hive worked well, for we had five acres [2 ha] logged and set fire to the same evening. On a dark night, a hundred or two of these large heaps all on fire at once have a very fine effect, and shed a broad glare of light for a considerable distance. In the month of July in the new settlements, the whole country at night appears lit up by these fires.

Hard work was followed by evenings of dancing and games:

> We managed to enjoy ourselves very much. After tea, dancing commenced, to the music of two fiddles, when the country-dances, reels and French fours were all performed with much spirit. The music was very good, the dancing indifferent.
>
> During the pauses between dances, some lady or

Fig. 16-12 A village dance in 1840.

gentleman would favour the company with a song. Then plays were introduced; such as hunt the slipper, cross questions and crooked answers, and several others in which forfeits had to be redeemed by the parties making mistakes in the game—a procedure of course productive of much noise, kissing, and laughter. Refreshments were handed around in great production, and the entertainment would end up with a dance.

USING YOUR KNOWLEDGE

16. Bees and dances were only two ways the pioneers enjoyed themselves. Suggest five other ways the pioneers could have spent their leisure time.

Conclusion

The people who went into the wilderness to carve out lives for themselves suffered many hardships. Were they successful? Read the following passage written by an early pioneer woman, Catherine Parr Traill, and decide for yourself:

> When we first came up to live in the bush . . . there was but two or three settlers near us and no roads out. . . . Very great is the change that a few years have effected in our situation. . . . A village has started up where formerly a thick pinewood covered the ground; we have now within a short distance of us an excellent saw-mill, a grist-mill and store, with a large tavern and many good dwellings.

From *The Backwoods of Canada* by Catherine Parr Traill.

THINKING IT THROUGH

17. In modern society, we sometimes hear about people who want to "return to the land." In general, this means taking up a pioneer way of life. They plan to grow their own food, make their own clothes, and provide for their own needs.
    a) Why do you think some people would want to live a pioneer sort of life?
    b) Make a list of the advantages of living a pioneer life (for example—no traffic jams!) and another list of the disadvantages (no hot water taps in the house!)
    c) Would you want to adopt a pioneer way of life? Give reasons for your answer.

INVESTIGATIVE REPORTER

18. Choose one aspect of pioneer life that interests you and find more information about it. Here are some suggested topics. Choose one of these or select your own topic:

a) school days
b) pioneer medicines and home cures
c) house-building
d) bees
e) role of churches

Present your information in any form that you want; for example, written report, pictures, models, short stories, posters.

Pronunciation key for English words

SYMBOL	EXAMPLE	[PRONUNCIATION. Parts of the word to be emphasized are in capital letters.] RESPELLING
a	bat	bat
ay	say, date, air	[say], [dayt], [ayr]
ah	all, car, lot	[ahl], [cahr], [laht]
eh	let, meant	[leht], [mehnt]
ee	see, hear	[see], [heer]
er	her, learn, fur	[her], [lern], [fer]
ih	sit	[siht]
ī	mīle	[mīl]
ir	sir	[sir]
oh	no, flow	[noh], [floh]
oi	oil, joy	[oil], [joi]
oo	boot, rule, through	[boot], [rool], [throo]
or	corn, door, store	[corn], [dor], [stor]
ow	cow, out, bough	[cow], [owt], [bow]
u	put, look	[put], [luk]
uh	fun, but	[fuhn], [buht]
yoo	few, cue	[fyoo], [cyoo]
ch	chin, beach	[chihn], [beech]
g	go, big	[goh], [bihg]
j	jet, giant, bridge	[jeht], [JĪ-ant], [brihj]
k	kite, cup, back	[kīt], [kuhp], [bak]
ks	tax	[taks]
kw	queen	[kween]
ng	song	[sawng]
s	say, cent	[say], [sehnt]
sh	she, conscious	[shee], [KAHN-shuhs]
th	that, death	[that], [dehth]
<u>th</u>	breathe	[bree<u>th</u>]
y	yet, union	[yeht], [YOO-nyuhn]
z	zeal, use	[zeel], [yooz]
zh	pleasure	[PLEH-zher]

Pronunciation key for French words

Vowels
(Sounds for which there are no English equivalents)

SOUND	SYMBOL	EXAMPLE	[PRONUNCIATION] RESPELLING
eu	œ (this is a little like the sound in "her")	seul	[sœl]
e, eu	eu (this is a little like the sound in "put")	le, je	[leu], [zheu]
u	u^e (to make this sound, purse your lips as if to whistle and try to say "ee")	rue	[ru^e]
oi	wah (this is a little like the sound in "water," but the lips must be a little more pursed)	voiture	[vwah-TU^{E}R]
ui	wee (this is a little like the sound in "week," but your lips must be a little more pursed)	oui	[wee]

Nasals
(These sounds should be made through your nose, but without actually pronouncing the "n" or "m")

SOUND	SYMBOL	EXAMPLE	[PRONUNCIATION] RESPELLING
an (m), en (m)	ah^n	dans,* vent	[dah^n], [vah^n]
on (m)	oh^n	bon	[boh^n]
ain (m), in (m)	a^n	pain, vin	[pa^n], [va^n]
un (m)	u^n	brun	[bru^n]

*The final consonant of a French word is not usually pronounced.

Glossary

allies People or countries that join together for a common purpose; for example, to fight against an enemy.

ancestors People you are descended from, such as great-grandparents, who lived in an earlier time.

Anglicize To make a group of non-English people as English-like as possible. This may mean teaching them to speak English and follow English customs.

anthropologist A person who studies the way of life or culture of groups of people in order to understand all humans.

archaeologist A person who studies the life of ancient peoples by discovering and examining their artifacts.

arms race Two or more nations try to gather the greatest number of weapons. They often do this to prepare themselves in case of war.

artifacts Things made by human work. Tools, weapons and pieces of sculpture are all examples of artifacts.

auction Public sale of things (or persons in the days of slavery) to the highest bidder.

bee A gathering at which neighbours work together at tasks such as barn-raising or harvesting. Bees were often social events; after the work was finished, people would eat, dance and play games.

blockade The blocking off of a city or region from contact with the outside world.

cabinet Advisors to the head of government.

censitaires Farmers of New France who rented land from a lord or seigneur. They were habitants. The rent they paid to the seigneur was called the cens.

charter A government grant that gives rights to a person in a written form.

Château Clique Nickname given by French-Canadians to members of the governor's council.

colony A settlement located far from the country that founded it and that still governs it.

confederacy A league or joining together of countries, states or tribes.

Confederation A union of Canadian colonies under one central government. The central government controls certain matters. Each colony, or province, however, still has its own government for local matters.

consensus Agreement about an issue by all people who will be affected by the issue.

constitution A set of laws or rules that say how a country will be governed.

council A group of people, usually appointed, who make decisions or give advice.

coureurs de bois French-Canadian trappers and fur traders.

culture The way of life of a people. Culture includes language, dress, foods eaten and art.

democracy A form of government where the people have the power to make decisions. They may do this through elected representatives.

deported Sent back to the country from which a person came.

dig An area that is being examined for artifacts and other clues about people of the past and their way of life.

discovery Anything that you find or learn about for the first time.

documents Sources of information such as letters, diaries and reports.

elected assembly A group of people chosen by voters to make laws.

election The process by which people choose representatives.

Europeans People from any country in Europe.

expulsion The act of forcing people to leave.

Family Compact Nickname given to a small group in Upper Canada that made the important political decisions.

Fenians A secret Irish brotherhood formed in New York to free Ireland from English rule. The Fenians' plans included capturing Canada and forcing England to free Ireland.

filles du roi Women brought to Canada from France to marry men settled in New France. This was part of France's plan to increase the population of the colony.

frontier Undeveloped region near a settled area.

government People who officially run the affairs of a country, province, region or town.

guerilla warfare A style of warfare in which small groups of hidden soldiers launch surprise attacks on the enemy.

habitant A farmer in New France. Also called a censitaire.

habitation A house. In the early days of New France it referred to a colony or settlement; for example, the habitation at Quebec.

heritage Something handed down from ancestors.

Huronia The area between Georgian Bay and Lake Simcoe in which the Huron Indians lived.

hypothesis An educated guess or unproved theory.

imperial Having to do with an empire. An imperial struggle is a struggle between two empires such as England and France.

Industrial Revolution The changes in society that resulted when machines and factories replaced hand labour.

industrialization The large-scale production of goods by machines in factories rather than by hand.

intendant Royal official in charge of a colony or settlement.

Inuit Native North American people who live largely in the far northern regions of the continent.

Jesuit Member of the Society of Jesus, a Roman Catholic religious order for men founded in 1534.

land granting The giving of land to a person by the government.

legend A story passed down through the generations. Legends deal with something that happened in the past. People usually believe that the stories behind the legends are true, but there is no way of knowing for sure.

legislative Having to do with making laws. A legislative council is a council that makes laws.

Loyalists Those people who remained loyal to Britain during the American Revolution.

Métis People of Indian and European ancestry. For example, the child of a French-Canadian father and an Indian mother is a Métis.

militia Ordinary citizens trained to help the army fight in times of emergency.

Minutemen Armed citizens of the Thirteen Colonies who were ready to fight British troops at a minute's notice.

missions Headquarters of a religious group, such as the Jesuits, that is trying to spread its beliefs.

monopoly Complete control of trade by one person or group.

municipal Having to do with the government for villages, towns and cities.

nation An established community of people who usually share a language, territory and culture.

native peoples The original inhabitants of Canada. Native peoples include Indians and Inuit.

New World The Western Hemisphere, including North and South America.

Northwest Passage A water route from the Atlantic to the Pacific Ocean through the Arctic.

outpost A settlement on a frontier or border.

parliament Name of the national legislature of Canada, the body that makes laws for the country.

Patriot A person who supported the rebellion of the Thirteen Colonies against Britain in the American Revolution.

Patriotes French word for "patriots," people who are loyal to their country. The term was used by the group of people who were against the British in Lower Canada in the 1830s.

pioneer In history, a settler in a new territory.

polling place The place where people go to vote.

press-gang A group who round up others and force them to serve in the army or navy.

privateer A privately-owned ship hired by governments in wartime to attack enemy ships. Merchant ships in particular were targets for privateers. This term is also used to refer to the commander of such a ship.

Proclamation Line Boundary of the Thirteen Colonies running along the Appalachian Mountains. The land west of the mountains was declared an Indian reserve.

propaganda Information used to convince people to accept a certain point of view. The information usually contains twisted facts, or presents only part of the story. Propaganda may take such forms as printed material, speeches and films.

radicals People who want very great changes at once.

rebel A person who revolts against the government or against any figure of authority and control.

rebellion An uprising of rebels against a government or other authority that they think is unjust.

records Anything that gives us information about people or events. Records can take the form of written accounts such as letters or books, or they may also be objects, such as tools.

Reformers People who try to bring about changes. This term was given to the people against the Family Compact in Upper Canada in the 1830s.

representation The action of a person or group acting on behalf of others. In government this means that elected or appointed members stand up for the rights and interests of the people they represent.

representative assembly A body of government in which laws are made by members who are acting on behalf of others.

representative government Government based on the election of representatives so that people have some say about their affairs.

responsible government A form of government in which the executive council (the governor's advisors) could be voted out of power by the elected assembly. This means that the assembly has control of the government; the governor and council cannot ignore the assembly's wishes.

right of search In wartime, the right a country has to search ships for deserters from the army or navy, for weapons, or for smuggled goods.

seigneur In New France, a lord who owned land and rented it to farmers.

seigneurial system A system of land-use in New France based on the feudal system of Europe. The king granted control of land to the intendant, who divided it among seigneurs, who rented it to the censitaires.

seigneury Name for the large block of land owned and controlled by a seigneur.

siege A military attack in which an enemy army surrounds a town or fort to cut off supplies. It involves bombarding the town in an attempt to force the people to surrender.

stalemate A situation between opposing parties in which things come to a standstill. In this state, no effective actions can be taken and no decisions can be made.

status quo The way things are at a certain period of time. For example, the political status quo of the 1830s was the set of attitudes, values and situations in politics that was commonly accepted at the time. The Reformers and Patriotes rebelled against the status quo, or the accepted way; they wanted radical changes in the system of government.

technology Tools, machines and ways of using them which provide a people with the things they want and need.

Tories　Name given to members of the Conservative Party. It is also the nickname given to people loyal to Britain during the American Revolution.

traditions　Beliefs, customs and practices handed down from generation to generation.

union　A combining or joining of parts.

U.S. Civil War　War fought from 1861-65, when Southern States tried to break away from the United States.

Vikings　Sea-adventurers and pirates from Scandinavia who traveled far and wide in the tenth and eleventh centuries, even to North America.

voyageurs　Employees of fur-trading companies who paddled freight canoes through the river systems of North America.

War Hawks　People strongly in favour of war.

Index

Acadia, 188-208. *See also* Nova Scotia.
   expulsion of the Acadians, 202-208, 220, 222
Adams, John, 285
Adams, Sam, 283, 285, 287
Alexander, Sir William, 178
Algonquins, 27, 108, 110, 112
American Revolution, 266, 274-293
Anse aux Meadows, L', 81-82
Argall, Captain Samuel, 192
Arnold, Benedict, 288
Artifacts, of early humans, 10-16
Aulnay, Charles de Menou d', 194, 195, 196, 198
Aulneau, Jean-Pierre, 132-134

"Bees," 356
Beothuks, 100-105
Biencourt, Charles, 192, 193
Blackfoot Indians, 61-66
Black Loyalists, 311
Bonaparte, Napoleon, 323, 324, 336, 339
Boston Massacre, 274-275
"Boston Tea Party," 283, 285
Boycotting, 283
Brant, Joseph, 299
Brant, Molly, 299-301
Brébeuf, Jean de, 113, 114
Brock, Sir Isaac, 328, 333, 334
Brûlé, Etienne, 93, 126-127
Brunet, Michel, 247
Butler, Colonel John, 299, 300

Cabot, John, 87-88
Carleton, Sir Guy, 264, 288, 305
Cartier, Jacques, 89
   meetings with Micmacs, 105-107
"Castine fund," 338
Cause and effect, in study of history, 31-37
Censitaires, 135, 137
Champlain, Samuel de, 7, 27, 90, 126
   establishment of Quebec, 124
   founding of Port Royal, 123
   relationship with Indians, 108-111, 112
Charles I (King of England), 178, 182
Charles II (King of England), 182, 183
Charlesbourg-Royal, 122
Chesnaye, Charles Aubert de le, 138-140, 142
Chronology, in study of history, 30
Clark, Louisa, 355
Columbus, Christopher, 78, 79, 83-86
Committees of Correspondence, 283, 287
Constitutional Act (1791), 268-269
Continental Army, invasion of Canada by (1775), 288
Continental Congress, 283, 284, 285
Cormack, William E., 104
Coureurs de bois, 127, 148, 149-151

Daughters of Liberty, 283
Declaration of Independence, 284, 285
Democracy, *See also* Elected assembly; Representative government; Responsible government.
   in Nova Scotia, 267
   in Quebec, 264
De Monts, 90, 123, 190, 191, 192
Dollard, Adam, 27-32

Early humans, 9-16
Economy, of New France, 137-142
Elected assembly, 262, 263, 264
   in Nova Scotia, 267
   in Upper and Lower Canada, 268-269
Elizabeth I (Queen of England), 167, 169
Explorers, list of, 93

Facts, 21-26. *See also* "Getting the Facts" section in each chapter.
   versus opinions, 25-26
Farming
   in New France (1750), 156-158
   pioneer farms, 349-355
   in Upper Canada during the War of 1812, 337
Fishing, 87, 175, 339
FitzGibbon, James, 331
Fort Beausejour, 203, 207
Fort building, 215
Fort Henry, 339
Franklin, Benjamin, 286
Frost, Sara, 305-308
Frost, William, 305
Fur trade, 87, 265
   in New France, 108, 112, 123, 138-139, 147-151, 155
   source of rivalry between French and English empires, 212, 213-214

Gaspé, 222
Gilbert, Sir Humphrey, 169
Government
   in English colonies in America, 180-186
   among the Iroquois, 56-58
   in New France, 137-142
   in Quebec after 1763, 254-270
   representative, 185-186, 268-269
   in Upper and Lower Canada, 268-269
Grand Banks, 87, 181
Greenland, 77, 79
Griffon (ship), 154
Guy, John, 100-102

Haldimand, Governor, 300, 314, 316
Halifax, 218-219, 222, 311, 318, 336
   elected assembly in, 267
   in the War of 1812, 337
Hall, Charles Francis, 94

Hancock, John, 285, 287
Henry VIII (King of England), 176
Herjolfsson, Bjarni, 79
Hessian fly, 352
Hudson, Henry, 93, 191
Hull, General William, 326, 328
Hurons, 27, 54, 56, 58-61
   Champlain's meeting with, 110-111
   effect of Europeans on, 60
   Iroquois attacks on, 112-113, 114
   trade among, 58, 59
   trade with French, 108, 112

Immigrants, after 1815, 352-353
Indians, *see also* Algonquins; Beothuks; Blackfoot; Hurons; Iroquois; Micmacs; Native Peoples; Pacific Coast Indians; Plains Indians.
   armed conflicts with whites, 255-256, 259, 324, 333
   British agreements with, 232, 259-260, 279
   contacts with Europeans, 60, 98, 99, 100-114, 117, 149-150, 151
   Palaeo-Indians, 13-15, 49
   tribes, 49-50
Ingstad, Helge and Anne, 82
Intendant, 135, 137
Intolerable Acts (1774), 281
Inuit, 49, 70-73
   explorers, 94-95
   inventions, 71-73
Ipilkvik, 94-95
Iroquois, 27-31, 54, 56-58, 60
   in American Revolution, 299-300
   contacts with Europeans, 108, 109, 110, 212
   government, 56-58
   war on Huronia, 112-113, 114

James I (King of England), 170, 178
Jamestown, 170
Jefferson, Thomas, 284, 285
Jessup's Rangers, 314
Jesuits, 112-113, 114, 132-134, 192
Johnson, Sir William, 299
Journal of discovery, 17

Karlsefni, Thorfinn, 100

Lalemant, Gabriel, 113, 114
La Salle, René-Robert Cavalier, Sieur de, 22, 93, 154
La Tour, Charles de, 193-199
La Vérendrye, 147
Law of Forfeiture, 312
Lawrence, Governor, 267
Leisure, in pioneer days, 356-358
Le Loutre, 219
Lescarbot, Marc, 127-128

Lexington and Concord, battle at, 283, 285, 287
Libraries, use of, 75
Logical thinking, 34-35
Long Sault, battle at, 28-32
Louis XIV (King of France), 155
Louisbourg, 215-217, 225-226, 278
Lower Canada, 268
Loyalists, 266, 268, 285, 286, 291, 293, 296-318

Madison, James, 326
Malecites, 51-53, 54, 55
Mance, Jeanne, 129
Manufacturing
   in New France (1750), 163-164
Mason, Captain John, 173-175
Massachusetts, 176-177, 179
Massachusetts Bay Colony, 177, 179, 185
Masts, 346
"Mayflower Compact," 185
Medicine bundle, 61-62
Mennonites, 286
Merchants, in New France, 161-164
Métis, 149
Micmacs, 51-53, 54, 55, 191, 192, 195
   contacts with Europeans, 105-107
Minutemen, 283, 285, 287
Missionaries, 112-113, 114, 132-134
Mohawks, 111, 299, 300
Montcalm, Marquis de, 224, 227, 230, 236
Montgomery, Richard, 288
Montreal, 27-29, 112, 148
Murray, James, 258-259, 262, 263, 264

Native peoples, 46-75. See also Algonquins; Beothuks; Blackfoot; Hurons; Indians; Inuit; Iroquois; Micmacs; Pacific Coast Indians; Plains Indians.
Navigation Acts, 277, 282
New Brunswick, 318
New England, 176-177, 179
Newfoundland
   Beothuk Indians in, 100-105
   discovery of, 77, 82, 100
   establishing settlement in, 173-175
   fishing off, 87, 175
   government in, 180-184, 185
Newfoundland Act, 183-184
New France, see also Quebec.
   boundaries and population of (1750), 131
   early settlers of, 125-129
   farming in, 156-158
   founding of, 122-124
   fur trade in, 108, 112, 123, 138-139, 147-151
   government and the economy in, 137-142
   growth of, 143, 155
   reactions to "conquest" in, 236-249
   Roman Catholic Church in, 130, 132-134, 246, 248
   seigneurial system in, 135-137
   town life in, 161-164, 165
Northwest Passage, 87
Note-taking, 43-44
Nova Scotia, 90. See also Acadia.
   democracy in, 267
   early attempts at settlement, 178
   movement of Loyalists to, 305-308, 317-318

Officers and enlisted men, 221
Ohio Territory, 212, 279, 281
Opinions versus facts, 25-26

Pacific Coast Indians, 67-70
Palaeo-Indians, 13-15, 49
Patriots, 285, 286, 287, 291, 302, 303
Pictures, use for study of history, 21, 22-23
Pilgrims, 176-177, 185
Plains of Abraham, 228, 229, 230
Plains Indians, 61-66
Polo, Marco, 84
Pontgravé, 108-110
Pontiac, 255-256, 259, 279
Port Royal, 122, 123, 128, 191-192
Potash, 345-346
Potlatch ceremony, 69
Poutrincourt, Jean de Biencourt de, 191-192
Press-gangs, 221, 337
Primary sources, 41-42
Prince Edward Island, 201, 283, 293, 298, 310, 313
Privateers, 336
"Proclamation Line," 232, 259-260, 279, 299
Puritans, 179, 185, 199

Quakers, 286
Quebec, see also New France.
   attack by colonial armies on, 283-284, 288, 289
   government after 1763, 254-270
   treatment disputed by 13 colonies, 278
Quebec (city), 124, 161-164, 215
   siege of, 226-230
Quebec Act (1774), 264-265, 281
Queenston Heights, battle of, 328

Raleigh, Sir Walter, 167, 169-170
Razilly, Isaac de, 194, 195
Reading, in study of history, 23-25
Records, historical, 7, 9
Religion. see also Mennonites, Pilgrims, Puritans, Quakers, Roman Catholic Church.
   among the Blackfoot Indians, 61-64

Representative assembly, 172
Representative government, 185-186
   in the Canadas, 265-266, 268-269
Research, 37-44
   note-taking, 43-44
   preparing questions, 40-41
   using the library, 75
   using primary and secondary sources, 41-42
   using textbooks, 38-39, 40
   writing a first draft, 75
Revere, Paul, 275, 285, 287
Rideau Canal, 339
"Right of discovery," 120, 122
Riverin, Denis, 149-151
River systems, and fur trade, 212, 213-214, 215
Roanoke Island, 167
Roberval, 122
Robson, John, 170-173
Roman Catholic Church
   in New France, 130, 132-134, 246, 248
   in Quebec after 1763, 262
Royal Proclamation of 1763, 259-260, 262
Rush-Bagot Agreement, 339

Sagas, 79, 80, 100
Saint John, New Brunswick, 308, 318
Ste. Marie (mission village), 112, 114
Salaberry, Charles de, 321, 334-335
"Salmon People," 67-70
Sawmills, 347
Secondary sources, 41-42
Secord, Laura, 330-331
Seigneurial system, 135-137
Seven Years' War, 219, 224-230
Shanawdithit, 104, 105
Shipbuilding
   in the Maritimes, 348
   in New France, 139-140, 163
Skills, used in the study of history, 20-44
"Skrellings," 100
Slavery
   and the American Revolution, 311
   in New France, 140
   in the 13 colonies, 289
Smuggling, 282
Sons of Liberty, 283, 285
Sources of information, 41-42
Spices, 84, 85
Stamp Act (1765), 281
Stereotyping, 99
Stobo, Robert, 229
Strickland, Samuel, 356
Sun Dance, 61, 62-64

Talon, Jean, 138-140, 142
Taxation, in 13 colonies, 278
Tea Act (1773), 281, 283
Tecumseh, 324, 328, 332-334
Textbooks, use of, 38-39, 40

Thirteen Colonies, 264, 265, 266, 275, 276. *See also* American Revolution.
  arguments with Britain, 277-279
Timber trade, 344-348
Tippecanoe, battle of, 324
Tobacco, 170, 171, 352
Tories, *see* Loyalists.
Totem poles, 67-69
Townshend Acts (1767), 281
Trade
  between Acadia and New England, 197
  among the Hurons, 58, 59
Traill, Catherine Parr, 358
Treaty of Paris (1763), 232, 257, 258, 291, 300
Treaty of Utrecht (1713), 201
Treaty of Versailles (1783), 324
Tribes, Indian, 49-50
Tukkolerktuk, 94-95

United States, 266, 293
Upper Canada, 268

Vancouver, George, 93
Vikings, 76-77, 78-82, 100
Vinland, 80
Virginia, 167, 169-170, 170-173
  government in, 185
Virginia Company, 170, 172
Visuals, *see* Pictures.
Voltigeurs, 334
Voyager I spacecraft, 3

"War hawks," 324
War of 1812, 320-340
Washington, George, 224, 283, 285, 288
Washington, D.C., attacked during War of 1812, 338

West Indies Company, 138, 139
"Western Charter," 182-183
Westward expansion, 324
Wheat farming, 352, 355
Wolfe, James, 221, 222, 226-230, 232, 236
Women
  among the Iroquois, 56-57, 299-301
  and the Loyalists, 299-301
  and pioneer settlement, 355, 358
  in Acadia, 195-196
  in New England, 185
  in New France, 129, 132, 140, 161-164
  in the War of 1812, 330-331, 337

Yorktown, battle at, 291

Sources

pp. 46-7 Based on *When the Morning Stars Sang Together* by John S. Morgan (Toronto: The Book Society of Canada Ltd., 1974) p. 32; p. 55 Based on *Glooscap and His Magic: Legends of the Wabanaki Indians* by Kay Hill (Toronto: McClelland & Stewart, 1963) pp. 17-25; p. 67 Story of the first fish from *The Salmon People* by Hugh McKervill (Sidney, B.C.: Gray's Publishing Ltd., 1967) p. 8; p. 67-8 Story of Edensaw from *Indiens Inuit Métis* by Hope MacLean (Ottawa: C.A.N.S.P., 1978) pp. 41-2; pp. 204-5 From *History of Nova Scotia* by G.G. Campbell (Toronto: Ryerson Press, 1948) pp. 125-6; p. 336 (top) Based on *The Atlantic Privateers* by John Leefe (Halifax: Petheric Press, 1978) p. 22; p. 337 (top) From *Laura Secord: The Lady and the Legend* by Ruth MacKenzie (Toronto: McClelland & Stewart, 1971) p. 33; p. 337 From *Halifax: Warden of the North* by Thomas Raddell (Toronto: McClelland & Stewart, 1971) pp. 144-51

Picture credits

p. 2 CP Picture Service; p. 5 (montage) Public Archives Canada (PAC) C5389, PAC C13584, PAC C61408; p. 8 and 10 Courtesy of The Newfoundland Museum, Historic Resources Division, Department of Culture, Recreation and Youth, Government of Newfoundland and Labrador; p. 12 and 14 Courtesy of the Royal Ontario Museum, Toronto, Canada; p. 22 Bibliothéque nationale du Québec; p. 26 Wide World Photo; p. 29 PAC C3018; p. 43 PAC C58632; p. 45 PAC C73678; p. 46 Manitoba Archives; p. 53 Metropolitan Toronto Library: T15 823; p. 58 PAC C30009; p. 60 Metropolitan Toronto Library: T16041; p. 62 Glenbow-Alberta Institute NA 2426-1; p. 63 PAC PA9318; p. 64 PAC C19000B; p. 66 PAC C6933, PAC C26182; p. 68 PAC 11216; p. 70 Anglican Church of Canada, General Synod Archives; p. 71 Hudson's Bay Company; p. 72 PAC C30923; p. 73 Hudson's Bay Company; p. 74 PAC PA 117148; p. 81 Parks Canada, Historic Properties, Halifax, N.S.; p. 89 Metropolitan Toronto Library: T15513; p. 94 From Capt. George E. Tyson, *Arctic Experiences* (New York, 1874), reprinted by permission from Keith J. Crowe, *A History of the Original Peoples of Northern Canada* (Montreal: Arctic Institute of North America and McGill-Queen's University Press, 1974); p. 104 and 105 Courtesy of The Newfoundland Museum, Historic Resources Division, Department of Culture, Recreation and Youth, Government of Newfoundland and Labrador; p. 106 National Gallery of Canada, Ottawa; p. 111 PAC C10486; p. 115 Hudson's Bay Company; p. 116 Metropolitan Toronto Library Board; p. 117 Courtesy of National Museum of American Art, Smithsonian Institution; p. 119 PAC C5933; p. 123 PAC C9711; p. 126 Confederation Life Collection; p. 128, PAC C3202; p. 130 PAC C5078; p. 132 PAC C11232; p. 136 (photo) Department of Energy, Mines and Resources, (map) PAC C54143; p. 141 PAC C29486; p. 144 photo by Robert C. Wheeler, Minnesota Historical Society; p. 147 Hudson's Bay Company; p. 148 Glenbow-Alberta Institute NA-1532-6; p. 150 PAC C82974; p. 153 PAC C15497; p. 156 National Gallery of Canada, Ottawa; p. 157 PAC C16952; p. 159 PAC C13476; p. 162 PAC C17875; p. 163 PAC C15784 and PAC C17059; p. 164 Notman Photographic Archives; p. 166 Metropolitan Toronto Library: T15874; p. 169 Confederation Life Collection; p. 172 Metropolitan Toronto Library Board; p. 174 PAC C3686; p. 177 PAC C921; p. 179 Metropolitan Toronto Library: T14870; p. 183 Metropolitan Toronto Library: T14859; p. 188 PAC C24347; p. 189 New Brunswick Department of Tourism; p. 192 PAC; p. 196 Courtesy New Brunswick Museum; p. 198 PAC C11237; p. 200 Acadian Historical Village; p. 203 PAC C73709; p. 206 PAC C19584; p. 210 (top) PAC C43, (bottom) Archives nationales du Québec, collection Initiale; p. 220 Reproduced from the Collections of the Library of Congress; p. 223 (from left to right) Metropolitan Toronto Library: T15426, PAC C5707, PAC C12417; p. 224 PAC C3697; p. 225 PAC C5907; p. 227 Metropolitan Toronto Library: T30420; p. 231 PAC C1078; p. 234-5 Archives nationales du Québec, collection Initiale; p. 255 PAC C11250; p. 256 Courtesy of The Royal Ontario Museum, Toronto, Canada; p. 264 PAC C6150; p. 267 Courtesy of The Royal Ontario Museum, Toronto, Canada; p. 269 Confederation Life Collection; p. 274 Reproduced from the Collections of the Library of Congress; p. 277 PAC C41370; p. 285 Metropolitan Toronto Library: T14933; p. 291 PAC C17507; p. 293 "Surrender of the Army of Cornwallis" by François Godefroy, Paris, 1784. The Daughters of the American Revolution Museum. Gift of Mary Washington Chapter, in honour of Mrs. Howard C. Van Arsdale. Photograph by Jean Martin; p. 294 Metropolitan Toronto Library: T14946; p. 297 Courtesy of New Brunswick Museum; p. 299 Metropolitan Toronto Library: T14943; p. 300 From: *United Empire Loyalists, Pioneers of Upper Canada*. Courtesy Mika Publishing Company, Belleville; p. 301 Metropolitan Toronto Library: T16554; p. 304 Reproduced from The Collections of the Library of Congress; p. 306 From *United Empire Loyalists, Pioneers of Upper Canada*. Courtesy Mika Publishing Company, Belleville; p. 308-9 Courtesy New Brunswick Museum; p. 310 PAC C9564; p. 317 Courtesy New Brunswick Museum; p. 324 Metropolitan Toronto Library: T16600; p. 328 PAC C70264; p. 329 PAC C276; p. 332-3 Metropolitan Toronto Library: T15255; p. 335 PAC C3297; p. 342 Norwich and District Historical Society, Painting by Ross Butler; p. 346 PAC C2409; p. 347-8 Courtesy of The Royal Ontario Museum, Toronto, Canada; p. 352 Photograph: the late R.R. Sallows, Goderich, Ontario. Reproduction: The Ontario Ministry of Agriculture and Food; p. 353 (cradle scythe) Norwich and District Historical Society; p. 354 Metropolitan Toronto Library: T15905